Prendergast

Milton

MORAN.

B. West

PAUL CORNOYER

TS. 1819.

Hovenden

HOMER

Th. Robinson

E. SHINN

A.H. Maurer

Whistler

W.C. Wall.

C Roesen

Geo Luks

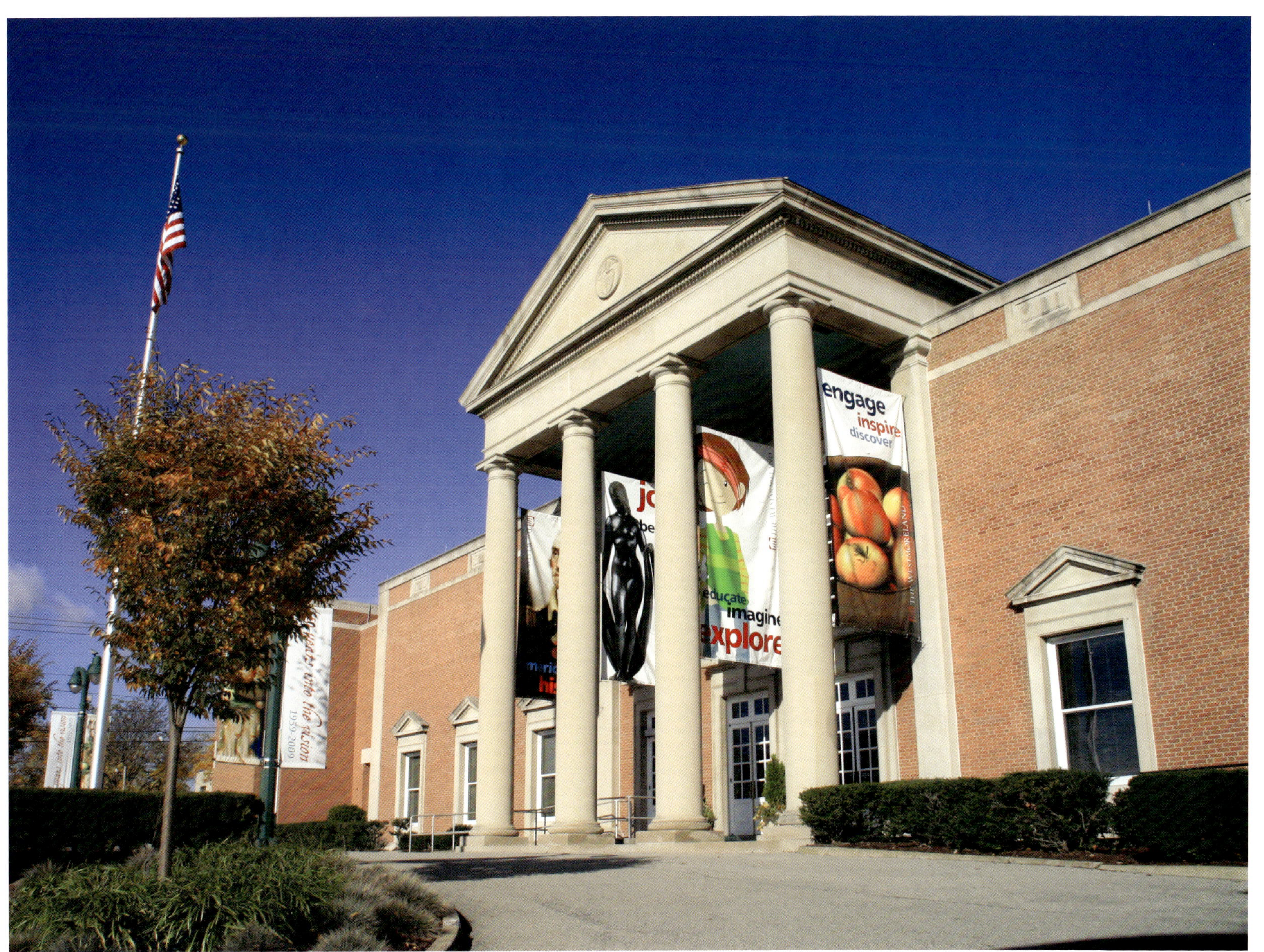
engage
inspire
discover
educate
imagine

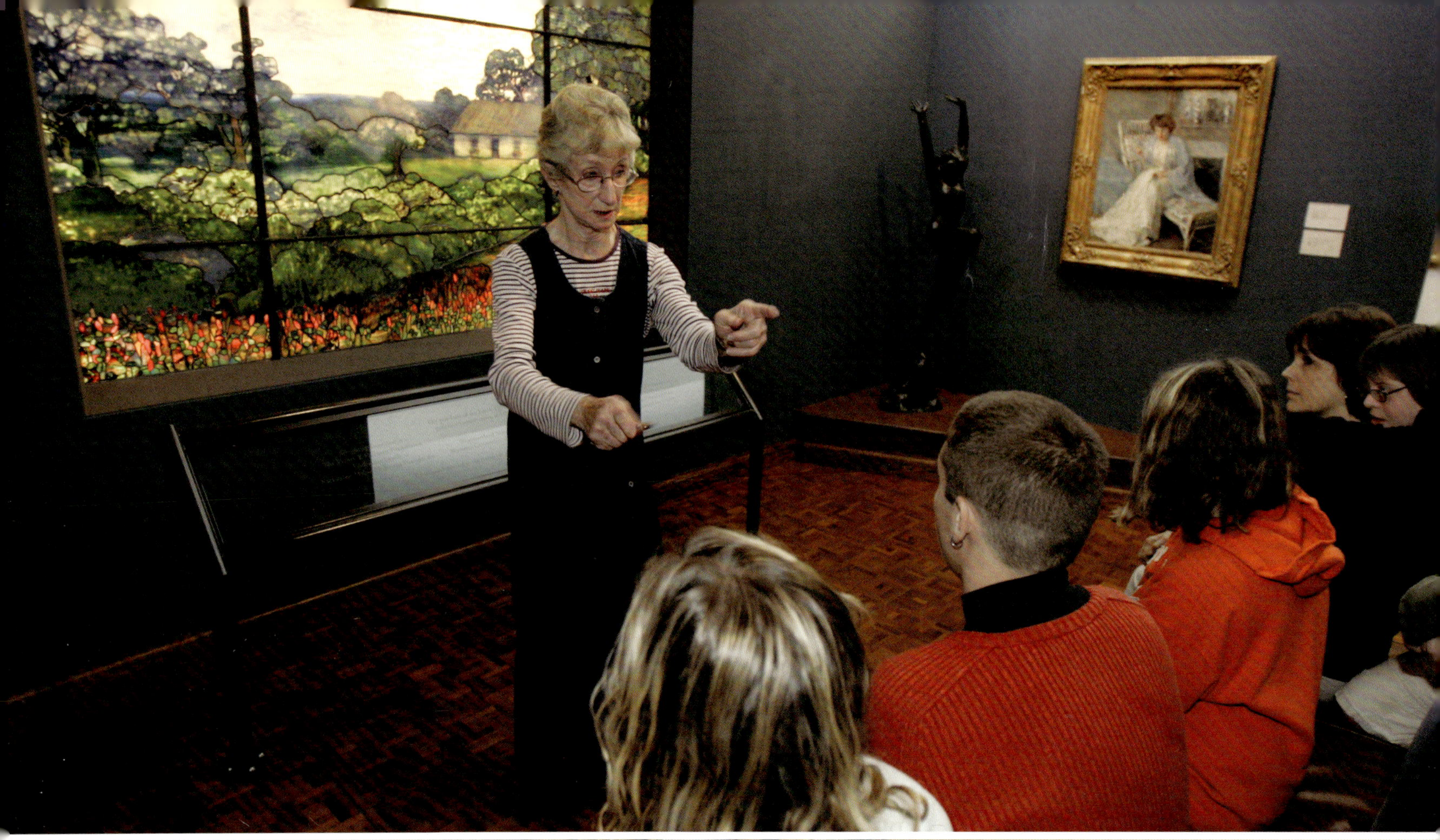

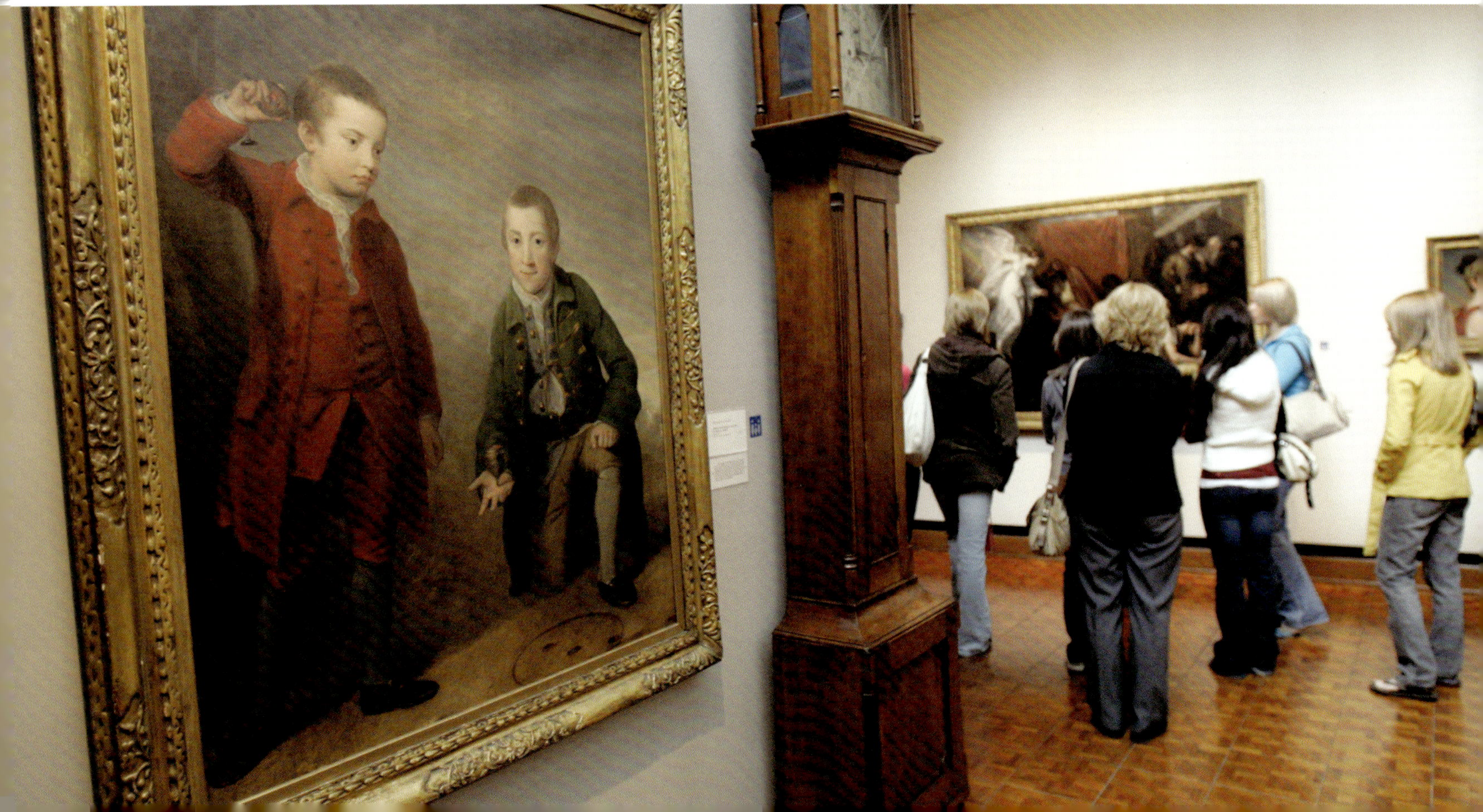

Picturing America

Signature Works from the Westmoreland Museum of American Art

Barbara L. Jones
with
Judith Hansen O'Toole & Harley N. Trice

Published by the
Westmoreland Museum of American Art
221 North Main Street
Greensburg, PA 15601

www.wmuseumaa.org

Produced by Chameleon Books
31 Smith Road, Chesterfield, MA 01012

Production director/designer: Arnold Skolnick
Production assistant: KC Scott
Copy Editor: Jamie Nan Thaman
Photography: Richard A. Stoner
Jacket Design: Chemistry, Pittsburgh, PA

Library of Congress Cataloging-in-Publication Data
A complete record is available from the Library of Congress

ISBN 0-931241-37-6

Paper: 128 gsm acid free Gold East Matt Artpaper
Typeface: Centaur
Printed in China by Oceanic Graphic Printing

This book is made possible with support from:
Richard King Mellon Foundation
Henry L. Hillman Foundation
The National Endowment for the Arts

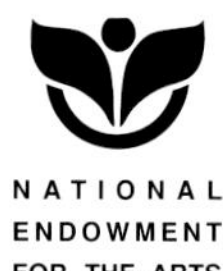

NATIONAL
ENDOWMENT
FOR THE ARTS

The Museum's name has changed since its inception to the following, all of which reference this institution under Selected Exhibitions within each catalog entry:

Westmoreland County Museum of Art (1959 – 1984)

Westmoreland Museum of Art (1984 – 1996)

Westmoreland Museum of American Art (1996 – present)

To our founder, Mary Marchand Woods
To our founding Director, Paul A. Chew, Ph. D.
To our volunteers and patrons, exemplified by Anne and Jack Robertshaw
To our Board of Trustees and Staff, past and present
To our future . . .

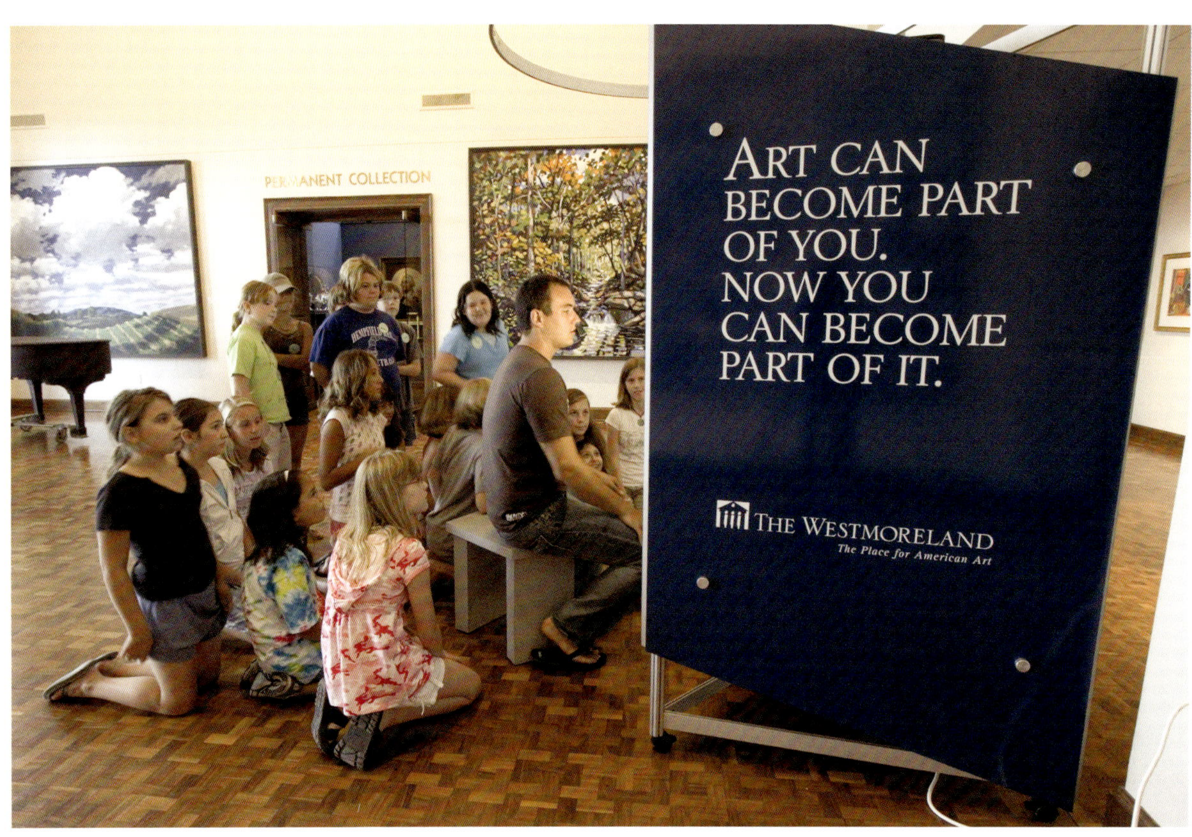
PERMANENT COLLECTION
ART CAN
BECOME PART
OF YOU.
NOW YOU
CAN BECOME
PART OF IT.
THE WESTMORELAND
The Place for American Art

One Nation under Track Lights

The above title was a finalist in our staff's pseudo competition to name this volume on the permanent collection. It is still one of my favorites which is why I appropriated it for this preface. Submitted by our preparator, P. J. Zimmerlink, whose role it is to install and light our collection, it speaks to our profession and to the specificity of the objects we hold in trust for our public.

Ultimately titled *Picturing America,* this is the second of four planned volumes dedicated to the permanent collection of the Westmoreland Museum of American Art. The first was *Born of Fire: The Valley of Work* (2006). The third and fourth, yet to be written, will address our works on paper and the Scalp Level school of landscape painting.

This volume replaces *The Permanent Collection: The Westmoreland County Museum of Art,* published in 1978 on the occasion of the Museum's 20th anniversary. That was two institutional name changes and over three decades ago, making this catalog long overdue.

It is surprising that the The Westmoreland was built without the stimulus of a collection in need of being housed, as is the case with so many museums of all disciplines. Yet in the early years, the collection grew quickly due to the vision of my predecessor and the accessibility of American art, both in price and quantity. Half a century later, the market in American art has dramatically changed as we now struggle against escalating prices and keen competition to fill gaps in and grow the collection.

Fifty years ago the Museum hired a Director/Curator, Paul A. Chew, who noted in his acknowledgements for the 1978 volume that demands of his "day" job prohibited his being able to "carry out the various research problems and essays" required for the task of writing the permanent collection catalog. Today, I am Director/CEO, reflective of my administrative and executive duties, and we have a Chief (and only) Curator, Barbara L. Jones, who is responsible for the calendar of travelling exhibitions and the installation and research needs of our permanent collection. She is ably assisted by Collections Manager, Douglas W. Evans, who maintains detailed object files on each item in our holdings.

We stand in collective awe of the curatorial fortitude Barbara summoned enabling her to triumph over innumerable details, frequent impediments, day-to-day job related distractions and time constraints, to produce this book. Such an astonishing example of pure stamina and dedication cannot be asked for or extracted through any external means. It can only be offered, as it was in this case, as a result of her passion for her field.

Our gratitude is as deep, if not deeper, than her fortitude.

Judith Hansen O'Toole
Director/CEO
June 2010

Acknowledgments

This catalog was a long-time in the making and indeed, long overdue. Published for the first time in 1978, the Museum's permanent collection has grown substantially over the past thirty-two years. It has been my privilege to work with this outstanding collection of American art and to play a role in its development for the past fifteen years.

I am indebted to many people for their assistance with this catalog, especially my co-authors, Judith Hansen O'Toole and Harley N. Trice. Not only is Judy the Museum's Director/CEO, but she is also an art historian and colleague who shares my passion for the art, and who can, remarkably, describe it using less words. My special thanks for her strength, leadership, and enthusiastic support of all the work we do as well as for her essays in this volume. Harley is a supportive board member and collector who shares our love of objects and this Museum. I thank him for contributing his expertise on the decorative arts and furniture and for his willingness to donate his time to this endeavor so that we are able to provide a more comprehensive view of the collection.

I have been privileged as well to work with an exceptional staff, and as a result of that, we have been able to execute many ambitious projects together. No exhibition or publication is produced by one person, and it is because of a dedicated team effort that we are able to accomplish all that we do. We share a common vision to ensure that the Museum becomes "the place for American art" and a destination for visitors to learn about the art of their own country. My heartfelt appreciation to all of them for their support in this, yet another ambitious project, specifically to Doug Evans, who expertly coordinated all of the photography for this volume and kept his sanity doing it; P.J. Zimmerlink, for his preparation of all the objects; Darlene Konvalinka, for her dedication and assistance with every aspect of this catalog; Judy Ross, for taking up the mantle of revisions in my absence and not going crazy, and for successfully market this volume to our audience; Amy Baldonieri for her never-ending encouragement and fundraising expertise; Pat Erdelsky for her diligent proofreading; Charlene Bidula for handling the technology; Katie Barnard and Maureen Zang for the creative education programming to come; Casey Wertz, my summer intern from St. Vincent College, for her careful reading of the manuscript; to our dedicated docent corps whose tours will continue to teach the public about this collection; and to Bruce Wolf, for his leadership as President and his sensitivity as a collector himself, and our Board of Trustees who encourage us in all we do.

A great many people in both the public and private sector gave freely of their time, advice, and assistance over the past two years. Together with my co-authors, I extend our sincere appreciation to them: Eric Baumgartner, Hirschl & Adler Galleries, Inc., NYC; Sam Berkovitz, Concept Art Gallery, Pittsburgh; Pat Boulware, Saint Louis Art Museum; Marisa Bourgoin, Archives of American Art, Washington, D.C.; R. David Brocklebank; Elizabeth Tufts-Brown, Carnegie Museum of Art; William Bunch, William Bunch Auctions & Appraisals, Chadds Ford, PA; Gretchen Burch, Sotheby's, NYC; Russell Burke; Peter W. Chillingworth; John Churchell; Janice Conner; Laura Domencic, Pittsburgh Center for the Arts; John P. Driscoll, Babcock Galleries, NYC; Nancy Druckman, Sotheby's, NYC; Patti Duff; Maryann Fausold, intern, Seton Hill University; Stuart Feld; Robert Gilliland, Gilliland Fine Art, Ligonier, PA; Laurence Glasco, University of Pittsburgh; Gary Grimes; Martha Hoppin; Connie Houchins; Arthur Humphrey; Becca Humphrey; Dana Jones; Ruthann Hubbert-Kemper, Pennsylvania Capitol Preservation Committee, Harrisburg; Susan Kriete, New-York Historical Society; Anne Kumer, Bryant Park Corporation, NYC; Frank Kurtik; Edward F. LaFond, Jr.; Leah Lehmbeck; Abby Leone, intern, Seton Hill University; Cheryl Leibold, Pennsylvania Academy of the Fine Arts; Dan Lilienkamp, St. Louis County Library; Ray Ann Lockard, Frick Fine Arts Library, University of Pittsburgh; Stephen May; Patrick McCormick, Butler Institute of American Art, Youngstown, OH; Laura McElherne, The Mary Cassatt Catalogue Raisonné Committee, NYC; Timothy Milford, St. Johns Academy; New York Public Library Reference Department; New York Public Digital Library; Marshall Price, National Academy of Design,; Rebecca Reynolds, North Shore Arts Association, Gloucester, MA; Marcia Rostek, Frick Fine Arts Library, University of Pittsburgh; Heather Semple, The Duquesne Club, Pittsburgh; Ralph Sessions; Graham Shearing; Shirley Silverman; Juliet Lea Hillman Simonds; John Smith, Archives of American Art, Washington, D.C.; David Wheatcroft; D. Wigmore Fine Art, Inc., NYC; Michael Preston Worley, R. H. Love Galleries, Chicago; Tina Zins; Philip Zimmerman; and a private collector.

My great appreciation to Richard A. Stoner for his, as always, expert photography of the art and objects; Jamie Nan Thaman, for her flawless editing; KC Scott and Bob Aller for their assistance with text and image details; and Arnold Skolnick of Chameleon Books, for his design, all-around patience and good nature these many months. To Richard King Mellon Foundation, Henry L. Hillman Foundation, and The National Endowment for the Arts, our funders, I thank them for their generous support, for without it this catalog could not have been realized. Judith Hansen O'Toole would like to thank her father, Chadwick C. Hansen, retired professor of American studies and author, who inspired her interest in art and museums; and her mother, Betty Jane, who inspired her in everything else.

And finally, my ongoing thanks to my partner, David Ludwig, who assists me in so many indecipherable ways, and who shares my love of this Museum and its collection.

Barbara L. Jones
Chief Curator
July 2010

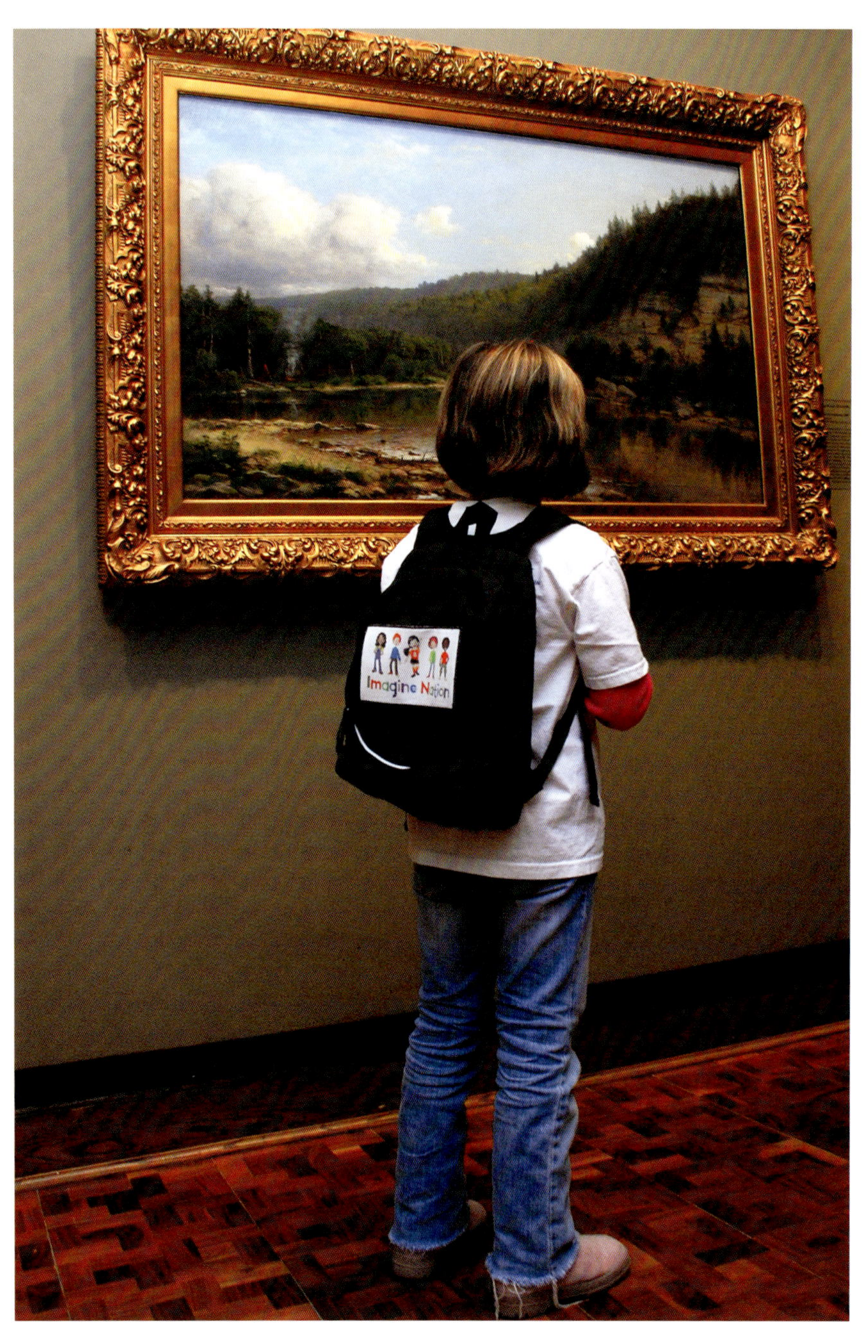
Imagine Nation

A History of The Westmoreland

At the crest of a hill in Greensburg, Pennsylvania, sits a structure of Georgian architecture, built of brick with limestone trim. Inside is an American art collection that rivals the finest in the nation. The Westmoreland Museum of American Art has stood at this site since it opened its doors on May 29, 1959, as a cultural oasis nestled in the foothills of southwestern Pennsylvania. More than fifty years have passed since The Westmoreland greeted its first visitor, which is cause for reflection and celebration—including the publication of this catalog, signature works from the permanent collection.

The Westmoreland's story begins with the vision of one woman, Mary Marchand Woods (1871–1953). As in many great stories, the protagonist is unassuming. Local lore reveals that once widowed, she was extremely thrifty, taking as her daily lunch each day a bowl of soup from the school cafeteria across the street from her Greensburg home on North Main Street. It must have come as a surprise when in 1949, Mary announced her decision to leave her entire estate to create a museum for the people of Westmoreland County. In that moment, the vision of one woman became the benefit of an entire community.

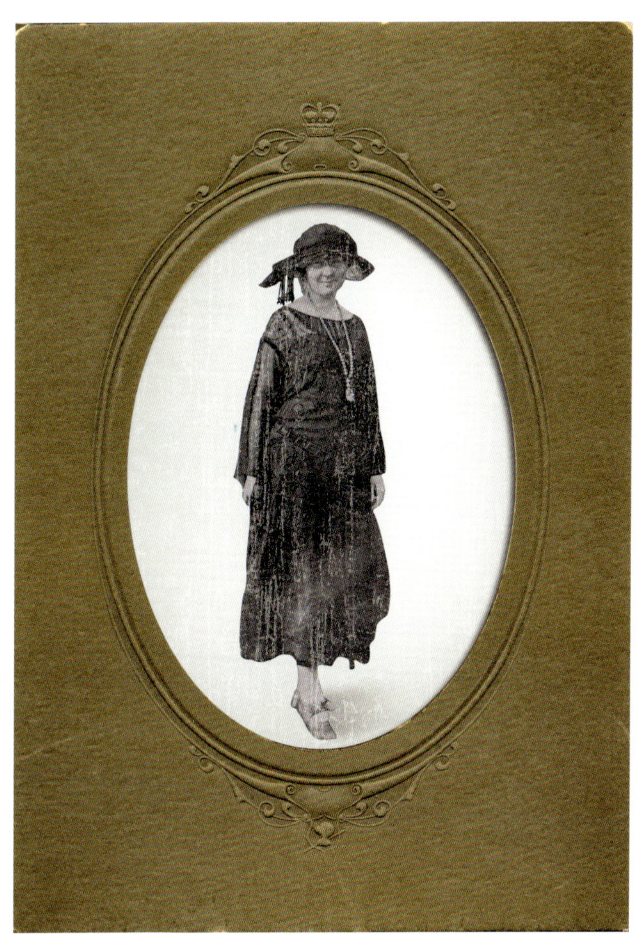

Mary had begun the process of organizing her estate as the Woods-Marchand Foundation after her husband, Cyrus E. Woods (1861–1938), passed away. She would dedicate the Museum in his memory but request no recognition by naming. Cyrus had had an impressive government career, serving as Pennsylvania state senator (1901–1908), United States minister to Portugal (1912–1913), secretary of the commonwealth (1915), U.S. ambassador to Spain (1921–1923) and Japan (1923–1924), and finally Pennsylvania's attorney general (1929). Mary traveled with her husband, enjoying the exposure to other cultures, but always returned to their house, positioned near where the Museum stands today. Mary lived there quietly until her death on January 28, 1953.

In the years following her death, plans for the Museum began to take shape. In addition to Mary's home, the site contained other homes, including that of Mary's grandparents, Mr. and Mrs. Albert G. Marchand, and the former Greensburg City Hall, all of which were purchased and razed to provide the Museum with an entire

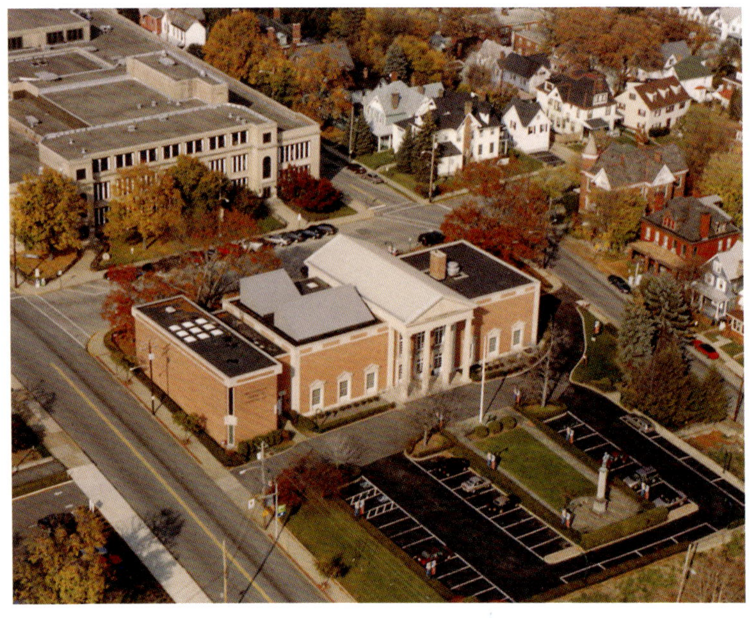

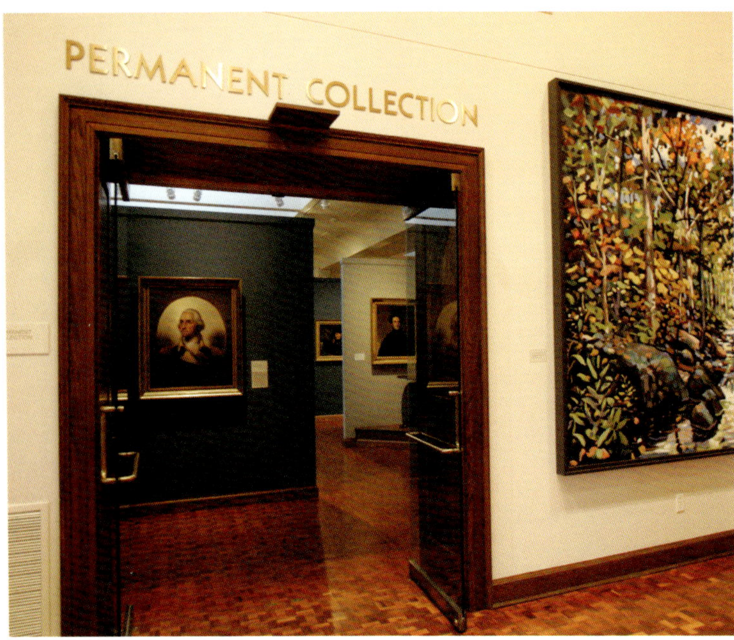

city block on which to build. After considering a series of proposed architectural designs, including one by a young Philip Johnson, the Board settled on the Georgian style presented by the Pittsburgh firm Sorber & Hoone.

The first board of directors meeting of the Woods-Marchand Foundation was held on June 15, 1950, at the Woods residence. Virginia E. Lewis, an art historian, curator and professor of fine arts, was appointed part-time director of the Museum on September 1, 1954, and served in that capacity until April 13, 1956. Construction of the building began on May 18, 1957, and the cornerstone was laid just over four months later, on September 20. Dr. Paul A. Chew was elected director of the Museum by the Board on December 5, 1957. A small staff moved into the unfinished building on December 1, 1957, and just eighteen months later, the Westmoreland County Museum of Art officially opened to the public.

While Mary left two million dollars to construct and endow the Museum, she had no art collection to bequeath. The Museum's focus, under Paul Chew, who served as both director and curator, became the collection and exhibition of American art. According to Chew:

> In my initial meeting with the Board of Directors, it was asked that I recommend a policy for forming a collection for this museum, at that time still under construction. There was no doubt in my mind that our policy should be to form a collection of American art. It is our aim to build towards an American art collection in general and specifically one of Pennsylvania art, with an emphasis on the western part of the state.[1]

When the Westmoreland County Museum of Art opened, the collection contained just seventy-eight works of art. The first twenty-nine objects were gifts from Mrs. Armistead Peter III in 1958, including twenty-one bronze sculptures made by her stepfather, sculptor Paul Wayland Bartlett (1865–1925). Rembrandt Peale's (1778–1860) *Portrait of George Washington* became the first painting to enter the Museum's collection in December of that year, followed by works by David Gilmour Blythe (1815–1865), Everett Shinn (1876–1953), Theodore Robinson (1852–1896), George Inness (1825–1894), and Robert Henri (1865–1929). The inaugural exhibition, *250 Years of Art in Pennsylvania,* was an ambitious undertaking that contained 428 objects, representing a who's who of distinguished

American art and artists. Gordon Bailey Washburn, director of the Department of Fine Arts at Carnegie Institute (now Carnegie Museum of Art), attended the first exhibition and commented that it was "Greensburg's good fortune in being given, in our materialistic age, a center where the things of the spirit might be nurtured." Mary Cassatt (1844–1926), Charles Willson Peale (1741–1827), Gilbert Stuart (1755–1828), John Neagle (1796–1865), David Gilmour Blythe, Thomas Moran (1837–1926), and Cecilia Beaux (1855–1942) were all included in that first exhibition and continue to be represented in the collection by one or more works.

In addition to the small collection, the new Museum contained four period rooms that, as requested in Mary's will, were furnished with personal objects from her family home which had stood on the site. It was her wish that the rooms replicate a typical western Pennsylvania Victorian setting, so that future generations might have an idea of how their nineteenth-century ancestors lived. The four Victorian rooms—study, parlor, dining room, and bedroom—were arranged en suite around a courtyard in the east side of the Museum. Three bay windows completed the "home" setting, one of which was used for the display of textiles. The rooms were dismantled in 1981, and the Mary Woods-Marchand Memorial Gallery (now the Mack-Woods-Marchand galleries) opened in mid-1982 to house selections from the growing permanent collection.

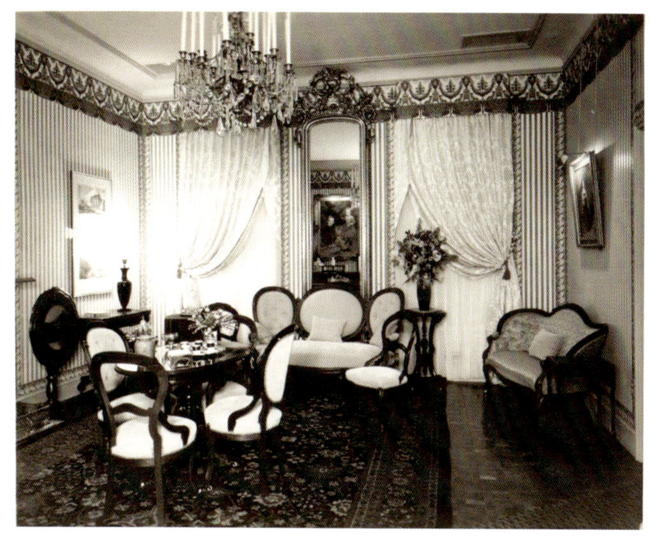

In keeping with its initial goal, the Museum's collection is national in scope, with a concentration on two hundred years of American art—1750 to 1950, extending to the present day in special collections, especially works on paper. The Museum is also the largest repository of southwestern Pennsylvania art in the country. Works by artists of the Scalp Level school, who painted the pristine natural landscape near Johnstown, Pennsylvania, and those constituting *Born of Fire*, depicting the region's scenes of industry, serve as complementary collections telling the story of how the commonwealth evolved from an agrarian to an industrial society. During the first twenty years of its existence, the Museum became well known for its collection of works by southwestern Pennsylvania artists, organizing its first exhibition and publishing the first catalog on the subject in 1981. Another ambitious undertaking, the exhibition included 304 paintings by 59 artists. As a result of its success, the Museum published *Southwestern Pennsylvania Painters*— a catalog featuring its own collection—in 1989. A second important exhibition and publication, *George Hetzel and the Scalp Level Tradition*, occurred in 1994,

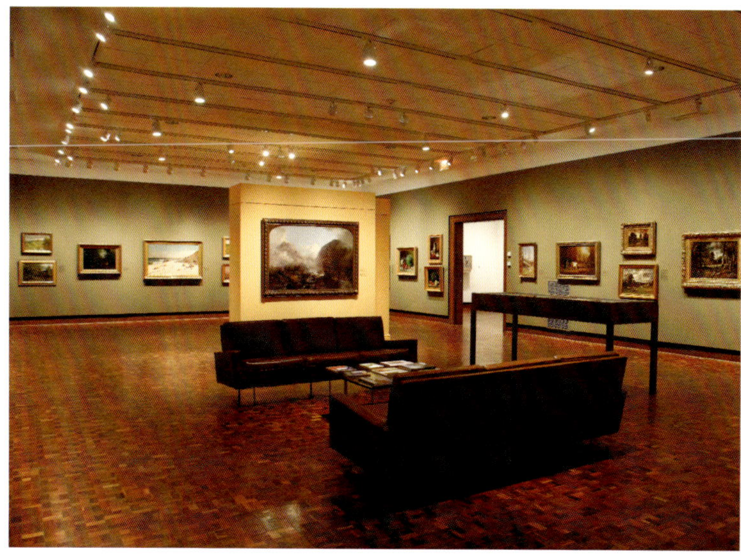

highlighting this regional school of artists.

Over the years, the collection has grown in various ways. William A. Coulter and Thomas Lynch, Esq., were the first and second Board members to recognize the importance of the Museum by establishing trust funds for the purchase of works of art, resulting in 132 gifts from the former and 78 from the latter to date. In 2002, William Jamison, a Greensburg architect, bequeathed over one million dollars for a fund to be designated for acquisitions. Each year the Westmoreland Society, a membership group, commits funds to purchase one or more works of art for the collection. The Women's Committee, celebrating its fiftieth anniversary in 2010, organizes fund-raising events that serve the mission of the institution, including acquisitions. The largest number of works came as gifts from individual donors, whose generosity helped build the collection substantially. Today the collection contains 3500 objects and is still

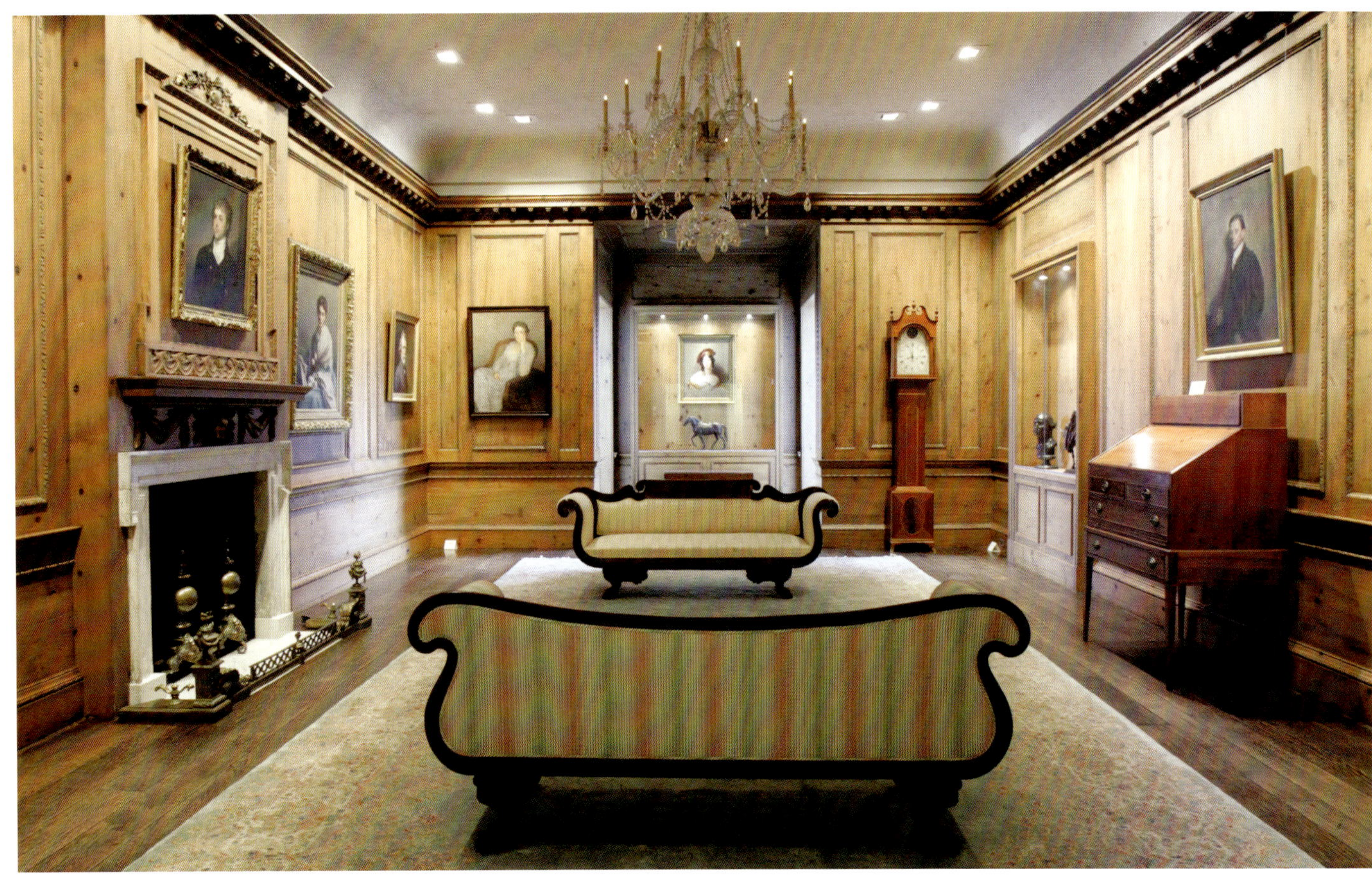

growing, filling in the gaps that will allow us to continue telling the story of American art to our audience, which now extends beyond Westmoreland County.

In 1968, the Museum added a west wing to house two mid-eighteenth-century pine-paneled rooms, a gift of the Scaife family. With that expansion came new space to house the art library and administrative offices. Ten years later, to celebrate the Museum's twentieth anniversary, the first permanent collection catalog was published. This catalog is only the second such publication.

In 1984, the word "County" was eliminated from the Museum's name in an effort to avoid any confusion regarding a nonexistent county affiliation. In order to more clearly define the Museum's collection to the public, the name changed once more in 1996 with the addition of the word "American."

The next chapter in the Museum's history began in 1993. The Museum's second director, Judith Hansen O'Toole, was hired, and a new long-range plan was established to leverage the Museum's unique collection and position the institution as an important cultural resource. Within five years, the Museum reasserted itself as a vital, forward-thinking institution and, in the process, hired its first full-time curator, marketing director, and director of development. The Campaign for Enriching the Public Experience, launched in 1997, surpassed its goal of $3.5 million and raised $4.7 million for a much-needed Museum interior renovation, which would provide for more effective galleries, allow for a reinstallation of the permanent collection, provide improved educational facilities, and contribute to the Museum's endowments.

The new millennium brought many positive changes. The Museum launched *Every Picture Tells a Story: Exploring Pennsylvania History Through Art* in 2001—a program that brings area fourth-grade students to the Museum to study Pennsylvania history through the collection, specifically through two semi-permanent exhibitions: *Southwestern Pennsylvania Landscapes* and *Born of Fire: The Valley of Work*. This program, which increased from one participating school in 2001 to over twenty in three counties, continues to grow in popularity among teachers, students, and administrators because of its important link to the state-mandated fourth-grade curriculum. In 2004, the Museum received the Pennsylvania Federation of Museums and Historical Organizations' Award of Excellence and the Westmoreland Historical Society's St. Clair Award for this program. Since the inception of *Every Picture Tells a Story*, the Museum

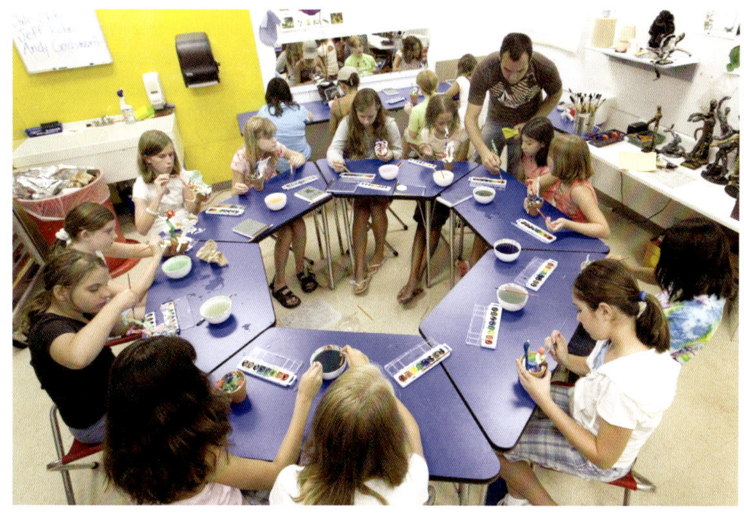

This is a paragraph about what I learned at the museum. I learned that scalp levelartist are very good at what they do. That was the most exciting trip I have ever went on! I learned that the steel industry produced alot of polution. Barry helped me notice that everyone is an artist. He helped everyone make steel industrys and and a neighborhood. That was the best experience ever I look foward to seeing you agin.

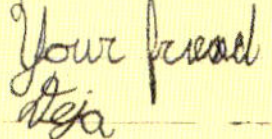
Your friend
Deja

has created two additional curriculum-based programs, for middle school and kindergarten students. The Westmoreland continues its commitment to education and to serving children and families through a new initiative launched in 2008: *Imagine Nation,* a fun, new way for kids and adults to experience American art.

In February 2004, the Museum was selected to be the lead episode of the eleventh season of the public television series The Visionaries. The thirty-minute segment featured the Museum's collection, accessibility, commitment to regional partnerships, and educational initiatives that were making a difference in the region. Of the 103 non-profit organizations profiled by The Visionaries, The Westmoreland was the first museum and only the second arts organization.

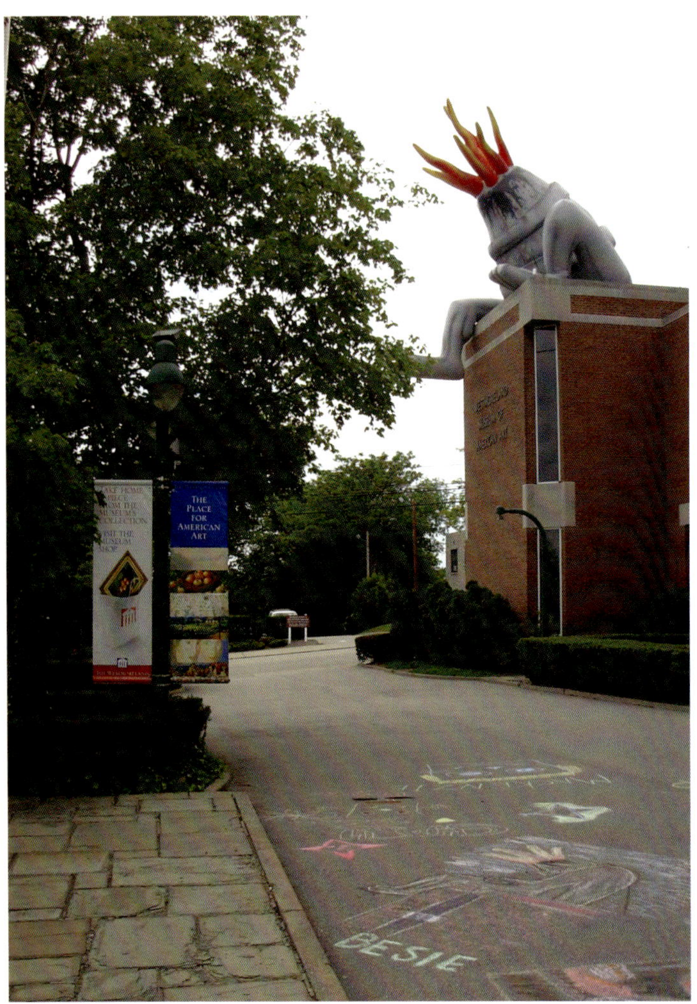

Outstanding exhibitions and additions to the permanent collection continued during this period, which coincided with a heightened national and even international interest in American art. Partnerships with collectors, museums, art historians, and donors from around the country brought greater visibility to the Museum, extending its geographic reach. By 2005, more than half the Museum's visitors were coming from outside Westmoreland County, and a national spotlight was bringing more attention to the Museum's collections.

After forging new paths in education, visitor experience, and collections, the Museum built a transatlantic bridge through the exhibition and product development project *Born of Fire.* Featuring the first-ever exhibition and catalog of the Museum's entire scenes-of-industry collection; a music CD; and a documentary DVD, the combined set tells the story of the art, music, and history of the Big Steel Era in our region. Sixty works from the *Born of Fire* collection traveled to the LVR-Industriemuseum in Oberhausen, Germany in 2007 for its European debut, connecting the Pittsburgh region with the world. It continued on to Chemnitz, Germany, and to Zabrze, Poland, in 2008 and 2009, before returning to Oberhausen, where twenty-nine works were featured in the exhibition *Feuerländer: Regions of Vulcan* at LVR as part of the Ruhr region's designation as the 2010 European Capital of Culture. "*Born of Fire* is not just about artists interpreting the visual spectacle that was the steel industry through their creative impulses. It is also about recognizing dreams, mental drive, a soul of fire, if you like, visions and what can become of them. In this case, naturally, the American dream. This dream is universal. Its vision surmounts borders and oceans. So let's inhale the past and exhale the future in this sense: may *Born of Fire* bring us pride in our past and enthuse us about the future."[3]

The year 2009 marked the fiftieth anniversary of the Museum. A yearlong celebration not only looked back on the accomplishments of the first half-century but became a launching pad to the next fifty years. Now, fifty-one years into the vision, The Westmoreland is exceeding the expectations of visitors and is acknowledged across the state—and in the nation—as a new model for art museums. In addition to increasing awareness about American art in general, The Westmoreland is a place to teach Americans about the art of their own country.

The Museum began as the idea of one, and has grown to inspire the lives of many. Mary Marchand Woods was a visionary, who had the foresight to meet a need for art and culture that she believed would benefit her community. The Westmoreland carries her vision into the future, continuing to expand our collection, our physical capacity, and our ability to serve as a destination for the public.

1 Paul A. Chew, *The Permanent Collection* (Greensburg, PA: The Westmoreland County Museum of Art, 1959), x.

2 Westmoreland County Museum of Art Bulletin, Fall 1959, 4.

3 Thomas Schleper, Leiter des LVR-Industriemuseum, Rheinisches Landesmuseum für Industrie-und Sozialgeschichte, Schauplätze Oberhausen, 2009.

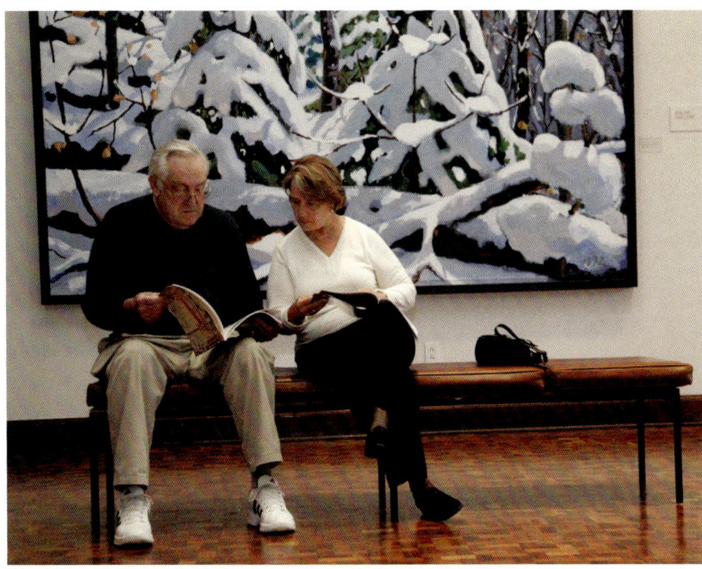

Captions

FRONTISPIECE:

Westmoreland Museum of American Art.
(Photography: Shirleah Kelly)

Page 2

TOP:

Volunteer docent Fran Lynch tells the story of the *Thomas Lynch Tiffany Window.* (Photography: Jason Cohn)

Bottom:

A group tours the permanent collection. (Photography: Jason Cohn)

Page 6

Students experience the Museum's story-telling kiosk.
(Photography: Larry Rippel)

Page 10

Imagine Nation Club member tours the gallery with one of our Discover Backpacks. (Skysight Photography)

Page 11

Museum founder Mary Marchand Woods

Page 12

TOP:

Aerial photograph of the Museum. (Jonathan Nakles Photography)

BOTTOM:

Visitors entering the permanent collection are greeted by Rembrandt's Peale's *Portrait of George Washington.* (Photography: Jason Cohn)

Page 13

TOP:

One of the period rooms on display when The Westmoreland opened in 1959.

BOTTOM:

A view of the exhibition, *Scenic Views,* a survey of works by Scalp Level school artists organized in 2009.
(Photography: Richard A. Stoner)

Page 14

The large paneled room houses portraits, sculpture and decorative arts from the permanent collection. (Photography: Jason Cohn)

Page 15

TOP:

Summer art campers paint sculptures during their week long activities.
(Photography: Larry Rippel)

BOTTOM:

The Museum receives many wonderful notes and letters from students who have visited.

Page 16

Opening festivities for the exhibition *Born of Fire* included "Bessie," an inflatable public art project. The anthropomorphic version of a Bessemer converter was designed by regional artist Steve O' Hearn.

Page 17

A couple shares an exhibition catalog on their visit. Behind them is Charles"Bud" Gibbon's *Winter Scene.* (Photography: Jason Cohn)

The Catalog

JOHN SINGLETON COPLEY (1738–1815)
Portrait of John Gardiner, c. 1758
Oil on canvas, 48 x 38 ¾ inches
Anonymous gift by exchange, 1987.17
Provenance: Gardiner Family; Tudor Gardiner; Hirschl and Adler Galleries, New York; Childs Gallery, Boston.

SELECTED EXHIBITIONS: Carnegie Institute, Pittsburgh, 1971; *American Portraits by John Singleton Copley*, 1975–76, *A Gallery Collects*, 1977 and *American Art from the Colonial and Federal Periods*, 1982, Hirschl & Adler Galleries, New York.

Named after his maternal grandfather, John Singleton Copley was born in Boston to Richard and Mary Singleton Copley on July 3, 1738. His father died shortly after his birth, and his mother was remarried in 1748 to Peter Pelham (c. 1695–1751), a well-know mezzotint engraver in the city. Copley's early education came from his stepfather, whose work he emulated in an early portrait engraving of 1753, made when he was just fifteen years old. It was the beginning of a prolific and successful career. Essentially self-taught, Copley trained his eye for minute details by using the graver's tools; copying anatomical plates from an encyclopedia; and studying the work of other artists, including that of John Smibert (1688–1751), Joseph Blackburn (c. 1730–c. 1778), and Robert Feke (c. 1705–1751)—all of whom had been prominent portraitists in Boston.

While living in Boston, Copley painted portraits of both Tory loyalists and Whigs, one of which is The Westmoreland's *Portrait of John Gardiner*, a self-proclaimed staunch Whig and the son of distinguished physician Dr. Sylvester Gardiner and his wife, Ann (Gibbons) Gardiner. Following his studies at the University of Glasgow, John Gardiner returned to Boston, working in the law office of Benjamin Pratt from 1755 to 1758. He was admitted to the Inner Temple in London in 1758, was called to the English bar in 1761, and practiced in courts on the Welsh circuit until 1768, when he left England for the island of Saint Christopher (St. Kitts) in the West Indies where he lived and practiced law, acting as attorney general during the French occupation of St. Kitts from 1781 to 1783."[1] Upon his return to America in 1783, Gardiner resumed his law practice in Boston and subsequently served as the District of Maine's representative to the Massachusetts legislature after his move to Pownalboro in 1786, where he had inherited a large farm from his father. Gardiner became known as a great barrister and an avid law reformer, and he was very active in local politics, including reforms that secured Maine's statehood. En route to the 1793 Massachusetts legislative session, he drowned when the schooner on which he was traveling sank off Cape Ann.

Copley painted this portrait early in his career, when he was about twenty years old. Above all other portraitists from eighteenth-century colonial America, Copley is known for his facility at capturing the likeness as well as the character of his sitters. With relentless attention to detail, he achieved a sophistication in his portraits that surpassed that of his contemporaries. Copley scrutinized his sitters and included personal details that inform the viewer of the subjects' unique personalities, social status, politics, or occupation. In this portrait, you find a successful barrister dressed for his profession, complete with powdered wig worn in the courtroom. Gardiner looks directly out at the artist while engaging the viewer with his body language. His facial expression, with his mouth poised in a tight-lipped smile and a glint in his eyes, suggests that he has a story to tell. His left hand rests on a large leather-bound law book, while his thumb holds his place in another book, implying that he has just been interrupted from his reading. With the index finger of his right hand, Gardiner directs the viewer's attention to the edge of the canvas, where a fragment of a mountain landscape is revealed. The heavy brown drape that comprises the background conceals any further information about the interior setting and heightens the illusion of three-dimensional space in the foreground. This compositional device was used by many artists of the period, and Copley frequently used a similar format for his professional portraits, many of which included a landscape view. It is unclear as to the location of the landscape. It had been assumed that the artist was referring to Gardiner's time in the West Indies, but the date of the painting does not corroborate that; thus, it may be a reference to the land that his father owned in Pownalboro on the coast of Maine. It is also possible that the artist is offering a clue to the sitter's preference for being outside as

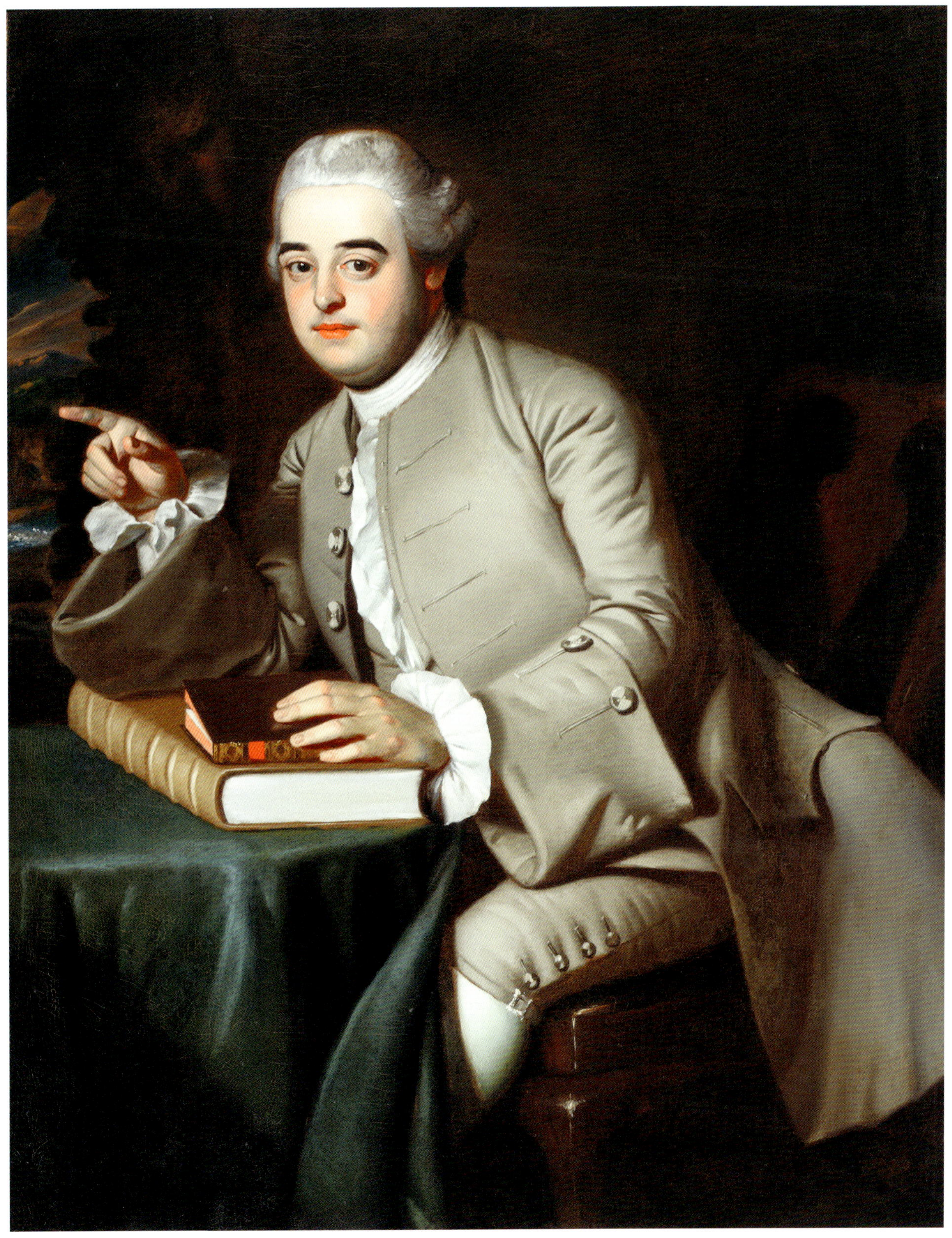

opposed to being cooped up inside, practicing law. By adding this exterior view to his formal portrait, Copley offers a third layer of information about the sitter, albeit inconclusive.

Copley was a master at manipulating color, light, and shadow to achieve the illusion of three dimensions, and one of his hallmarks can be seen in this portrait in the myriad folds of the fabric, for which he distinguishes the differences in type and sheen of Gardiner's suit coat and breeches, the ruffled front and cuffs of his shirt, and the table covering. And although the artist would become even more skilled at painting such details after he left America for England, the buttons, needlework, and buckle details as well as the light reflecting off his fingernails reveal Copley's skill at differentiating between one surface and the next. Around the same time, Copley painted a portrait of Gardiner's sister Ann; and in later years, a portrait of his father.[2]

When this portrait was reproduced in Jules Prown's catalogue raisonné of the artist's work in America, it was assigned the date c. 1768 by the author.[3] However, when *Portrait of John Gardiner* was presented to The Westmoreland in 1987, Prown reviewed the painting after it had been cleaned and felt it to have been created about a decade earlier. The Westmoreland also owns *Study of a Cherub* (1961.157), a blue chalk drawing by the artist.

Copley married Susanna Clarke (nicknamed Suky), the daughter of a rich Tory merchant, in 1769. The artist was painting in Boston in the years preceding the American Revolution—a turbulent period in colonial America's history. Although he tried to remain neutral, he became indirectly mixed up in the brewing hostilities that led to the Boston Tea Party through his father-in-law, Richard Clarke, as he was an agent for the East India Company and one of the owners of the tea that was dumped into Boston Harbor on December 16, 1773.

While the artist achieved considerable success in this country, he felt stifled by painting only likenesses and believed he had a higher calling—to make history paintings, considered nobler and filled with didactic content. As a Tory and thus caught in a difficult political situation, Copley left America for Europe in June 1774, studying masterworks in Italy and France before settling in London in 1775, where he became associated with both Sir Joshua Reynolds (1723–1792) and the American expatriate Benjamin West (1738–1820), who had left America in 1760. Suky and the rest of his family joined him there that year. Copley had sent one of his masterworks, a portrait of his half brother Henry Pelham, or *Boy with a Squirrel* (1765, Museum of Fine Arts, Boston), to the Society of Artists exhibition in London in 1766, where it was seen by Reynolds, then president of the Royal Academy, and West, who criticized its "hardness in drawing, coldness in the shades." Both artists urged Copley to travel to Europe to study "before it was too late in life, and before [his] manner and taste were corrupted or fixed by working in [his] little way in Boston."[4]

Although he would regret his decision later in his life, he became an expatriate, never to return to his native soil. Copley turned to his higher aspiration of history painting in London and, like West, painted historical events of both the distant past and the modern era. One of his first masterpieces, *Watson and the Shark* (1778; National Gallery of Art), documents an episode that took place just three decades earlier in the life of a young Brook Watson, who was attacked by a shark in Havana harbor in 1749.

After suffering a stroke, Copley died in London on September 9, 1815, at the age of seventy-seven. While he continued to paint until 1810, his reputation suffered, as did his work. However, his six-decade-long career, four of which were spent in London, resulted in some of the most accomplished portraits in the history of American art.

BLJ

1 For in-depth information on John Gardiner see: T. A. Milford, *The Gardiners of Massachusetts: Provincial Ambition and the British-American Career* (Durham, NH: University of New Hampshire Press, 2005. The Westmoreland's *Portrait of John Gardiner* is the cover illustration on the paperback edition.

2 See Jules David Prown, *John Singleton Copley: In America*, 1738–1774 (Cambridge, MA: Harvard University Press, 1966), vol. 1, plates 39 and 318.

3 Prown, vol. 1, plate 193.

4 Richard McLanathan, *The American Tradition in the Arts* (New York: Harcourt, Brace & World, Inc., 1968), 94.

Chippendale Slant Front Desk, c. 1765
Probably Philadelphia
Walnut with poplar and pine or cedar
38 x 43 ½ x 21 inches
Anonymous Gift by Exchange, 1990.34
Provenance: Estate of the Honorable Livingston Biddle, Philadelphia, Pennsylvania.

The rococo style of furniture in America is known as Chippendale, after London cabinetmaker Thomas Chippendale, whose pattern books of extremely ornate furniture were published in the mid-eighteenth century and became popular with American cabinetmakers, particularly in Philadelphia. This style departed from the graceful, curved lines of the earlier Queen Anne style by expressing energy through asymmetrical naturalistic carved ornamentation. The shell-carved interior of The Westmoreland's *Slant Front Desk*, as well as the undulating concavity of the small interior drawers below, bring visual excitement to an otherwise plain façade of drawers.

The rococo style is also expressed in this piece by the lively figuring, or grain, of the native Pennsylvania walnut used for the lid and exterior drawers of the case, and its ornate brass hardware. The carving, figured wood, and fancy brass combine to excite the eye. All of these design choices represent costly options, as shown in the eighteenth-century Philadelphia cabinetmakers price books, which indicate that the extra costs for carving and choice woods were significant. In this context, it is interesting to note that carving on The Westmoreland's desk was also lavished on a surface not normally visible: the door behind the interior central prospect door. This concealed interior door has a shell identical to the five shells across the desk interior and is part of a removable unit concealing three secret drawers. In addition to the carved shells, the vertical document drawers flanking the prospect door are carved with flutes.

This is not, however, the most expensive desk that could have been ordered at this time. Imported mahogany from the West Indies was then available in Philadelphia, and it was more costly than native walnut. A customer could also order a bookcase to fit on top of the desk, with wood-paneled, glazed, or mirrored doors. Finally, a fancy cornice of scrolls or pediments, enriched with carved ornamentation, could also have been added to the bookcase at extra expense.

The cabinetmaker who made this desk did not sign or label it, which was not uncommon in Philadelphia. In some rare instances, cabinetmaker invoices or account books have survived from which attributions can be made. Another virtually identical six-shell desk from the same shop recently reappeared on the market, having been previously sold at auction in 1929 at the famous Reifsnyder sale[1] This cabinetmaker may have worked just outside Philadelphia, since some design aspects of the desk differ from those of mainstream Philadelphia work. The ogee feet of The Westmoreland's desk, for example, are taller and of a different shape than those typical of "downtown" cabinet shops. In addition, the design of the carved shells is more geometric than naturalistic, suggesting the cabinetmaker may have carved them himself.[2] Interestingly, most carvers were immigrants lately arrived from England or Germany, who frequently worked for cabinetmakers as independent contractors.

The provenance of The Westmoreland's *Slant Front Desk* includes the Honorable Livingston Biddle, who was descended from Charles Biddle (1745–1821), vice president of the Supreme Executive Council of Pennsylvania. Charles's mother, Mary Scull Biddle, was the daughter of the surveyor-general of Pennsylvania, Nicholas Scull.

HNT

1 See Sotheby's *Important Americana:* New York, 22 & 23 January 2010, Sale 8608, lot 515.

2 See Wallace Nutting, *Furniture Treasury* (Cambridge, MA: University Press, 1928), vol. I, pl. 638, for a less sophisticated Pennsylvania desk with identical shell carvings.

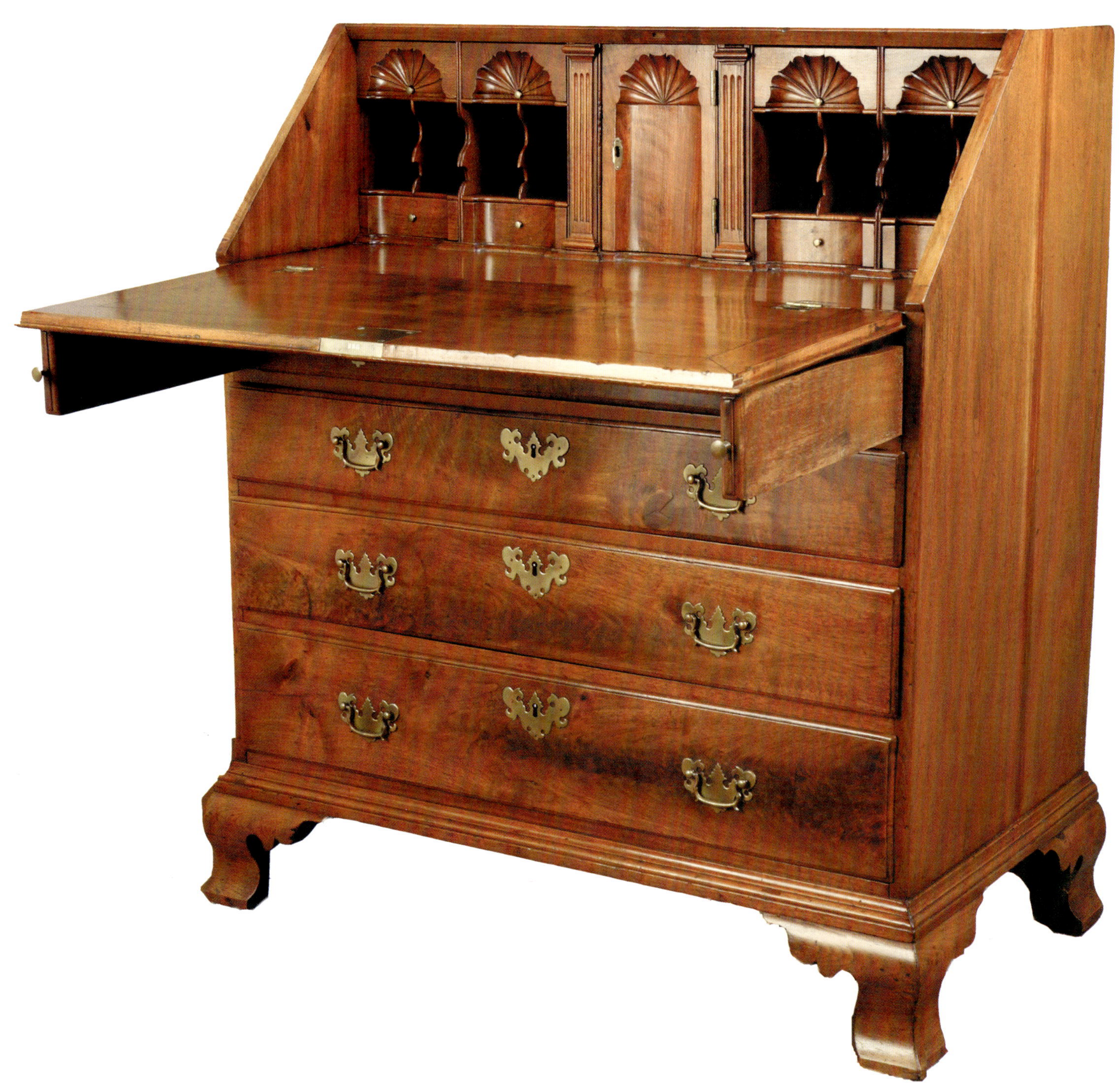

JOHANN KARL SCHEIBELER (w. 1769–1800)
Taufschein for Jacob Kuntz, 1789
Hempfield Township, Westmoreland County, Pennsylvania
Ink and watercolor on laid paper, 16 ¼ x 12 ¾ inches
Signed and dated: Karl Scheibeler Schoolmaster Hempfield Township Westmoreland County 1789
Gift of the Mary Marchand Woods Estate, 1960. 533
PROVENANCE: Mary Marchand Woods, Greensburg, Pennsylvania.

SELECTED EXHIBITIONS: *250 Years of Art in Pennsylvania*, Westmoreland County Museum of Art, 1959; *The Pennsylvania Germans: A Celebration of Their Art, 1683–1850*, Philadelphia Museum of Art, 1981; *A Sampler of American Folk Art from Pennsylvania Collections*, Westmoreland Museum of Art, 1989; *Made in Pennsylvania: A Folk Art Tradition*, Westmoreland Museum of American Art, 2007.

Fraktur art is a product of two medieval European traditions. It is a writing style that used printed, or fractured, gothic letters rather than cursive writing, and combined this calligraphy with pictorial decorative elements in the manner of the medieval illuminated manuscript. Fraktur art also expressed spiritual values through religious text and celebration of family. Among the various forms of fraktur are birth and baptismal certificates (*geburts und taufschein*), house blessings (*haussegen*), spiritual clocks, New Year's greetings, awards of merit, songbooks, book plates, writing samples (*vorschriften*), and the occasional marriage certificate.[1]

The great influx of immigrants from Germany and Switzerland beginning in the late seventeenth century brought fraktur to Pennsylvania. Seeking freedom from political and religious persecution, these immigrants arrived in Philadelphia, and many settle in Greensburg and other areas west of the Allegheny Mountains. Large numbers also settled in Ohio, West Virginia, Virginia, Maryland, North Carolina, and Ontario, Canada. These German settlers tended to form communities around a church. Most were farmers, but some were schoolteachers and artisans, including weavers, blacksmiths, and cabinetmakers.

Fraktur flourished in Pennsylvania from about 1750 to 1850. The Ephrata Cloister was the earliest German school in Pennsylvania, and it has a rich fraktur tradition. Because the early German settlers tended to have communal societies, German remained their principal language well into the nineteenth century, and probably 90 percent of Pennsylvania fraktur is written in German rather than English.

The schoolmaster was the primary fraktur artist. He taught writing to his students, often by providing samples of religious texts to be carefully copied. Fraktur art was not taught as part of the school curriculum but was practiced by the schoolmaster, or a professional scrivener, to earn extra money. Fraktur were treasured by recipients as family records, and as such they were seldom framed for display; instead, these records were often pasted on the inside of a blanket chest lid, rolled inside the till, or folded for storage in a book or family bible.

Western Pennsylvania had an important fraktur tradition that was largely unknown until 1986, when the first scholarship on Westmoreland County fraktur was published.[2] By this time, The Westmoreland already had a significant collection—a dozen fraktur by six western Pennsylvania artists. In 2007, the Museum exhibited forty-nine western Pennsylvania fraktur and subsequently acquired the Joy and R. David Brocklebank Collection of western Pennsylvania fraktur consisting of more than 250 examples.

By the late eighteenth century, Greensburg had a significant population of German immigrants who established their own schools. Johann Karl Scheibeler is the earliest fraktur artist working in Westmoreland County whose work has been identified. Based on recorded examples, he was active in the county from 1784 to 1793. Before coming to Westmoreland County, he worked in Egypt, Lehigh County, Pennsylvania (w. 1774–1775), and Frederick County, Maryland (w. 1779).[3]

The first school in Greensburg was a German church school that was part of the Harrold Settlement, located three miles southwest of Greensburg. The first schoolmaster there was Balthazer Meyer, who performed lay baptisms from 1772 until 1792. "His records are fine specimens of penmanship in

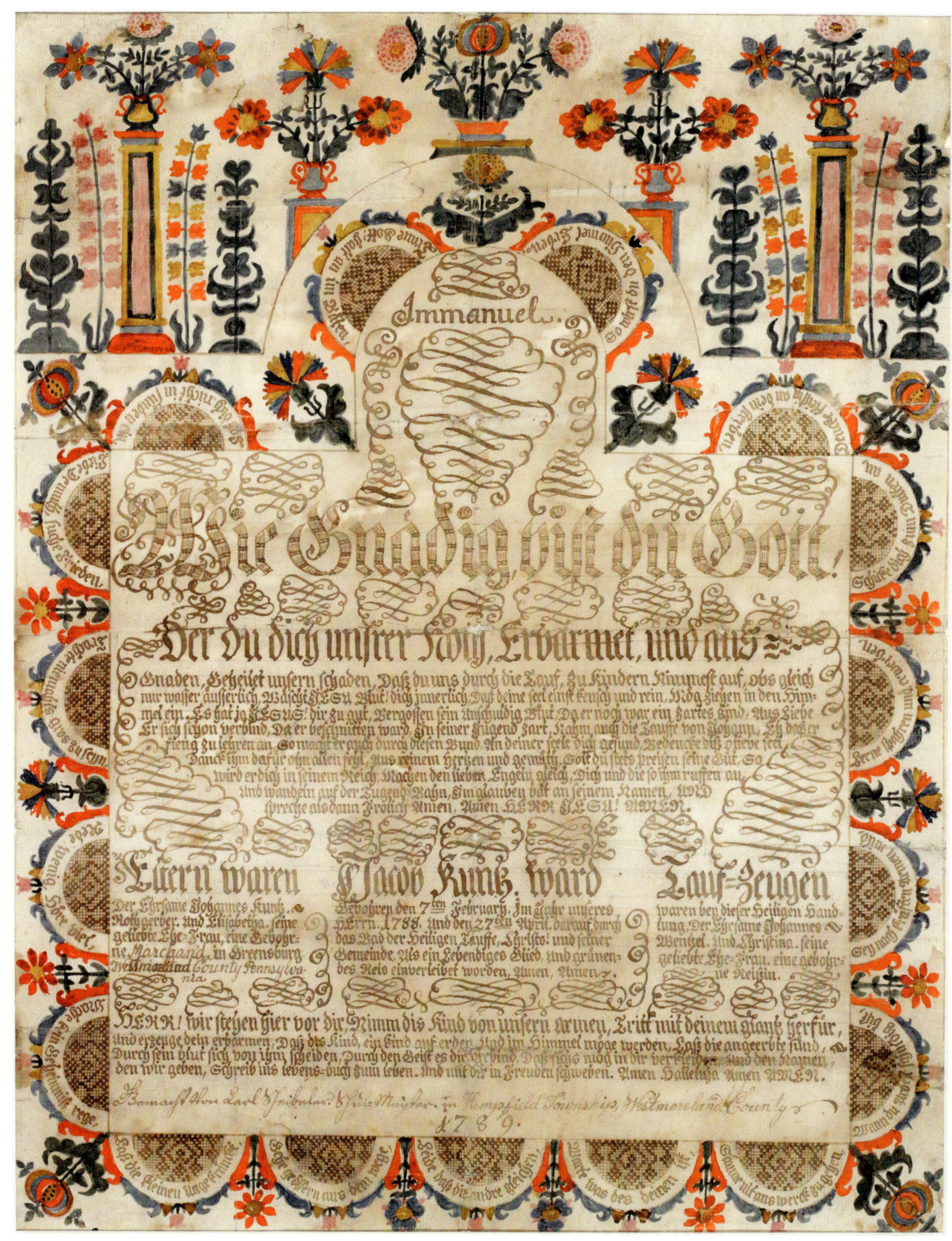
Immanuel
Wie Gnädig bist du Gott!
Der du dich unser Gnädig Erbarmet, und aus Gnaden, Geheilet unsern schaden, Dass du uns durch die Tauf, Zu Kindern Nimmest auf, obs gleich nur wasser äusserlich, Wäscht JESU Blut! dich innerlich, Dass deine seel einst keusch und rein, Mög ziehen in den Himmel ein. Es hat ja JESUS! dir zu gut, Vergossen sein unschuldig Blut, Da er noch war ein zartes Kind, Aus Liebe Er sich schon verbind, Da er beschnitten ward, In seiner Jugend zart, Nahm auch die Tauffe von Johann, Eh daher fieng zu lehren an, So macht er auch durch diesen Bund, An deiner seele dich gesund, Bedencke diss o liebe seel, Danck ihm dafür ohn allen fehl, Aus reinem Hertzen und gemüth, Solt du stets preisen seine Güt, So wird er dich in seinem Reich, Machen den lieben Engeln gleich, Dich und die so ihm ruffen an, Und wandeln auf der Tugend-Bahn, Im glauben bat an seinem Namen, Und spreche alsdann Frölich Amen, Amen HERR JESU! AMEN.
Eltern waren
Der Ehrsame Johannes Kuntz. Rothgerber. und Elisabetha. seine geliebte Ehe-Frau, eine Gebohrne Marchand. in Greensburg. Westmoreland County Pennsylvania
Jacob Kuntz. ward
Gebohren den 7ten February. Im Jahr unseres HErrn. 1788. und den 27ten April. darauf durch das Bad der Heiligen Tauffe, Christo! und seiner Gemeinde, Als ein Lebendiges Glied, und grünendes Reis einverleibet worden, Amen, Amen.
Tauf-Zeugen
waren bey dieser Heiligen Handlung, Der Ehrsame Johannes Wentzel. und Christina. seine geliebte Ehe-Frau, eine gebohrne Reisin.
HERR! wir stehen hier vor dir, Nimm dis Kind von unsern armen, Tritt mit deinem glantz herfür, Und erzeuge dein erbarmen, Dass dis Kind, ein Kind auf erden, Und im Himmel möge werden, Lass die angeerbte sünd, Durch sein blut sich von ihm scheiden, Durch den Geist es dir verbind, Dass sichs mög in dir verkleiden, Und den Namen den wir geben, Schreib ins lebens-buch zum leben. Und mit dir in Freuden schweben. Amen Halleluja Amen AMEN.
1789.

the German, and with those of his successors, covering a period of 90 years, carefully made, are intact."[4] The reference to "fine specimens of penmanship" suggests that Meyer was also a fraktur artist.

Johann Karl Scheibeler was identified as an early schoolteacher in a local history published in 1927: "While Balthaser [sic] Meyer, probably did not at first teach beyond the Harrold neighborhood, Karl Scheibler [sic], also an expert penman, and a veteran of the Revolutionary War, taught in and around Greensburg just following the Revolution and he became the successor of Balthazer Meyer, later at Harrolds."[5] The same early Greensburg history illustrates a baptismal certificate by Scheibeler for John George Eisaman, described as one of the earliest carpet and coverlet weavers in Greensburg, and both the taufschein and Eisaman are pictured.[6]

Scheibeler's baptismal certificate for Jacob Kuntz is the most elaborate of those in The Westmoreland's collection. It combines semicircular border devices and numerous colorful floral elements with lengthy text and calligraphic ink flourishes. Scheibeler is one of the few artists to record the father's occupation in his baptismal certificates. The text identified Jacob's father as Johannes Kuntz (a tanner) and his mother as Elisabetha (Marchand), and lists both the date of his birth (February 7, 1788), and his baptism in the same year (April 27). In addition, Scheibeler lists the witnesses, including the wife's maiden name, thus providing a genealogical record that can be traced further.

Eight fraktur signed by, or attributed to, Scheibeler are illustrated in *Made in Pennsylvania: A Folk Art Tradition,* seven of which are part of the Joy and R. David Brocklebank Collection at The Westmoreland.

HNT

JOHN GEORGE BUSYAEGER (1774–1843; w. 1805–1841)
Taufschein for David Landis, 1825
Hempfield Township, Westmoreland County, Pennsylvania
Ink and watercolor on paper, 15 1/16 x 12 5/16 inches
Signed and dated: J. George Busyaeger Westmoreland County State of Pennsylvania 1825
The Joy and R. David Brocklebank Collection through the William Jamison Art Acquisition Fund, 2008.151
PROVENANCE: Private Collection, Adamsburg, Pennsylvania; Joy and R. David Brocklebank.

SELECTED EXHIBITIONS: *Made in Pennsylvania: A Folk Art Tradition,* Westmoreland Museum of American Art, 2007.

John George Busyaeger was born in Heidelberg, Germany, in 1774 and arrived in America in 1803.[7] Church records indicate that Busyaeger taught at the Brush Creek Settlement near Greensburg.[8] Busyaeger was the most prolific of the Westmoreland County fraktur artists, with more than fifty recorded signed fraktur. Eight of his fraktur, including a spiritual clock, are illustrated in *Made in Pennsylvania: A Folk Art Tradition.*[9] Busyaeger also made at least two marriage certificates, one of which is in The Westmoreland's collection (2008.213).[10]

The vast majority of Busyaeger fraktur are written in German and designed in a horizontal format composed of a simple decorative border of tulips, leaves, and pinwheel flowers, with a covered urn in the center of the top border. The birth and baptismal certificate for David Landis departs from this standard format in several important respects: it is written in English rather than German, it is vertical rather than horizontal, and it is visually more complex and interesting. The decoration does not merely frame the writing but highlights the text by dividing it into four parts. Additionally, the decorative vocabulary has been expanded to include colorful architectural columns in the upper corners, which support vases with plants, including blue thistles. The central green wreath is also a device not found in most of Busyaeger's work.

The recorded Landis family history suggests its westward migration from eastern Pennsylvania. David Landis, the subject

Chest over Drawers, c. 1790
Pennsylvania, probably Berks County
Painted tulip poplar with pine [feet restored]
47 ¼ x 28 ¾ x 21 ¾ inches
Gift of Mr. and Mrs. Paul Euwer in honor of
Carolyn Lynch, 1977.23
Provenance: Mr. and Mrs. Paul Euwer, Greensburg, Pennsylvania.

Selected Exhibitions: *Pennsylvania Folk Art*, 1700–1865, Southern Alleghenies Museum of Art, Loretto, Pennsylvania, 1978; *A Sampler of American Folk Art from Pennsylvania Collections*, Westmoreland Museum of Art, 1989.

The immigration of Germans to Pennsylvania began in 1683 with the arrival of Francis Daniel Pastorius and several other families, who founded Germantown just north of Philadelphia.[1] On the voyage from Europe, most people brought their possessions with them in a chest with locks to protect money and other valuables. The chests were quite simple, constructed of six boards including a hinged lift top, and most were painted to protect the wood.

This simple horizontal chest, also referred to as a "dower chest," was the most important piece of furniture in the early Pennsylvania German household, with each adolescent child and adult member owning one. The chest of drawers with a vertical case was an English furniture form that did not become popular with German immigrants until the mid nineteenth century.

Chests made in Pennsylvania German communities were commonly constructed of soft wood painted with colorful traditional designs. Typical motifs were flowers, hearts, creatures, and human figures. Background surfaces were painted a solid color or were sponge decorated or grain painted to look like expensive hardwood.

Frequently, the front was painted with two or three architectural panels of lighter color than the rest of the case. These arched or square panels were often filled with colorful decoration. Some chests were inscribed on the front with the owner's name and the date. Unfortunately, it was not common practice for the Pennsylvania German makers to sign their work. An exception to this general rule was the furniture of the Mennonite cabinetmakers of Soap Hollow, Somerset County, who frequently signed their work. (See entry for *Soap Hollow Chest of Drawers.*) However, in the absence of a maker's signature or mark, it is still possible to attribute painted decoration to certain Pennsylvania counties based on reliable family ownership histories of chests with similar decoration.

The Westmoreland's *Chest over Drawers* has several distinctive motifs, including painted architectural columns and panels that appear on other Pennsylvania German chests. The vertical heart borders and the black pinwheel flowers are also distinctive. Nine published examples of chests with all of these particular motifs have been attributed to Berks County, Pennsylvania, with inscribed dates ranging from 1786 to 1803.[2]

The case of The Westmoreland's chest is beautifully decorated with sponged or mottled brown paint with fan designs. Blue green paint has been applied in the same manner to the drawer fronts. The lower portion of the case containing the drawers is painted bright red, as are portions of the architectural columns flanking the arched panels and the arches themselves. The lid is painted with the same decoration as that on the front of the chest, although much of the color has faded over time. Since these chests were used to store valuable items such as jewelry, money, and important family documents including fraktur, they usually had at least one locking mechanism. This chest has three types of locks: a large interior crab or bear-trap lock to secure the lid, a small metal key lock for each of the two large drawers, and a concealed wooden locking mechanism for the small central drawer. This last mechanism consists of a vertical wooden rod attached to the inside of the backboard of the chest, which extends down to engage the back of the small drawer. This rod must be manually raised from inside the chest to release the drawer.

The interior of the case has a till attached to the left side of the chest composed of three thin boards; a bottom, a front, and a lid. Tills sometimes contain drawers and secret compartments. Fraktur were often kept rolled inside the till or pasted on the inside lid of a chest. Simple wrought-iron strap hinges attach the lid of this chest to the inside backboard of the case.

HNT

1 Monroe H. Fabian, *The Pennsylvania-German Decorated Chest* (Trenton, NJ: Main Street Press, 1978), cat. 68.

2 Fabian; cat. 64, 66, 68–73. Based on the painted decoration, three may be by the same hand as The Westmoreland's chest: No. 69 in the collection of the Metropolitan Museum of Art, and Nos. 70 and 73, both with Israel Sack, Inc. provenance.

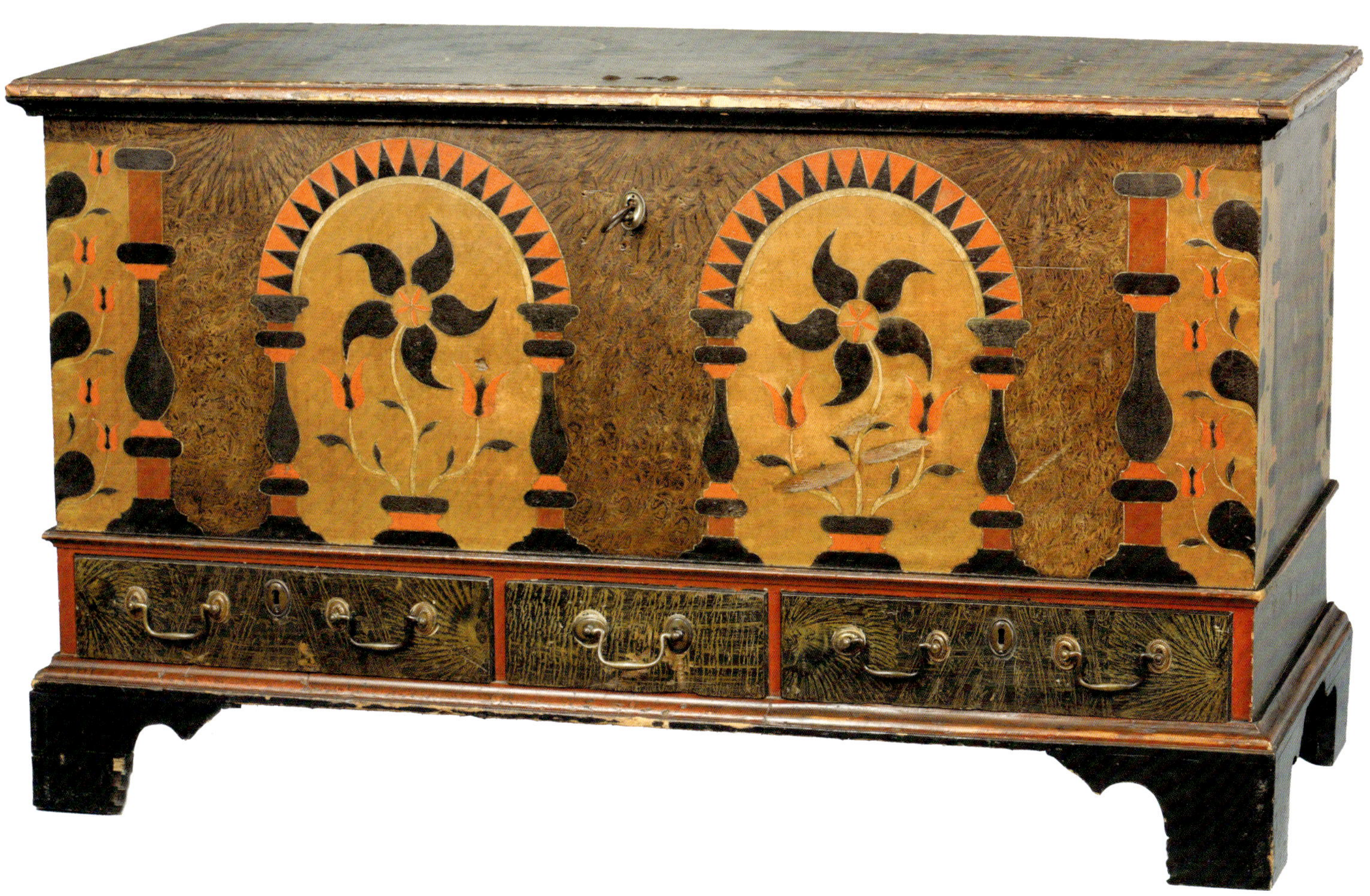

HENRY WISE (1763–1831; w. 1802–1814)
Tall Case Clock, c. 1805
Greensburg, Pennsylvania
Case: cherry with chestnut
Movement: eight-day iron and brass with strike
Dial: silvered sheet-brass
99½ inches high (case) [feet and base molding restored, finials missing]
Gift of John Barclay Jr., 1983.53
Provenance: John Barclay Jr., Greensburg, Pennsylvania.

The earliest clocks made in America date from the first decade of the eighteenth century. The dials of these clocks were made of imported brass with applied and engraved decoration. The silvered sheet-brass dial of this tall case clock is unique among clocks made in western Pennsylvania because this frontier region was incapable of supporting clockmakers until the end of the eighteenth century, when the less-expensive white-painted iron dial had long replaced the brass dial. Clocks were extremely costly because they required the skills of several artisans: a clockmaker to assemble the brass movement and dial, an engraver to ornament or finish the dial, a cabinetmaker to make the wood case, and a carver to add decoration. Thus, a tall clock was not only a practical means of telling time but also a symbol of wealth for friends and visitors to admire.

The beautifully engraved dial of this clock, with its two birds, whimsical human face, and extensive foliation, is signed "Henry Wise/Greensburg." Henry Wise was listed in the tax records of Greensburg as a clockmaker, watchmaker, and silversmith from 1802 to 1814.[1] The clock was probably made soon after he arrived in Greensburg. According to a descendant, Henry Wise was born in either Virginia or Maryland.[2] He signed a deed in 1788 stating that he was a resident of the "town and county of Bedford [Pennsylvania]." Around 1791, he purchased land in Greensburg where the courthouse now stands. He was married to Barbara Rohrer of York, Pennsylvania and had four children, one of whom, John H. (w. 1813–1829), was also listed in Greensburg as a silversmith and watchmaker.[3] Unfortunately, no silver made by Henry Wise has been recorded, and only a single fiddleback coin silver teaspoon—marked "J. H. Wise" in a serrated rectangle—is known by his son John.

Possible explanations for Wise's use of an elaborate brass dial for this clock are that it was made for himself or a family member; if that were the case, the significant additional cost of the brass dial and its extensive engraving would not have been a concern[4]

The engraved face on the dial arch is a recent discovery. Long before the clock entered the Museum's collection, a round silvered disk had been attached to the front of the dial arch covering the engraved face. This disk was engraved with a sundial, an urn, and an adage: "Time passeth away / like a shadow." The engraving on the disk, however, does not appear to be by the same hand that engraved the dial; it is not as refined and lacks its ornate flourishes (see detail). Upon examination of the movement, three piercings were observed in the back of the dial arch. When the disk was removed, the face emerged (see detail). A relative of the donor recalled having heard about young girls being frightened by a face on the dial; perhaps that is why the disk was added.

The most common embellishment of a dial arch was a "moon dial," which continuously turned to display ships, landscapes, and phases of the moon. Clockmakers in New England sometimes substituted a rocking ship in the dial arch by attaching a metal device with a painted sailing ship to the pendulum so that the ship rocked back and forth with each swing of the pendulum. Much rarer, however, is a face in the dial arch with rocking eyes, which our clock apparently had based on physical evidence. Three piercings with pairs of fastener holes—some threaded—above and below each eye probably supported a device with painted eyes and mouth attached to the pendulum rod. A Philadelphia tall clock by Burrows Dowdney, c. 1770, made for Philadelphia silversmith Thomas Shields, has a painted face in the dial arch with eyes that rock with each movement of the pendulum.[5] These features could easily frighten children.

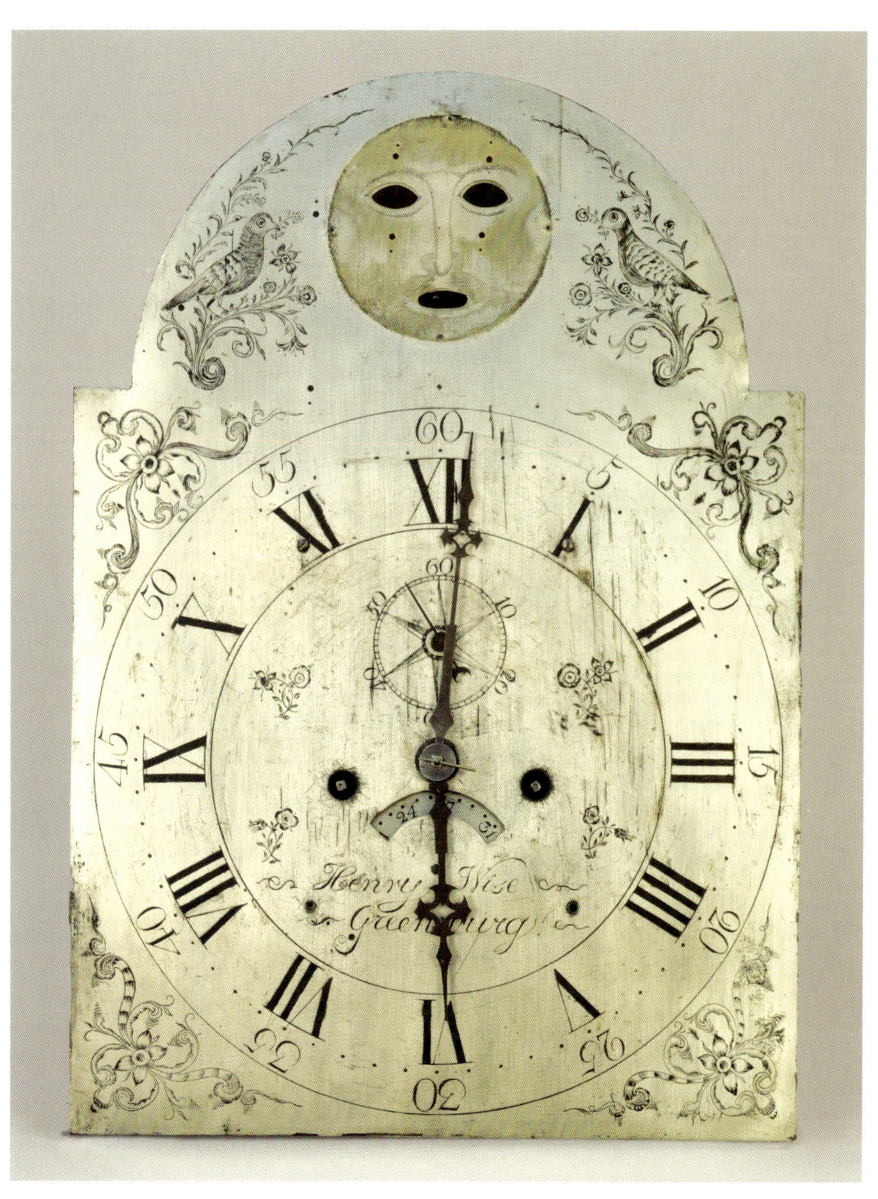
Henry Wise

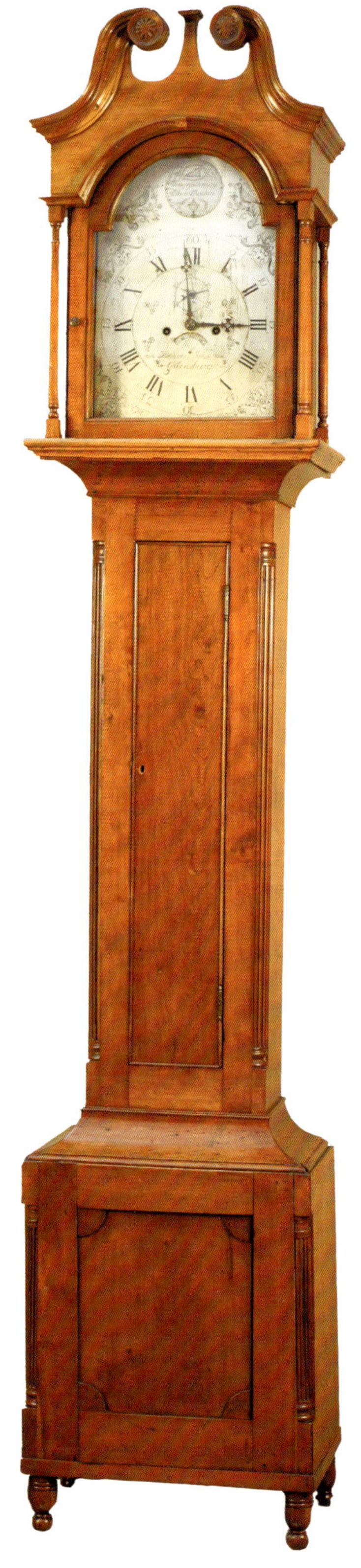

The cherry case of the Wise clock is in the Chippendale style, which was popular in America from the mid-eighteenth century to about 1785. The Chippendale characteristics of the case include the carved rosettes at the ends of the scrolled arches on the hood, and the carved fluted quarter columns on the front corners of the waist and the base.

Henry Wise was not the only clockmaker working in Greensburg in the late eighteenth century. Jacob Hugus (1769–1833), is recorded as a clockmaker working here from 1799 to 1805.[6] A tall clock with a white-painted dial signed by Hugus was loaned to The Westmoreland's inaugural exhibition, *250 Years of Art in Pennsylvania*, in 1959.[7] The case of the Hugus clock is also in the earlier Chippendale style. Clockmaking in nearby Pittsburgh began roughly around the same time, c. 1800, but Pittsburgh clockmakers were quicker to adopt the new neo-classical style for clock cases, which substituted inlay for carved decoration.[8]

HNT

1 James Biser Whisker, *Pennsylvania Clockmakers, Watchmakers, and Allied Crafts* (State College, PA: Jostens Printing and Publishing 1990), 135.

2 Correspondence with Shirley H. Silverman, on deposit in the Henry Wise Tall Case Clock object file, Westmoreland Museum of American Art.

3 Whisker, *Pennsylvania Clockmakers*, 135.

4 The clock was bequeathed to the Museum in 1983 by James Barclay Jr., in whose house it stood since at least 1934, when it was appraised for insurance purposes. Preliminary research suggests the Wise and Barclay families may have been related.

5 William H. Distin and Robert Bishop, *The American Clock* (New York: E.F. Dutton & Co., 1976), 20–21.

6 Whisker, *Pennsylvania Clockmakers*, 69.

7 Paul A. Chew, *250 Years of Art in Pennsylvania* (Greensburg, PA: Westmoreland County Museum of Art, 1959), 59, plate 165.

8 Edward F. LaFond Jr., "Southwestern Pennsylvania Clockmaking," *Made in Western Pennsylvania: Early Decorative Arts* (Pittsburgh, PA: Historical Society of Western Pennsylvania, 1983), 43–55.

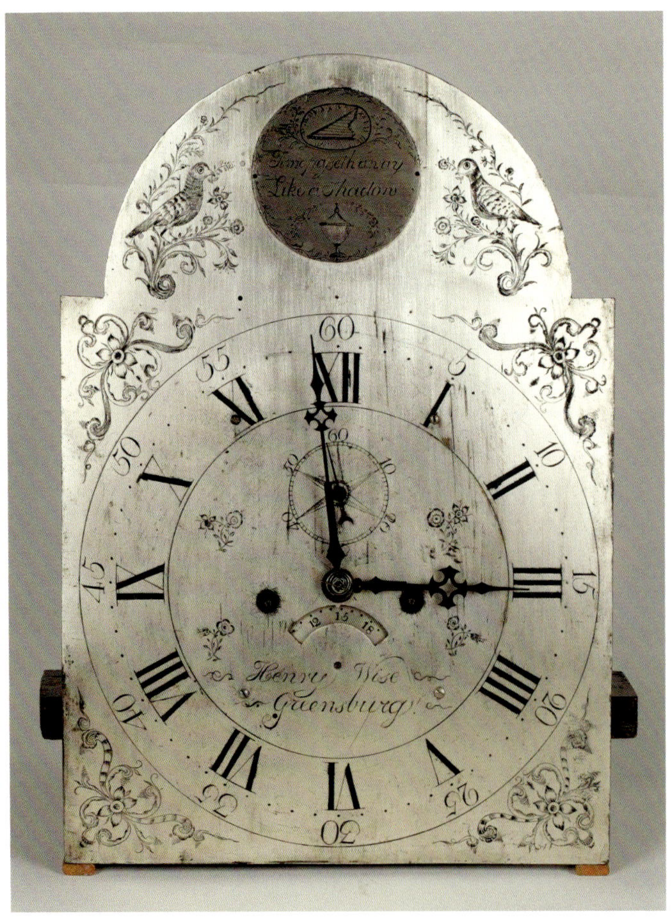

BENJAMIN WEST (1738–1820)
King Priam, 1808
Oil on canvas, 47 x 69 ¾ inches
Signed and dated lower center
Gift of the William A. Coulter Fund, 1968.3
Provenance: Family of the Artist; Robert Frank, London; French and Company, New York.

Selected Exhibitions: Royal Academy, London, 1808; British Institution, London, 1809, 1816; *Benjamin West, 1738–1820,* Graham Gallery, New York, 1962; *A Feast for the Eyes: Treasures from the Westmoreland Museum of American Art,* Woodmere Art Museum, Philadelphia, Pennsylvania, 1998.

Born in rural Springfield, Pennsylvania, southwest of Philadelphia, Benjamin West became the first native-born American artist to achieve international recognition and acclaim. A child of Quakers, he was entirely self-taught until the age of twenty-two, when—sponsored by American patrons—he set sail for Italy in 1760, to begin his initial art studies among the works of Italian Renaissance and baroque masters. He then traveled on to London, where he achieved such success that he settled there permanently in 1763, never to return to his homeland. Together with Sir Joshua Reynolds (1723–1792), he was a founding member of the Royal Academy of Arts in 1768. West succeeded Reynolds as the organization's second president, serving from 1792 to 1805. He was reelected in 1806 and served until his death in 1820. West was appointed historical painter to the court by King George III in 1772, just three years before the outbreak of the American Revolution, providing him with an annual income and freeing him from traditional portrait commissions. In 1791, he would become surveyor of the king's pictures, a post that he also held until his death. West was engaged to marry Elizabeth Shewell of Philadelphia before he left America, and he sent for her in 1764. Married in London, they spent the rest of their lives there, raising two sons together, one of which was named after West's friend Benjamin Franklin.

West served as an important mentor to other American artists who crossed the Atlantic to study the great masters of Europe. His studio was host to several generations of American artists, and West's influence was vast, spreading to future generations of artists who traveled to England to study, including John Singleton Copley (1738–1815), John Trumbull (1756–1843), Charles Willson Peale (1741–1827), Rembrandt Peale (1778–1860), and Gilbert Stuart (1755–1828), all of whom would establish distinguished reputations in their own country. When West died in London at the age of eighty-one, he was buried with great honors in St. Paul's Cathedral, next to his friend Reynolds.

The Westmoreland owns two oil paintings by Benjamin West. His *Portrait of an English Gentleman* (1959.56) was one of the first works of art to enter the collection, a gift from Messiers Hirschl and Adler (now Hirschl & Adler Galleries), who would establish an ongoing relationship with the Museum, resulting in fifteen gifts over the years. This painting represents the artist's earlier, more reserved style of portraiture; King Priam, on the other hand, reveals the artist's interest and acclaim in the field of history painting. Grand historical themes referencing the distant past were the norm for this type of painting, expounded by the Royal Academy and considered the highest ranked style of painting in the hierarchy of noteworthy subjects at the time. Seen as the noblest form of art, history painting documented a period or specific event in history that conveyed a didactic message to its viewers to teach a religious, nationalistic, or ethical moral. West would revolutionize history painting forever in 1770 when he commemorated a contemporary event in his 5 x 7 foot *Death of General Wolfe* (National Gallery of Art, Canada). The Battle of Quebec, which he depicted, had occurred just eleven years before on September 13, 1759. His cast of characters are dressed in modern military uniforms, abandoning the costumes of classical antiquity that were the style for this type of painting, as they were thought to be timeless. West portrayed both past and modern events in his history paintings. *William Penn's Treaty with the Indians* of 1771 (Pennsylvania Academy of the Fine Arts) not only depicts an event of the recent past but also celebrates the New World and his connection, and perhaps

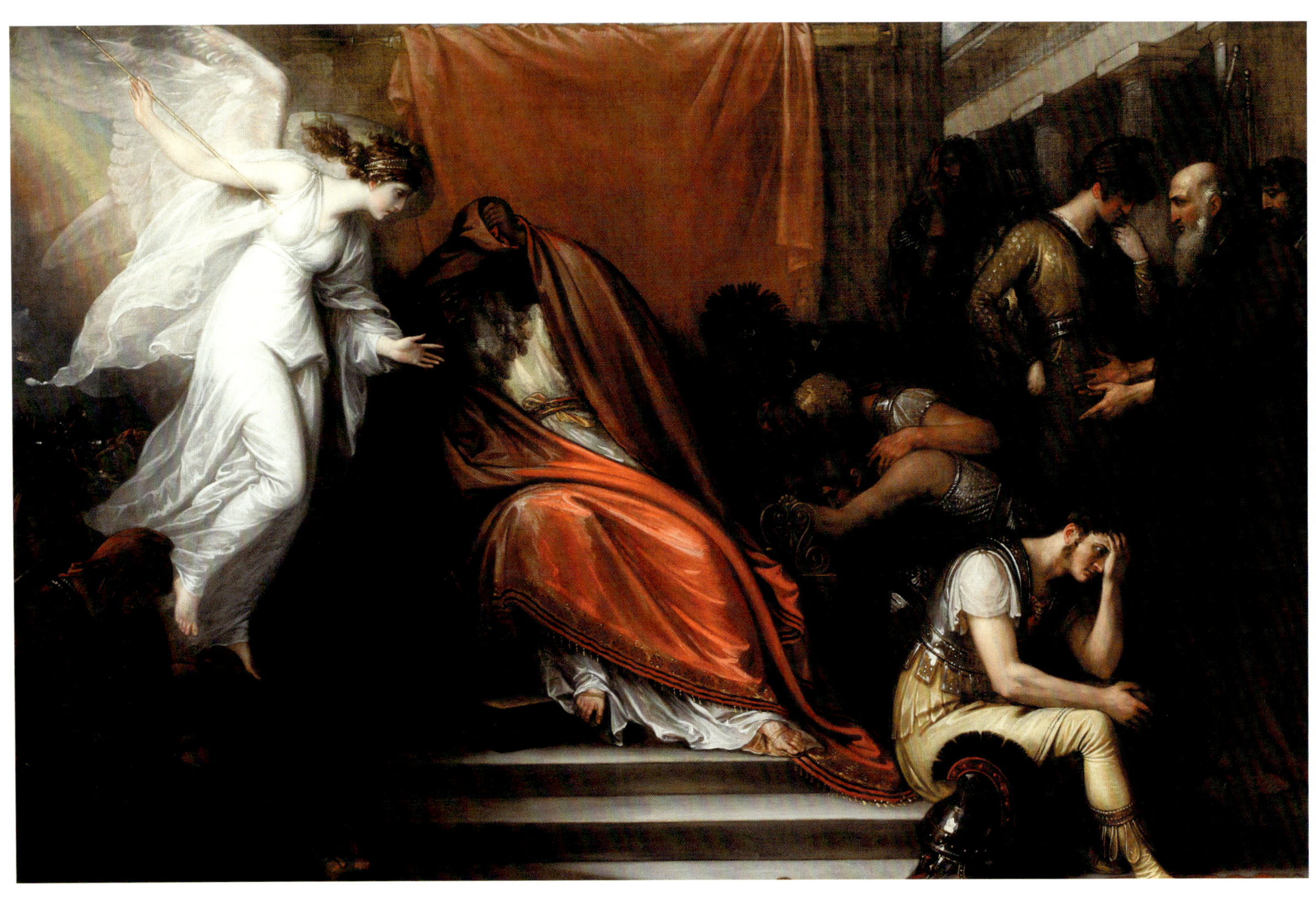

nostalgia, for his birthplace.

In *King Priam*, West portrays mythological drama on an epic scale in this nearly 4 x 6 foot painting. The subject is based on Homer's *Iliad* and illustrates the moment in which King Priam is told of the fate of his son Hector, who was dragged to death behind the chariot of Achilles during the Trojan War. An angelic Iris, messenger to Zeus, hovers by the king's side, informing him of the events that have taken place:

> *Then down her bow the winged Iris drives,*
> *And swift at Priam's mournful court arrives:*
> *Where the sad sons beside their father's throne*
> *Sat bathed in tears, and answered'd groan with groan;*
> *And all amidst them lay the hoary sire,*
> *(Sad scene of woe!) his face, his wrapp'd attire*
> *Conceal'd from sight; with frantic hands he spread*
> *A shower of ashes o'er his neck and head.*[1]

Iris symbolically brings Hector's death with her in the miniature vignette of his demise shown behind her. The severity of the event is illustrated in the classical postures of Hector's fellow warriors on the king's right and left, who mourn his loss, their bodies collapsed in despair. Grief overwhelms the remaining participants, including Priam's other two sons, who surround the king, their emotion meant by the artist to carry over into the sentiments of the viewer. Other members of Priam's court are situated to the left of the distraught king, cast in shadow by the mantle the king pulls over his head as Iris delivers her dire message. Idaeus, Priam's companion, is seen at the far right, his hands extended to the king, offering comfort.

West created his complex composition in a pyramidal format, with all the action of the scene contained within a central triangular structure. Strong diagonals direct viewers' eyes through the scene, allowing them to "read" the narrative set before them. Outside the triangle, in the upper-left background, another event is being played out, in which viewers are witness to Achilles dragging Hector's body behind his chariot and Aphrodite anointing the body with oil to protect him from harm. This small scene and the larger one parallel each other, revealing the past and present simultaneously. This painting was presumably commissioned by West's patron Thomas Hope, who had ordered three paintings from the artist in 1805; there is no record that the third work was ever delivered.[2] West offered the painting to the Pennsylvania Academy of the Fine Arts in Philadelphia in 1809, but it was declined. Achilles had been the artist's subject in an earlier and just as ambitious canvas painted in 1805.

Sketches for this painting of *King Priam* are known to exist, one of which is owned by Swarthmore College. The Westmoreland also owns a pen-and-ink drawing by West of the *Madonna and Child with Saint John* (1968.16).

West was a self-assured artist who rose to prominence early in his career, and his success in England carried over to America, where he remains one of the most important expatriate artists of the colonial period.

BLJ

1 Alexander Pope, "The Redemption of the Body of Hector," *The Iliad of Homer*, book 24, eBooks@Adelaide, The University of Adelaide Library, South Australia.

2 Helmut von Erffa and Allen Staley, *The Paintings of Benjamin West* (New Haven: Yale University Press, 1986), 254–55.

WILLIAM RICE (1777–1847), attributed
Tavern Sign Board, c. 1815
Probably New England
Paint on pine, 23 5/8 x 28 ½ inches (Lion side)
Gift of Friends of the Museum, 1965.3

Selected Exhibitions: *A Sampler of American Folk Art from Pennsylvania Collections,* Westmoreland Museum of Art, 1989; *All God's Creatures: Man and Beast in Early America,* Fraunces Tavern Museum, New York, 1999; *The Gift of Art,* Westmoreland Museum of American Art, 2009.

Illustrated: *A Sampler of American Folk Art from Pennsylvania Collections,* Westmoreland Museum of Art, 1989, Cat. 251, 41; Helene Smith, *Tavern Signs of America: History,* (Greensburg, PA: McDonald/Sward Publishing Co., 1989), front and back covers; Helene Smith, *Tavern Signs of America: Catalog* (Greensburg, PA: McDonald/Sward Publishing Co., 1989), 39.

Pictorial trade signs played an important role in eighteenth and nineteenth-century America, due to the fact that many people were unable to read as a result of the scarcity of public education until the mid-nineteenth century. Henry David Thoreau recognized that tavern and trade signs were an effective way to attract attention and business: "some to catch him by the appetite, as the tavern and victualling cellar; some by the fancy, as the dry goods store and the jeweller's; and others by the hair, or the feet, or the skirts, as the barber, the shoemaker, or the tailor."[1]

The visual messages conveyed by the eagle and lion on opposite sides of The Westmoreland's tavern sign were patriotic. The lion with a crown was a traditional depiction from English heraldry; however, here the lion's crown is missing, communicating the diminished status of England after the Revolutionary War.

The eagle on the other side of the Museum's sign was an even more patriotic symbol. Congress adopted the bald eagle for use on the Great Seal of the United States in 1782, and it became a popular motif for tavern signs.[2] Here the eagle is shown with outstretched wings, a form often referred to at the time as the "spread eagle." The eagle was a powerful icon of the new republic, although Benjamin Franklin and Thomas Jefferson reportedly disagreed over the designation of a national bird, with Franklin favoring the turkey, and Jefferson the eagle.

A trade sign with a lion or an eagle was a common signal of a tavern or public house, where travelers and businessmen could stop to eat, drink, and discuss topics of interest. Taverns also served as convenient places to conduct public meetings. At the Sign of General Butler tavern in Pittsburgh, representatives of the federal government met several times with angry local residents in an effort to negotiate an end to the 1794 Whiskey Rebellion.

Greensburg had taverns as early as the late eighteenth century, according to Helene Smith, an authority on the history of tavern signs. "Already in 1786 there were four taverns or more in Greensburg. . . . Some of the taverns were known as Sign of the Spread Eagle, Sign of the Cross Key, White Hawk Inn, Sign of Captain Lawrence, Sign of George Washington and the like."[3]

The Westmoreland's tavern sign is in remarkable condition for its age, especially considering that it would likely have hung outside to attract travelers, thereby exposing it to damaging weather.

Following the Revolutionary War, some tavern keepers replaced their signs bearing royal insignia with more patriotic symbols by simply turning them around and painting an eagle or another patriotic figure on the reverse side.[4] It would seem more likely, however, that the offending symbol would have simply been painted out. Examination reveals that earlier images on both sides of The Westmoreland's sign have been painted over. The lion covers an indistinct blue image inside a white oval partially visible to the right of the lion's head. Similarly, the spread eagle was painted over an image of an American shield; a profile of an eagle, facing left, with its head and tail partially visible; and small blue stars, all of which are still faintly visible to the left of the current eagle's head.

The Westmoreland's unsigned tavern sign has been attributed to William Rice (1777–1847), who was active in Massachusetts from 1806 to 1815, and in Hartford, Connecticut, from 1816 to 1847.[5] Rice began business in 1806 with a shop in Worcester, Massachusetts, where he was engaged in both sign painting and house painting. After moving to Hartford

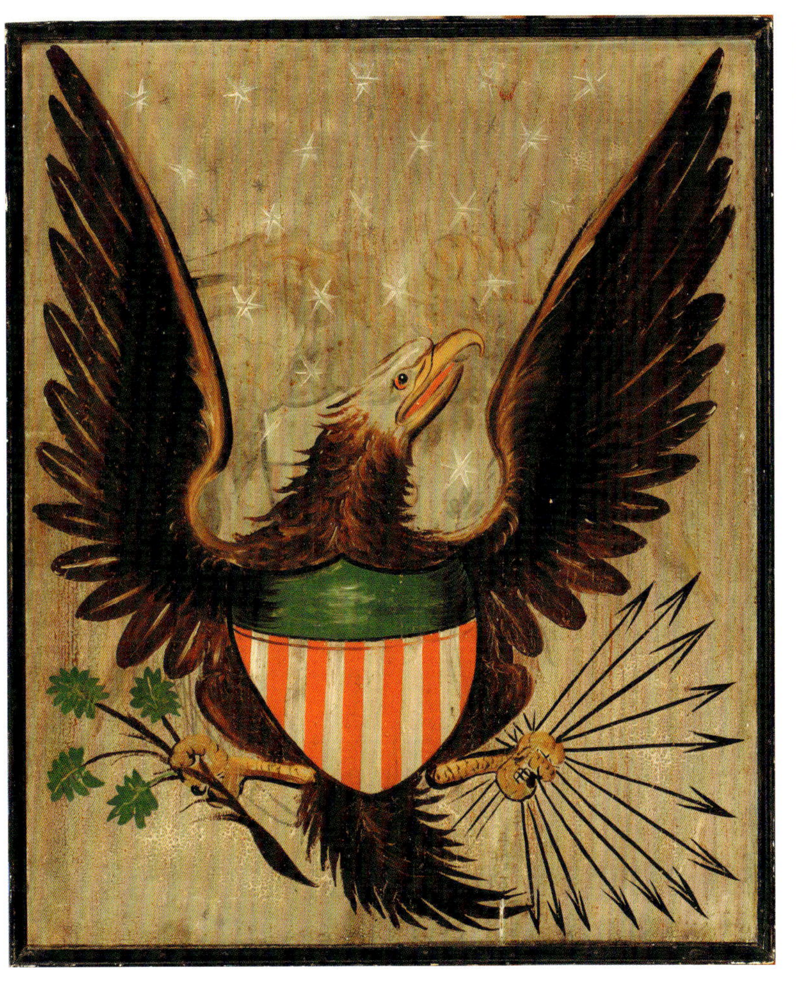

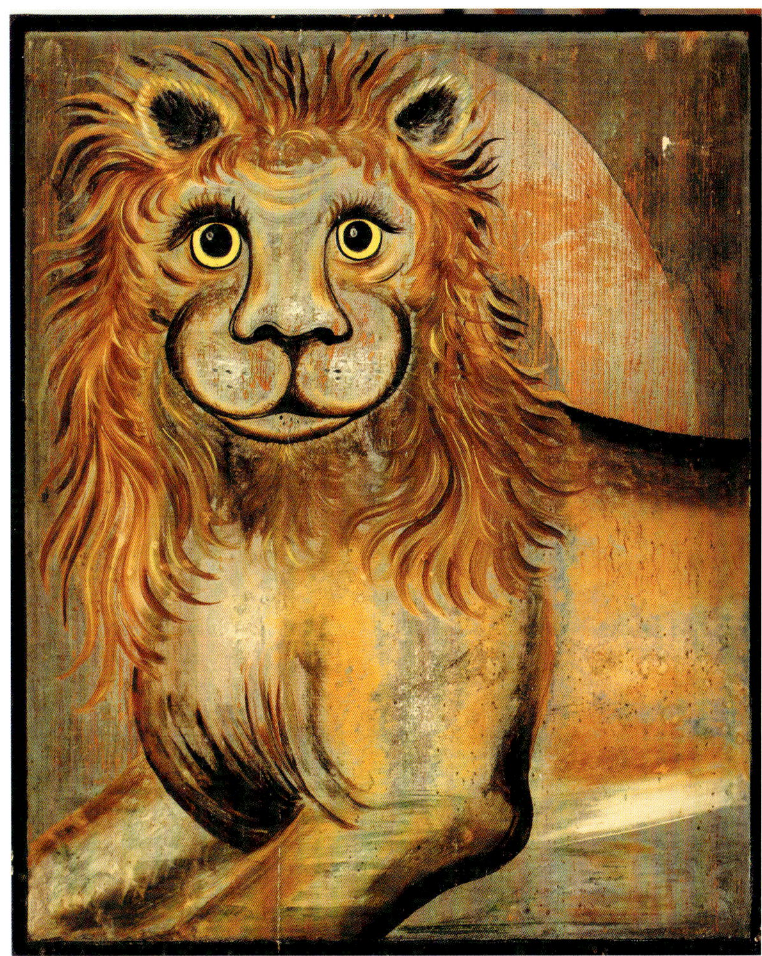

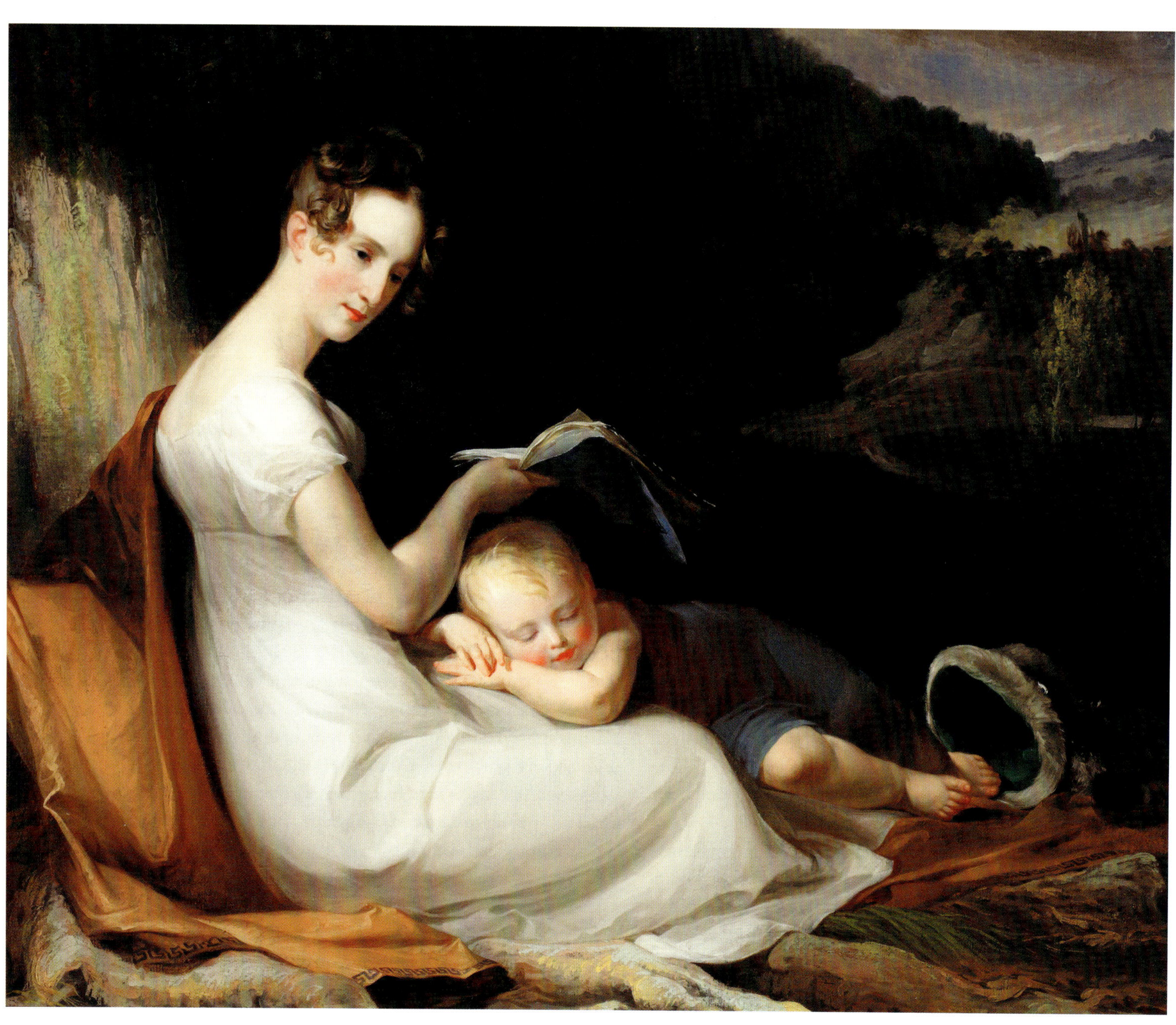

will be found with the artist (at least by the sitter) if he improve the appearance."[1] The painting—one of the earliest to enter the collection—came to The Westmoreland as a gift in 1960, descending from a private collection in Philadelphia. A second oil painting by Sully in the Museum's collection elegantly portrays *George Washington Harris* who was a merchant in Baltimore and Philadelphia (1993.51). It is evident when seeing the two portraits together that the artist's flattery extended as much to his male subjects as it did to his female sitters.

Sully painted and taught at the Pennsylvania Academy of the Fine Arts, where he was named academician in 1812 and served as its director for fifteen years. He remained an active member of the organization, directly involved with the instruction of emerging artists. In 1838, on a commission from the Society of the Sons of St. George in Philadelphia, he returned to England to paint his most famous portrait—that of a life-size young Queen Victoria. When Sully died in Philadelphia on November 5, 1872, at the age of eighty-nine, his logbook contained over twenty-six hundred paintings and miniatures that he made over the course of his seventy-year career. Written in 1851, his book, *Hints to Young Painters, and the Process of Portrait-Painting as Practiced by the Late Thomas Sully,* was published posthumously by his heirs in 1873. The book was perhaps his way of helping artists like himself succeed in the art world. A memorial exhibition consisting of 235 of his portraits was held at the Pennsylvania Academy of the Fine Arts on the fiftieth anniversary of the artist's death in 1922.

BLJ

1 Michael David Zellman, *American Art Analog*, vol. 1, 1688–1842 (New York: Chelsea House, 1986), 96.

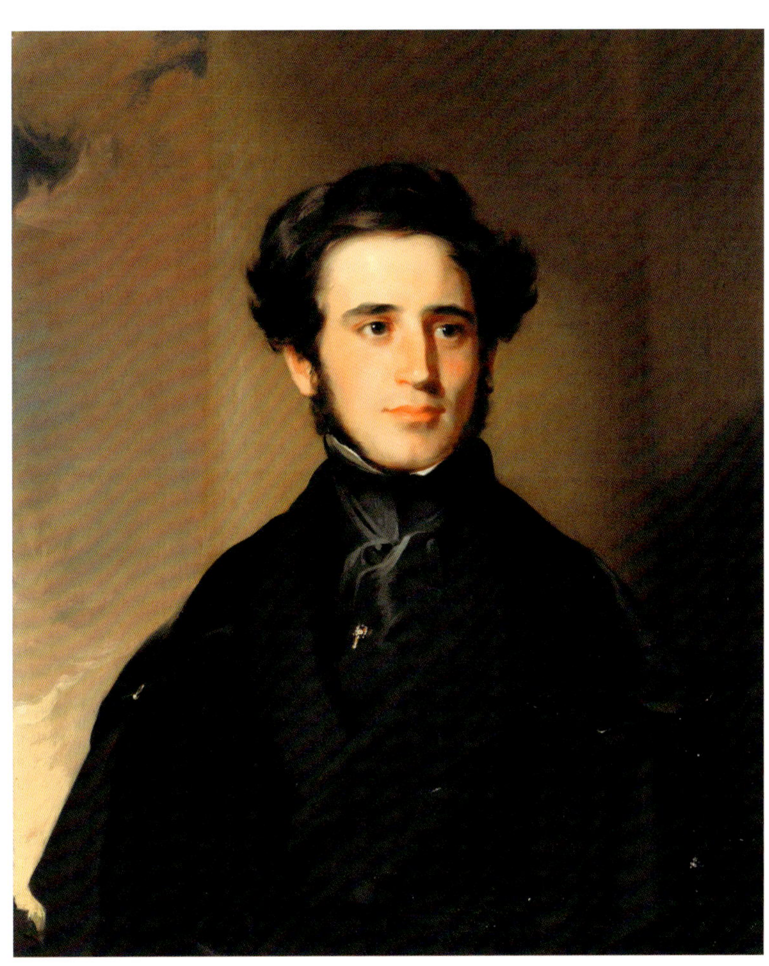

George Washington Harris, 1837
Oil on canvas mounted on masonite, 30 x 25 inches
Gift of the Westmoreland Society, 1993.51

REMBRANDT PEALE (1778–1860)
Portrait of George Washington (Porthole type), c. 1824
Oil on canvas, 36 x 29 inches
Signed lower left
Gift of the William A. Coulter Fund, 1958.37
Provenance: Thomas Harris Powers, Colorado; M. Knoedler & Co., Inc., New York.

Selected Exhibitions: *Peale Memorial Exhibition*, Pennsylvania Academy of the Fine Arts, Philadelphia, 1923; *Mr. President*, Dallas Museum of Fine Arts, 1956; 250 *Years of Art in Pennsylvania*, Westmoreland County Museum of Art, 1959; Henry Clay Frick Fine Arts Department, University of Pittsburgh, 1963; *Three Centuries of American Art*, Philadelphia Museum of Art, 1976; *Pennsylvania Painters from Commonwealth Collections*, William Penn Memorial Museum, Harrisburg, Pennsylvania, 1979; *A Feast for the Eyes: Treasures from the Westmoreland Museum of American Art*, Woodmere Art Museum, Philadelphia, 1998.

The Westmoreland's first painting acquisition, Rembrandt Peale's *Portrait of George Washington*, was purchased in February 1958, fifteen months before the Museum opened to the public. Named after the seventeenth-century Dutch master, Rembrandt was the second son of Charles Willson Peale (1741–1827), the patriarch of Philadelphia's first and most influential family of artists, and founder of one of the country's first museums of natural history and art. Born in Bucks County, Pennsylvania, and one of seventeen children—many of whom were also named after artists—he was the son whom Charles most counted on to continue the portrait tradition. Trained by his father, with whom he shared a studio space in the Philadelphia museum, Rembrandt's career was launched when Charles arranged to have George Washington pose for him in 1795. In turn, the younger Peale looked to the country's first president to help him gain a secure reputation and hoped that the portrait—dubbed the "port-hole portrait" because of the trompe l'oeil oval stonework framing the sitter—would become the official likeness of the father of our country. According to the artist: "Neither satisfied with my father's, nor Trumbull's, nor Pine's, nor Wertmuller's, nor Stuart's, nor my own,—I made repeated attempts to fix on canvas the idea which was so strong in my mind, by an effort of combination, chiefly of my father's and my own studies." After sixteen unsuccessful attempts, "the portrait known as the 'Port Hole Washington' achieved what he had set out to do."[1] Peale himself referred to the portrait as "The Standard National Likeness," his *Patriae Pater*. Although an image of Washington by painter Gilbert Stuart (1755–1828) was chosen instead as the "official" likeness, Rembrandt Peale made good use of his painting by creating at least seventy-nine replicas of it during the 1840s and 1850s at the request of various collectors.[2] He often lectured on "Washington and His Portraits," successfully increasing his portrait commissions and providing himself with a continuous income. Washington was not his only commercial success, however. In 1820, he had painted an enormous twenty-four-foot canvas called *The Court of Death* (Detroit Institute of Arts), from which he earned a considerable sum by taking it on tour.

In 1802, Peale traveled to England with his father, who was exhibiting the mastodon skeleton he had unearthed. While there, he studied briefly at the Royal Academy in London with Benjamin West (1738–1820). In 1808, Charles sent him to Paris to paint portraits of twelve distinguished Frenchmen for his museum in Philadelphia. Napoleon invited Rembrandt to become his court painter, and although Peale declined the invitation, he did paint an equestrian portrait of the emperor. He remained in France for a year, studying the masterworks at the Louvre and, for a short time, studying with neoclassical painters Jacques-Louis David (1748–1825) and Francois Gerard (1770–1837).

Rembrandt was an early founder of the Pennsylvania Academy of the Fine Arts, becoming an academician in 1812 and serving on its board of directors from 1811 to 1813. Following even further in their father's footsteps, he and his older brother Raphaelle (1774–1825) opened a museum in Baltimore in 1797.

The artist's first and only sitting with Washington came when he was just seventeen years old. Washington was so popular as a subject for portraits at that time that he often sat for more than one artist simultaneously. About one such session that included Charles, Raphaelle, and Charles's brother, James (1749–1831), Gilbert Stuart was said to have commented that Washington was being "Pealed all around."[3]

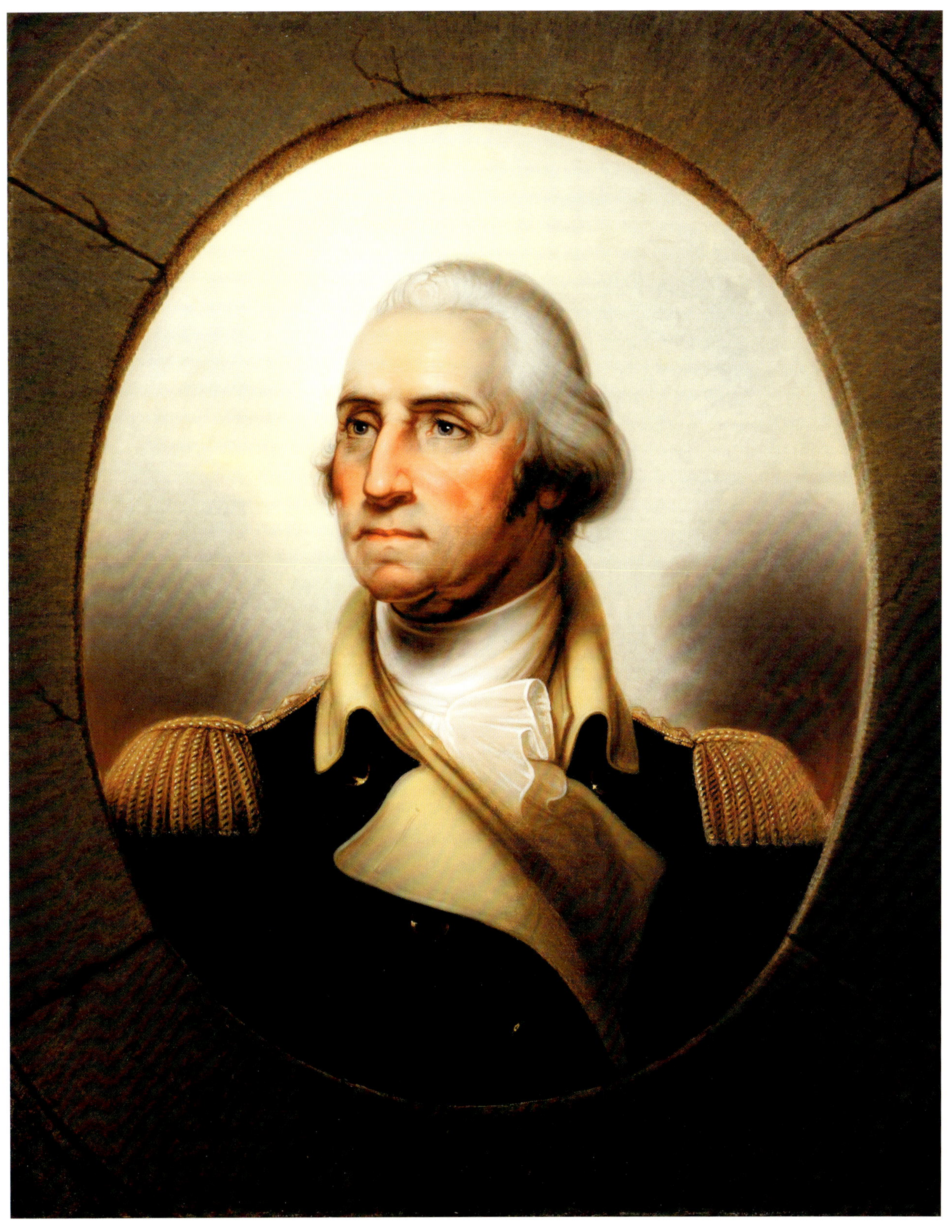

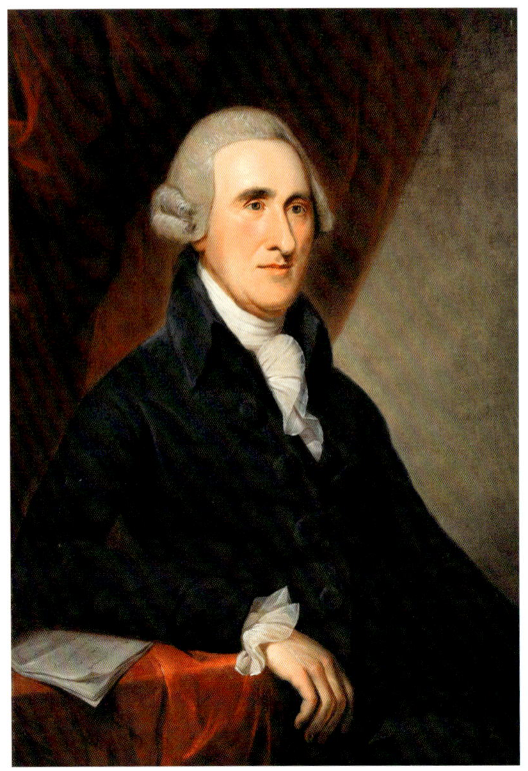

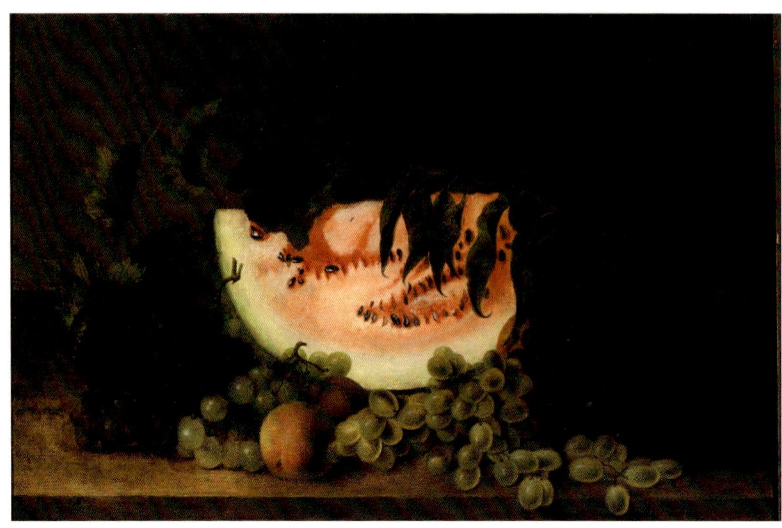

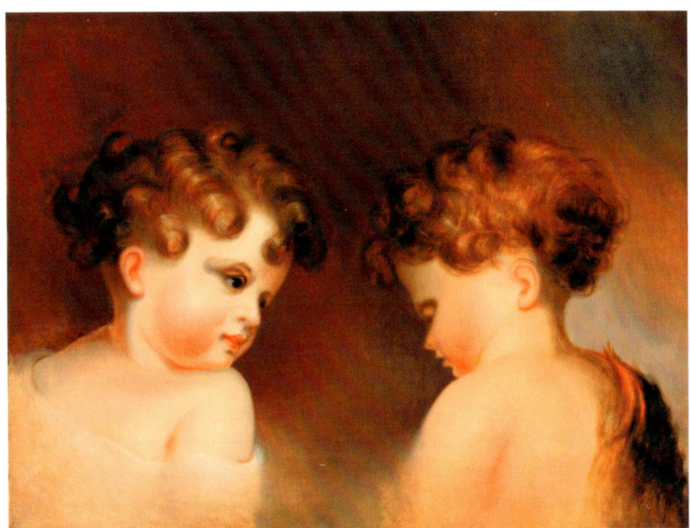

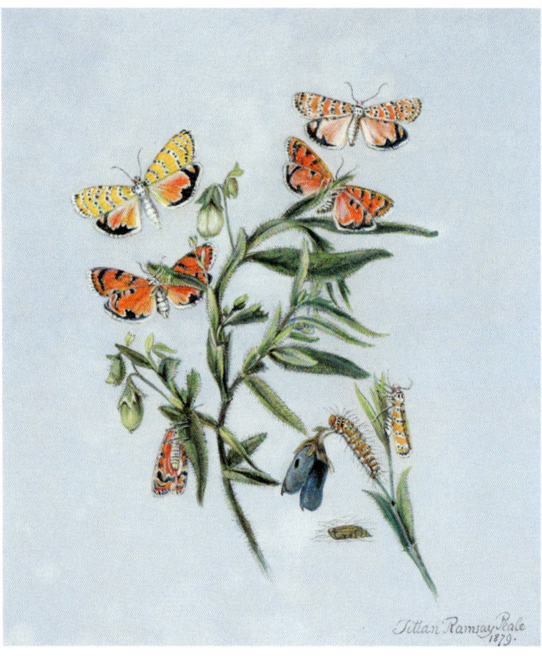

(TOP) Charles Willson Peale (1741–1826), *Portrait of Thomas McKean*, 1776
Oil on canvas, 35 ½ x 26 ¼ inches
Mary Marchand Woods Memorial Fund, 1964.106

(BOTTOM) Mary Jane Peale (1827–1902), *Children*, 1882
Oil on canvas, 18 x 24 inches
Gift of Hirschl and Adler Galleries, New York, NY, 1969.1

(TOP) Rubens Peale (1784–1865). *Still Life with Watermelon*, 1863
Oil on canvas, 18 ½ x 27 ¼ inches. Gift of the Mary Marchand Woods Foundation, 1986.150

(BOTTOM) Titian Ramsay Peale (1799–1885)
Still Life with Flowers and Insects, 1879
Watercolor on paper, 9 ½ x 8 3/8 inches
Mary Marchand Woods Memorial Fund, 1959.32

Peale began his work on what he hoped would be the "definitive" portrait of Washington in 1823. His inspiration in using the heroic pose and simulated stonework frame came from European prints, where it was used to signify the importance of the sitter. The military uniform that Peale used most often was replaced in some versions of the portrait with the dark suit of a statesman. The original—a much larger version, measuring 69 ½ x 52 ½ inches—shows the first president dressed in his black velvet senatorial robe. In this smaller copy, Washington is bathed in a soft, golden light, flattering the sitter with especially rosy cheeks while also calling attention to Washington's age—he was sixty-three in 1795—with the depiction of his double chin. Washington's intense blue eyes gaze out to his right, as if in the midst of serious thought rather than engaged with the artist. The faux painted porthole reveals the appropriate cracks of age, not only reflecting the historic symbolism of the portrait but also calling the viewer's attention to the status of the sitter as a military hero and the father of his country. Peale created his portrait when nostalgia for the country's first president and Revolutionary War hero was at its height and images of him were in demand. Pictures of Washington were reproduced and disseminated to the masses through the print medium, especially by the leading lithographers of the period: Currier and Ives and Louis B. Prang.

Peale's portrait of Washington is in fact a composite image, based on the portrait he created during the 1795 sitting, his father's portrait painted at the same time, the portrait bust by French sculptor Jean-Antoine Houdon (1741–1828), and other images of the first president, including those of Stuart. The example owned by the Museum was exhibited in the *Peale Memorial Exhibition* in 1923 at the Pennsylvania Academy of the Fine Arts in Philadelphia; it was also chosen for the bicentennial exhibition, *Three Centuries of American Art*, at the Philadelphia Museum of Art as one of the finest examples of this subject.

The Westmoreland owns four additional works by the Peale family of artists. Charles Willson Peale's *Portrait of Thomas McKean* (1964.106) was painted in 1776, the earliest of six portraits he made of McKean who served as governor of Pennsylvania from 1799 to 1808. Given by McKean to his daughter Elizabeth as a wedding present, the portrait remained in the family before coming to the Museum through the Mary Marchand Woods Memorial Fund in 1964. An exquisitely simple arrangement of fruit in *Still Life with Watermelon*, 1863 (1986.150), by Rubens Peale (1784–1865), was painted just two years prior to the artist's death. In 1810, Rubens succeeded his father as administrator of the Peale Museum in Philadelphia; twelve years later, he took over supervision of his brother Rembrandt's museum in Baltimore. His only daughter, Mary Jane Peale (1826–1902), painted her idealized cherubic *Children* in 1882 (1969.1). While not specific portraits, her image imparts a romanticized notion of the innocence of childhood. *Still Life with Flowers and Insects* (1959.32)—a watercolor on paper by the youngest of Charles's sons, Titian Ramsay Peale (1799–1885)—reveals his career path as a naturalist.

Peale painted many other portraits in addition to those of Washington, including other heroes of the Revolution and statesmen such as Thomas Jefferson, James Monroe, Andrew Jackson, and the Marquis de Lafayette, achieving the significant reputation for which his father had hoped.

BLJ

1 Quoted from notes accompanying the sale paperwork from M. Knoedler & Co., Inc., February 11, 1958. Artist file, Westmoreland Museum of American Art.

2 The "official" likeness of Washington that Stuart painted from life in 1796 is referred to as the *Athenaeum Portrait* (National Portrait Gallery, Smithsonian Institution and Museum of Fine Arts, Boston) and is reproduced on the one-dollar bill. Stuart also created copies of his Washington portrait, painting over one hundred money-maker replicas, which he referred to as his "hundred dollar bill portraits." Charles had also created replicas of his paintings of Washington. The original version of Rembrandt Peale's *Porthole Portrait of George Washington* was sold to the federal government in 1832 and resides in the United States Senate Collection, currently hanging in the office of the vice president. One copy of this larger version exists; his subsequent replicas were made smaller, similar in size to The Westmoreland's portrait.

3 Lillian B. Miller, *In Pursuit of Fame: Rembrandt Peale, 1778–1860* (Washington, DC: National Portrait Gallery, Smithsonian Institution, 1992), 32.

ELIZABETH EICHAR (1824–1913)
Pictorial Sampler, 1837
Inscribed: The School of Harriet Price in Mount Pleasant, PA
Silk on linen, 16½ x 16¾ inches
Gift of James Trosch, Kennett Square, PA, 1998.4
Provenance: Heritage Center Museum, Lancaster, Pennsylvania; James Trosch, Kennett Square, Pennsylvania.

SELECTED EXHIBITIONS: *Made in Pennsylvania: A Folk Art Tradition*, Westmoreland Museum of American Art, 2007.

This needlework sampler was made by Elizabeth Eichar in 1837, when she was thirteen years old. Most American samplers contain only the name of the maker, her age, and the fabrication date. This one is unusual because it also identifies the town where the sampler was made as well as Elizabeth's instructor: "the school of Harriet Price in Mount Pleasant, PA."[1]

Young girls made samplers to learn their alphabet and their numbers. These simple needlework exercises were known as band samplers, since they contained alphabets and numbers in rows, or bands. Needlework was also important for teaching girls how to make and repair clothing and other family textiles. Some girls went on to make "fancy" samplers depicting landscapes, houses, animals, and people. Because these pictorial samplers were complex, they were usually made under the direction of skilled teachers, who sometimes supplied their students with designs to follow. The influence of these teachers can be seen most readily in the appearance of similar designs or formats in samplers by different makers in different years. The Mary Tidball School samplers from Allegheny County are all very large in format, and particular motifs reappear. Three samplers by different girls from an unknown Allegheny County school, referred to as the Star School because of a cluster of star-like motifs above the same three-story brick house on each, range in date from 1820 to 1828.[2] Finally, two published Pittsburgh samplers from the Mary Callan School depicting similar buildings, one of which is marked "Academy," are closely related to the design of an English sampler from 1823 by Eliza Mitchell, in which the building is marked "Ferrier" and has a horse standing next to it, waiting to be shod.[3]

Elizabeth Eichar's *Pictorial Sampler* is very well designed, another indicator of formal instruction. Her brick house is placed in the center at the bottom flanked by two people, trees, and flowers. A third person appears in the doorway, and a horse grazes at far left. The scene is framed with a meandering floral vine. Two baskets with stylized contents flank religious verse in the middle. The house is complete in outline, but only the left side has been finished, using red thread to suggest brick. Similarly, the tree to the right of the house has been outlined but not completed unlike its counterpart on the left.

Although there is virtually no information on the maker or her teacher beyond the inscriptions on the sampler, we know something about Mount Pleasant during this time period. Westmoreland County was established in 1773 and divided into eleven townships, one of which was Mount Pleasant Township. The town of Mount Pleasant was laid out by 1797 and was incorporated as a borough in 1828. At that time, it had a population of about three hundred, ranking second in size in Westmoreland County only to Greensburg. In addition to farming, Mount Pleasant Township had several iron furnaces, including Alexander McClurg's Mount Pleasant Furnace on Jacobs Creek, built about 1810. Both English and Germans settled here, including William Wall—the father of artists William Coventry Wall (1811–1886) and Alfred S. Wall (1825–1896)—who emigrated from England in the early 1820s. (See William Coventry Wall entry in this catalog for information on the Wall family).

The first school in Mount Pleasant was a log structure known as the Bennett Schoolhouse, built about 1800. As was true for the rest of the county, the early schools were for boys only; public schools for girls would come later. Minutes of the Mount Pleasant School Board, published in the *Mount Pleasant Journal*, recorded a motion on April 6, 1838, for the establishment of two schools, one for males and the other for females.

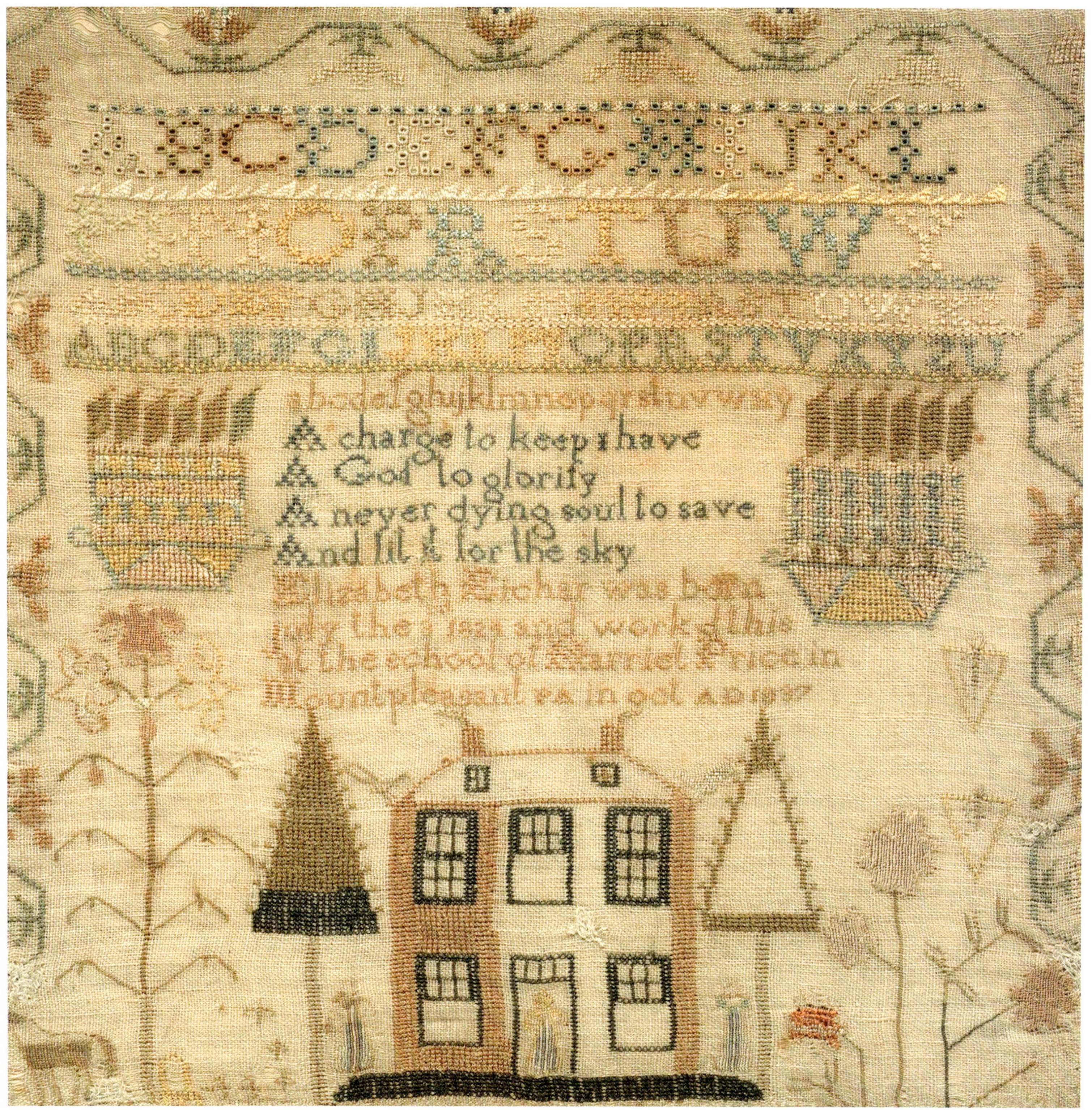
A charge to keep I have
A God to glorify
A never dying soul to save

By May 28 of that year,

> [t]he committee to obtain a female teacher made a report that their efforts were unsuccessful, and ask[ed] to be discharged. The request was granted. The president, on behalf of the committee to obtain a male teacher, reported that John Harrold can be had at a salary of $23 per month.[4]

On March 6, 1840, it was reported that "Mrs. Farrell will take charge of a school for one month at a salary [of] . . . $12."[5] Therefore, Harriet Price's school must have been private since it predates this attempt to establish a taxpayer-funded school for females.

A second Harriet Price School pictorial sampler is in a private collection. It is inscribed: "Lucinda Kampf was born May the 6th 1825 and worked this at the school of Harriet Price in Mount Pleasant PA sept AD 1837."[6] Made in the same year as the Eichar sampler, the Kampf sampler contains the exact same verse, a similar house flanked by trees, a tethered horse to the left, and a single figure standing in the front door. Only two other pictorial samplers from Westmoreland County have been published: one by Eliza Kuhns, dated 1814 and inscribed "Greensburg"; and the other by Rebekah McClure, dated 1824 and inscribed "Westmoreland County."

HNT

1 This school was incorrectly identified as the school of Margaret Price in *Made in Pennsylvania: A Folk Art Tradition* (Greensburg, PA: Westmoreland Museum of American Art, 2007), 37, 44.

2 *Made in Pennsylvania: A Folk Art Tradition,* 41.

3 Ibid., 40; M. Finkel & Daughter, *Samplings* 20 (2001): 15.

4 Jill B. Cook, ed., *A Town That Grew at the Crossroad* (Scottdale, PA: Laurel Group Press, 1978), 68.

5 Ibid.

6 See Bonhams' *Fine European and American Furniture and Decorative Arts: Monday June 14, 2010,* San Francisco, Sale 18254, lot 5033.

JOHN F. FRANCIS (1808–1886)
Fruit and Wine, 1858
Oil on canvas, 25 x 30 inches
Signed and dated lower right
Anonymous gift, 1978.16
Provenance: John Griffen; Mrs. John Griffen; Ester L. Griffen; Fanny Pennypacker; Hirschl and Adler Galleries, New York; Dr. John J. McDonough, Youngstown, Ohio.

SELECTED EXHIBITIONS: *Retrospective of a Gallery*, Hirschl and Adler Galleries, New York, 1973; *A Panorama of American Painting: The John J. McDonough Collection*, New Orleans Museum of Art, 1975–1976; *Pennsylvania Painters from Commonwealth Collections*, William Penn Memorial Museum, Harrisburg, Pennsylvania, 1979; *A Salute to Pennsylvania's Artistic Heritage*, Pennsylvania Historical and Museum Commission, Harrisburg, Pennsylvania, 1979; *A Feast for the Eyes: Treasures from the Westmoreland Museum of American Art*, Woodmere Art Museum, Philadelphia, Pennsylvania, 1998.

John Francis has emerged as one of the most important still life artists of the nineteenth century, situated as he was between the Peale family, who dominated the field in the early part of the century, and William Merritt Chase (1849–1916), whose talent marked the late century. The Peale family of painters had elevated still life to a worthy place in the hierarchy of painting subjects, and as such, the nineteenth century saw an explosion of still life painters and patronage. Americans turned away from the grand manner style of the European art tradition in favor of subjects that they felt expressed more of an American spirit.

Born and trained in Philadelphia, Francis would certainly have seen the work of the Peale family, especially Raphaelle Peale (1774–1825), who was the most celebrated for his still life paintings. However, like many artists of his era, Francis chose to pursue portraiture early on, turning to still life painting later in life. As an itinerant portrait painter, he traveled to Washington, D.C.; Delaware; Tennessee; and central Pennsylvania during the 1830s and 1840s. He turned to still life painting around 1850, and his most productive work in this vein occurred after his move to central Pennsylvania, where he most likely encountered the work of immigrant painter Severin Roesen (1815–c. 1872), a European-born master of the art. Francis had moved to Jeffersonville in 1866, and he lived there until his death in 1886. However, there are no paintings known by him that are dated after 1879.

By the middle of the nineteenth century, several factors contributed to the rise in popularity of still life as subject matter: the purchase of still life paintings by affluent middle-class patrons to decorate their dining rooms; the exhibition, distribution, and sale of still life paintings to the public by the American Art-Union; and the arrival into the United States of foreign still life specialists, such as Roesen. Still life arrangements could be set up in the studio, when inclement weather might prohibit painting the natural landscape, and were easier to deal with than the sitters for portraits. Chromolithographs made after still life paintings, published by leading lithographic firms Currier and Ives in New York and Louis B. Prang in Boston, also played a role in their dissemination. The predominance of still life as subject matter in painting is evidenced by the large number included in major exhibitions of the mid-to-late nineteenth century throughout the northeast.

Francis developed a highly personal style using tabletop arrangements, which often featured a dessert or luncheon theme in a domestic setting. He reveals his mastery of the "luncheon picture" in The Westmoreland's painting *Fruit and Wine*, an elaborate grouping of variously shaped objects that recall the sophistication of seventeenth-century Dutch still life paintings. Often, as in the Museum's example, the table is set before an open window, giving the scene an ambiguous feeling somewhere between the indoors and outdoors. Set on a white linen cloth, open bottles of red and white wine, partially filled glassware, a large basket of fruit, quartered oranges, nuts, and biscuits are all to be enjoyed by some unseen guests. While at first glance the abundance of objects may seem randomly placed, they are in fact thoughtfully arranged in this harmonious and balanced composition. With them, the artist leads the viewer's eye through his composition, from the Wedgwood blue pitcher at the far left, up over the large napkin partially

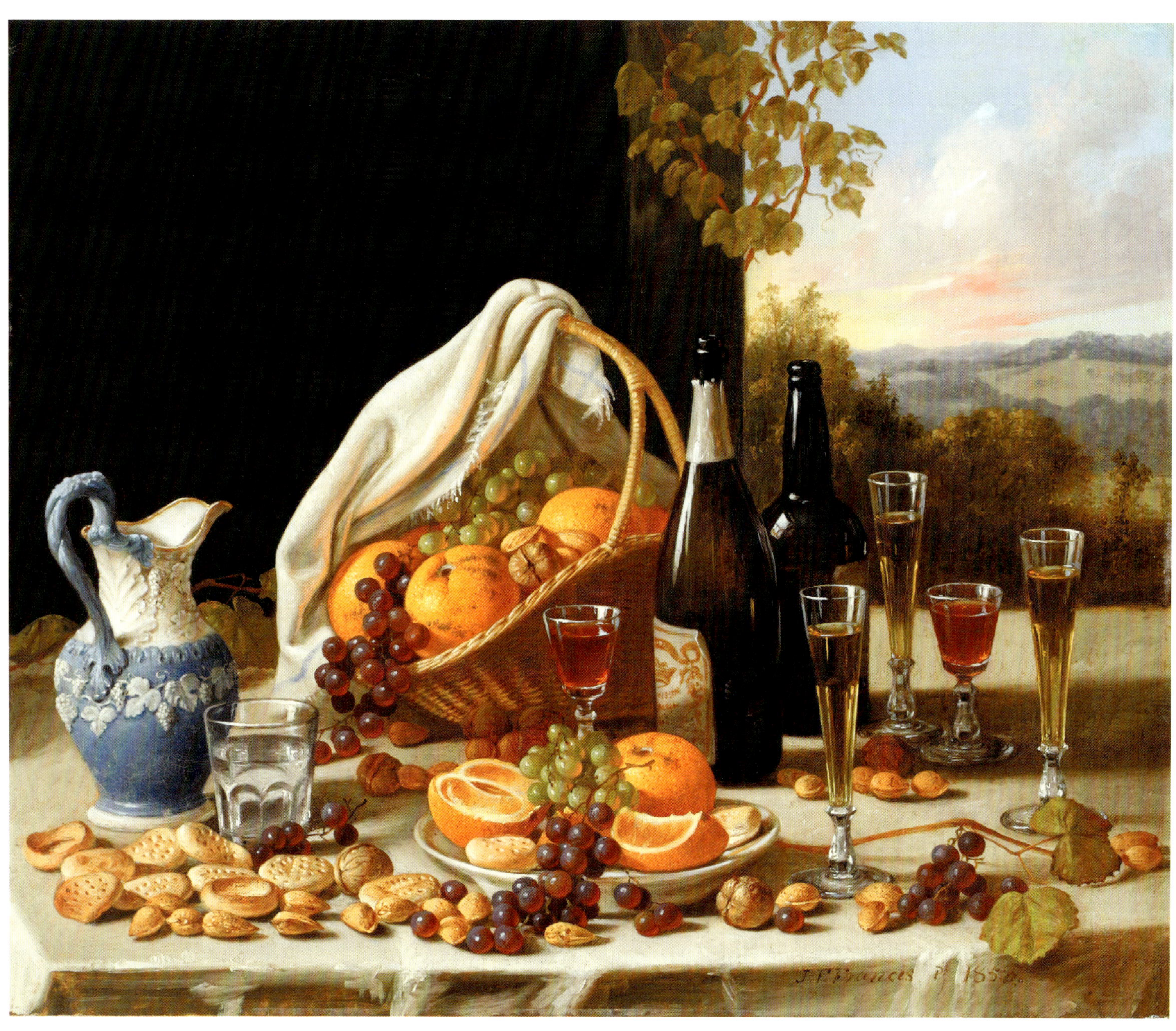

obscuring the basket of fruit, to the curvilinear basket handle, then snaking through the various wine bottles and glasses, around the curve of the plate, and finally back to the glass of water. The artist's arrangement of champagne flutes in particular has often been compared to musical notes on a score. Francis's primary interest is in the shapes and tactile qualities that are unique to each of his chosen objects. He contrasts hard surfaces with soft, and rough textures with smooth, while showing both the dimpled outside skin of the orange and its pliable, colorful flesh inside. Grapes spill out of the basket, connecting its contents with those lying on the tabletop. The artist's vibrant coloration and complex patterning, together with his brushwork, create and sustain interest in the composition. Setting up a rhythm with the various shapes, heights, and colors of his objects, he achieves a pleasing harmony of the whole. Francis—who never placed his still life arrangements directly in nature, as other artists frequently did—references nature by incorporating the central Pennsylvania landscape through an open window, seen at right. Grape leaves lying on the table and still growing on the vine that frames the window enhance this effect by bringing the outdoors inside. His placement of objects suggests depth within the composition's rather shallow foreground, yet he accomplishes a sense of deep space by extending the background to the distant horizon beyond. The idea of creating truthful records of nature with scientific accuracy was espoused through the writings and aesthetic theories of John Ruskin (1819–1900) through his multivolume treatise on art, *Modern Painters,* first published in London and introduced to America in the late 1850s.[1] These truth-to-nature principles, readily transferred to still life painting and championed by the American Pre-Raphaelites, were widely disseminated in America through the *Crayon,* a periodical published between 1855 and 1860. Francis began incorporating landscape into his still life arrangements around 1858, which reveals that he was indeed receptive to such ideas.

Francis often rearranged the same objects for other canvases, such as his *Luncheon Still Life* (c. 1860, Smithsonian Museum of American Art), which is a virtual replica of The Westmoreland's *Fruit and Wine,* with only slight variations. While Francis's compositions are generally very complicated, like *Fruit and Wine,* his later still lifes incorporate fewer objects and are more in keeping with his early work and similar in style to that of the Peale family.

Francis exhibited in the Pennsylvania Academy of the Fine Art annuals in 1847, 1855, and 1859, and the American Art-Union sold many of his fruit pieces; nevertheless, the artist was relatively unknown during his lifetime. His work, however, has since played a significant role in the revitalization of still life painting in America.

BLJ

1 *Modern Painters* was published in five volumes between 1843 and 1860.

DAVID GILMOUR BLYTHE (1815–1865)
The Young Musician, c. 1858–1860
Oil on canvas, 30 ½ x 21 inches
Signed on wall, left center
Gift of the William A. Coulter Fund, 1958.34
Provenance: Newhouse Galleries, New York; Mr. Joseph Katz, Baltimore; Hirschl and Adler Galleries, New York.

SELECTED EXHIBITIONS: 250 *Years of Art in Pennsylvania*, Westmoreland County Museum of Art, 1959; *Art Across America*, Munson-Williams-Proctor, Utica, New York, 1960; Henry Clay Frick Fine Arts Department, University of Pittsburgh, 1963; Butler Institute of American Art, Youngstown, Ohio, 1964; William Penn Memorial Museum, Harrisburg, Pennsylvania, 1972; *19th and 20th Century Regional Painters*, Westmoreland County Museum of Art, 1976; *The World of David Gilmour Blythe* (1815–1865), National Collection of Fine Arts, Smithsonian Institution, Washington, D.C., 1980–1981; *Southwestern Pennsylvania Painters*, 1800–1945, Westmoreland Museum of Art, 1981; *From Kane to Quinn, Part II*, Pittsburgh Center for the Arts, 1996; *Selections from the Westmoreland Museum of American Art*, Governor's Residence, Harrisburg, Pennsylvania, 1998.

Born near East Liverpool, Ohio, David Gilmour Blythe was essentially self-taught as a painter, although his first training came in wood carving when he was apprenticed at age sixteen to Joseph Woodwell, a Pittsburgh wood-carver and father of the Scalp Level landscape painter Joseph Woodwell (1842–1911). Beginning in 1837, Blythe served as a carpenter in the U.S. Navy on the *USS Ontario*. Following his discharge in 1840, he earned a living as an itinerant portrait painter in eastern Ohio and western Pennsylvania before settling in Uniontown in the winter of 1846. One of his most famous commissions was a 9-foot statue of General Lafayette, which he carved between 1847 and 1848 for the dome of the Fayette County Courthouse in Uniontown.[1] The artist's most ambitious undertaking was a 300-foot panorama entitled *The Great Moving Panorama of the Allegheny Mountains* (whereabouts unknown), which he toured in Maryland and Virginia before ending its tour in Pittsburgh in 1851. Mounted on rollers, the great expansive image unfolded before the viewer one scene at a time, much like the first motion pictures.

Blythe lost his young wife, Julia, to typhoid in 1849 after just one year of marriage, setting him on a path of depression and alcoholism. He left Uniontown in 1851 for East Liverpool, Ohio before settling five years later in Pittsburgh, where he found ample subject matter for his brush. The artist painted prominent citizens, but his subjects of choice were vagrants, thieves, drunkards, beggars, and homeless street urchins who made up the sociopolitical fabric of industrial Pittsburgh, which at the time was suffering from an overpopulation of immigrants without jobs or housing to accommodate them. He portrayed politics and the legal system, calling attention to its inhumanity and injustice to man. And when he painted the upper class, he portrayed them in less-than-flattering depictions. Blythe's genre subjects are harshly realistic and often humorous descriptions of life in the city, as interpreted by his sharply satirical wit. His paintings are filled with direct or implied symbolism that assails the viewer with meaning.

His paintings of ragamuffin children reflect the lower economic urban environments in which Blythe himself lived, where mothers and children were forced to work the streets to help support themselves. In *The Young Musician*, a boy takes a moment to play his mouth harp after selling the contents of his basket. In paintings such as this one, Blythe portrays the squalor and poverty that was prevalent in sections of the city in pre–Civil War America. An article entitled "Bad Taste" in the *Pittsburgh Gazette* describes an artist's choice of subject matter:

> We really wonder what class of our citizens it is which buys such paintings as that of "The Drunkard," exhibited in Gillespie's window on Wood Street. It is a good representation of a disgusting object, and although much talent may be displayed in portraying a character of this kind, we cannot help thinking that the time and talents of the artist are thrown away, particularly since there are scenes of beauty all around, well calculated to call forth the finer feelings of our nature. Painting is one of Beauty's handmaidens, and though sometimes it may be allowable for an artist to revel in the horrible, still, we think that he should eschew the disgusting. One thing is very certain, that the keepers of the pot houses, where alone such paintings are admissable [sic], will take good care not to suffer them to be brought into their bar rooms, and certainly no man of taste would hang in his parlor.[2]

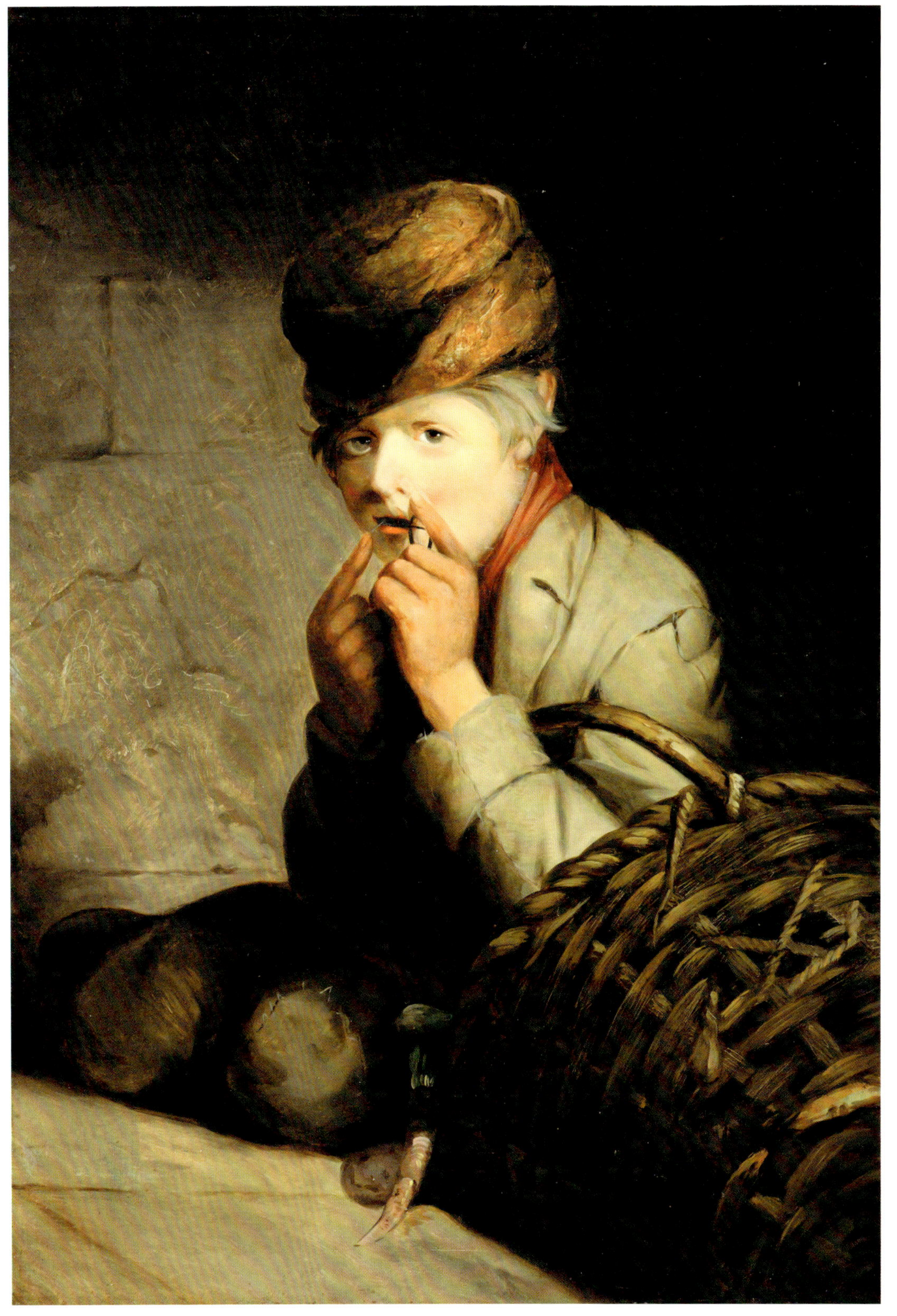

SEVERIN ROESEN (c. 1815–c. 1872)
Still Life with Fruit, not dated
Oil on canvas, 36 x 50 inches
Signed lower right
Museum purchase and the William A. Coulter Fund, 1980.78
Provenance: Dorthea M. Crosby, Pennsylvania.

SELECTED EXHIBITIONS: *Private Worlds: 200 Years of American Still Life Painting, Aspen Art Museum,* 1996—1997; *A Feast for the Eyes: Treasures from the Westmoreland Museum of American Art.* Woodmere Art Museum, Philadelphia, Pennsylvania, 1998.

Severin Roesen is perhaps one of the best known and admired American still life painters of the nineteenth century. Despite this fact, almost nothing is known about his life and training. It is believed that he came to America, as did many Germans, in 1848 to escape the civil unrest occurring in his native country. To date, attempts to identify his birthplace and year of birth have been fruitless. Even more surprising is the fact that the circumstances of his death are also unknown. His reputation has been built on the remarkable number and quality of the paintings he produced in a twenty-some-year period—well over three hundred.

Although Roesen's birth records have not been located, the census taken in 1860 in Huntingdon, Pennsylvania, lists an artist of that name at forty-four years of age residing in Miller's hotel. Huntingdon is an agricultural community nestled along the banks of the Juniata River about one hundred miles west of Harrisburg—a likely stopping point for Roesen between Harrisburg and Williamsport, as he traveled through Pennsylvania searching for a suitable community in which to settle. From that record, the artist's birth year can be determined to be 1815 or 1816.

It has been assumed that Roesen was born in Cologne, Germany, for two reasons: St. Severin is Cologne's patron saint, and an artist named Severin Roesen exhibited a "floral piece" there in 1847. The following year, Severin Roesen is listed for the first time in the annual directory of New York City. Three still lifes by the artist, one floral and two fruit compositions, were included in 1849 in the second annual exhibition of the Maryland Historical Society, indicating his immediate entry into the art world. Roesen's paintings were also included in sales records for the American Art-Union from 1848 until the union's closing in 1852, with paintings going to collectors as far away as Boston, New Orleans, and Charleston.

Roesen's compositions appealed to American audiences of the mid-to late-nineteenth century. They symbolized the country's natural beauty and physical bounty and, akin to the landscapes being produced at the same time, addressed a sense of national gratitude for that bounty. By that time, many second-and third-generation Americans were well established, with growing middle and upper classes in the market for fine objects. Roesen's style varied only somewhat during the twenty-four-year period of his known activity. *Flower and Fruit Still Life* (1848; The Corcoran Gallery of Art), is his earliest known dated painting. It is compositionally more attuned to his Dutch predecessors and employs a gentle "S" curve around which the still life objects are arranged. Whether stimulated by his exposure to American still life artists, who tended to employ less artifice in their compositions, or conceding to market demands, his later work employed a pyramidal structure, giving the resultant still life less a sense of dynamism than of stability.

Shortly after his arrival in the United States, Roesen married his countrywoman, Wilhelmina Ludwig, and the couple had three children: Louisa, Wilhelmina, and Oscar. The last year that Roesen is listed in New York's city directory is 1857, a year marked by a troubled economy in the city. These circumstances perhaps caused the artist to leave New York City in an attempt to locate a healthier economic climate in which to promote his work and support his growing family. However, by 1860, Mina Roesen lists herself in the city directory as a widowed seamstress, a way of saving face since her separation from Roesen was by then permanent.

Roesen traveled westward through Pennsylvania, stopping only briefly in Harrisburg before going on to Huntingdon and finally settling in Williamsport by 1860. It was in this flourishing logging town that Roesen spent the last twelve years of his life as a painter and teacher. The community contained a large

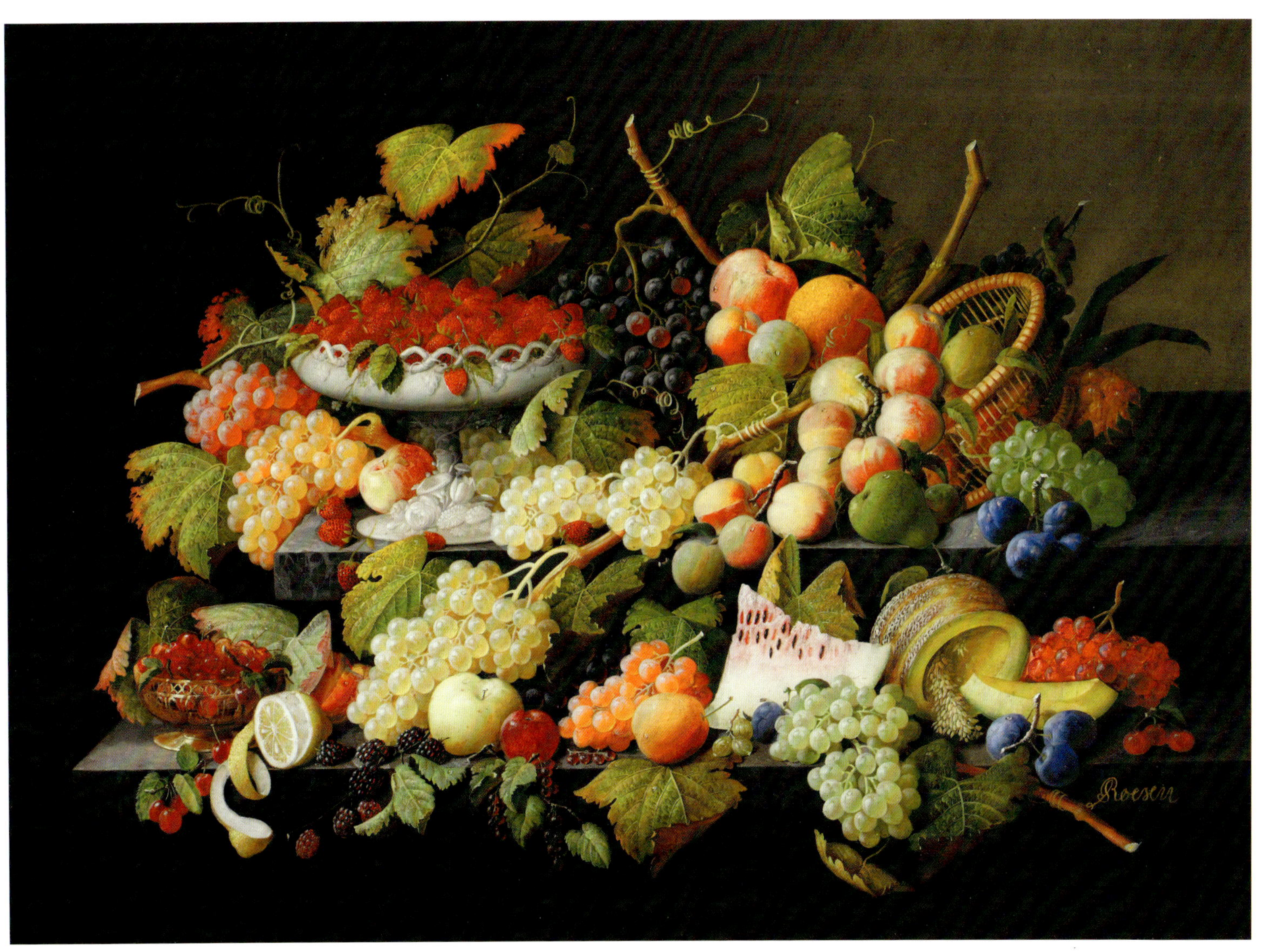
Roesen

number of German immigrants, which would have been attractive to the artist, as well as a growing upper class with new mansions in need of decoration. A testament to this activity is the growth of the city's population—from 1,615 in 1850 to 27,132 by 1890. Roesen stayed in various boarding houses and hotels, subsisting primarily by means of a barter system, documented by many families whose descendants still live in the area. One small painting retains a note tucked inside the frame from its original owner, describing it as having been accepted in trade for a pair of trousers.

Roesen's style is clearly evident in The Westmoreland's *Still Life with Fruit,* a large work showing his mastery of technique and composition. Using a brilliant palette, Roesen paid close attention to detail in rendering each piece of fruit, achieving a highly finished paint surface with little evidence of the artist's hand. The footed dish of strawberries is decorated with a floral motif in reference to Roesen's other favored still life subject. The artist's work typifies the Victorian aesthetic of *horror vacui,* which called for an almost overwhelming proliferation of objects arranged in various containers and laid directly on marble ledges. Large canvases such as this one date from his Williamsport period, intended for a grand residence or hotel.

The artist was characterized as a "genial, well-read, and generous" man, whose studio was often filled with visitors enjoying his company and sharing his love of good tobacco and beer.[1] A Williamsport newspaper article published twenty-three years after he left the city described his living quarters as having "about a hundred" paintings in various stages of completion.[2] This, combined with the fact that his compositions rely on a variety of formulaic objects and groupings, points to his technique as being dependent not on studies from life but on previous sketches, notes, and memory.

Despite Roesen's popularity and productivity while in Williamsport, he departed abruptly for reasons unknown to us. The last city directory in which he is named dates from 1872. No death records or notices have been located, and his whereabouts thereafter continue to be a mystery. Further, a volume on Williamsport's history published in conjunction with the nation's centenary makes no mention of the painter in a section listing other artists who contributed to the city's cultural well-being.[3]

The quality and volume of Roesen's life's work stand in place of biographical details, institutional associations, awards, and distinctions, as they do for all artists once facts are set aside and the body of work is considered alone.

JHO'T

1 *Williamsport Sun and Banner,* June 1895.

2 Ibid.

3 *History of Lycoming County,* Philadelphia, 1976.

GEORGE FREDERICK BENSELL (1837–1879)
Rip Van Winkle, not dated
Oil on canvas, 50 x 39 ½ inches
Signed lower right
Gift of the Western Pennsylvania Conservancy, Pittsburgh, from the Dorothy Kantner Estate, in memory of George and Lila B. Hetzel, 1977.129
Provenance: The Artist; George Hetzel; Lila B. Hetzel; Estate of Dorothy Kantner; Western Pennsylvania Conservancy, Pittsburgh.

Selected Exhibitions: *Dutch New York: The Roots of Hudson Valley Culture*, Hudson River Museum, Yonkers, New York, 2009–2010.

George Frederick Bensell was a painter known for his genre scenes, landscapes, and historical paintings. A lifelong resident of Philadelphia, he exhibited annually at the Pennsylvania Academy of the Fine Arts from 1856 to 1868. While still students, he and his younger brother, the artist Edmund Birckhead Bensell (1842–1894), together with four other artists, formed the Philadelphia Sketch Club (PSC) in 1860. He served as the club's first president, and it was in his studio that they held their first meetings. He served as president two more times and remained a member until his death. The PSC remains active today, located on Camac Street in Philadelphia. Also with his brother, he created the illustrations for James Dabney McCabe's *Great Fortunes and How They Were Made* in 1871, and made a series of oil paintings illustrating themes from Shakespeare. Bensell studied at the Pennsylvania Academy of the Fine Arts in 1858 and with the artist James Reid Lambdin (1807–1889). He was also a member of the Pennsylvania Academicians, an advisory body to the Academy's board, elected as an associate in 1860 and as a full academician in 1864.[1] Bensell married Josephine Crissman in 1871, and together they had three children, all of whom died at a young age.

Bensell's painting *Rip Van Winkle* demonstrates the artist's skill at combining a detailed landscape painting with a narrative portrait, re-creating Washington Irving's timeless tale. While in England in 1819, Irving (1783–1859) published *Rip Van Winkle* as a short story in his book *The Sketchbook of Geoffrey Crayon*, which also included *The Legend of Sleepy Hollow*. It was the first book by an American author to gain international acclaim.

According to the legend, Rip Van Winkle lived in a small village in New York State at the foot of the Catskill Mountains. He was an amiable fellow but a lazy husband, and to avoid the hard work on his farm and escape his wife's nagging, one day he decides to go hunting with his faithful dog, Wolf. In the midst of his climb up the mountain, he comes upon a peculiar little man toting a heavy keg. Rip helps him carry it deep into the woods, where they come upon a group of odd-looking men playing the game of nine-pins. They thank Rip for his help and invite him to quench his thirst with the mysterious contents of the keg, and after consuming one too many drinks, Rip falls into a deep sleep under a shady tree—a sleep he believes was for only one night but which actually lasted twenty years! When Rip awakes after two decades, his dog is nowhere to be found; his beard is a foot long; his hair has turned gray; and his leggings, shoes, and gun stock are rotted away. Worried about how angry his wife is going to be, he hurries down the mountain to his village, which he finds has also dramatically changed. The image of King George III on the sign over the inn has been replaced by an image of George Washington. Rip had slept through the Revolutionary War. The town had grown, and so had its population. No one recognizes him anymore. And although his wife has died, Rip is reunited with his adult son and daughter and his grandchildren, bringing the story to a happy conclusion.

Bensell's narrative painting depicts the moment when a bewildered Rip has just awakened from his long nap, looking startled at his own appearance as a craggy old man with a foot-long beard, tattered clothes, and rotted rifle, as described in Irving's story. His head is bald, yet what remains of his hair is shoulder length, and his fingernails have grown inches. All of the details of his appearance after twenty years are realistically rendered, and the mountainous landscape behind him seems as wild and removed from civilization as its lone occupant. Bensell focuses his attention (and the viewer's) on the main

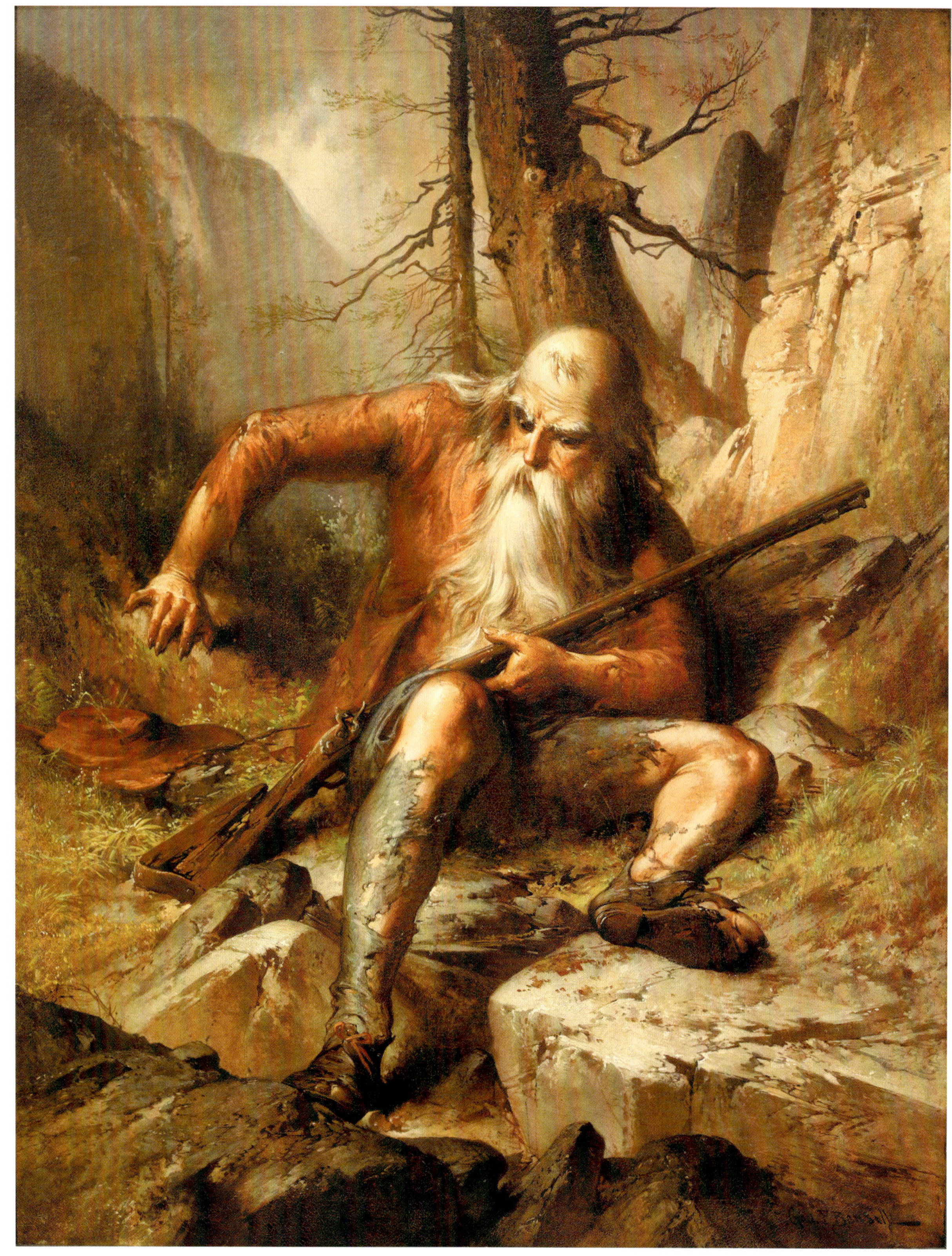

character of the story, setting his life-size figure of Rip at the very center of the composition, accentuated by the light streaming down on him. The figure of Rip is animated as he begins to rise to his feet and takes stock of his situation.

Irving's tale of Rip Van Winkle was a popular subject and captured the attention of worldwide readers as well as other artists of the period. John Quidor (1801–1881) describes different aspects of the story in his two paintings, *Rip Van Winkle and His Companions at the Inn Door of Nicholas Vedder* (1839; Museum of Fine Arts, Boston) and *The Return of Rip Van Winkle* (1849; National Gallery of Art, Washington, D.C.).

Rip Van Winkle was formerly owned by southwestern Pennsylvania artist George Hetzel (1826–1899), leader of the Scalp Level school of landscape painting, who purchased it in Philadelphia when he lived there in 1869. The painting descended in his family to his daughter Lila B. Hetzel (1873–1967), also an artist, and then to his granddaughter, Dorothy Kantner (1905–1977), who was the art critic for the *Pittsburgh Sun-Telegraph.*

Bensell was on the path to a promising career when it was cut short by his untimely death in 1879 in Philadelphia at the age of forty-two. The twenty-two page poem *The Artist's Dream* (1867), written by Bensell and Samuel W. Duffield (1843–1887) and illustrated by his brother, Edmund, is in the collection of the Historical Society of Pennsylvania in Philadelphia.

BLJ

1 The original twenty-three Pennsylvania Academicians were elected by the Board of Directors on 13 March 1812. Limited to forty members, they were responsible for selecting professors and curators. The group was disbanded in 1871. My thanks to Cheryl Leibold for this information. See Cheryl Leibold, *In the Service of Art: A Guide to the Archives of the Pennsylvania Academy of the Fine Arts* (Philadelphia: Pennsylvania Academy of the Fine Arts, 2009).

JEREMIAH H. STAHL (1830–1907) (attributed)
Chest of Drawers, 1867
Soap Hollow, Somerset County, Pennsylvania
Cherry and tulip poplar, painted and decorated
38 7/8 x 59 x 19 ¾ inches
Inscribed: "KB"
Gift of the Westmoreland Society, 2003.3
Provenance: Robert Meyers, Johnstown, Pennsylvania; Private Collection, Massachusetts.

Selected Exhibitions: *Made in Pennsylvania: A Folk Art Tradition*, Westmoreland Museum of American Art, 2007.

Illustrated: Charles R. Muller, *Soap Hollow: The Furniture and Its Makers* (Groveport, OH: Canal Press, 2002), cover, 76; *Made in Pennsylvania: A Folk Art Tradition* (Greensburg, PA: Westmoreland Museum of American Art, 2007), 4.

This bright red and black painted chest of drawers with gilt stenciled decoration and elegant scrolled backboard is an iconic example of nineteenth-century Germanic folk art from western Pennsylvania. It was made in Soap Hollow, a small remote valley in Conemaugh Township, Somerset County, Pennsylvania, where at least eight Mennonite cabinetmakers worked from 1836 into the twentieth century making distinctive furniture by hand and decorating it with paint. In nearby Johnstown, Cambria County, factories were producing low-cost machine-made furniture throughout most of this period. Fortunately, that technology had no apparent impact on the Soap Hollow cabinetmakers.

Soap Hollow furniture has several distinctive features, most of which are present in this chest of drawers. First and foremost is the scrolled backboard, found without significant variation on every recorded chest of drawers from 1850 until 1883. (The earliest known Soap Hollow chest of drawers, dated 1836, never had such a backboard.) Second is the persistence of style. The style of this chest of drawers is essentially Sheraton, having paneled ends, turned feet, a shaped skirt, five tiers of drawers, and half-round top moldings, and did not significantly change for fifty years. Third is the use of stencils for both decoration and inscriptions. On this particular piece, the stenciled ornamentation includes birds, potted plants, floral wreaths, and an inscription consisting of a date over the initials of the owner. Another characteristic feature of Soap Hollow furniture is that much of it is signed by the maker. Most Pennsylvania German ("Pennsylvania Deutsch") furniture from southeast and central Pennsylvania is unsigned. Although this chest is not signed, it is attributed to Jeremiah H. Stahl based on certain design details from several signed pieces.

Eight Soap Hollow cabinetmakers have been identified by signed pieces using the phrase "Manufactured by . . . " preceding the maker's name or initials stenciled on the front. These signed pieces enable attribution of unsigned pieces through consistent decoration choices. For example, stenciled squirrels are motifs seen to date only on work by the Livingston family (w. 1853–1874). Similarly, horses are associated with the work of John Sala (w. 1850–1859), and hearts frequently appear on the furniture made by Peter K. Thomas (w. 1861–1867).

Although this chest lacks a maker's name stenciled on the front, several design choices make him easily identifiable. Foremost is the bright red color of the case, known as Chinese Red. Jeremiah Stahl's furniture exhibits the most creative use of color, sometimes substituting dark green for black on feet and side panels, and sponged background for grained or flat case color. Another colorful detail is the yellow painted line on each drawer edge. Stahl's signed pieces have stenciled borders or frames around dates and owner initials, such as those on the side panels of The Westmoreland's *Chest of Drawers.* This piece is attributed to Stahl also on the basis of its date of manufacture, 1867, which fits into a timeline developed from a group of signed and dated examples which gives working dates for Stahl of 1865–1874, with only Peter K. Thomas overlapping in 1867.[1]

Jeremiah H. Stahl was born in Conemaugh Township. In the 1870 census, he was listed as a carpenter, and later tax records list him as a farmer. He is believed to have apprenticed under John Sala (1819–1882), one of the earliest identified Soap Hollow makers. Next to Stahl's house, as shown on a map of

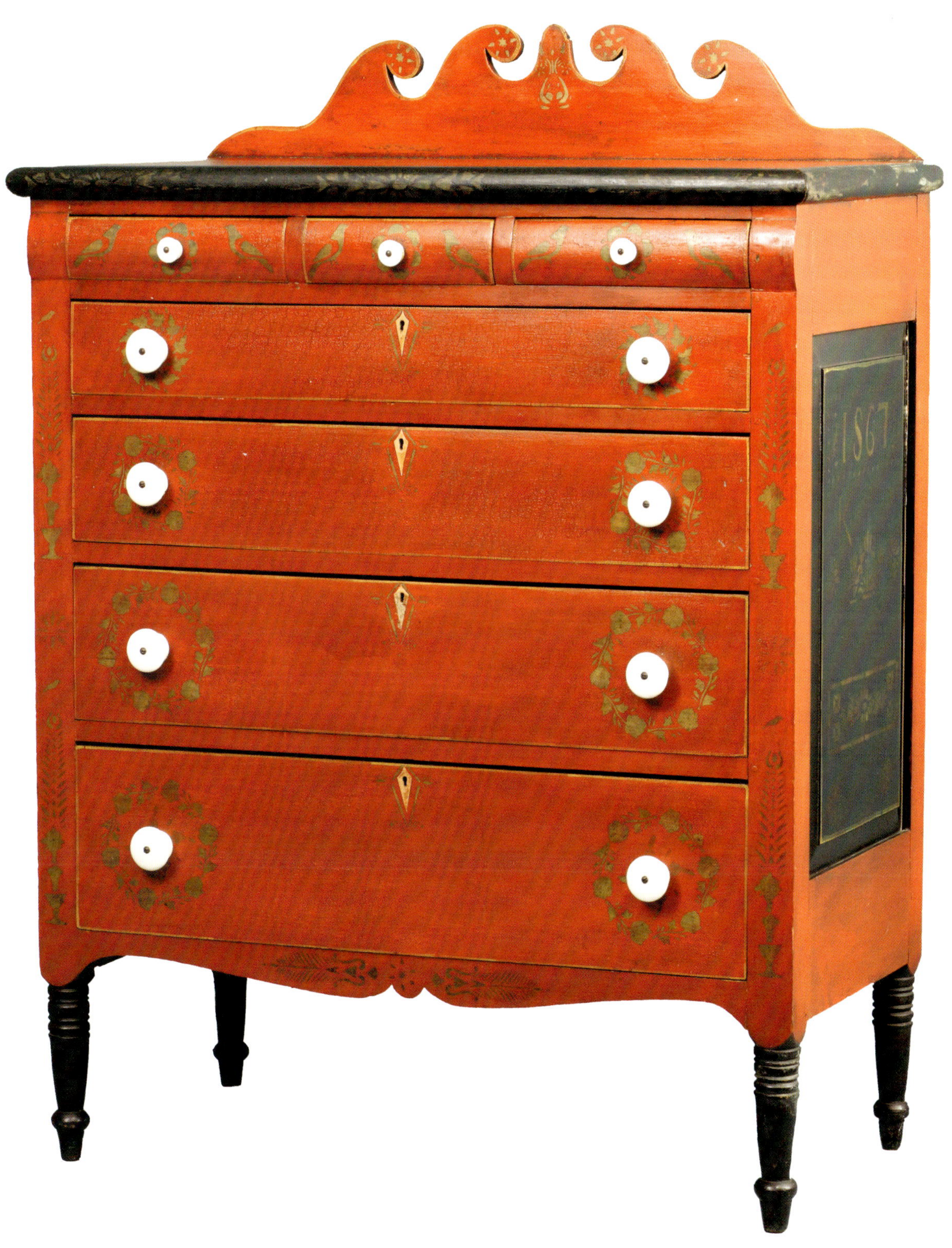
1867

Conemaugh Township in an 1876 county atlas, is a building identified as a carpenter shop.[2] It is possible that some or perhaps all of the Soap Hollow furniture production occurred there. Stahl moved in 1880 to Kent County, Michigan, where he died.

The chest of drawers as a form for Soap Hollow furniture is interesting for two reasons. First, it is a distinctly English form rather than a German one. Germans preferred blanket boxes and schranks (wardrobes) to chests of drawers, or at least to painted chests of drawers.[3] Consequently, very few painted Pennsylvania German chests of drawers are known. Second, Soap Hollow chests of drawers all have the graceful scrolled backboard, which appears on no other American furniture and whose origin remains a mystery. One writer referred to it as a "double swan neck pediment" and speculated that it may have been adapted from the scrolls found on the hoods of tall case clocks.[4]

While the overall form of the Soap Hollow chest of drawers varied little over fifty years, minor design elements did change. For example, drawers were originally fitted with pressed glass knobs.[5] Beginning in the mid-1860s, white ceramic knobs, like those on our chest, replaced glass knobs. The form of the small drawers in the top tier of drawers changed at about the same time, from flat-face to curved-face, as on our example. The other significant style change appears in the decoration in the 1870s, when Victorian transfers or decals began to replace stenciled decoration. Despite these gradual design changes, construction techniques remained the same. Dovetailed drawers, hand-planed surfaces, and turned feet continued to be hallmarks of this distinctive furniture.

In addition to chests of drawers and blanket boxes, Soap Hollow craftsmen produced miniature blanket boxes, sewing stands, corner cupboards, hanging cupboards, tall clocks, flat-wall cupboards, stands, lifttop desks, beds, chairs, and what seems to be a unique cupboard over drawers dated 1870.[6] More than seventy signed pieces have been recorded, including eleven by Jeremiah Stahl.[7]

A similar but earlier tradition of distinctive German paint-decorated furniture existed in southeastern Pennsylvania in an area known as Mahantongo Valley or Schwaben Creek Valley in Schuylkill and Northumberland Counties from about 1789 to 1838. These furniture forms are like Soap Hollow, but the painted decoration and inscriptions are largely freehand or stamped rather than stenciled, and the chests have only four drawers and lack scrolled backboards.[8]

Finally, there is a second decorated furniture tradition in Somerset County related to Soap Hollow. A father and son partnership, Jacob (1796–1883) and Elias (1832–1910) Knagy, is credited with Sheraton style grain-painted and stenciled furniture.[9] The Knagys worked from about 1841 to 1882, and they often signed their furniture on the exterior, but only with initials. Unlike Soap Hollow decoration, the owner's name is usually spelled out rather than in initials only.

Three pieces of Soap Hollow furniture from a private collection were included in the Museum's 1989 exhibition *A Sampler of American Folk Art from Pennsylvania Collections*, and fifteen pieces made up the furniture section of the exhibition *Made in Pennsylvania: A Folk Art Tradition*, organized by The Westmoreland in 2007.[10]

HNT

1 Charles R. Muller, *Soap Hollow: The Furniture and Its Makers* (Groveport, OH: Canal Press), 10.

2 Ibid, 4. Map illustration from *County Atlas of Somerset, Pennsylvania* (New York: F.W. Beers, 1876).

3 Monroe H. Fabian, *The Pennsylvania-German Decorated Chest* (New York: Universe Books, 1978), 26.

4 Scott T. Swank, *Manufactured by Hand: The Soap Hollow School* (Loretto, PA: Southern Alleghenies Museum of Art, 1993), 3.

5 When this chest of drawers entered the collection, it came with three white ceramic knobs on the three rolled drawers, and brown Rockingham knobs on the four graduated drawers. The Museum replaced the brown ones with white ones to reflect its appearance when it was made.

6 Muller, *Soap Hollow*, 28–29.

7 Ibid, 89.

8 Cynthia V. A. Schaffner and Susan Klein: *American Painted Furniture* (New York: Clarkson N. Potter Inc., 1997), 142–43.

9 Ibid, 145.

10 *A Sampler of American Folk Art from Pennsylvania Collections* (Greensburg: Westmoreland Museum of Art, 1989), catalog nos. 155, 156, 169; *Made in Pennsylvania*, 4, 6–13.

WILLIAM COVENTRY WALL (1811–1886)
View Along the Allegheny Near Aspinwall Pa., 1867
Oil on canvas, 26 ½ x 47 ¾ inches
Signed and dated lower left
Gift of Jack and Suzanne Shilling and Family, 2008.136
Provenance: Private Collection; Debra Force Fine Art, Inc., New York.

SELECTED EXHIBITIONS: *Scenic Views: Painters of the Scalp Level School Revisited*, Westmoreland Museum of American Art, 2008.

The oldest of three members of the Wall family active as painters in southwestern Pennsylvania in the nineteenth century, William Coventry Wall was born in London on December 8, 1811.[1] He immigrated to the United States with his parents and younger sister in the early 1920s, where they settled in Mount Pleasant, a small community 45 miles southeast of Pittsburgh.[2] Wall's father, also named William, made his living as a stonemason and gilder.

Largely self-taught, W. C. Wall, as he is known, was surrounded by artists, including his father, who had trained as a painter. By the early 1840s, Wall had married and moved to Pittsburgh, busying himself there with several enterprises, including theatrical scene painting, making illustrations of historical sites and events, and portraiture. To further support himself and his young family, he opened a framing and art supply store, perhaps initially associated with the precursor of the J. J. Gillespie Gallery, which became a gathering place for the city's painters.[3] A contemporary newspaper article describes Wall as a "plain and fancy portrait and picture frame manufacturer" who also "neatly gilded and repaired" frames and sold paintings and engravings, including portraits by his own hand.[4] He was known to generously extend credit to his artist-customers and was by all accounts a successful businessman.

In 1845, Wall woke to witness the devastating fire that destroyed most of Pittsburgh that year, including his own store and that of his father-in-law. Sketches made at the scene became paintings and later lithographs, which were widely distributed. *Pittsburgh after the Fire of 1845, from Birmingham* and *Pittsburgh after the Fire of 1845, from Boyd's Hill* are both in the collection of the Carnegie Museum of Art. Wall's reputation was thus made, and by 1847, his occupation—according to the city directory—indicated that he had successfully transitioned from business owner to landscape painter. He exhibited at the annual exhibition of the Pennsylvania Academy of the Fine Arts in 1855 and again in 1885, the year before he died. The only artist member of the managing committee of the Pittsburgh Art Association's first annual exhibition, he became an important figure in Pittsburgh's developing art world.

W. C. Wall's first sketching trip may have been to rural Fayette County, south of Pittsburgh, with fellow artist Trevor McClurg (1816–1893) in 1853. Later, Wall associated with George Hetzel (1826–1899), leader of what became known as the Scalp Level school in the latter half of the nineteenth century. With McClurg among them, this group spent their summers escaping the city's dirty industrial neighborhoods to paint en plein air in the nearby countryside of western Pennsylvania. There, cultivated farmland and undeveloped forests awaited their brushes. Wall developed a style based on direct observation and careful transcription, resulting in precise, detail-filled, and usually brightly colored compositions. The precision with which his images are rendered, along with their general lack of atmospheric perspective, gives his paintings a look bordering on the naive. Sketchbooks filled with careful pencil drawings, sometimes enhanced with white and black pastel or gouache, served as reference for his work. The Westmoreland owns one such sketchbook (1999.12), which includes his preparatory study for *Cottage Beside a Stream, Autumn* (1997.10). Wall began experimenting with photography as early as 1856 and may have used this medium as reference for his work in oil. He was also known to complete small versions of a scene and later work the composition into a more ambitiously scaled canvas.

Although he was known for painting pure landscapes, Wall completed many pieces—including *View Along the Allegheny Near Aspinwall Pa.*—that have a narrative motif or motifs. In this case, several different vignettes of activity within the composition serve as visual subplots. We see a farmer and his wife surveying their farmhouse across a harvested field; a factory busy with activity; and a river bustling with small

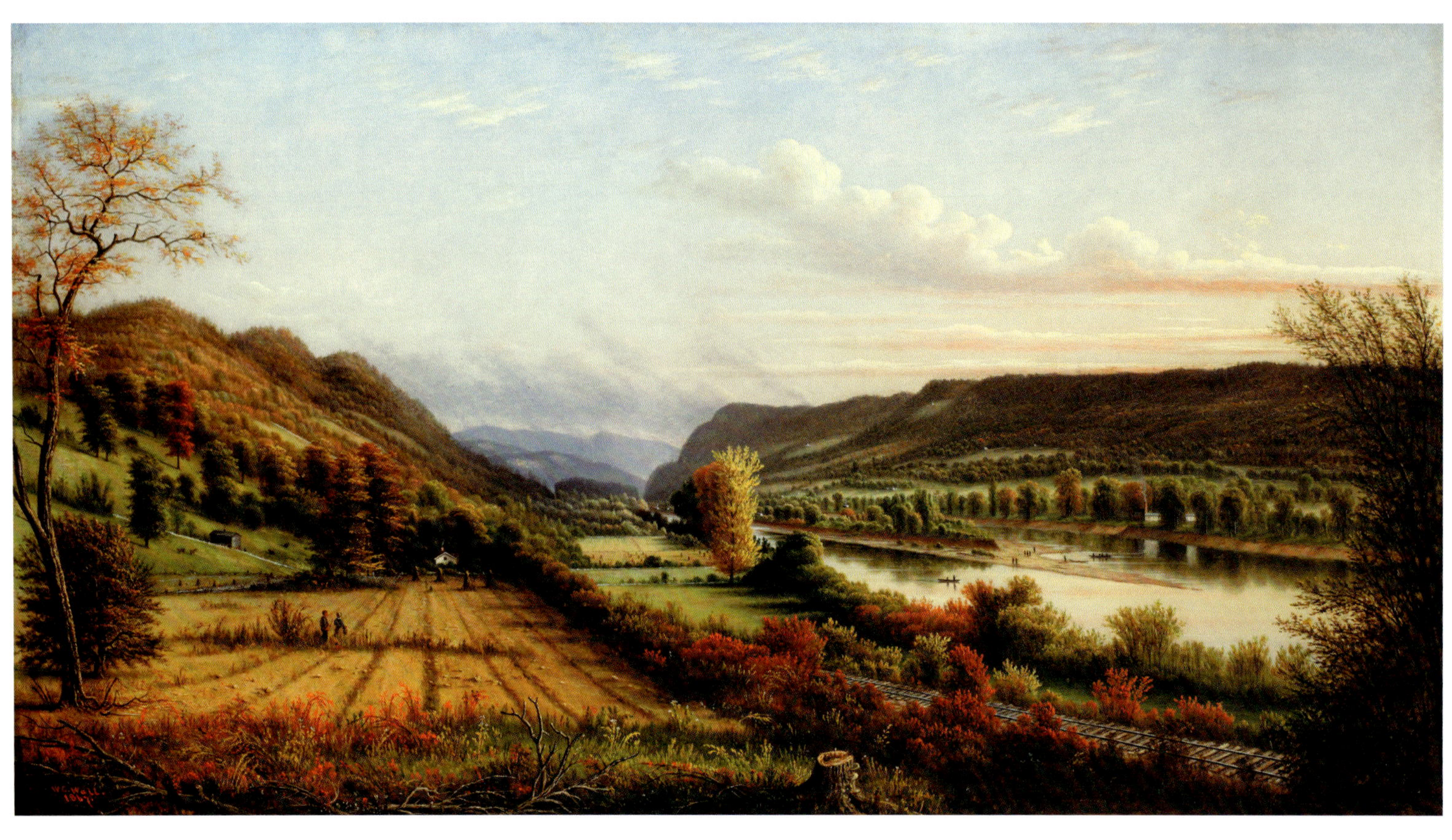

craft. Wall's orderly arrangement of man's activities within the vastness of nature reflects harmonious cohabitation.

Wall demonstrates his knowledge of nineteenth-century landscape metaphors by juxtaposing a tree stump—a symbol of man's early impact on nature—with a railroad track nearly hidden by the undergrowth—a symbol of the industrial revolution to come. The brilliant yellow tree at the composition's central focal point indicates the glory of autumn, the season most visibly marked by change. The panoramic format, with the upper third devoted to a vast blue sky, is a hallmark of Wall's style.

Research has revealed that the location is a point on the right bank of the Allegheny River six miles above Pittsburgh, at the small community of Sharpsburg, looking upriver to Aspinwall.[5] The current view from that site is not only very much changed but substantially obscured by the Highland Park Bridge. The railroad tracks were laid by the Western Pennsylvania Railroad in 1866 along an old canal route. Six Mile Island can be seen in Wall's painting, and the farm has been identified as that of James O'Hara, Esq.—a patriarch of the Darlingtons, a prominent Pittsburgh family.[6] Painted in 1867, in the prime of Wall's oeuvre and just two years after the Civil War ended, the scene exudes the warm tranquillity and domesticity characteristic of Wall's best work.

JHO'T

1 His brother, Alfred S. Wall (1825–1896), and Alfred's son, A. Bryan Wall (1861–1935), were also painters. Wall's birth year has previously been recorded as 1810, but a genealogical record recently located in London by Wall's relative, Dr. Betty Jane McWilliams, establishes this later date.

2 Mount Pleasant, settled during the French and Indian War, is one of the oldest communities in southwestern Pennsylvania and the childhood home of Henry Clay Frick (1849–1919).

3 J. J. Gillespie Company, the name of the gallery when it was established in 1832, remains in operation today after 178 years, now located in the community of McMurray, fifteen miles south of Pittsburgh.

4 Unidentified and undated newspaper clipping, artist file, Westmoreland Museum of American Art.

5 Research by Frank J. Kurtik and Gary Grimes, 2009, artist file, Westmoreland Museum of American Art.

6 Three Mile Island is also known as Guyasuta Island, after the Seneca brave said to have guided the young George Washington in 1753.

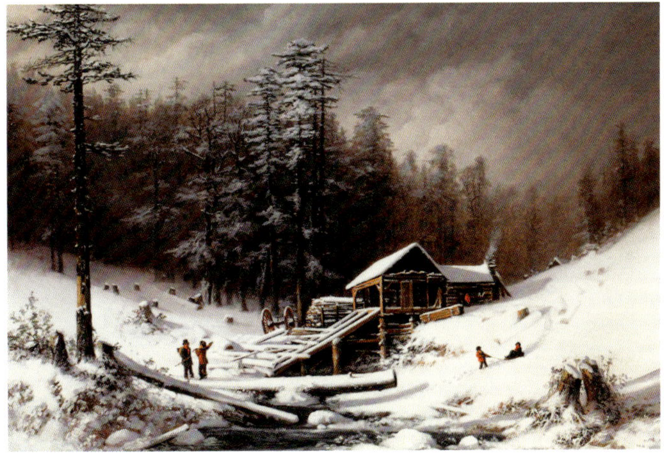

Alfred S. Wall (1825–1896), *Old Saw Mill*, 1851
Oil on canvas, 38 x 57 inches
Gift of the Woods-Marchand Foundation, 1986.262

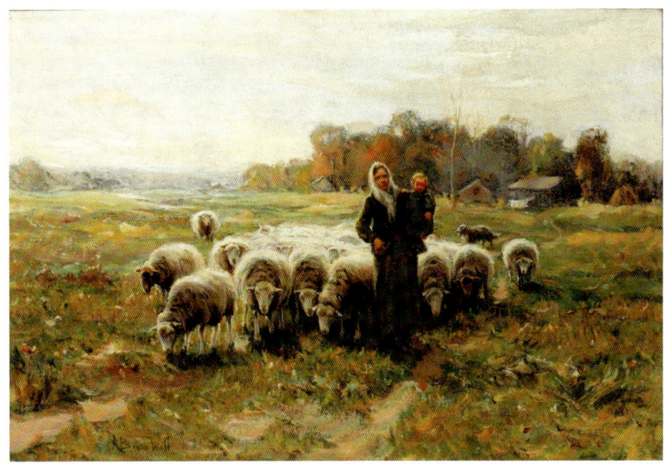

Alfred Bryan Wall (1861–1935)
Shepherdess with Sheep and Child, n.d.
Oil on canvas, 20 x 30 inches, Museum purchase, 1980.89

WILLIAM THOMPSON RUSSELL SMITH (1812–1896)
Aqueduct of the Pennsylvania Canal below Harrisburg, PA, 1868
Oil on canvas, 23 x 35 ½ inches
Signed and dated lower right
Gift of the William A. Coulter Fund, 1961.142
Provenance: Private Collection; Kennedy Galleries, New York.

Selected Exhibitions: University Art Gallery, University of Pittsburgh, 1963; Butler Institute of American Art, Youngstown, Ohio; 1964; Pennsylvania Historical and Museum Commission, Harrisburg, 1979; Southern Alleghenies Museum of Art, Loretto, Pennsylvania, 1996.

> When so many painters have painted such a variety of landscape with all forms of arrangements of features it is difficult to seem always original in ones own work; and, indeed, to avoid any appearance of mannerism and repetition, it is well to take the main features of your composition or pictures directly from nature: this I have long striven to do.[1]

Although he achieved widespread acclaim for his drop curtains and scenic sets for theaters in Philadelphia, in New York, and along the eastern seaboard, William Thompson Russell Smith thought of himself first and foremost as a landscape painter. Nature and the landscape always played an integral role in his theater commissions. Theater critics, artists, and theatergoers alike praised his ability to paint scenery with such accuracy that they sometimes preferred his creations to the performance. Critics felt that this particular type of painting prepared Smith for "high excellence in other departments of art." Smith must have agreed, since he produced his first professional scene painting for the opening of the Pittsburgh Theater at age twenty-one and continued to paint theater commissions for nearly fifty years of his sixty-five-year career.

Russell Smith gravitated early to painting nature, recalling that as a child he drew from his mother's china plates decorated with landscapes. His romantic sensibility toward the landscape developed early as well, from his first seven years in a castle in Scotland, where he was born, to his travels in a Conestoga wagon from Philadelphia to Indiana County (near Blairsville), where he lived until 1822, when his family moved to Pittsburgh. Western Pennsylvania was essentially wilderness when Smith's family made their way across the state in 1819. This trip instilled in him his love for the natural landscape. Smith kept an autobiographical journal from 1836 to the 1890s, in which he described his experiences as an artist, and it is from these writings that we learn of his preference for and appreciation of wild nature: "I have always had great fondness for river scenery, especially that which has been unspoiled by the axe and plough."

After completing only seven quarters of high school, Smith received three years of formal art training from the leading portrait painter, James Reid Lambdin (1807–1889), with whom he studied while in Pittsburgh. During his career, Smith occasionally painted portraits on commission, as well as for friends and family members. The Westmoreland's *Self-Portrait*, painted when Smith was seventy-five, portrays a self-assured and distinguished artist who had been making art for over sixty years. Essentially self-taught, Smith deliberately combined the exact details found in nature—every branch, blade of grass, flower, shrub, rock formation—with the softer, atmospheric effects of light, as it filtered through and softened trees, foliage, and background alike. With his palette, he attempted to remain as true to nature as possible, perhaps inspired by the writings of artist-critic John Ruskin (1819–1900), who directed artists to nature to find the truth there, and to draw or paint it in all its magnificent detail. Smith carefully studied the landscape, its topography, and local color so as to re-create it as he saw it. As a boy, he made several camera obscuras that he "could put his head into . . . and contemplate the charming effect of the brilliant landscape cut off by the dark surroundings from all extraneous objects," allowing him to view only a portion of the landscape in an unobstructed and focused manner.

Smith elaborated on his fidelity to nature in his journals, which served as his painting bible. To ensure a faithful record, he itemized everything he saw in writing, whether it was another painting or simply details of the landscape, describing the sites he sketched. He recorded skies, mountains, water, trees, plants, atmosphere, and even the meteorological conditions that existed so that he could replicate each exactly as he had found it. His notes about color reveal how exhaustively

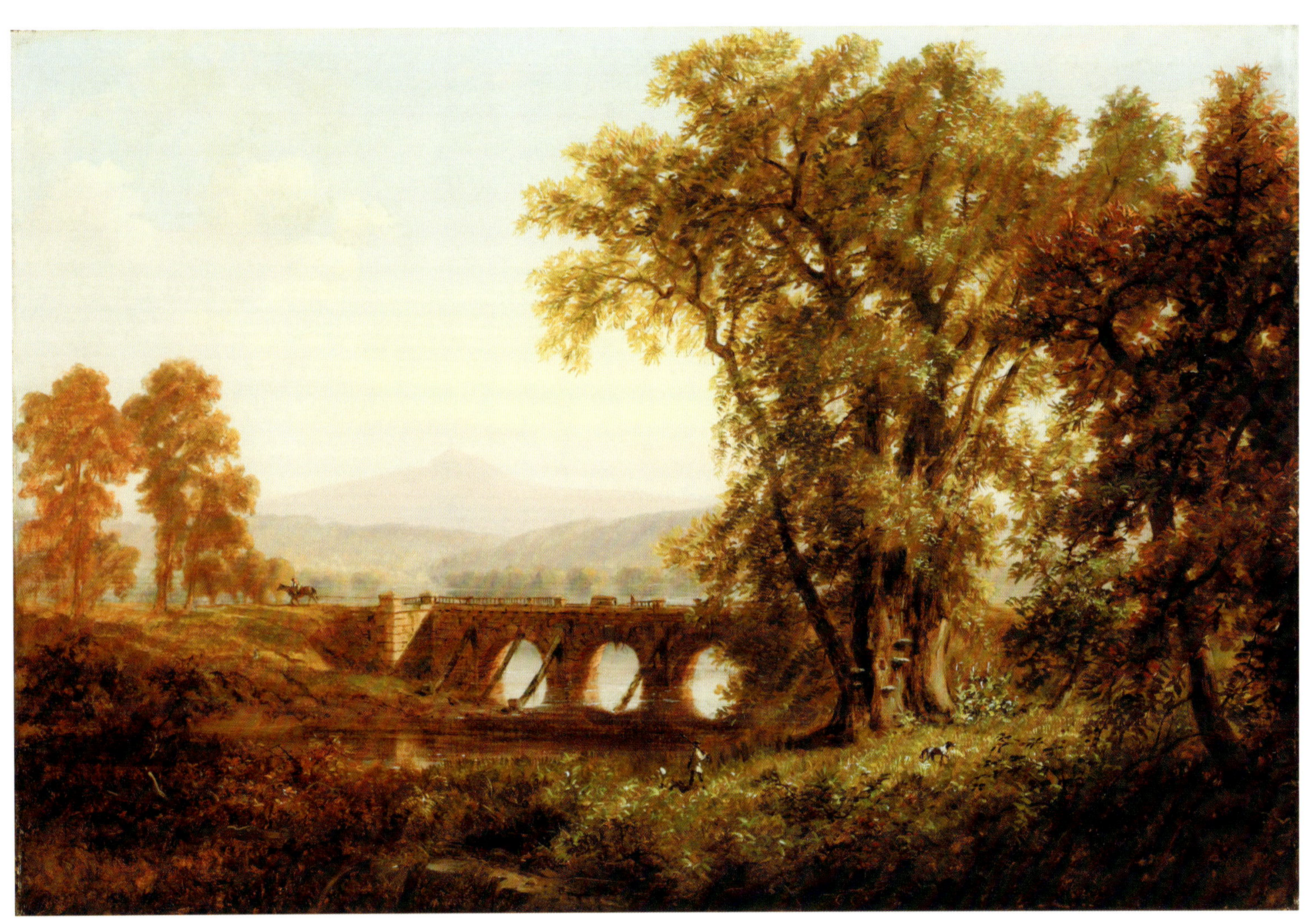

he analyzed a scene before he committed it to canvas. Samples of color pigments are indicated in the margins. He even fabricated his own paint case so that he could paint out in the open air. Smith repeatedly references the eighteenth-century French artist Claude Lorrain (1600–1682), whose compositional formula was universally adopted by Smith's contemporaries. This formula, which focuses the viewer's attention and directs the eye, is clearly evident in the way Smith ordered his compositions. He also indicated his admiration for J. M. W. Turner (1775–1851) and Salvator Rosa (1615–1673), whose work he encountered directly when he was in Europe. Nature, however—as his primary source of inspiration—allies him more closely with his contemporaries: the Hudson River school painters in America and the Barbizon school in France. Both groups were united philosophically with their love for nature and their desire to paint its picturesque beauty. With Smith's truth-to-nature principles, combined with his interest in light and shadow and atmospheric effects, his paintings appear to be a congenial marriage of the two schools.

The artist's obsession with such acute observation was likely the result of his travels as an illustrator, making geological and topographical sketches for William B. Rogers's survey of Pennsylvania (c. 1841) and Virginia (1844). Fourteen years later, he made sketches to illustrate *The Geology of Pennsylvania: A Government Survey* (1858), some of which he later developed into paintings. His scientific drawings were used to accompany lectures on the subject by many scientists and geologists that he knew, including British geologist Sir Charles Lyell, and Benjamin Silliman, founder of the *American Journal of Science and Arts*.

In his paintings, Smith's nature is part settled and part wilderness. He always gravitated to the natural landscape, moving from Philadelphia, where he worked, to a rural environment north of the city to live and paint. He designed two homes in the course of his life, Rock Hill in Branchtown (1841) and the castle-like Edge Hill in Montgomery County (1854), where he lived for the remainder of his life. In spite of his busy career with theater commissions, he always made time to paint landscapes. In July and August of each year, he took walking tours to the mountains and along the Juniata and Susquehanna rivers to absorb and make sketches of scenes he would later transfer to canvas in his studio.

In *Aqueduct of the Pennsylvania Canal below Harrisburg, PA* Smith reveals his interest in both the engineering feat of the aqueduct as a means to transport boats over land, and the surrounding landscape. The human figures in the scene—a man on a horse pulling a flatboat across the aqueduct, and a hunter with his dog in the foreground—are miniscule when compared to the landscape surrounding them. Although clearly subordinated to the natural environment, these figures participate in it as well, the former utilizing a man-made device to complement nature, and the latter making use of the landscape as a resource. Raking light directs our attention to this dual activity.

Although it seems to have been his preferred terrain, Smith did not restrict his landscape painting to Pennsylvania views. Following the path of the Hudson River school painters, the artist extended his painting trips to Lake George, Lake Champlain, Mount Chocorua, the White Mountains, the James and Shenandoah rivers, and Owl's Head, Maine. Smith did not consider these trips family vacations but business trips, during which he would generate enough sketches to enable him to continue making landscape paintings. In his travels through Europe, he visited England, Scotland, France, Italy, Switzerland, and Holland. From the volumes of detailed notes and oil and pencil sketches he brought back from these trips, Smith generated hundreds of paintings. He referenced many of his European sketches for theater sets that required architectural ruins, castles, or other historically accurate details. The Westmoreland owns five paintings by Russell Smith, two of which are Italian landscapes.

Throughout his lifetime, Russell Smith was an active participant in the art scenes of Philadelphia, New York, and Boston. He was an extremely prolific artist, and a large body of his work survives in both public and private collections. The broad range and variety of it, added to the volumes of notes and sketches, testify to the artist's ambitious efforts to document his life and the life around him. He made art for nearly sixty-five of his eighty-four years and wrote about every aspect of it. He married fellow artist Mary Wilson (1819–1874) in 1838, and their union produced two children, Xanthus and Mary, who also became artists. As his obituary indicates, Smith continued painting until his death on November 8, 1896. His love of nature and his desire to preserve it on canvas remained to the end: a finished landscape was found on his easel the day after he died.

BLJ

1 William Thompson Russell Smith, unpublished autobiography, *Smith Family Papers*, 1880-1884 (New York: Archives of American Art, microfilm), volume 5, reels 2036-2037.

(THOMAS) WORTHINGTON WHITTREDGE (1820–1910)

Home by the Sea, c. 1872
Oil on canvas, 14 ½ x 22 5/8 inches
Signed lower right
Gift of the William A. Coulter Fund, 1960.6
Provenance: Victor Sparks, New York.

Selected Exhibitions: Henry Clay Frick Arts Department, University of Pittsburgh, 1963; *Worthington Whittredge,* Ringling Museum of Art, Sarasota, Florida, 1989-1990.

Born in Springfield, Ohio, Thomas Worthington Whittredge was the son and last child of a former sea captain turned farmer.[1] He left home at age seventeen and went to Cincinnati. There he worked for his brother-in-law as a house and sign painter. He later traveled to Indiana and West Virginia, working first as a daguerreotypist and later as a portraitist, but in 1834 he decided to concentrate on landscape painting. Financial assistance from wealthy art collectors he befriended in Cincinnati enabled him to go to Europe in 1849. Arriving first in Paris, he was disappointed to find no one there with whom he cared to study landscape painting. Venturing to Düsseldorf, he lived with landscape painter Andreas Achenbach (1815–1910) and accompanied Karl Friedrich Lessing (1808–1880) on several nature-sketching trips. He studied with them in what is termed The Düsseldorf School, receiving a thorough indoctrination in drawing and landscape and in romantic depictions of the sublime, wild aspects of nature. In all, Whittredge spent ten years working abroad in Germany; Switzerland, where he painted alongside Albert Bierstadt (1830–1902); France, where he saw landscapes of the Barbizon school; and Italy, where he settled in Rome in 1854.

Whittredge returned to the United States taking a studio in the newly opened Tenth Street Studio Building in New York City in 1859 along with Albert Bierstadt and other members of the Hudson River school, of which he was considered a member. The design of the building allowed for private studios in addition to public areas for exhibition and discussion, thereby affording an atmosphere of camaraderie among the tenants.[2]

Applying his talents to native landscapes, including those traditionally visited by artists along the Hudson River valley and New England's coastline, Whittredge found greater commercial success than he had with European subjects. His style tended toward the picturesque, favoring the earth tones employed by the Düsseldorf school and choosing harmonious subject matter. Bucolic farms, tranquil shorelines, gentle mountains, and pleasant weather conditions were among his favorites. His popularity grew quickly and in 1861 he became a member of the National Academy of Design. Like others of the Hudson River school's second generation, he eventually journeyed westward, seeking fresh, different material for his brush. The first of three trips between 1866 and 1871 was made in the company of Sanford Robinson Gifford (1823–1880) and John Frederick Kensett (1816–1872). The three traveled through Nebraska, Kansas, and Colorado, and into New Mexico along the eastern Rocky Mountains. There Whittredge found inspiration in the vast, essentially untouched purity of plains and mountains. Sketches from this and subsequent trips became the basis for major easel paintings created later in the Tenth Street Studio Building.

Still drawn to the seacoast, perhaps influenced by his father's first vocation, Whittredge summered in Rhode Island whenever possible. In the 1870s and 1880s, he completed seven versions of *Home by the Sea,* based on a scene in Newport—a location that held great nostalgia for the artist. Throughout his childhood in Ohio, his siblings and father regaled one another with sentimental remembrances of the northeastern coast, which he alone among them had not experienced. When he visited the area later, he noted, "I had heard much of it and the neighborhood surrounding it when I was a child, and many things I saw seemed perfectly familiar to me, although never seen before. Many years had passed since I had heard stories related of such-and-such a house, or this cranberry patch, or that whaling ship coming in laden with oil. . . . In short it was the land of my forefathers."[3]

Newport was a destination for many artists, including Kensett and Martin Johnson Heade (1819–1904), the latter also a resident of the Tenth Street Studio Building and well known to Whittredge. Newport was also already established as a summer haven for the wealthy when Whittredge painted his series related to *Home by the Sea.* Impressive mansions being built

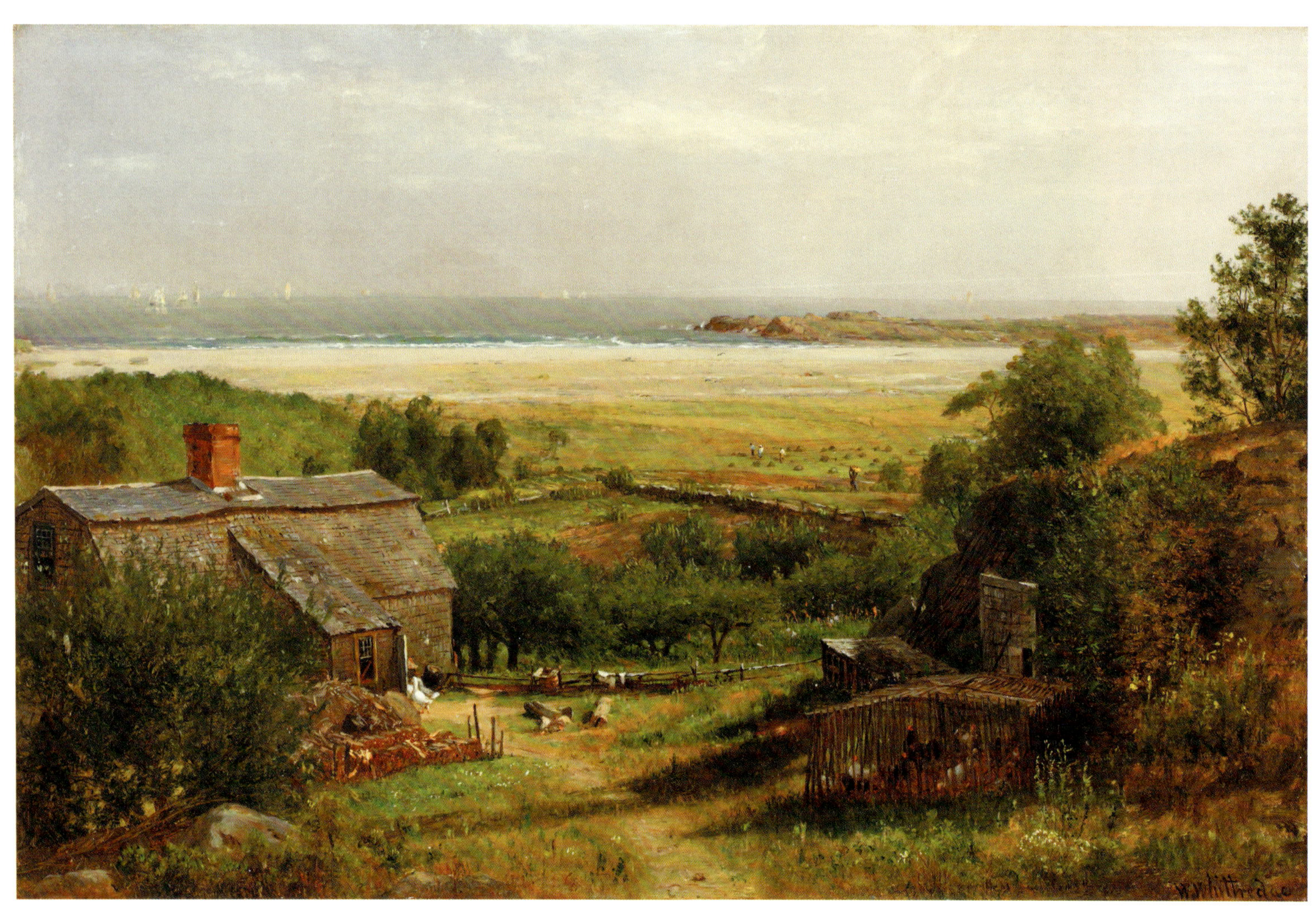

concurrent to Whittredge's visits included architect Richard Morris Hunt's personal residence, known as Sunnyside (1870–1871); Boston architect Russell Sturgis's design for the artist Edward Darley Boit (1840–1915), known as the Rocks (c. 1870); and Henry Hobson Richardson's massive Queen Anne style "cottage" for Bostonian F. W. Andrews and his family.

Whittredge's choice of a dilapidated colonial-era farmhouse as the subject for The Westmoreland's *Home by the Sea* reveals his interest in recalling an earlier, simpler time. A nostalgic choice and perhaps a biographical one, the scene includes both a farm and the sea. The seven extant versions of this view are painted from varying perspectives. Three of them date from 1872; and the others, between 1876 and 1885, indicating a longtime fascination on the part of the artist with this homestead. A detailed drawing by Whittredge of Whitehall, the eighteenth-century Newport home of Bishop George Berkeley, identifies the building, which was still a working farm when Whittredge sketched and painted it.[4] He carefully rendered details of the structure, which was a typical colonial New England farmhouse—a style experiencing a revival of interest in the latter half of the nineteenth century. In contrast to the palatial summer homes being built nearby, Whitehall was a humble, functional dwelling. At least two of the other versions show workers in the process of haying, with fully laden horse-drawn wagons returning from the fields. All versions contrast farmland with ocean and sky in varying proportions.

The Westmoreland's version is a detailed oil sketch, signed by the artist in the lower right, for a much larger painting now in the collection of the Addison Gallery of American Art.[5] The farmhouse is nestled in the lower-left corner of the composition, across a worn, dirt path from a well-populated chicken coop. Fences surround an orchard beyond, the fields of which give way first to sandy beach and then to water, where sailboats on calm seas articulate the horizon line. Trees are dressed in the full, dark green foliage of summer, under pale blue skies decorated with wisps of clouds. Westward-leading shadows and the figure of a woman feeding geese from the farmhouse doorway (more distinct in the larger version) indicate the time of day as dawn. Whittredge carefully records the foreground fauna, delighting in a more painterly handling of pigment in the smaller version, which reveals his facility in the oil medium. The entire scene is bathed in a soft golden light, a specialty and hallmark of the artist. Whittredge manages to avoid any sense of hackneyed sentimentality in this quaint genre scene, imbuing his image instead with a sense of well-being and authenticity.

Whittredge died at the age of eighty-nine in Summit, New Jersey, where he and his family lived the last thirty years of his life in a home he called Hillcrest.

JHO'T

1 Whittredge dropped Thomas from his name in 1855.

2 The studio building, designed by Richard Morris Hunt, was an innovative structure built specifically for artists, writers, and architects, with studio rooms laid out around a central gallery. Home to several generations of artists, including Winslow Homer (1836–1910) and William Merritt Chase (1849–1916), it was located at 51 West Tenth Street between Fifth and Sixth avenues and is credited with making Greenwich Village an arts community. It was torn down in 1956.

3 John I. H. Baur, ed., *The Autobiography of Worthington Whittredge: 1820–1910* (New York: Arno Press, 1969).

4 The location of the drawing is currently unknown; photograph at Munson-Williams-Proctor Arts Institute, Utica, New York.

5 *Home by the Sea*, 1872, oil on canvas, 36 1/8 x 54 1/8 inches, Museum Purchase, 1943.173. Addison Gallery of American Art, Phillips Academy, Andover, Massachusetts.

GEORGE INNESS (1825–1894)
The Coming Shower, c. 1873
Oil on canvas, 12 ¼ x 18 inches
Signed lower left
Gift of the William A. Coulter Fund, 1958.38
Provenance: Schenck Art Gallery, New York, 1879; Babcock Galleries, New York; Findlay Galleries, New York; Mr. Casablanca, Long Island, New York; Mrs. Peter Lloyd, Chagrin Falls, Ohio; M. Knoedler & Company, Inc., New York.

SELECTED EXHIBITIONS: Butler Institute of American Art, Youngstown, Ohio, 1964; Henry Clay Frick Fine Arts Building, University of Pittsburgh, 1963.

George Inness was born on a farm near Newburgh, New York, and grew up in Newark, New Jersey, where his father, by then a prosperous businessman, ran a grocery store. Inness had epilepsy, a disease much misunderstood at the time. His delicate health and distracted nature caused him to underperform at school. In order to divert him from his early-evidenced artistic ambitions, his father set him up in business. However, the young Inness showed little interest and aptitude for the world of commerce. He left home to become apprenticed to a map engraver—Sherman & Smith—having always had an interest in prints and fine illustrations. In fact, he would spend hours studying and copying old prints, thereby honing his skills as a draftsman.

At the age of eighteen, Inness convinced his father to let him study in New York, but his poor health did not permit him to manage the arduous classes at the National Academy of Design. Instead, he apprenticed briefly with the French landscape painter Régis François Gignoux (1816–1882), a proponent of the Hudson River school. Inness knew and admired the work of Thomas Cole (1801–1848) and Asher B. Durand (1796–1886), leaders of the Hudson River school, and initially developed a style aligned with theirs. In fact, he often wished he could combine in his own work the "lofty striving" he saw in Cole with the "more intimate feeling of nature" in Durand.[1] These early canvases by Inness showed panoramic views executed with attention to detail, faithfulness to nature, and an attempt to evoke in paint specific natural phenomena, including weather conditions, seasons, and times of day.

Remarkably, Inness began exhibiting with the National Academy in 1844, the same year he opened his first studio in New York. At the same time, the American Art-Union promoted several of his engravings. In 1847, he made his first sale for $100.[2] This and other early positive responses to his work provided Inness the incentive to make his first of many trips to Europe in 1851. There he took up residence in Florence, but on subsequent trips he worked in France, where he came to know the work of the French Barbizon school of landscape painters and especially the landscapes of their leader, Jean-Baptiste-Camille Corot (1796–1875). The Barbizon painters differed from the American landscape school in that they favored a more intimate, painterly approach to nature, often forgoing detail in favor of mood. Inness began to introduce some of these stylistic tenets into his own work, feeling that the minute details of his earlier work did not sufficiently allow for artistic imagination and expression of the mystery that nature inspired in him.

Inness quickly rose to a prominent position in the art community, had an established list of patrons, and was elected to membership in the National Academy of Design in 1853. His quirky, unpredictable personality and substantial ego sometimes meant the loss of sales and relationships, but these had no impact on his trajectory. His paintings began to take on an individualistic quality, making nearly impossible the categorization of his work as demonstrating realism, impressionism, or any other prescribed "ism." Compounding this, Inness's introduction and conversion in the early 1860s to the Swedenborgian Church affected his style. It became charged with rich, luminous colors laid over one another in thick impasto and in forms that tended to oscillate, mimicking movement and the transitory quality of nature, light, and atmosphere

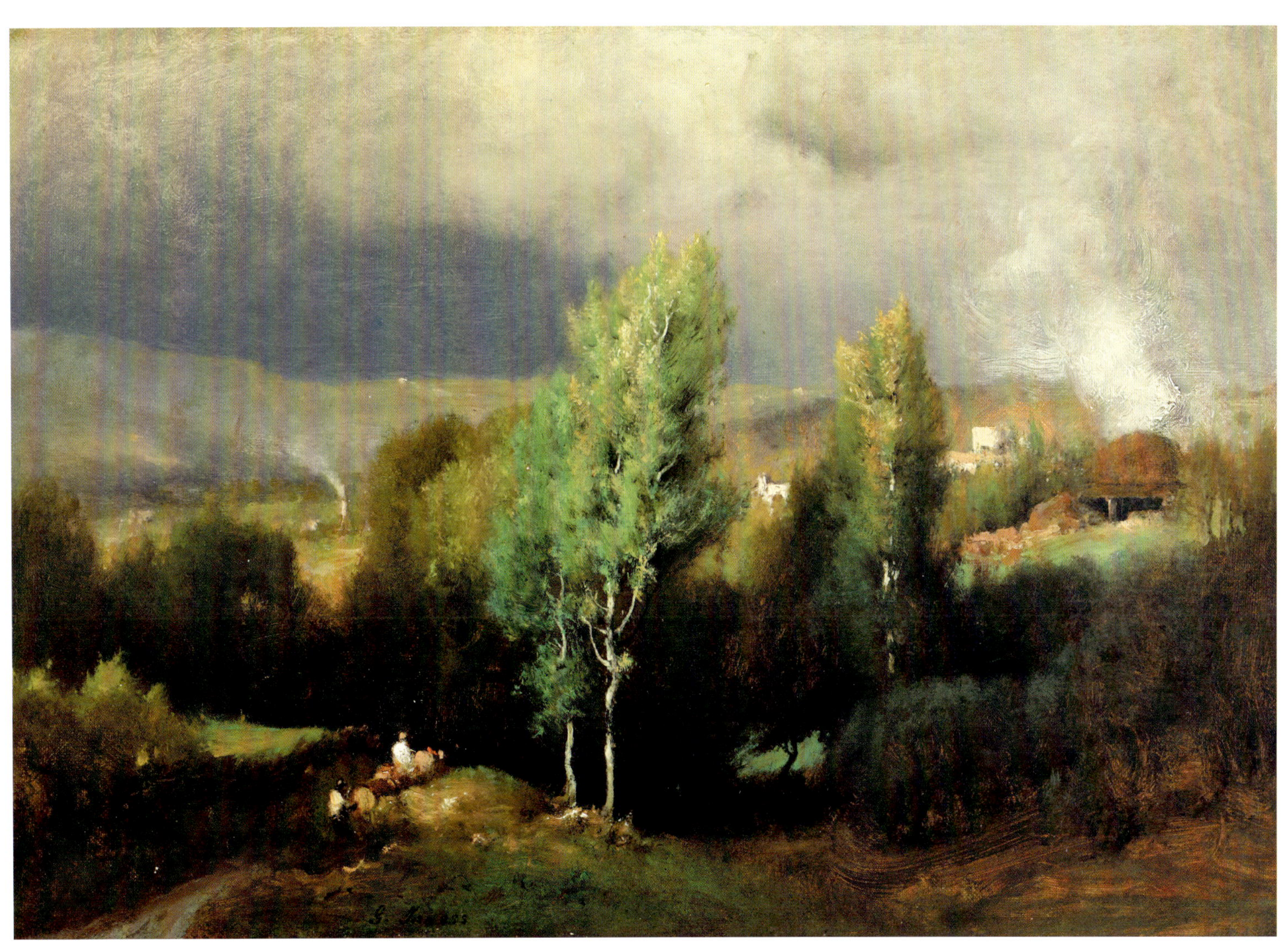

rather than depicting a single moment in time.[3] Imaginative, emotional, and mysterious reveries, they were equal parts artist's creative imperative and evocation of an omnipresent and accessible God. These later works fused sky with earth, trees with landscape elements, to reveal this restless, spiritual presence. Inness's keen powers of observation, which had formerly been expressed through the detailed rendering of nature, were now being put to work to make the intangible visual.

The poeticism of this later work achieved significant critical acclaim for Inness in his later years. However, with this new vision came a near constant urge to return to each canvas to adjust one area, which would inevitably lead to a repainting of the entire composition. Paint layers thickly applied could occasionally improve the image, but they sometimes became muddled, rendering the composition lost.

In *The Coming Shower*, Inness captured transitory light effects produced by rapidly changing weather conditions. The dramatic scene is charged with the storm's virulent energy, foreground trees cast into bright light against the darkness of the forested hills behind. The viewer cannot help but feel the thrilling yet dangerous sensation of being in the midst of such a storm, so evocative of its effects is Inness's depiction. We feel akin to the travelers, seen in the composition's lower left, as they approach their continued journey with trepidation. Because the artist spent much of 1870–1875 traveling to a variety of locations within Italy and France, this canvas most likely depicts the Italian landscape—perhaps near Perugia, where he summered in 1871 and 1873, or Albano, in the Alban Hills outside Rome, where he summered in 1872. The diminutive figures and structures resemble those dotting the landscapes of Claude Lorrain (1600–1682)—a French painter active mainly in Italy, whose works Inness greatly admired. Inness was in the habit of making sketches from nature, which he would transform into paintings in his studio. The particular freshness of this piece, along with its scale, suggests that it may have been substantially completed on site.

In the summer of 1878, Inness moved his family to Montclair, New Jersey, to escape the constant demands of the New York art world and to enjoy the countryside he so loved to paint. He had come to have differences with the art establishment in New York, particularly with the academy, which he felt had become too large in membership and too disparate to continue to be a leadership organization. At a time when followers of the Hudson River school were beginning to fall out of favor, Inness still enjoyed a steady income from sales of his work, affording him the ability to expand and remodel the home he had purchased and add a studio to the property. In 1850, he had married Elizabeth Abigail Hart (1833–1903), to whom he was devoted, and they had six children. Among them was a son, George Inness Jr. (1854–1926), also a landscape painter, who worked in the studio alongside his father, to both men's pleasure. The Montclair studio was also sometimes shared by Inness's son-in-law, the sculptor Jonathan Scott Hartley (1845–1912), whose family lived next door.

Inness continued his European travels, and he died in Scotland in 1894, after visits to Paris, Munich, and Baden-Baden. His body was returned to the United States, where it lay in state at the National Academy, a signal of the great admiration in which he was held by his fellow artists. Two hundred and forty paintings from his estate were auctioned the following year at the Union League Club in New York, where many works commanded high prices for the era.

Inness was an artist's artist. His work is still current today, having a seemingly timeless appeal, which explains why many contemporary painters continue to find inspiration in his enigmatic landscapes.

JHO'T

1 George Chambers Calvert, "George Inness: Painter and Personality," *Bulletin of the Art Association of Indianapolis, Indiana, The John Herron Art Institute* 13 (November 1926): 37.

2 The American Art-Union operated from 1840 to 1851 in New York City with the goal of educating the American public about the best in American art. It sold reproductions, conducted auctions, and held annual meetings of its membership.

3 Emanuel Swedenborg (1688–1772) was a Swedish scientist, philosopher, and theologian whose writings became the basis for the Swendenborgian Church, whose tenets include the beliefs that our material and spiritual lives coexist as one, and that the spiritual world is evidenced in nature.

THOMAS MORAN (1837–1926)
Tower Falls and Sulphur Mountain, Yellowstone National Park, 1874
Watercolor on paper, 10 x 14 inches
Signed with artist's monogram and dated lower left
Verso in script: Artist's description of the site
Gift of Dr. Walter Read Hovey, 1978.87
Provenance: Kennedy Galleries, New York; Dr. Walter Read Hovey.

SELECTED EXHIBITIONS: *Paintings and Graphics from the Walter Read Hovey Collection*, Westmoreland County Museum of Art, 1973; *The Gift of Art*, Westmoreland Museum of American Art, 2009.

Born in Bolton, England, Thomas Moran came to the United States with his family in 1844 at the age of seven. While still a teenager, he spent four years in the Philadelphia shop of Scattergood and Telfer, where he learned wood engraving—a detailed technique that would serve him well in his later work. Wood engraving, the medium of choice for illustrators at that time, produced crisp, clean lines for accurate reproduction. This new process, developed in the 1850s, replaced drawings that were incised into copper or steel plates. Moran drew directly on his wood blocks to achieve the best outcome, which meant his drawings were destroyed after the blocks were printed; as a result, few of Moran's sketches remain. From 1860 to 1861, Moran lived and studied with the prominent Philadelphia engraver John Sartain (1808–1897), and it was from him that Moran would gain his knowledge of quality publications. Moran also created etchings and lithographs during his career, and throughout the 1860s he worked steadily as an illustrator and fine artist, publishing images in a range of periodicals and books of the time. Essentially self-taught as a painter, he made the first of two trips to England in 1862 to study the works of J. M. W. Turner (1775–1851), making reproductions of his paintings.

Tower Falls and Sulphur Mountain, Yellowstone National Park was one of a series of watercolors that Moran created while traveling with Dr. Ferdinand V. Hayden, the geologist who led the 1871 U.S. Geological Survey into the region, which, within a year, would become the country's first national park. Sponsored by the Department of the Interior, it was a systematic investigation conducted by scientists, engineers, and photographer William Henry Jackson (1843–1942).[1] While not the artist of record, Moran went along as an unofficial member of the survey team. At the time, Moran was an established artist and was seeking new material for an illustration commission for *Scribner's Monthly* magazine, which shared the cost of the artist's trip with the Northern Pacific Railroad, whose guidebooks he illustrated.

Prior to the Hayden expedition, the Yellowstone region was described as a "hellish place of smoking geysers, boiling springs, and satanic sites." Afterward, however, "with stunning images display[ing] both the beauty and the color of the unusual formations, scientific data about the area's geology, and a new prospect for the region as the first national park, publicity shifted to a celebration of its marvels."[2] During the 1871–1872 session, a bill was introduced in Congress that set aside "a tract of 55 x 65 miles about the sources of the Yellowstone and Missouri Rivers and dedicates it and sets it apart as a great national park or pleasure-ground for the benefit and enjoyment of the people."[3] The bill became law on March 1, 1872, reserving 3,575 square miles as a public park.

This watercolor, together with fourteen others that Moran made after the 1871 expedition, constituted a forty-five page portfolio that was reproduced in 1876 as chromolithographs by the Boston lithographic firm Louis Prang & Company for publication in *The Yellowstone National Park and the Mountain Regions of Portions of Idaho, Nevada, Colorado and Utah*. These high-quality chromolithographs were the first color images to be printed of the first national park and its environs. The portfolio brought images of the American west to the people of the rest of the country, showing them places where most would never travel and garnering a new public appreciation for the region.[4] Dr. Hayden wrote the text that accompanied Moran's watercolors and described each locale to the viewer. The series of chromolithographs were exhibited in the galleries of the Centennial Art Building of the Centennial Exposition in

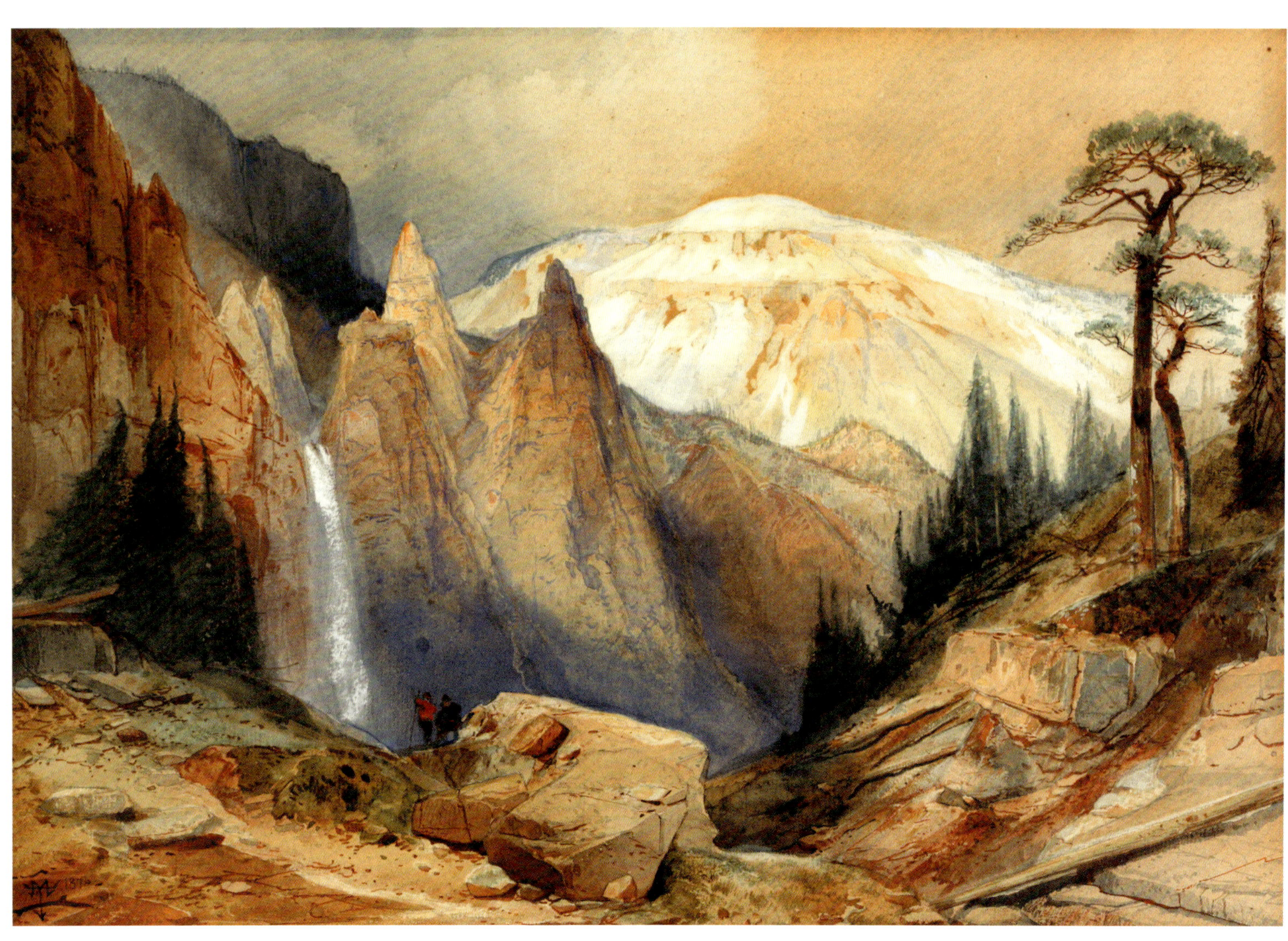

Philadelphia during the summer of 1876. When Prang produced the Yellowstone portfolio, he was the leading chromolithographic publisher in America. He and Moran were the perfect partners for this endeavor, as they both had knowledge of printmaking and publishing. Chromolithographs, published by Prang and also by Currier and Ives in New York, created a new appreciation of color images by the public and, since they were sold at affordable prices, made owning a work of art accessible to a broader public.

Seen at left, Sulphur Falls—a prominent feature of Tower Creek, a tributary of the Yellowstone River—plunges 132 feet to the creek bed below. Moran has included the winding creek as it wends its way down the mountain above the falls. A distinguishing feature of the site are the two rows of basaltic rocks that form a bluff wall that rises four to five hundred feet above the river below, which is not seen. These walls extend for two miles; the first row is fifteen to twenty feet high, with the second reaching up to thirty feet. The tower-like masses of breccias framing the falls are another unique feature of the site, eroded over time into strange formations that resemble gothic spires. The expansive white dome of Sulphur Mountain looms in the background at the center. Hayden's vivid description of the site culminates with: "Tower Creek marks the lower end of the Grand Canon [*sic*] of the Yellowstone, and the interest which it excites by reason of the grand scenery surrounding it is still further enhanced from the fact that there are several sulphur springs in its vicinity."[5] Two hikers, miniscule in relation to the grand natural wonder before them, can be seen at rest from their journey through the rugged terrain, taking a moment to enjoy the spectacular vista before them. Moran situates himself behind them, thus allowing the viewer to be part of the hiking party taking in the sublime scene. In his lengthy inscription on the back of the watercolor, Moran describes the colors he saw: "Beneath these columns lies a strata of calcareous deposit intermixed with sulphur & iron giving the most delicate & beautiful tints of red & yellow. . . . The impression on the eye is one of dazzling beauty, the whole mountain always being relieved against the sky as a mass of light." With a color palette that mimics his direct experience with the color and light conditions, Moran has created a picture-postcard of this remarkable place, accurately portraying both the topographical aspects of the site and its breathtaking natural beauty. The site is still intact today and remains a significant tourist destination within the park.

Moran made quick field sketches and took photographs during his travels through Yellowstone, giving him accurate records of each site from which to create finished watercolors when he returned to his studio, as the later 1874 date attests. A tiny 3 3/8 x 5 ½ inch sketch of *Tower Falls and Sulphur Mountain* owned by the Gilcrease Museum in Tulsa, Oklahoma, is gridded for enlargement and could very well be the preparatory study for The Westmoreland's larger watercolor. The chromolithograph made after Moran's watercolor is in the collection of the Joslyn Art Museum in Omaha, Nebraska.

Tower Falls and Sulphur Mountain, Yellowstone National Park was given to the Museum in 1963 by Dr. Walter Read Hovey, who was an art historian, professor of art, and director of the Department of Fine Arts at the University of Pittsburgh. He was a member of The Westmoreland's founding board of trustees from 1959 to 1980, and was made an honorary life trustee in 1980. The university continues to give the Walter Read Hovey Art History Memorial Fund Award annually to advance the career of graduate students. A second work in the collection, *Bridge in the Pass of Glencoe, Scotland* (1985.56), an etching of 1888, references Moran's visit to that region.

Thomas Moran's excursion with Dr. Hayden in 1871 was the first of the artist's many sketching trips to the western territories of the United States, which earned him his reputation as a preeminent landscape painter. Dubbed "the father of the national park system," he took his final trip to Yellowstone in 1924, when he was eighty-eight years old.[6] The artist traveled extensively throughout his lifetime and exhibited regularly at the Pennsylvania Academy of the Fine Arts in Philadelphia and at the National Academy of Design in New York, becoming a full academician there in 1884. After a long and prolific career, Moran died in Santa Barbara, California, in 1926 at the age of eighty-nine.

BLJ

1 Jackson's photographs of the same areas support the accuracy of Moran's views.

2 Joni L. Kinsey, *Thomas Moran's West: Chromolithography, High Art, and Popular Taste* (Lawrence: University Press of Kansas, 2006), 60.

3 F. V. Hayden, *The Yellowstone National Park and the Mountain Regions of Portions of Idaho, Nevada, Colorado and Utah* (Boston: L. Prang and Company, 1876; repr. Tulsa: Gilcrease Museum, 1997), 11.

4 For images of the other fourteen chromolithographs, see Kinsey, *Thomas Moran's West*, 205.

5 F.V. Hayden, *The Yellowstone National Park*, 27.

6 Donald Dale Jackson, "Go West, Moran," *Smithsonian*, October 1997, 68.

JAMES BRADE SWORD (1839–1915)
Silver Thread Falls, Pennsylvania, 1874
Oil on canvas, 60 x 48 inches
Signed and dated lower right

Gift of the Westmoreland Society, the William Jamison Art Acquisition Fund, and additional contributions from Mr. and Mrs. David G. Assard; Mr. and Mrs. James S. Beckwith III; Mr. and Mrs. Alan Berk; Mr. and Mrs. Sam Berkovitz; Mr. and Mrs. Charles H. Booth Jr.; Mr. and Mrs. Lawrence S. Busch; Mr. and Mrs. Peter Cecconi Jr.; Mr. and Mrs. B. Patrick Costello; Mr. and Mrs. John W. Douglas Jr.; Mr. and Mrs. Paul J. Evanson; Mr. and Mrs. G. Joseph Frederick; Mr. and Mrs. Charles W. Gibbons III; Mr. and Mrs. Terence L. Graft; Mr. and Mrs. Richard Hendricks; Mr. and Mrs. John Howat; Mr. and Mrs. James Isbister; Dr. and Mrs. Peter Jannetta; Mrs. Robert Kilgore; Mr. and Mrs. D. Scott Kroh; Mrs. Rose Mack; Mr. and Mrs. Charles G. Manoli; Mr. David J. Millstein, Esq.; Mr. Thad Mosley; Mrs. Barbara Nakles; Mr. and Mrs. Kevin O'Toole; Mr. and Mrs. James L. Parker; Mr. and Mrs. John A. Robertshaw Jr.; Mr. and Mrs. James F. Ross; Dr. and Mrs. Karl W. Salatka; Ms. Teruyo P. Seya; Mr. and Mrs. Jack W. Shilling; Mrs. G. Albert Shoemaker; Mr. and Mrs. Andrew J. Sordoni III; Mr. Rudolph Stanish; Mr. and Mrs. Harry A. Thompson II; Mr. and Mrs. John L. Wandrisco; and Mr. Jeffry J. Williamson, 2008.135

PROVENANCE: Private Collection, Pennsylvania; Private Collection, New York; Babcock Galleries, New York.

This exhibition-sized canvas may be the most important extant work by James Brade Sword, a member of the last generation of Hudson River school painters active in the late nineteenth century. It may also be his masterpiece. Unseen by the public in over a century, this painting descended by inheritance through two private collections before being recently rediscovered at auction just prior to entering the Museum's collection. The work's expansive composition invites the viewer to enter the falls from the vantage point of the artist as he stood to observe and record the scene. If one were to visit the same dramatic falls today, the view would be much the same. Spared from the encroachment of civilization, they are located in the Delaware Water Gap National Recreation Area near Milford, Pennsylvania, and are one of the two highest waterfalls in the Pocono Mountains, the other being Dingmans Falls.

Born in Philadelphia, raised in the Portuguese-settled Macau in the People's Republic of China, and back in the United States by puberty, Sword worked as a civil engineer until enrolling in the Pennsylvania Academy of the Fine Arts in 1861, at the outset of the Civil War. Like his contemporary landscape painters, Sword traversed the American Northeast, recording its landscapes with an eye for detail and a sense of awe for the natural world in all its guises. Lake George, Martha's Vineyard, and the Rhode Island coast served as subjects for his brush. Scenes were often identified by season (*September Morning*) or weather conditions (*Foggy Weather*) rather than by location, indicating the artist's interest in capturing climatic and atmospheric effects on the landscape rather than referencing specific places. Sword later came under the private tutelage of William Trost Richards (1833–1905), another master landscape painter, whom he may have accompanied on sketching excursions during the summer months. His work also reveals the influence of the leader of the Hudson River school's second generation of painters, Asher B. Durand (1796–1886), who, among other stylistic innovations, preferred interior views of the landscape to the panoramic vistas composed by earlier proponents of the school. Fidelity to nature was another shared attribute of the two. Sword was also an accomplished genre and portrait painter, who became a distinguished member of Philadelphia society and was a founding member of the Art Club of Philadelphia[1]

The large dimensions of this work suggest its significance. Artists of the nineteenth century painted on this scale to ensure a prominent position at exhibitions, where walls were crowded and smaller-to-mid-sized pieces were often skied (hung so high as to be unavailable for proper viewing). *Silver Thread Falls* may have been one of two paintings Sword painted in preparation for exhibition during the nation's centennial in 1876. The subject, no doubt first studied from life and captured in numerous pencil and oil sketches, records the majesty of America's wilderness, a theme much celebrated as the nation approached its one-hundredth birthday.

Framed by a large tree trunk on the right and a cascade of boulders on the left, the falls have been reduced to a slender, late-summer trickle, fully deserving of their name: a silver thread barely capable of having an impact within such a

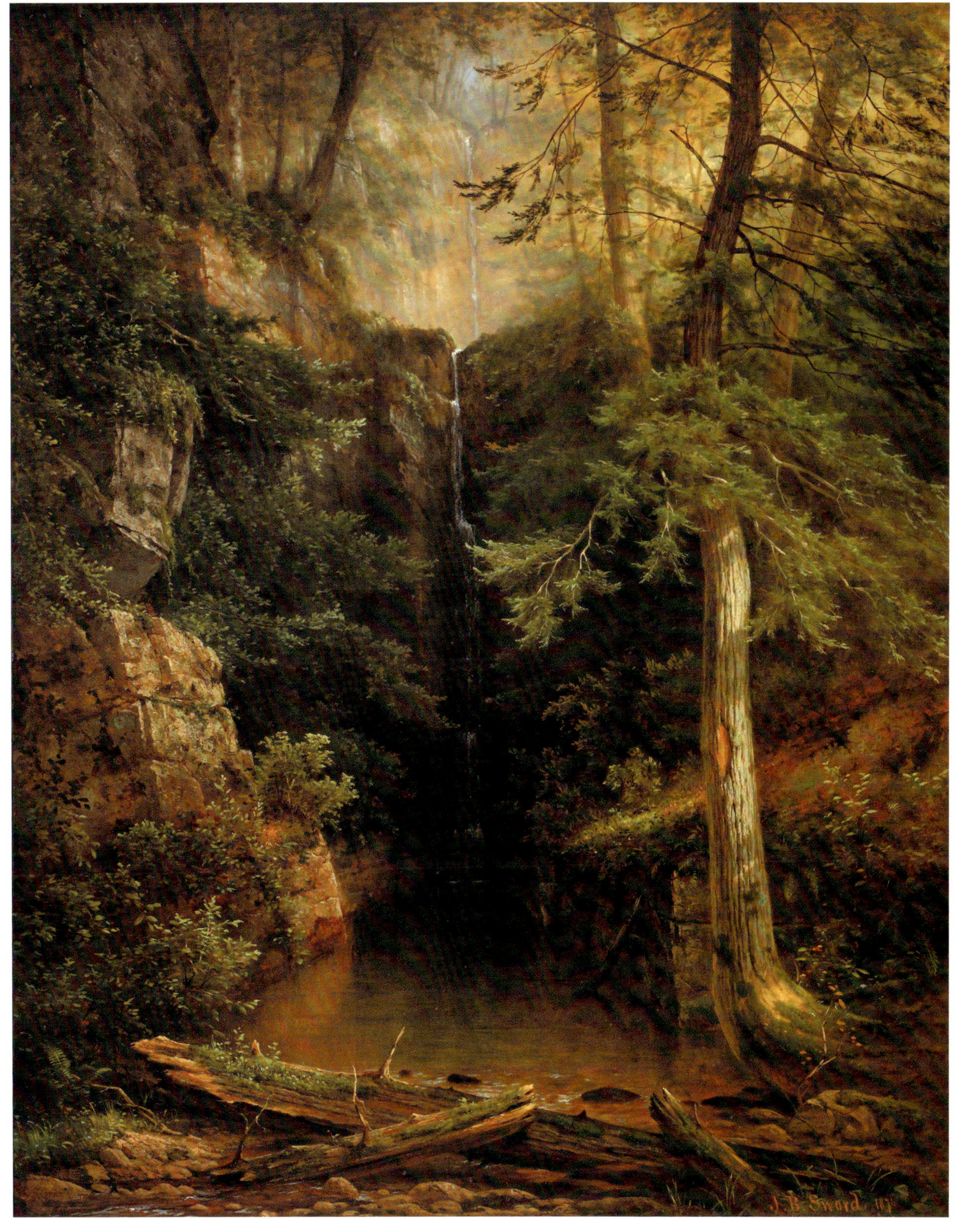
J. B. Sword

WILLIAM MICHAEL HARNETT (1848–1892)
Philadelphia Public Ledger, 1880
Oil on canvas, 10 x 14 inches
Signed and dated lower left
Anonymous Gift by Exchange, 1986.395
Provenance: Kennedy Galleries, New York.

Selected Exhibitions: *William M. Harnett,* Metropolitan Museum of Art, New York, 1992–1993; *A Feast for the Eyes: Treasures from the Westmoreland Museum of American Art,* Woodmere Art Museum, Philadelphia, Pennsylvania, 1998; *Silent Things, Secret Things: Still Life from Rembrandt to the Millennium,* Albuquerque Museum, 1999–2000.

Born in Clonakilty, County Cork, Ireland, William Michael Harnett came with his family to America in 1849, when he was not quite a year old. Raised in Philadelphia, he began his artistic career as a silver engraver—a skill that paved the way for the exacting detail he accomplished later in his still life oil paintings. Harnett studied at the Pennsylvania Academy of the Fine Arts (PAFA) before moving to New York in 1869, where he studied at the Cooper Union and the National Academy of Design while continuing his work as an engraver. By 1875, he was able to abandon the engraving trade and devote himself full time to painting. The following year, he was back in Philadelphia, where he resumed his studies at the PAFA, studying with realist Thomas Eakins (1844–1916). He made his first trip to Europe in 1880, traveling to London, Munich—where he applied to the Royal Academy of Fine Arts but was rejected—and Paris, before returning to New York in 1886.

Harnett began to exhibit his paintings in 1875, yet recognition did not come to him for nearly half a century after his death, his reputation built during the late 1930s and 1940s as a result of the international movement of surrealism. Edith Halpert of the Downtown Gallery exhibited his work in 1939, but as the fast-paced art world moved on to new and different styles, Harnett once again faded into the background. It was not until the publication of extensive research on still life painters by both Alfred Frankenstein and William H. Gerdts that the work of Harnett and his fellow tromp l'oeil artists garnered the recognition and attention they deserved.[1]

Trompe l'oeil painting—translated as to "trick the eye" in French—was Harnett's forte, characterized by dark backgrounds, precise detail, and nearly invisible brushwork. His subjects, usually readily available everyday objects, are set in a shallow pictorial space very close to the picture plane, furthering the illusion of three-dimensionality by often projecting into the viewer's own physical space. Creating the three-dimensional illusion in painting was a popular device used by artists during the late nineteenth century. According to Gerdts, in their day, trompe l'oeil paintings were "looked upon as mere trickery, amusing for their eye-fooling deceptiveness, but . . . unrelated to the purpose of 'true art.'" When discussing the work of painter Alexander Pope (1849–1924) in *Brush and Pencil* in 1901, critic Howard J. Cave referred to this type of painting as: "tricks of the palette rather than strong conceptions ably expressed."[2] Harnett was inspired by the precision of old master still life painting, especially the work of seventeenth-century Dutch artists, and as this was a type of painting also sought after by collectors, it was a path well-suited to the artist.

Philadelphia Public Ledger is a prime example of Harnett's expertise in painting in the trompe l'oeil tradition. His selection of man-made objects are painted life-size and seem incredibly real, as if the viewer could reach into the painting to extract them. The artist's attention to detail demonstrates both his technical abilities with the brush and his acute powers of observation. He painted the salt-glazed stoneware mug with the right heft and texture; rendered the Meerschaum pipe appropriately delicate; and created a worn line on the book of *Longfellow's Works,* indicating its use and age. The bits of ash and spent matches give the arrangement a sense of the human touch that went into creating it, yet no sign of the artist's hand is present. The artist's emphasis is entirely on the reality of the objects. One of the matches extends outside the picture plane, into the viewer's space, further enhancing the three-dimensional illusion. Harnett would have you believe that the owner of the objects has folded his newspaper and left the scene a mere moment before the painting was begun. Thus, he adds to the narrative, composing a near portrait of the

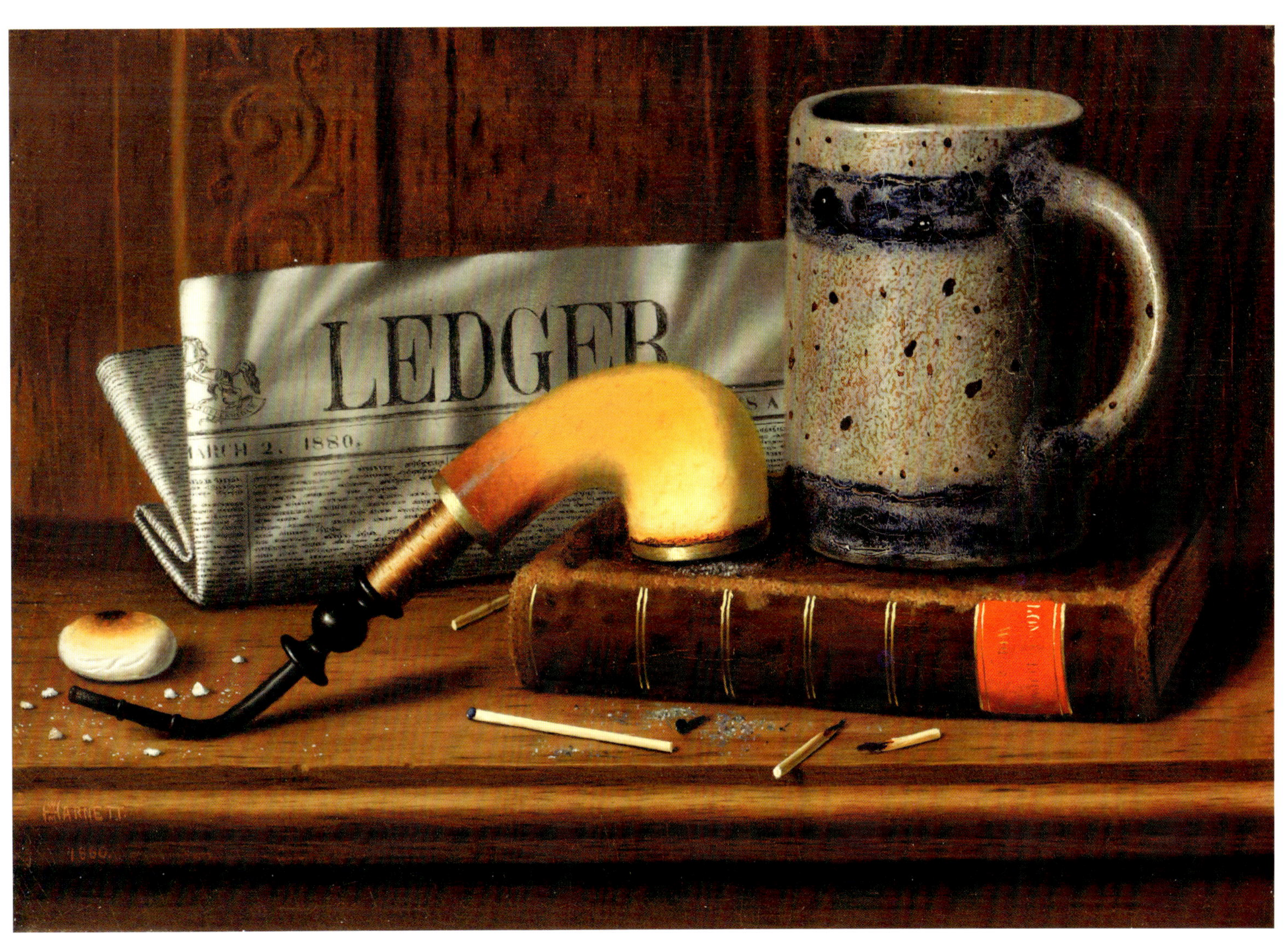
LEDGER
1880.

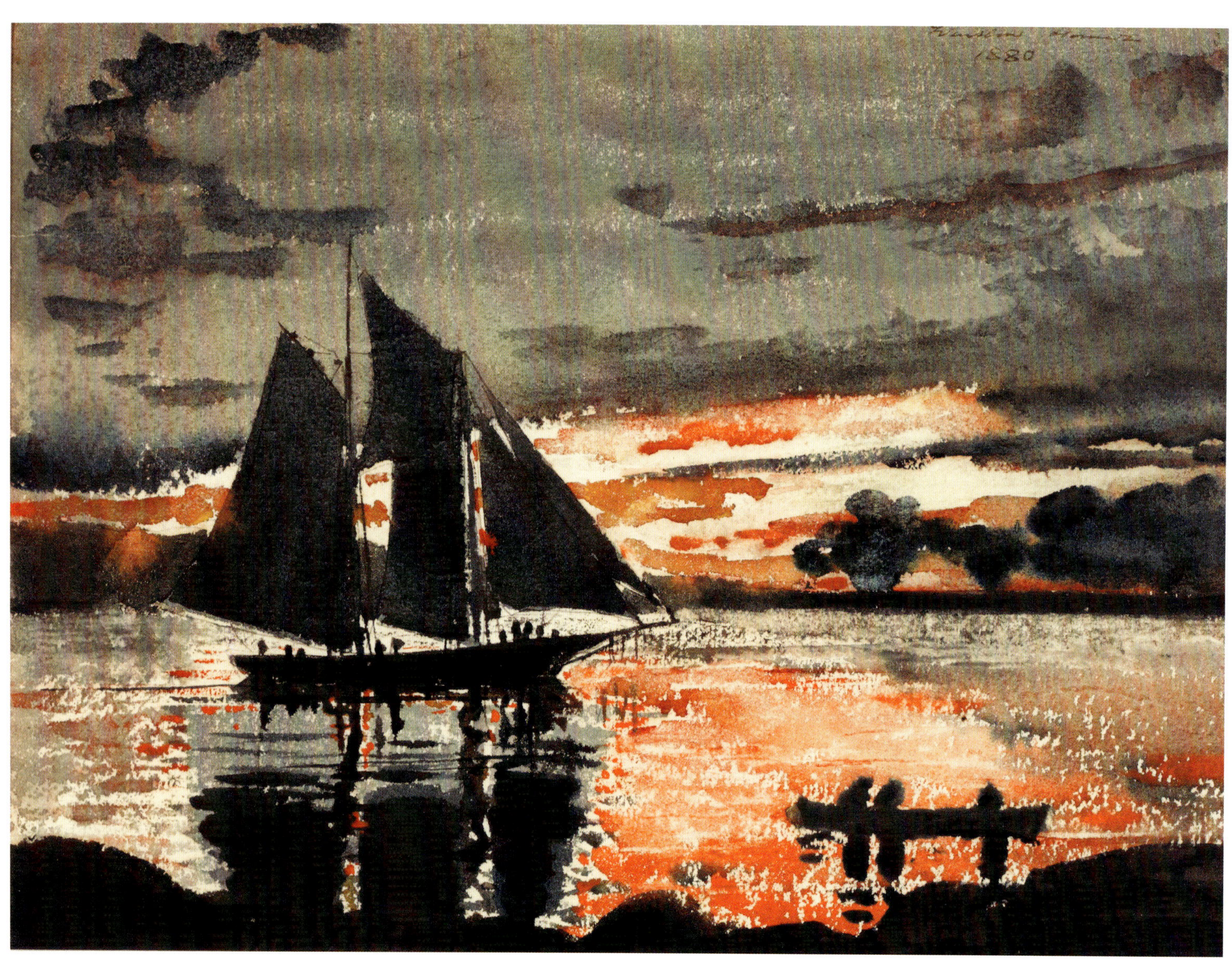

from others. Working with a drybrush technique in transparent washes of color, he layered pigment onto a rough-grained paper from light colors to dark, employing the color and texture of the paper to create highlights of diminishing sunlight as it reflected off the water's surface. His underdrawing of graphite is evident and references his original sketch marks for the schooner. In *Sunset Fires*, you can see the effects of the artist's hand as it first moved lightly and then with heavier pressure, laying pigment on the paper. Some areas are fully saturated, while in others, his brush barely skims the surface. This technique of making use of the white of the paper as his third color was a change from his earlier working method in which he applied white pigment to achieve highlights.

Homer explored color much like a chemist, following the color theory of Michel Eugène Chevreul (1786–1889) as it was published in the English translation of his book, *Chevreul on Colours: the Laws of Contrast of Colour and their Application to the Arts* (John Spanton, 1858). Chevreul studied color under changing light conditions, and combined colors to achieve the greatest contrasts or closest harmonies in his pictures. Homer referred to his copy of Chevreul's book as his bible, and revealed his interest in times of day in his 1880 watercolors. He carefully studied types of light—man-made, moonlight, sunset, and reflected. According to Homer, "You must not paint everything you see. You must wait, and wait patiently until the exceptional, the wonderful effect or aspect comes. Then, if you have sense enough to see it—well, that is all there is to that."[3]

Writing of *Sunset Fires* and three other watercolors, Tedeschi states, "These demonstrations of pure expressive force of color are an indication that Homer was increasingly challenging himself against the model of J. M. W. Turner (1775–1851). Increasingly, too, he seems to have wanted to paint something modern, and at this moment, in 1880, the 'new' art was that of Whistler and the Impressionists."[4]

Of his group of Gloucester watercolors that depict different stages of the sun descending into the ocean, each one contains its own atmospheric effects. In *Sunset Fires*, the setting sun bathes the entire scene in crimson light, reflecting so intensely off the water that it gives the appearance of fire. The artist has eliminated all extraneous details, creating a composition that is exquisitely simple, consisting of just a few objects and painted in a limited color palette of red, yellow, blue, and black. The paint is fluidly applied in broad brushstrokes and softly blended from one shade of red to the next. All of the watercolors that Homer created during the summer he spent on Ten Pound Island were shown together in December of that year at Doll & Richards Gallery in Boston. Although Homer was not always celebrated for his watercolor technique in his day—his watercolors were sometimes criticized as seeming unfinished—he is now recognized as one of the most innovative masters of the medium.

Sunset Fires is one of the most frequently requested paintings in The Westmoreland's collection for loan to other museum exhibitions; as such, it has traveled extensively in the United States and Europe. In addition, the Museum owns one etching and four wood engravings by Homer.

The tranquillity of Homer's 1880 watercolors are in sharp contrast to the paintings he made the following year after settling in Cullercoats, on England's North Sea, where he would stay until 1882, witnessing the violence of the sea and how it impacted the residents of the fishing village. Not long after his return, Homer rekindled his love of nature and his observations of the sea in its many moods when he left New York in 1884 to live permanently at Prouts Neck, on the Atlantic coast just south of Portland, Maine. He remained there until his death in 1910, creating a body of work that reflects the magnificence and sheer power of the sea.

BLJ

1 For a complete chronology of Homer's life, see Nicolai Cikovsky Jr. and Franklin Kelly, *Winslow Homer* (New Haven: Yale University Press, 1995).

2 Martha Tedeschi with Kristi Dahm, *Watercolors by Winslow Homer: The Color of Light* (New Haven and London: The Art Institute of Chicago / Yale University Press, 2008), 198. This book, which accompanied an exhibition of the same name, provides an excellent in-depth examination of Homer's varied approaches to the watercolor medium.

3 John W. Beatty, "Recollections of Winslow Homer, 1923–24," in Carl Little, *Winslow Homer and the Sea* (San Francisco: Pomegranate Artbooks, 1995), 70.

4 Martha Tedeschi with Kristi Dahm, *Watercolors by Winslow Homer*, 74.

JOSEPH WOODWELL (1843–1911)
Seascape, Magnolia, MA, 1887
Oil on canvas, 40 x 60 inches
Signed and dated lower left
Gift of the Mary Marchand Woods Memorial Fund, 1986.201
Provenance: John W. Kephart, Glad Wyne, Pennsylvania.

SELECTED EXHIBITIONS: *The Gift of Art,* Westmoreland Museum of American Art, 2009.

Joseph Woodwell was born in Pittsburgh, the son of wood carver Joseph W. Woodwell. Born one year before Mary Cassatt (1844–1926), the two were to become artists and friends, although each followed different paths in their artistic pursuits.

Encouraged by his family to seek an education in the arts, young Joseph first studied informally with the genre painter David Gilmour Blythe (1815–1865), also of Pittsburgh. At the age of seventeen, about the same time that he exhibited in the first Pittsburgh Art Association exhibition (1859), Woodwell left for Europe, enrolling at the Académie Julian in Paris, an atelier popular with American art students who wanted to benefit from critiques by the best of the artists of the École des Beaux-Arts. Woodwell also traveled extensively, stopping at many of Europe's major cities, where he visited museums and met other artists, including the popular American genre painter Daniel Ridgway Knight (1839–1924), who befriended him.

Woodwell's most important experience in France came from his association with the Barbizon school of landscape painters—precursors of the impressionist movement. It was through them that he developed a love of painting in nature, later stating, "To understand painting, you must understand Nature, and to understand Nature you must have a love for her."[1] He established a lifelong friendship with the influential French landscape and genre painter Camille Pissarro (1830–1903) and met many of the other major artists of the time, including Claude Monet (1840–1926) and Pierre-Auguste Renoir (1841–1919). In France, he developed a sensitive and introspective style, which he applied to his landscape subjects, often employing a dark, earth-toned palette. His in situ oil sketches demonstrate his ability to capture detail without slavish rendering but with a lightness of brushwork and a discerning eye.

Upon his return to Pittsburgh in 1867, Woodwell divided his time between art and the hardware business—Joseph Woodwell Company—that he inherited from his father.[2] He quickly became a leader in the arts in Pittsburgh, among both artists and fellow businessmen whom he encouraged to invest in the arts. He was a founding member of the Carnegie Institute (now Carnegie Museum of Art) Board of Trustees, served on its Fine Arts Committee for five years, and was chairman at the time of his death in 1911. He exhibited regularly in the Carnegie Internationals and in the annual exhibitions of the Pennsylvania Academy of the Fine Arts, in addition to contributing to exhibitions in New York, Paris, and other venues.

Woodwell traveled extensively throughout his life, painting such iconic American scenes as Niagara Falls and Yosemite Valley, while also visiting swamps in Florida and redwood forests in California. His frequent companion on these excursions was his daughter, Johanna Knowles Woodwell [Hailman] (1871–1958), who became a leading artist and patron in her own right. An avid correspondent, he maintained national and international relationships with artists he met during his travels. One such friendship with Thomas Eakins (1844–1916), prominent American painter and teacher at the Pennsylvania Academy of the Fine Arts, resulted in Eakins painting his portrait in 1904,(Carnegie Museum of Art) the same year that Woodwell won a bronze medal for a painting at the World's Fair in St. Louis.

Another location of which Woodwell was fond was the small community of Scalp Level, near Johnstown, Pennsylvania, to which he traveled with other Pittsburgh artists, including George Hetzel (1826–1899), acknowledged leader of the Scalp Level school. Modeled somewhat on the Barbizon colony and somewhat on the sketching excursions shared by the artists of the Hudson River school, Scalp Level provided ample opportunity for studying nature. There Woodwell made wonderful

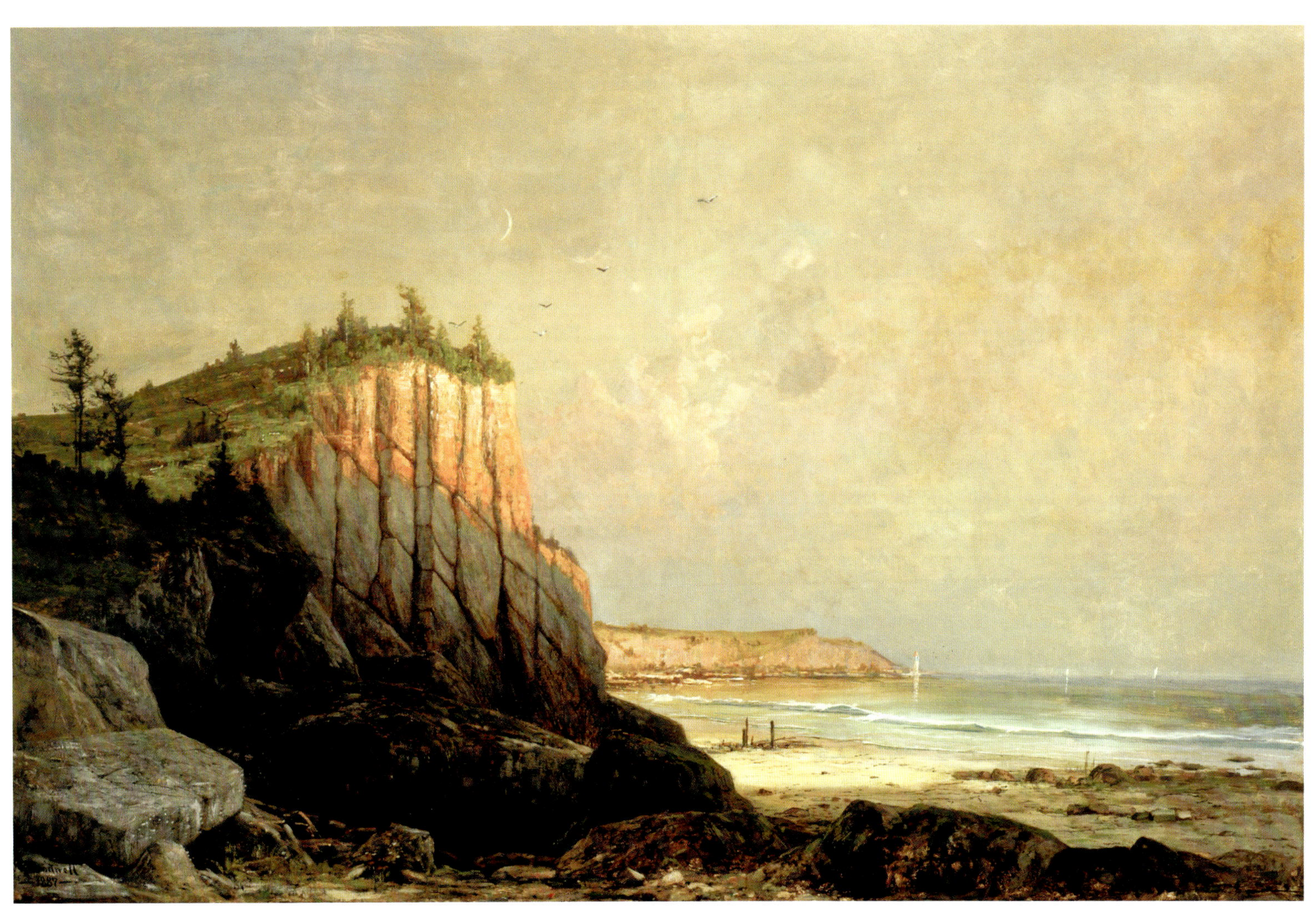

THOMAS HOVENDEN (1840–1895)
Death of Elaine, 1882
Oil on canvas, 46 x 71 inches
Signed and dated lower right
Gift of the Mary Marchand Woods Memorial Fund, 1985.25
Provenance: Descended from the artist; Peabody Institute, Baltimore, Maryland; Kennedy Galleries, New York.

SELECTED EXHIBITIONS: *Fifty-seventh Annual Exhibition,* National Academy of Design, 1882; Peabody Institute Gallery of Art, Baltimore, 1900; *Aspects of American Art: The Institute's Founding Years, ca.* 1870–1900, Staten Island Institute of Arts and Sciences, 1982; *Continuity and Diversity in American Art in the Nineteenth and Twentieth Centuries,* 1984; *Thomas Hovenden: American Painter of Hearth and Homeland,* Woodmere Art Museum, Philadelphia, Pennsylvania, 1995; *A Feast for the Eyes: Treasures from the Westmoreland Museum of American Art,* Woodmere Art Museum, 1998; *Rave Reviews: One Hundred Years of Great American Art,* National Academy of Design, New York, 2000–2001.

One of three children, Thomas Hovenden was born in Dunmanway, County Cork, Ireland, on December 23, 1840, to Robert and Ellen Bryan Hovenden. Both of his parents died during the potato famine, when Hovenden was just six years old; he was placed in an orphanage, where he received his early education and apprenticeship opportunities in wood carving and gilding. The tradesman with whom he apprenticed paid for him to take evening classes at Cork School of Design. Completing his education there, he immigrated to the United States during the Civil War in 1863, joining his older brother, John, in New York. He supported himself as a picture-frame maker during the war years and created illustrations for *Harper's.* He was admitted to night classes at the National Academy of Design (NAD), studying there from 1864 to 1868. While there, he met Baltimore artist Hugh Bolton Jones (1848–1927). In 1868, the two artists moved to Baltimore where they shared a studio.

Hovenden exhibited at the Maryland Academy of Art, where early patrons William T. Walters and his business partner, John W. McCoy, recognized the young artist's talent and not only urged him to study in Europe but financed it as well. In 1874, at the age of thirty-three, he sailed for France, where he studied under Jules Breton (1827–1906) and for a year in the studio of École des Beaux-Arts instructor Alexandre Cabanal (1823–1889). In Paris, he was forced to practice drawing for months before being allowed to paint, and he still studied the antique cast much like he was required to do at the NAD. During the summer of 1875, Hovenden traveled to the Brittany village of Pont-Aven, joining a colony of American artists including Robert Wylie (1839–1877), who led the colony; Daniel Ridgway Knight (1839–1924); and Helen Corson (1846–1935). In the fall of 1878, he followed Corson to Paris and turned from painting the landscape and life of the Breton peasants to painting historical and romantic subjects. They married in 1881, the year they returned to the United States, and settled in Plymouth Meeting, Pennsylvania, on her family's homestead. The couple had a son, Thomas Jr., and a daughter, Martha (1884–1941), who became a sculptor.

Hovenden believed art had a social purpose and expressed elevated moral or symbolic meaning. His genre scenes were revered for their naturalism and attention to detail as well as their ability to stir deep emotions in viewers. One such painting was his faithful recording of Alfred Lord Tennyson's love story based on Tennyson's literary poem, "Lancelot and Elaine," published in *Idylls of the King* in 1859. This tour de force painting reveals the moment when the court of King Arthur gathers around the body of Elaine, the "Lily Maid of Astolat," who has died of a broken heart over her unrequited love for Sir Lancelot, who cannot return her affections because he is in love with Arthur's wife.

Measuring nearly four by six feet, the ambitious canvas took the artist three years to complete, begun while he was in Paris in 1879 and completed in his New York studio in 1882. The emotional tale is vividly played out in the scene, with Elaine's lifeless body lying on a death bed at the very center of the composition, brightly illuminated as if with a spotlight from above. She is surrounded by King Arthur and his queen, Lady Guinevere to her right, and Sir Lancelot and Sir Galahad standing at the head of the bed. The love triangle is revealed as Lady Guinevere looks lovingly at Elaine while Sir Lancelot

into Rh
shown i
an emp
Th
serene a
recorde
conditi
orb car
clear. T
turns p
against
the wat
the pro
pebbles
water a
of a m
light, th
only th
is given
to the e
Bri
and sav
moder
exhibit
Macbe
promo
artists
and ur
spendi
overloo

I Judit
ran agro
the sever
naming

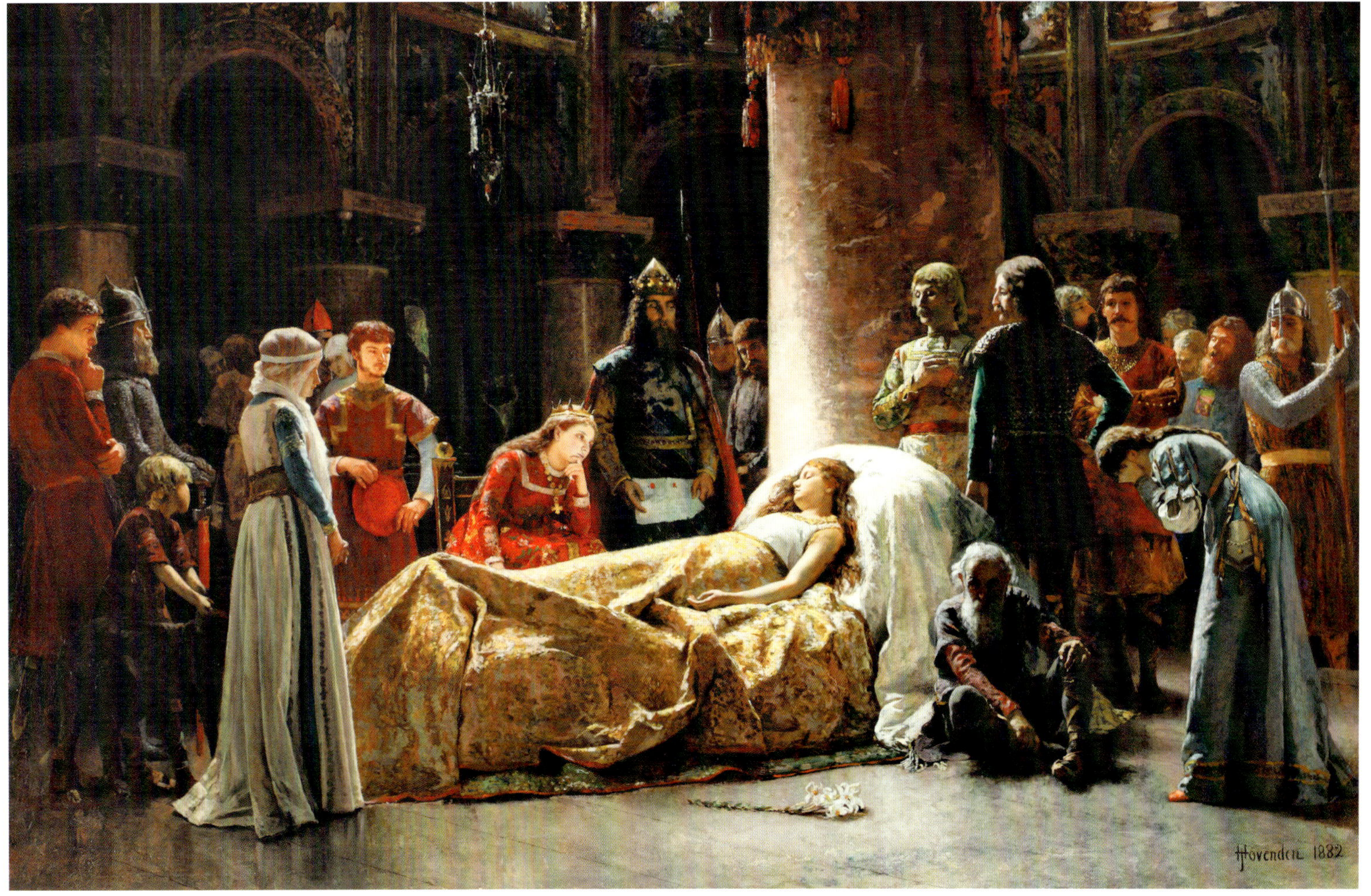

CECILIA BEAUX (1855–1942)
Mrs. John Wheeler Leavitt (Cecilia Kent), 1885
Oil on canvas, 45 ½ x 34 inches
Signed and dated lower left
Gift of Mary Eliza Drinker Scudder and Thayer Scudder in honor of Philip Drinker and Susan Aldrich Drinker, 1996.10
Provenance: Mary Eliza Drinker Scudder and Thayer Scudder, Altadena, California.

SELECTED EXHIBITIONS: *Cecilia Beaux and the Art of Portraiture*, National Portrait Gallery, Washington, D.C., 1995; Westmoreland Museum of American Art, 1996.

Eliza-Cecilia Beaux was born on May 1, 1855, in Philadelphia, and was orphaned when her mother, Cecilia Kent Leavitt Beaux, died just twelve days after her birth. In his grief, her father, Jean Adolphe Beaux, returned to his homeland of France, leaving his two young daughters in the care of his wife's family in Philadelphia. Cecilia and her older sister, Aimée "Etta" Ernesta were raised by her grandmother and two maternal aunts—Eliza and Emily—and Emily's husband, William Foster Biddle. They encouraged Beaux (nicknamed Leilie) in her artistic endeavors, took her to art exhibitions, and were supportive in her pursuit of a career. Beaux's father returned to Philadelphia in 1857 but never established a close relationship with his two daughters. However, he instilled in Beaux a desire to see Paris for herself, which she would beginning in 1888.

Beaux had no formal art training outside the home until she was sixteen, receiving her first drawing lessons from Catherine Ann Drinker (1841–1922), her Uncle William's cousin, who was a historical painter. She later studied with William Sartain (1843–1924) in Philadelphia at the Pennsylvania Academy of the Fine Arts (PAFA), where she was registered from 1876 to 1878. Thomas Eakins (1844–1916) was teaching there at the time, and although Beaux never took classes from him, his presence was impossible to escape; Eakins's interest in the human psyche appears as an important element in Beaux's portraits.

Her first masterwork was *Les derniers jours d'enfance* (1885, Pennsylvania Academy of the Fine Arts), a portrait of her sister and her sister's first-born son, Harry. The portrait launched Beaux's career in portraiture when it won the Mary Smith Prize at PAFA that year. The painting was shown at the Paris Salon of 1887, prompting Beaux to further her art studies in France.

The Westmoreland's portrait of her grandmother Leavitt was painted in 1885. For this portrayal, Beaux presents her eighty-seven-year-old grandmother sitting in a chair in her patio garden in west Philadelphia. Enclosed by a brick-wall backdrop and removed from the urban environment surrounding her, Mrs. Leavitt concentrates on her knitting. A red geranium blooms in the clay pot next to her; its spindliness suggesting that the growing season has just begun or is just ending. Grandmother Leavitt's profile pose recalls the famous portrait *Arrangement in Grey and Black No. 1: Portrait of the Artist's Mother* (1871, Musée d'Orsay, Paris) by James A. McNeill Whistler (1834–1903), while her attention to detail and the near monochromatic palette reflects an awareness of Eakins's objective realist style.[1] Her hands are delicately rendered to reveal the veining under her paper-thin skin. It is a touching portrayal of the woman who was an enduring force in the artist's life.

At the age of thirty-two, Beaux made the first of seven trips to France, where she would abandon the dark tonal palette of browns and blacks that dominated her early efforts for a light-filled, vibrant palette of pinks, whites, lavenders, and yellows, and her application of paint became more fluid and textural. Between 1888 and 1889, she studied at the Académie Julian, and at the Académie Colarossi. She spent the summer and early fall of 1888 painting en plein air at the American artist colony in the fishing village of Concarneau on the coast of Brittany. There she worked with fellow Philadelphia artist Alexander Harrison (1853–1930), an expatriate who declared "she puts brains in her work, and that is what few women do—I can tell you."[2]

Upon returning home, Beaux set up a studio in Philadelphia and was soon a highly sought-after portraitist to Philadelphia's high society. Like Mary Cassatt (1844–1926), eleven

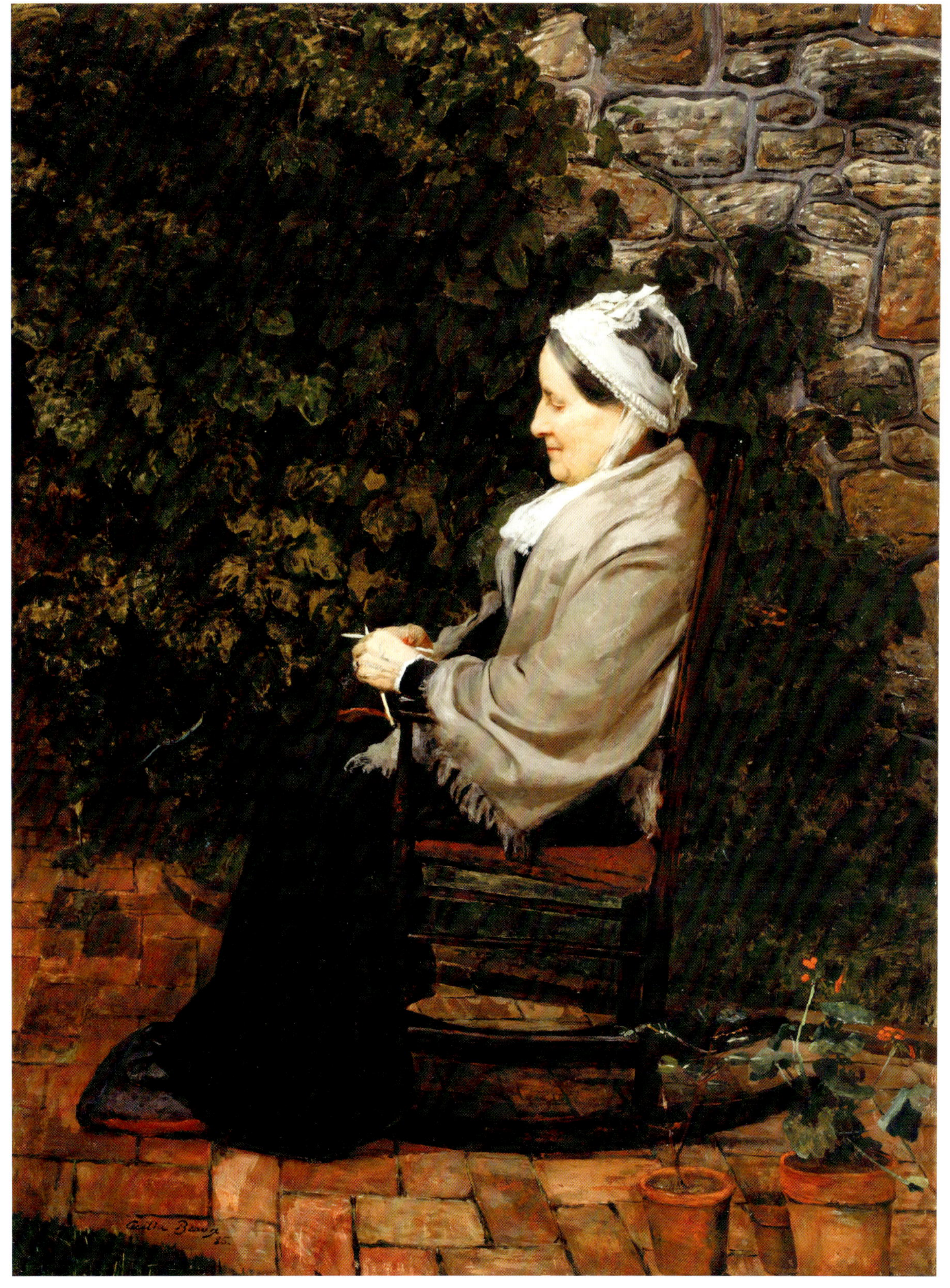

years her senior, Beaux defied Victorian-era conventions by turning down marriage proposals so that she could pursue her calling to be a full-time artist, as she felt that marriage and a career were incompatible. From 1905, she maintained a home and studio—Green Alley—in Gloucester, Massachusetts, where she said she "would finally find . . . not rest . . . but a new life."[3]

Beaux rivaled fellow portraitist John Singer Sargent (1856–1925), just one year her junior, as a leading painter of high-society portraits in New York, where she settled in 1900. Like Sargent, Beaux captured both the character and the style of her subjects; but unlike him, she rarely flattered her sitters, painting straightforward, realist likenesses. She captured joy, anxiety, mystery, innocence, and status in hundreds of portraits of men, women, and children. According to the artist, "I paint the goodness of men and women, however deeply it may be hidden away."[4]

The Museum also owns Beaux's *Still Life with Fruit* (1977.2), thought to be the only pure still life made by the artist, although she often incorporated still life objects as accessories in many of her portraits. The Westmoreland also owns the Victorian sofa (1999.20) that Beaux used at Green Alley.

Beaux became the first full-time female faculty member of PAFA where she taught from 1895 to 1916, even after moving to New York in 1900. She was elected an associate member of the National Academy of Design in 1894, achieving full academician status in 1902. She received the Mary Smith Prize from the Pennsylvania Academy four times, as well as a Gold Medal of Honor in 1898 for her artistic achievements. From the Carnegie Institute (now Carnegie Museum of Art) she received a bronze medal in its inaugural Carnegie International exhibition in 1896, followed by a gold medal the next year. In 1899, she was again recognized by the Carnegie Institute, winning the Medal of the First Class for her double portrait *Mother and Daughter* (1898, Pennsylvania Academy of the Fine Arts). In his speech during the opening of the exhibition, William Merritt Chase (1849–1916) proclaimed, "Miss Beaux is not only the greatest woman painter, but the best that has ever lived. Miss Beaux has done away entirely with sex in art."[5] Despite the intended compliment, Beaux hated this remark because it pigeonholed her as a "woman painter." In 1922, the League of Women Voters listed her as one of America's Twelve Greatest Living Women.[6]

In 1924, Beaux made her last trip to Europe, where she broke her hip. This disability and her development of cataracts would ultimately be responsible for the end of her artistic career. That year, the Uffizi Gallery in Florence, Italy, honored Beaux by commissioning a self-portrait for its Medici collection, the first American woman invited to do so. Because she could no longer paint steadily, she turned her attention to lecturing and writing, eventually publishing her autobiography, *Background with Figures*, in 1930.

Cecilia Beaux died at Green Alley on September 17, 1942, at the age of eighty-seven. Although she painted over three hundred portraits during her career and had an international reputation, Beaux was essentially forgotten for some fifty years following her death.[7] Beaux's work was rediscovered in recent years. She is now justly recognized as one of the country's leading portraitists.

BLJ

1 Whistler's painting was shown at PAFA in 1881, and one assumes that Beaux saw it there, as it was a very popular exhibition.

2 Alice A. Carter, *Cecilia Beaux: A Modern Painter in the Gilded Age* (New York: Rizzoli, 2005), 87.

3 Cecilia Beaux, *Background with Figures* (Boston: Houghton Mifflin Company, 1939), 339.

4 Tara Leigh Tappert, "Choices—the Life and Career of Cecilia Beaux: A Professional Biography" (diss., George Washington University, 1990), 300, quoted from Stephen May, "Cecilia Beaux: Portrait of the Gilded Age," *American Arts Quarterly*, fall 1998, 36.

5 William Merritt Chase, "Greatest Woman Painter: Art Jury Awards Miss Cecelia [*sic*] Beaux First Prize," *Public Ledger*, November 3, 1899, in Beaux Papers, Archives of American Art, microfilm 428, frame 1669, from Sylvia Yount, *Cecilia Beaux: American Figure Painter* (Atlanta: High Museum of Art / University of California Press, 2007), 77.

6 Yount, *Cecilia Beaux*, 184. See same publication for an in-depth chronology compiled by Alison Bechtel Wexler, 174–85.

7 Her friend Thornton Oakley (1881–1953) published his memoir of the artist in 1943, and Catherine Drinker Bowen discusses her Aunt Cecilia in her book *Family Portrait* (1970).

CHARLES LINFORD (1846–1897)
The Afterglow, 1887
Oil on canvas, 24 x 36 inches
Signed and dated lower left
Gift of the Constance Mellon Bequest, 1985.17
Provenance: Douglas Waite, Petoskey, Michigan.

Other than for being born in Pittsburgh, details of Charles Linford's family background and upbringing are unknown. He trained with George Hetzel (1826–1899), a prominent landscape and still life painter in the city. While still an amateur painter, Linford joined in the camaraderie and inspiration of the Gillespie Group, a loosely knit association of artists—led by Hetzel. They met almost daily at Pittsburgh's J. J. Gillespie Gallery to discuss art and art theory.

Although Hetzel is the acknowledged leader of the Scalp Level school of landscape painters, Linford is credited with being the first artist to discover the region for which the school was named, and to recognize its great potential for artists.[1] Scalp Level—a small town near Johnstown, Pennsylvania—was then surrounded by lovely farmlands, virgin forests, and several picturesque creeks. In 1866, Linford, just twenty years old, and attorney John H. Hampton, legal counsel to the Pennsylvania Railroad, invited Hetzel to join a fishing and sketching expedition to the region. After his introduction to its charms, Hetzel would return every summer, escaping industrialized Pittsburgh to paint the rural beauty of Scalp Level. He introduced it enthusiastically to other artists and students, making it a favorite retreat for two generations of painters, as well as a congregating point for like-minded landscape painters.

Linford, like his colleagues, painted out-of-doors; however, he is not known to have explored other subject matter—specifically still life or portraiture—as did his fellow painters in the winter months. Instead, throughout his career, he concentrated on landscape painting. Favoring birch trees in his compositions, he drew from the great stands no longer plentiful in the woods of southwestern Pennsylvania. Linford also chose to depict autumn scenes rather than spring and summer views favored by most other artists. Although the earlier, lush green seasons were sometimes recorded by Linford's brush, his preferred palette contained russet, brown, gold, and dark green.

A follower of the French Barbizon painters, Linford closely observed nature in intimate, wooded settings. He purchased a painting by the Barbizon school's leader, Jean-Baptiste-Camille Corot (1796–1875), at the auction of the Chapman Collection in New York in 1875. Corot's work was much sought after by Americans, and Linford sold the painting four years later to Pittsburgh collector C. H. Wolff. Wolff owned more than a dozen paintings by Linford, including some painted after the artist left Pittsburgh, indicating that the collector and painter maintained communications.[2] Andrew Carnegie was among other prominent city businessmen who owned works by the artist.

A comparison between Corot and Linford confirms their similar palette choices and preference for interior rather than panoramic views of nature, and also reveals their similar techniques of paint application. A critic wrote of Linford, "He has a habit of laying the color on with a paddle instead of a brush, and does not seem to be very particular whether the colors are mixed or pure. This may seem like a reckless way of painting, but it is not a bad way. It gives the picture strength, and imparts realistic effects to many of its features, especially to rough-barked trees and the like." The review concluded by stating, "Mr. Linford's work now commands the attention of clever art critics, and is receiving favorable comment."[3]

The Afterglow is a dramatic painting of sunset in the woods painted in Linford's brusque manner and ruddy palette. The woods are without figures, either human or wildlife, yet the deeply rutted dirt road and split-rail fence are silent testaments of man's attempts to organize and tame the natural environment. The road and fence lead the viewer's eye deep into the forested interior toward the source of light. The setting sun bathes the scene in a luminous red light evoking enchantingly the painting's title. Linford was in Scalp Level with Hetzel the year this painting was executed; accordingly, it

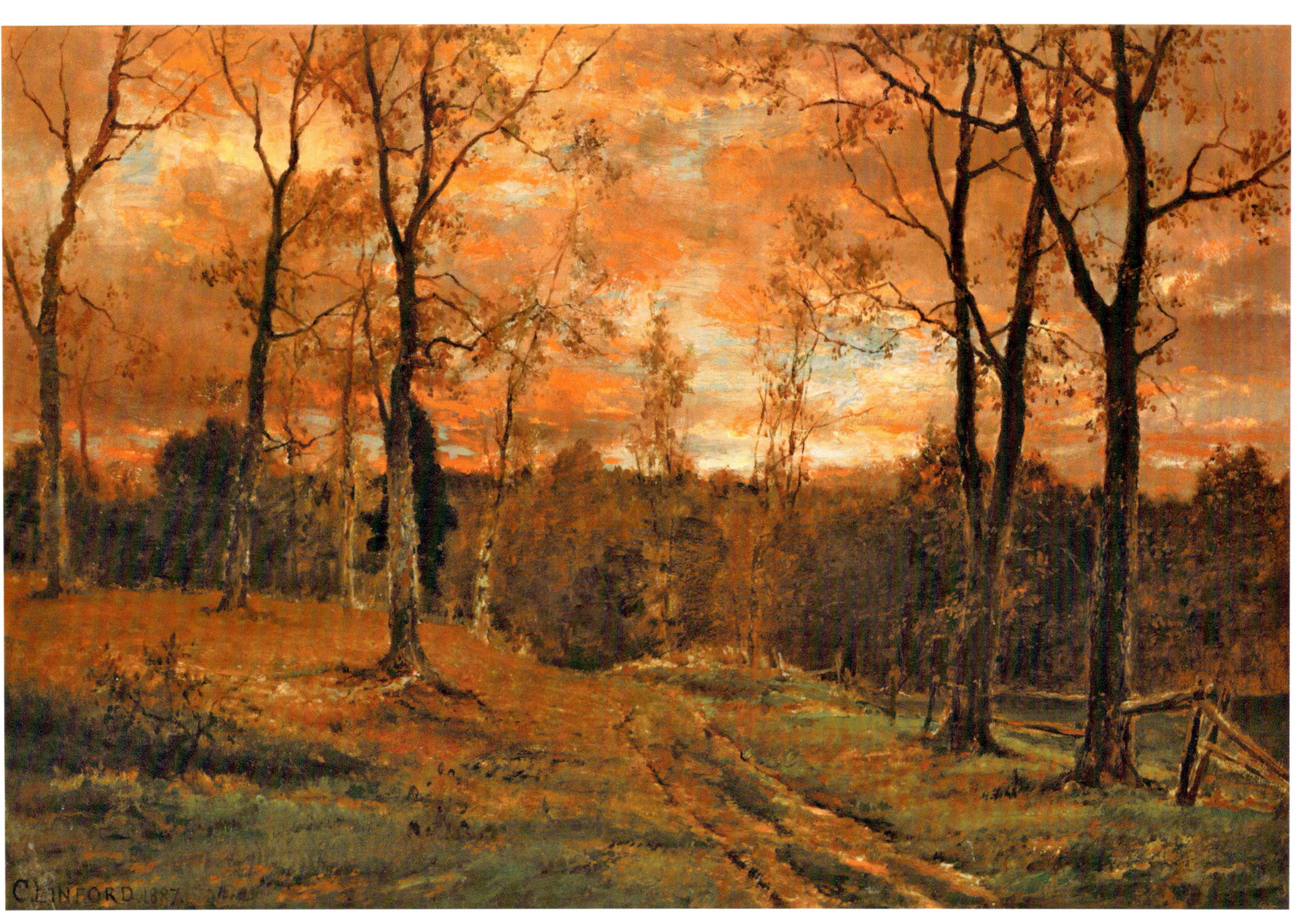
C LINFORD 1887

seems likely that the painting represents that region.

Before age thirty, Linford had become an integral part of Pittsburgh's art scene: he was among those who formed the Art Society of Pittsburgh in 1873. Despite this success, or perhaps because of it, the artist moved to Philadelphia in 1877. Other artists had made this move east, including his mentor, George Hetzel, who lived there with his family in 1869, returning to Pittsburgh after just one year. The move would position Linford closer to established art institutions with access to a greater number of collectors, thereby providing better opportunities to exhibit and sell his work. Linford resided in Philadelphia until 1893, exhibiting at the Pennsylvania Academy of the Fine Arts nearly every year until he left. He also exhibited at the National Academy of Design in New York during this period (1878, 1879, and again in 1890), selling work to collectors in both cities. In 1896, he contributed two landscape paintings—Solitude and Autumn, Pocona [sic] Valley—to the first Carnegie International. After 1893, Linford divided his time between Pittsburgh; New York City; and Plainsfield, New Jersey, where he died in 1897 at only fifty-one years of age. He is buried in Pittsburgh's Allegheny Cemetery.

Linford is one of three artists of the Scalp Level school described in the comprehensive, three-volume study by noted art historian William H. Gerdts, published in 1990. Along with George Hetzel and Joseph R. Woodwell (1843–1911), Gerdts notes Linford's status as a student of Hetzel and member of the Gillespie Group: and reproduces his painting *Birch Trees, Scalp Level, PA* (1980.68).[4]

JHO'T

1 See entry on George Hetzel in this volume for more information on the Scalp Level school.

2 Wolff was an important Pittsburgh collector, whose taste set the standard for other moneyed city residents. Of the Scalp Level painters, he particularly favored Linford. He was also a collector of the Barbizon school and European genre paintings.

3 Erasmus Wilson, *Quiet Observations* (New York: Cassell & Company, 1886), 385–86. The writer's reference to a "paddle" could mean either a flat, broad brush used for broad brush marks or, more likely, a type of wooden paddle used by sculptors for shaping clay.

4 William H. Gerdts, *Art Across America: Two Centuries of Regional Painting* (New York: Abbeville Press, 1990), vol. 1, illustration no. 1.291, 288.

THEODORE ROBINSON (1852–1896)
In the Garden, c. 1889
Oil on canvas, 18 x 22 inches
Gift of the William A. Coulter Fund, 1958.36
Provenance: George A. Hearn; Macbeth Gallery, New York; C. L. Baldwin; Frank Dudensing; Victor D. Spark, New York.

SELECTED EXHIBITIONS: *Paintings by Emil Carlsen, Theodore Robinson and J. Alden Weir,* Macbeth Gallery, New York, 1923; *The Impressionist Mood in American Painting,* The American Academy of Arts and Letters, New York, 1958; American Academy and National Institute of Arts and Letters, New York, 1959; Henry Clay Frick Fine Arts Department, University of Pittsburgh, 1963; Butler Institute of American Art, Youngstown, Ohio, 1964; *A Salute to Pennsylvania's Artistic Heritage,* Pennsylvania Historical and Museum Commission, Harrisburg, 1979; *American Impressionist Exhibition,* Henry Art Gallery, University of Washington, Seattle, 1980; *Impressionism: An American View,* Westmoreland County Museum of Art, Greensburg, 1983; *The Figural Images of Theodore Robinson, American Impressionist,* Paine Art Center and Arboretum, Oshkosh, Wisconsin, 1987; *Normandy, The Cradle of Art,* Nassau County Museum of Art, Roslyn, New York, 1994; *Theodore Robinson,* Owen Gallery, New York, 2000; *Flowers Observed/Flowers Transformed,* Andy Warhol Museum, Pittsburgh, 2004; *In Monet's Light: Theodore Robinson at Giverny,* Baltimore Museum of Art, 2004–2005.

One of the earliest paintings to enter The Westmoreland's collection before the Museum opened its doors to the public, *In the Garden* represents one of the artist's works that he painted in Giverny, France. Born in Irasburg, Vermont, and raised in Evansville, Wisconsin, Theodore Robinson's artistic career began at the Chicago Academy of Design, where he studied from 1869 to 1870, but he moved east to study at the National Academy of Design in New York in 1874. From there he made his first of many trips to Paris in 1876, where he studied in the independent studio of Emile Auguste Carolus-Duran (1838–1917) and, after passing his exams, with Jean-Léon Gérôme (1824–1904) at the École des Beaux-Arts. In 1877, one of his paintings was accepted at the Paris Salon, where his work would be shown again in 1880, 1887, 1888, 1889, and 1890. Robinson returned to the United States in 1879 and was resettled in New York by 1881, where he assisted fellow artist John LaFarge (1835–1910) with murals and decorative painting. Robinson returned to Paris in 1884, spending summer and fall months in the countryside outside the city, and also traveling to Holland and England. His first introduction to Claude Monet (1840–1926) occurred at Giverny in 1885, but it was during his second visit to the artist in 1887 that their friendship began. The pair established a close relationship, documented both in Robinson's personal diaries and through their correspondence. Monet had only just discovered the picturesque village northwest of Paris for himself in 1883 and had relocated there. Robinson appreciated his friendship with Monet, writing in his diary after one visit in 1892: "Monet was cordiality itself—it's very pleasant to think that I have a place in his affections."[1] Referring to Monet as the Master, Robinson relied on him for critical commentary and advice on his own work. Out of his association with this leading impressionist, Robinson's style underwent a major transformation, moving from primarily figural subjects painted in a subdued, darkened palette with little or no texture to figures and landscapes composed of rich impasto and light, high-key colors. Inspired by Monet, Robinson investigated the effects of varying conditions of light and atmosphere on his subjects. In Giverny, he combined figures and landscapes in one composition, but as his interest in impressionist theory increased, his palette lightened and the landscape alone became his primary focus. Robinson visited Giverny over the course of seven years, between his first trip in 1885 and his last in 1892. He would spend winter months back in New York, where he completed paintings begun during his trips abroad.

Robinson exhibited with the Society of American Artists, the American Watercolor Society, and the National Academy of Design in New York, as well as with the Pennsylvania Academy of the Fine Arts, where he also taught in 1895. His first impressionist paintings were shown at New York's Society of American Artists in 1889, and he was one of the first generation of American artists not only to embrace the modern style but to introduce it in this country.

The Westmoreland's *In the Garden* was painted during the artist's early years of experimenting with the new techniques of impressionism. In a light-pastel color palette of blues,

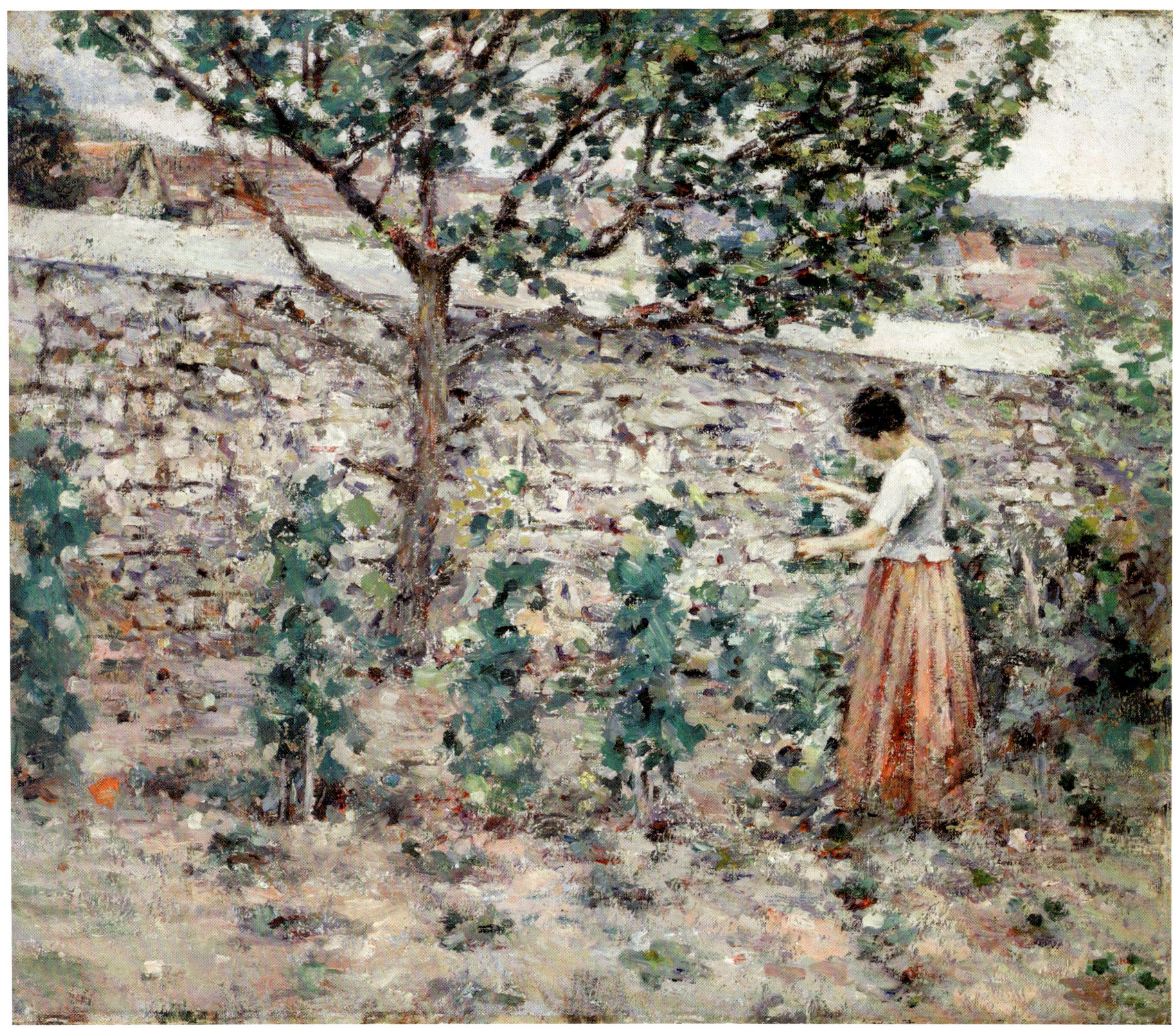

lavenders, pinks, and yellows, Robinson depicts a peasant woman tending pole beans in her small kitchen garden behind her home in Giverny. The garden depicted is a particular place, identified by Robinson in his diary as Gill's garden, a site that he repeated in a number of his landscape compositions of the village. The model is likely Marie, who was a favorite and frequently modeled for the artist in Paris and Giverny. Cyanotypes in the collection of the Terra Foundation for American Art show that the artist photographed his models to use in his paintings, and Marie, who appears in those images, shares similar features with the model in the Museum's painting. She appears in other Giverny paintings, including *La Vachère* (1888, The Baltimore Museum of Art), and *The Layette* (1892, The Corcoran Gallery of Art), in which Gill's garden also served as a backdrop. In this painting, forms dissolve in myriad broken strokes of color, and although the figure of the woman is more solidly modeled, which sets her apart from her surroundings, she exists in a sea of energized brushwork. Monet is known to have said, "nothing stands still," and Robinson's paintings reflect that notion. His surfaces are alive with built-up layers of color that capture a specific moment in time. The walled-in space of the garden concentrates the viewer's attention on the shallow foreground, where all of the activity takes place, pushing everything to the front of the picture plane. Robinson concentrates on the textural energy of the wall, the garden plants, and the figure. Just over the stone wall, the artist includes a glimpse of the neighboring properties in the village and the high horizon line in the distance, a common element in Robinson's Giverny landscapes. Intimate spaces like this one were often found behind houses, reserved for either decorative flower gardens or functional vegetable gardens. Like his early views of Giverny, *In the Garden* is cast in an overall subdued light that washes the scene evenly, muting the pastel color palette and creating a synthesis of the whole. The large tree to the left and the woman at right create focal points and balance the composition. Undertones of light blue and green throughout contribute to the composition's uniformity. This painting is not dated, but similarities with the lighting conditions of other paintings of this period suggest that it was probably made around 1889. His later landscapes are bathed in brighter light, containing sharper contrasts of light and shadow.

The personal diaries that Robinson kept of his day-to-day activities allow us to more fully understand his thoughts, his ideas about art, his feelings, his travel experiences, and his working methods, leaving an invaluable resource to the art world.[2] Robinson's health was always problematic due to acute asthma that had plagued him since he was a young adult. After his 1892 trip to Giverny, his health deteriorated and prevented a return to France in his remaining years, during which time he continued to paint the rural landscape, including that of his native Vermont. Robinson corresponded for the last time with Monet on February 6, 1896, as he would succumb to a severe asthma attack in New York less than two months later on April 2. Dying much too young, the artist was just two months' shy of his forty-fourth birthday. In 1946, fifty years after Robinson's death, a major exhibition of his work was mounted by the Baltimore Museum of Art.

BLJ

1 Theodore Robinson to Julian Alden Weir, 25 May 1892, Weir Family Papers. Referenced in Sona Johnston, *In Monet's Light: Theodore Robinson at Giverny* (Baltimore: The Baltimore Museum of Art, 2004), 62.

2 Theodore Robinson Diaries, 1892–1896, Frick Art Reference Library, New York.

LEVI WELLS PRENTICE (1855–1935)
Apples in a Brown Hat, c. 1890
Oil on canvas, 12 ¼ x 18 inches
Signed lower left
Gift of the Westmoreland Society, 1995.49
Provenance: Private Collection; Berry-Hill Gallery, New York.

SELECTED EXHIBITIONS: Berry-Hill Gallery, New York, 1993; *Nature Staged: The Landscape and Still Life Paintings of Levi Wells Prentice,* The Adirondack Museum, Blue Mountain Lake, New York, 1993; *A Feast for the Eyes: Treasures from the Westmoreland Museum of American Art,* Woodmere Art Museum, Philadelphia, Pennsylvania, 1998.

Born on December 18, 1851, in Harrisburgh, Lewis County, New York, Levi Wells Prentice grew up on a farm just outside the "blue line" that would circumscribe the Adirondack Park when it was established in 1892. He was the second son of Samuel Wells Prentice and Rhoda S. Robbins, who moved the family to Syracuse in 1870, where young Levi made his artistic debut and would live until 1879. The *Syracuse Journal* enthusiastically followed Prentice's artistic activities closely, reporting his exhibitions, his painting trips to the Adirondacks, and the duration of those visits. Although he made only four known trips to the Adirondacks between 1873 and 1877, those trips were highly productive and earned him a substantial reputation as an Adirondack artist.

When Edwin R. Wallace "advertised" Prentice as a "promising young artist" in his *Guide to the Adirondacks* in 1875, Prentice had already been painting the Adirondack landscape for nearly four years. It is curious to note that Wallace listed Prentice on a page with India rubber goods for sportsmen; a hotel; a portable camp stove, and a map of the Adirondack wilderness. The ad ran in the next five editions, until 1880, just after Prentice left Syracuse. The paintings Prentice left behind as records of his travels enable us now, over 130 years later, to retrace the artist's movements throughout the Adirondack region and identify the sites he documented. Prentice would spend nearly twenty years of his career depicting the picturesque mountains, lakes, and woodlands of the North Woods wilderness. His direct encounters with that region resulted in more than one hundred known paintings of that pristine natural world.

Self-taught as an artist, Prentice learned by looking at reproductions and the work of other artists, including the chromolithographs of Louis B. Prang and Currier and Ives. His formulaic composition—the interrelationship between foreground, middle ground, and background, connected by lake reflections—his methodical attention to detail, and his vocabulary of elements—calm lake, blasted tree, unfurling birch bark—reveal the influence of the Hudson River school of painters, but his paintings do not convey the same moral tone. His style of painting was marked by an intense realism heightened by skill in rendering texture, color, and form. Sharply focused and rigidly delineated hard-edged forms and high-key color combinations became his trademark.

Prentice painted every locale in which he lived. While in Syracuse, he not only traveled to the Adirondack Mountains but traveled east to Sherburne on the Chenango River, in addition to documenting the landscape that surrounded the city. His paintings help us retrace his moves from Syracuse to Buffalo, where he lived from 1879 to 1883. There he married Emma Roseloe Sparks in 1882 and painted at least three known views of Niagara Falls and the natural gorge at what is now Letchworth State Park. From Buffalo, he moved to Brooklyn, where he lived for twenty years between 1883 and 1903. His two children, Leigh Wells and Imogene, were born there in 1887 and 1889 respectively. While no Brooklyn landscape scenes are known, he did paint seascapes along the north shore of Long Island, where his mother lived at the time.

Concurrent with his move to Brooklyn, Prentice turned rather abruptly from landscape to still life, concentrating on subjects both set in interiors and found directly in nature. In the early 1880s, Brooklyn had its own artistic identity and enjoyed an enthusiastic and active art community. The Brooklyn Art Club and the Brooklyn Art Guild were two organizations available to artists living in the borough, but it was the Brooklyn Art Association, established in 1861, that offered primary support to artists through its spring and fall juried art exhibitions. While no records indicate that Prentice participated in the semi-annual exhibitions, they offered him the opportunity to

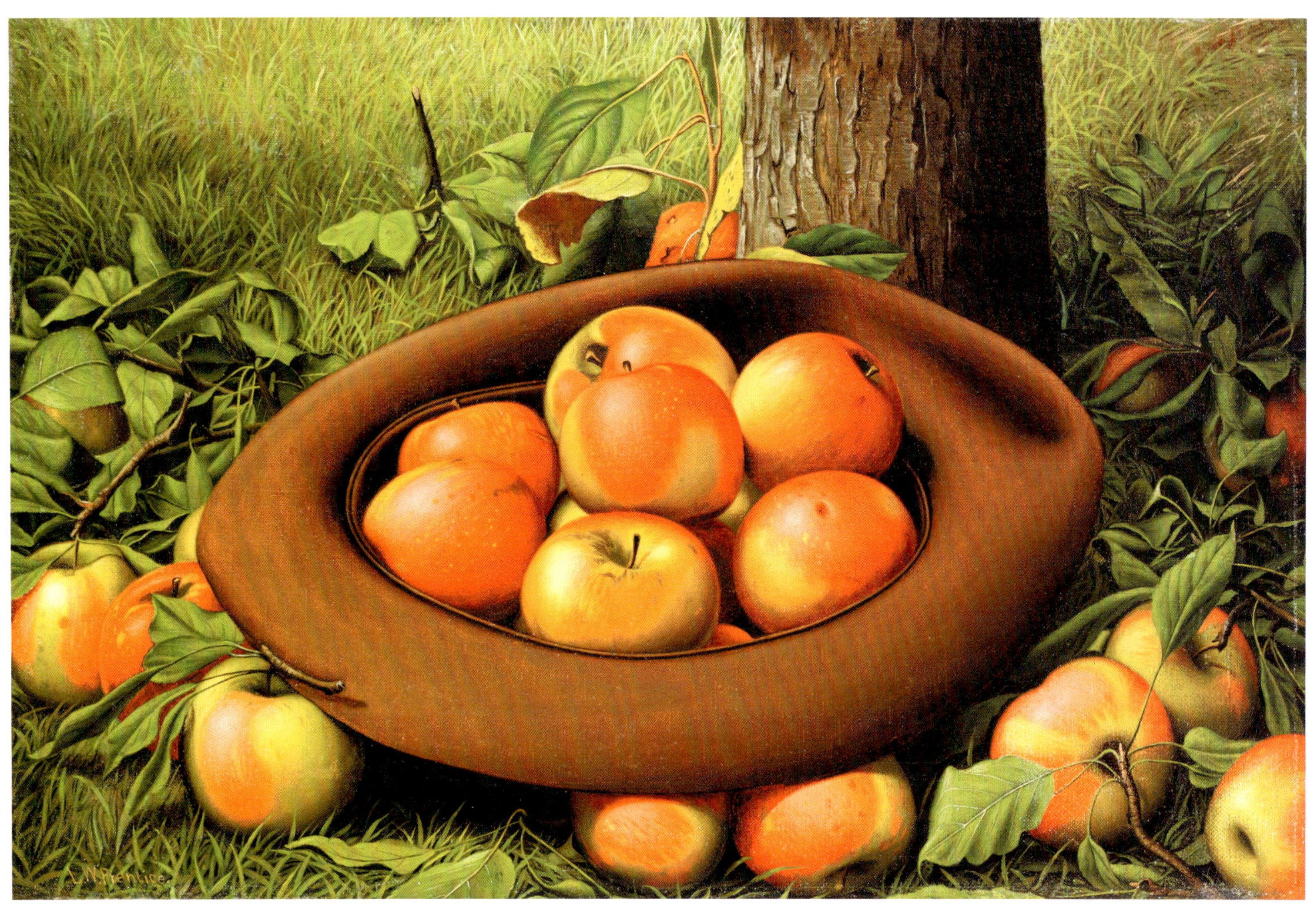

see the work of a great many of his contemporaries working in Brooklyn and the United States. Thomas Eakins (1844–1916) was an instructor for the art school of the association in 1883, and William Merritt Chase (1849–1916) conducted painting classes there from 1891 to 1895. Still life was an established and sought-after genre, as checklists of the association confirm, and Prentice took advantage of it, eager to embrace a new mode of expression that would allow him to continue to earn a living from his art. William Mason Brown (1828–1898) and Joseph Decker (1853–1924) were two leading still life painters living in Brooklyn while Prentice was there.

Apples in a Brown Hat shows the artist's favorite fruit, which he painted in myriad ways many times—on a tabletop, under a tree, or still growing on a bough. His apples are not glorified, beautiful, or perfect; instead, they appear as they are in nature, complete with bruises, gouges, and bumps. Prentice paid meticulous attention to detail, and this obsession, as well as his thoughtful arrangement of elements in his still lifes, carried over from his careful study of the natural landscape. He followed the truth-to-nature principles of John Ruskin (1819–1900), the English artist and critic who instructed artists to go to nature directly for everything they needed in their art: "Every class of rock, earth, and cloud, must be known by the painter, with geological and meteorological accuracy."[1] Ruskin believed that a finished work of art was an accumulation of the facts, and, as a result, the truth. The vibrant colors, hard-edged forms, and sharply focused details in this painting are stylistic components that together form Prentice's trademark style and, as with his landscapes, lend his work a curiously primitive yet contemporary air. This heightened reality allies him with trompe l'oeil still life specialist William Michael Harnett (1848–1892). Prentice painted at least three known variations of apples in a brown hat as well as fruit gathered in an assortment of other hats. It was common practice for him to reuse and recycle the same objects into different arrangements. The date of *Apples in a Brown Hat* can be approximated as c. 1890 because the painting compares favorably with other dated works in which the same attention to detail, accentuated color, and three-dimensional volume is so carefully delineated. One of the artist's best examples of the subject is *Apples in a Tin Pail* (1892; Museum of Fine Arts, Boston). His earliest dated still life is 1884.

From Brooklyn, Prentice moved his family to Philadelphia, where he is first listed in the city directories in 1905. While he would remain there for the remainder of his life, he split his time between Philadelphia and a studio that he had built near Bridgeport, Connecticut, essentially abandoning his family for many months of the year. When he died on Thanksgiving Day in 1935, his obituaries in the Philadelphia newspapers eulogized him as primarily an Adirondack landscape painter: "As a landscape painter and interpreter of the best in American natural scenery, Mr. Prentice had few peers. He was known and honored wherever art is worshipped for his unusual talent in depicting the glorious lake and mountain beauty of the Adirondacks particularly. The passing of Mr. Prentice well may be universally mourned. The world at this time is in sad need of men of his caliber, men who worship at the shrine of truth and beauty and can look beyond petty acquisitions of the day to scenes of grandeur and glory which will never pass away. Yet, though he is gone, his spirit and his works shall not soon let America forget him."[2] An interesting description, as Prentice was literally unknown after his relocation to Brooklyn and Philadelphia. Beyond his short-lived burst of fame in Syracuse in the 1870s, where he was praised as a "master" and "rare genius," for some thirty-five years after his death, Prentice was indeed forgotten. With the resurgence of interest in representational subjects in the 1970s, his art, especially his still life paintings, began once more to be recognized and are still highly sought after today.

BLJ

1 John Ruskin, *Modern Painters* (New York: John Wiley & Sons, 1885), Preface to the 2nd Edition, xvii.

2 "Death Claims Levi W. Prentice," *Philadelphia Journal of Commerce*, vol. no. 10, Saturday, 7 December 1935, 9.

WILLIAM MERRITT CHASE (1849–1916)
Lady in Pink,[1] c. 1892
Oil on canvas, 24 x 20 inches
Signed upper right
Gift in memory of G. Albert Shoemaker by his wife, Mercedes, 1995.23
Provenance: The Artist; Mrs. William M. Chase; Helen Chase Storm; Jackson Chase Storm; Grand Central Art Galleries, New York; Mr. and Mrs. G. Albert Shoemaker, Pittsburgh.

Selected Exhibitions: *American Realism, 1880–1980*, Liberty Bank, Oklahoma City, 1980.

The oldest of six siblings, William Merritt Chase enjoyed a happy childhood with loving parents. Born in what is now Ninevah, Indiana, his family moved to Indianapolis when Chase, whom they called Merritt, was thirteen. His father discouraged his interest in art; to please him, Chase joined the navy apprentice program in Annapolis, Maryland, in 1867. After quickly determining that he was not navy material, he enlisted his father's help to extract him from the program, resulting in a stay of only three months. In 1869, he convinced his father to let him study art at the National Academy of Design in New York. After a year, Chase left the academy and went to St. Louis—where his family had moved—to help with their financial situation. In 1872, with the backing of several local businessmen who saw promise in the young artist, Chase left St. Louis to study in Munich. Among the other American art students he encountered there were Frank Duveneck (1848–1919) and John Twachtman (1853–1902), with whom he became lifelong friends. Together they enjoyed their studies, the café/cabaret lifestyle of young art students abroad, and ready access to the works of the old masters.

It was in Munich that Chase first began to collect objets d'art—furniture, paintings, and decorative pieces that would later fill his famously decorated studio in New York City. In addition to creating an opulent ambiance, these items would be put to use in his paintings, serving as backdrops for his portraits and the basis for still life studies. Acquisitive in nature and sensitive to beautiful objects of all kinds, Chase continued to add to this collection throughout his life and his many travels. He was known to generously loan items to his students and fellow artists for their own tableaux or still life arrangements.

On his return to New York in 1878, two significant events occurred: he took a studio in the Tenth Street Studio Building, and he began teaching at the newly opened (1875) Art Students League. The studio would evolve into an extension of Chase as both artist and social creature, giving him a distinctive persona within the New York art world. His teaching would prove to be a lifelong passion through which he would give young artists the encouragement he himself craved but never received from his family.

A dapper man with a theatrical flair, Chase employed a series of African servants whom he dressed in exotic costumes, often topped with a red fez. A menagerie of macaws and cockatoos, and English or Russian greyhounds, inhabited his studio, which was host to elaborate dinner parties, poetry readings, and musical performances. Even in the early days, when he was on a starvation budget, Chase and his friends found ways to engage in these sorts of activities. They were generous colleagues, often lending one another money when they sold a painting, and forgetting who owed whom in between.

Chase's talent as a painter, compassion for other artists, acceptance and encouragement of individual styles, and warm nature earned him the respect of his peers. Artists and students alike sought him out and were rewarded with invitations to his studio gatherings. He was central to an era of artistic excitement in New York, when artists were returning from Europe and establishing studios, bringing the bohemian experience of Europe to Manhattan. New art associations were being formed, including the artist-run Society of American Artists, founded in 1877 as a reaction to the conservatism of the National Academy. Chase served as president of this organization from 1885 to 1895. He and others, including

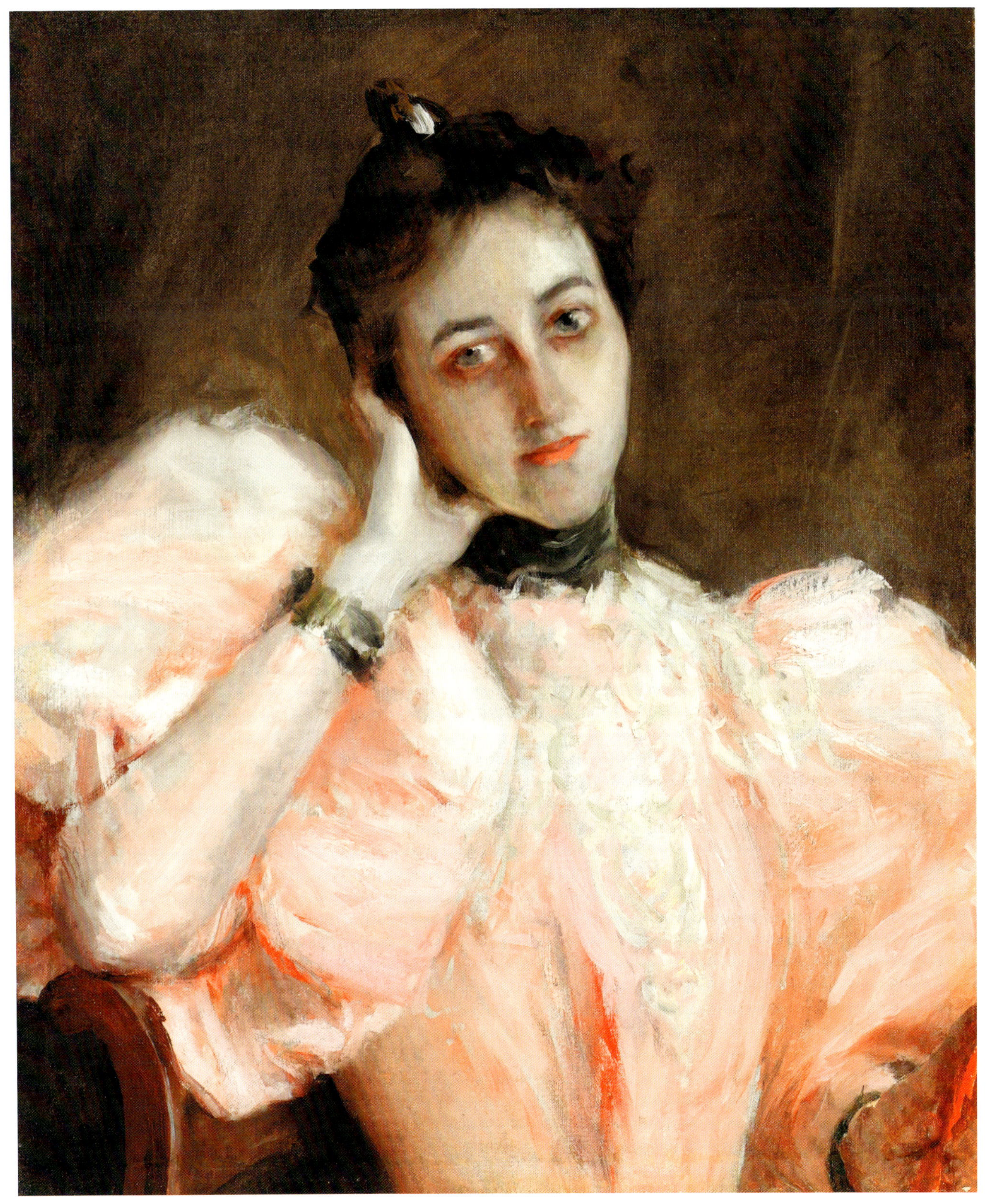

Twachtman, formed the Tile Club, meeting weekly for dinner and the decoration of tiles in the arts and crafts tradition.

In 1881 and 1882, Chase traveled to Europe with a number of artist friends, stopping in Holland, Spain, Germany, and France, where he visited the American expatriate painter Mary Cassatt (1844–1926). By 1887, he had settled again in New York and married his beau of several years, Alice Gerson, whose sister Virginia, is the likely subject of The Westmoreland's portrait.

Based on portraits known to be of Virginia, Ron Pisano cites a similarity in the arch of the eyebrows and bridge of the nose.[2] He also notes that the painting remained in the family's possession until 1980, further evidence of the sitter being a relative. The portrait was made shortly after Chase won the Gold Medal at the Paris Exposition of 1890 and after the death of his year-old son, William Merritt Chase Jr., in 1891.[3] That same summer, Chase established the Shinnecock Summer School of Art in Southampton, Long Island, where he could also engage in landscape painting. The picturesque area is one of sand dunes, beach grasses, and beautiful summer light overlooking Peconic Bay. Chase and his family looked forward to returning to the area every summer for years. Virginia likely sat for her brother-in-law in the summer of 1892, when the family's new home at Shinnecock Hills, designed by Chase's friend, Stanford White was completed.

The portrait reveals the surety of Chase's brush and its painterly result, especially in the pale pink fabric and ivory lacework of the sitter's dress. His ability to capture human expression is not limited to facial features but extends to pose. The casual gesture of her arm, slight smile, and pensive eyes reveal the subject's ease and familiarity with the painter. The dark background, devoid of any architectural or decorative setting, serves to focus our attention on the woman's sensitive features.

In 1896, Chase opened the Chase School of Art in New York, which he operated only until 1898, when he sold it and its name was changed to the New York School of Art. He held numerous teaching positions, including at the Brooklyn Art School, the Art Institute of Chicago, and the Pennsylvania Academy of the Fine Arts in Philadelphia, thereby affecting innumerable students throughout his lifetime. In addition to teaching fine art at the Pennsylvania Academy, he lectured on various subjects, including "Great Portrait Painters" (1902) and "Whistler, the Man and His Art" (1905)—about his good friend and fellow painter, who had died two years previously. While maintaining an active schedule of painting and exhibiting, he also continued his travels abroad. He was honored in 1915 with a one-man exhibition at the Panama-Pacific International Exposition in San Francisco.

In Chase's last days, he asked his wife, who maintained a bedside vigil, to recount her experiences in European galleries. Together they passed the time until Chase's death by sharing visual memories of masterpieces, thus lifting the artist's spirits and transporting his mind to the subject that had occupied his life.[4] Private funeral services followed by burial in the Gerson family plot in Brooklyn were held for this much revered man, who had touched many lives and affected several generations of American painters.

JHO'T

1 This painting has previously been referred to as *Lady in a Pink Dress*. The title has been changed to reflect the relevant entry in Ronald G. Pisano, Carolyn Lane, and D. Frederick Baker, *The Complete Catalogue of Known and Documented Work by William Merritt Chase (1849–1916)*, vol. 2, *William Merritt Chase: Portraits in Oil* (New Haven and London: Yale University Press, 2006), OP.184, 100.

2 Ibid.

3 In 1895, Chase and his wife lost a second son, John Rudolph Chase, born in 1894. His other children—Alice (b. 1887), Dorothy (b. 1891), Hazel (b. 1893), Helen (b. 1895), Robert (b. 1898), Roland Dana (b. 1901), and Mary (b. 1904)—survived into adulthood.

4 Katharine Metcalf Wolf, *The Life and Art of William Merritt Chase* (New York: Scribner's Sons, 1917), vi.

JOHN GEORGE BROWN (1831–1913)
Maid of the Hills, c. 1900
Oil on canvas, 30 x 25 inches
Signed and copyrighted lower left
Gift of Mrs. Paul B. Ernst, 1981.78
Provenance: Mrs. Paul B. Ernst, Pittsburgh, Pennsylvania.

SELECTED EXHIBITIONS: National Academy of Design, New York, 1901.

John George Brown was born in Bensham, England, and became an American success story, combining an entrepreneurial spirit with artistic excellence to create a signature body of work. Despite showing an early talent, Brown was discouraged from art by his father. He instead apprenticed as a glassworker while taking evening drawing classes from engraver and Pre-Raphaelite painter William Bell Scott (1811–1890). By 1853, Brown had moved to London and begun life as a portrait painter when he decided to immigrate to America. Once there, he settled in Brooklyn, where he temporarily resumed his trade in the glass industry, taking night classes in fine art at the Graham School of Art in Brooklyn and at the National Academy of Design in New York, where he studied life drawing and drawing from the antique with Thomas Seir Cummings (1804–1894).

Soon after his arrival in the United States, Brown began securing a place for himself in the contemporary art world by painting subject matter not approached by others, or at least not approached in the same manner or with the same skill. The newsboys and bootblacks who peopled his neighborhood were subjects for his brush, and the canvases that resulted proved to be popular with New York audiences. Nearly a generation older, Pittsburgh painter David Gilmour Blythe (1815–1865) painted figural types from the same socioeconomic class but did so with a pointed satirical humor that never appears in Brown's versions. Instead, Brown gave his young sitters a wholesome, approachable quality, often with a humorous anecdotal twist. He made his reputation on a canvas titled *The First Cigar* (location unknown), in which a young boy is seen leaning against a lamppost, his face sickly ashen as one of his companions removes the cigar from his lips and another blows smoke in his face.

Brown's training as a figure painter naturally led him to find appealing and willing subjects among those around him. Although he painted a wide range of people, of all ages and both genders, he has become pigeonholed as a painter of shoeshine boys and other young salesmen of the streets, perhaps because those images were, and remain to this day, his most popular. Brown copyrighted his paintings, converting them into prints that sold extremely well and, along with his paintings, earned him a very good living. By 1860, he opened a studio in Manhattan's Tenth Street Studio Building, where he worked for over fifty years. When interviewed in 1904, Brown recalled the "many good fellows gone who have made these walls echo with their laughter. There was Homer D. Martin bubbling over with quaint, funny speeches; there was George Inness with his Swedenborgian theories—the Beards, Sanford Gifford, Kensett, McEntee," and others.[1]

Brown was a dedicated and prolific painter despite an accident in infancy in which his right hand was severely scalded, rendering the last three fingers practically useless.[2] He produced twenty to thirty paintings a year while maintaining an active exhibition schedule and assuming prominent roles in New York's art associations. In 1863, he was elected a member of the National Academy of Design, where he served as vice-president from 1899 to 1903. He served as president of the American Watercolor Society from 1887 to 1904. He maintained his associations in Brooklyn, where he was a founding member of the Brooklyn Art Social—a men's professional club—in 1859, and held membership in the Brooklyn Art Association.

In Brown's best-known compositions, the artist works with a shallow picture plane, often positioning his figures against a wall or building, or simply placing them against a dark background to cut off any distant view or perspective. This technique served to focus attention on the figures while creating in them a greater sense of three-dimensional presence than if they had been portrayed in a deeper spatial plane. In *Maid of the Hills,* Brown employs another method of drawing attention to his main character: that of situating three-quarters of her figure above the horizon line, thereby casting her as

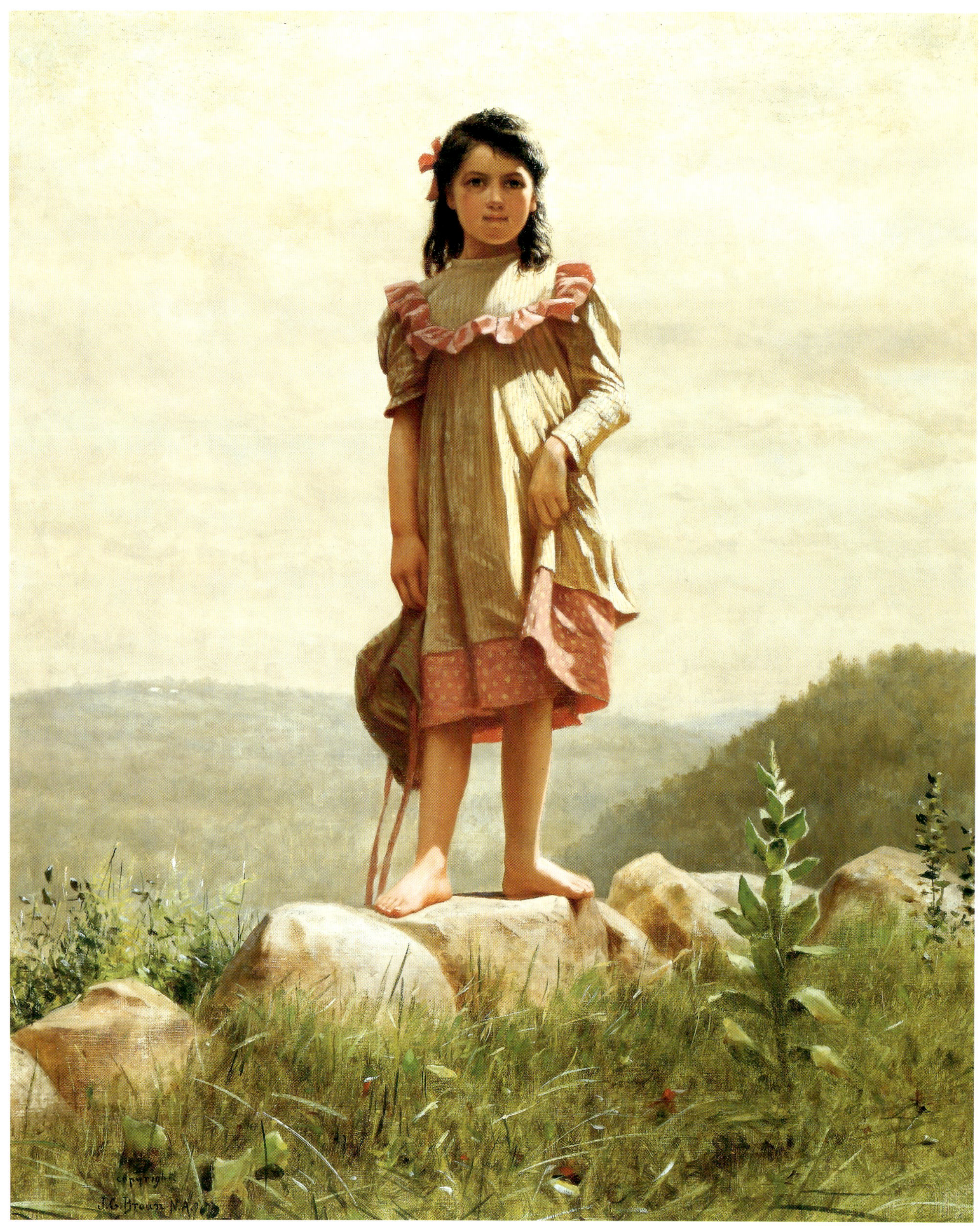
Copyright
J.G. Brown N.A.

heroic in scale.

Like many of Brown's figures, the girl pictured here is a preteen yet appears self-assured and wise beyond her age. A slight smile crosses her lips, and her eyes cast a confident gaze forward. Although not depicted in the humble garments of many of Brown's urban street urchins, this rural counterpart is still plainly dressed—perhaps in her Sunday best—in a coral-colored dress, with a matching ribbon decorating her hair and a bonnet in her hand. Her bare feet are clean and uncut. She stands with the sun at her back, half her figure cast in shadow as she pauses, or poses, for a moment, skirt hem in hand and looking down at the viewer. We can tell it is a summer day not only by her dress but by the warm, golden haze that fills the sky and the tangled growth of meadow at her feet. Prominent among the plants is the mullein in the right foreground, its verticality mimicking that of the maid, as both intersect the otherwise horizontal elements in the composition. The plant was used by landscape painters of the nineteenth century to symbolize good luck and prosperity, often being placed at the gate to a homestead or on the entrance to a well-worn trail or road. Here the plant's attributes are conferred on the young girl as she is figuratively and literally poised atop her world, like the mullein about to blossom, stepping from childhood to womanhood.

During the period that this painting was completed, Brown was summering near Rutland, Vermont. His practice was to make studies during the summer months, which he would then work into more finished compositions in his studio. Because *Maid of the Hills* was exhibited in the spring of 1901, it was most likely begun the previous summer. A related painting, *Study from Nature for "Maid of the Hills,"* with the same dimensions but slightly different compositional details, was included in Brown's estate sale of 1914. The absence of the present version in that sale indicates that it had been sold prior to the artist's death. Although Brown is best known for his paintings of young boys, he frequently employed female figures, especially in rural scenes.[3]

Brown's skill is evidenced in his ability to capture light as it plays against the girl and the landscape elements in which she is depicted. The painting's effect is one of sharp realism, yet the artist's brushwork is actually painterly and fluid. The palette is exceptionally sophisticated and pleasing in its use of coral as a base for the sky, the rocks, and even the distant mountains and foreground foliage, before becoming strongly evident in the young girl's dress. These artistic devices reveal a particularly sensitive and accomplished painter.

Pure landscape painting was a lifelong passion of Brown's, who searched New Hampshire's White Mountains and the region surrounding the Hudson River valley, among other places, for subject matter. These landscapes sometimes found their way to the backgrounds of his figural work, as in this canvas.

A popular teacher and successful painter, Brown died in 1913, the same year that saw the groundbreaking New York Armory exhibition, which introduced European modernists to American audiences and would dramatically change the direction of art in the United States.

JHO'T

1 "J. G. Brown, Painter of Street Boys, Dies," *New York Times*, February 9, 1913.

2 Ibid.

3 Martha Hoppin, *The World of J. G. Brown* (Chesterfield, MA: Chameleon Books, 2010).

ALBERT FRANCES KING (1854–1945)
Still Life with Onions, Brown Jug and Mackerel, not dated
Oil on canvas, 14 x 23 inches
Signed lower right
Museum purchase, 1980.32
Provenance: Gary Grimes, Pittsburgh, Pennsylvania.

Unlike many of the older, European-born artists with whom he associated, A. F. King, as he was known, was a native of Pittsburgh, part of a new generation of American artists. Rumored to have started painting at the age of nine, he later studied with fellow painter and friend Martin B. Leisser (1846–1940), known informally as the Dean of Pittsburgh painters.[1] Credited along with A. Bryan Wall (1861–1935) for bringing the aesthetics of the Scalp Level school into the twentieth century, King was a generation younger than most of the artists in that group.

In a photograph taken in July 1887, A. F. King's grinning visage is the youngest of five thrust out of a single window in a rustic Scalp Level farmhouse. The other four are fellow artists Horatio Stevenson (1854–1912), George Layng (1867–1931), Joseph Woodwell (1843–1911), and their leader, George Hetzel (1826–1899). The photograph is a record of their camaraderie as well as their excursion that summer for the purpose of landscape painting. As recorded in a newspaper interview, King was "a dreamer and [caught] nature's moods with a skillful brush—this for his own pleasure."[2] However, as much as he enjoyed his warm-weather jaunts into the Laurel Highlands, he made his living as a portrait painter and was most successful in this endeavor. Many distinguished Pittsburgh families, including the Carnegies and the Fricks, commissioned portraits from King, who accommodated them with good likenesses in formal poses. Dorothy Kantner of the *Pittsburgh Sun-Telegraph* noted that at the age of eighty-three, King "is still the one to whom many turn for portrait work. His hand is just as steady, his ability to secure a likeness just as infallible."[3]

According to oral history, King and Hetzel came to an agreement that the former would concentrate on portraits and the latter on landscapes. This pact allowed both to produce still lifes, a subject of which they were both fond. Still life was a natural partner to landscape painting in the nineteenth century, with many artists choosing to paint both. King sometimes depicted dead game and fruit subjects in a natural setting, on the forest floor as if they were just felled by either a hunter's bullet or a gatherer's hand. More often he would compose them in a domestic setting, especially in the format known as "kitchen pictures," with ingredients laid out on a wooden tabletop, ready for the preparation of the evening meal.

Still Life with Onions, Brown Jug and Mackerel is just such a picture, painted with the attention to verisimilitude common to nineteenth-century still life tradition. The specific qualities of each object, including the translucent crispness of the onion skin and the shimmering texture of the fish scales, are carefully rendered. The dark background, a convention carried over from the European tradition, serves as a foil to the foreground objects, while the brown jug serves to anchor the composition. With the objects clustered close to the front of the shallow picture plane, King creates the effect of being able to reach out and touch them. The position of the fish tail is such that it appears to jut out beyond the flat painted surface and enter the viewer's three-dimensional space. Called trompe l'oeil, French for "trick the eye," this is another element popular in nineteenth-century still life painting that King often incorporated into his work. Although King painted a variety of subject matter, he favored watermelons and fruits of summer, often positioning an object, sometimes a knife, at a diagonal to serve as a trompe l'oeil element.

It is said that when King completed a portrait and enjoyed the sitter's company, he would give him or her a miniature still life, no more than the size of a postcard, as a thank you for a good sitting and an enticement to purchase a larger version. About a dozen of these small compositions are extant and show King at his highest skill for the amount of detail contained within them.

A. F. King lived to see modern art movements, which he never adopted and, in fact, railed against to younger artists, warning them "against the evil of giving way to fads and fashions."[4] He felt the new styles lacked the ability to touch the

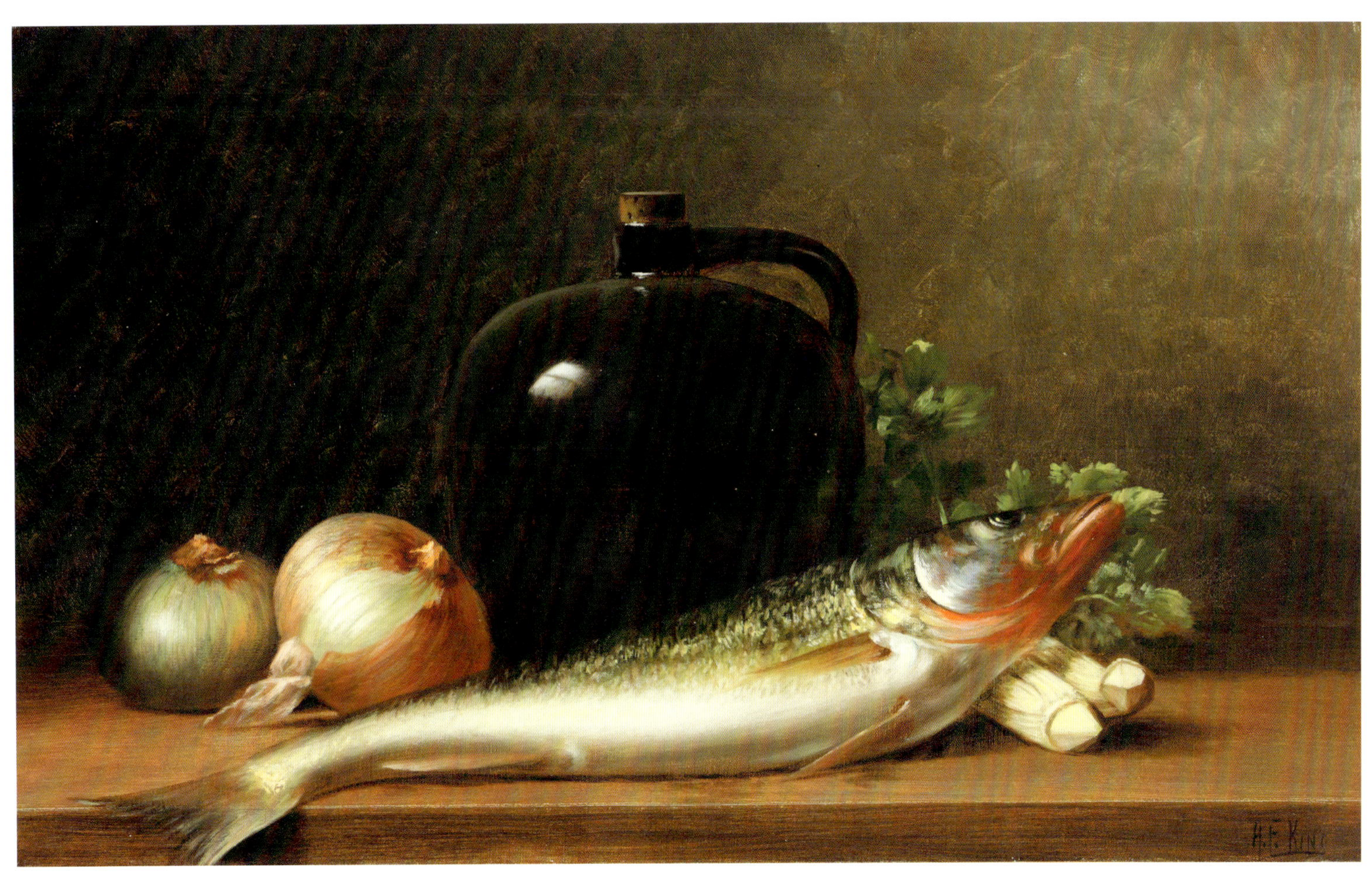

soul, as had the Scalp Level style of landscape painting. Despite this, his later paintings are executed with a looser handling of paint, perhaps an accommodation to impressionism. John Beatty (1850–1924)—fellow artist and first director of the Carnegie Institute (now Carnegie Museum of Art)—took King to Scalp Level around 1917 to see what the area looked like. King had not visited since the Johnstown Flood of 1889 and was disappointed to find that between coal mining and other commercialization, it had lost most of its pictorial charm.

As his older colleagues passed away, King was left with a great nostalgia for the community of artists with whom he had formerly engaged. His younger contemporaries tended not to congregate but to work more independently. In the 1920s, he stopped sending paintings to exhibitions, discouraged by the number of rejections from prior years, including those from the Carnegie Internationals. Thinking about retirement, he and his wife left Pittsburgh for Omaha to live with one of their sons in 1936, but they returned after just two years, having missed the environs of southwestern Pennsylvania.

Celebrated as a veteran Pittsburgh painter but feeling like a lonesome old-timer in an age of artistic experimentation, King died at the home of his son Albert in the city's East End, on February 4, 1945. He was buried in an unmarked grave in Homewood Cemetery.

JHO'T

1 This title reflected Leisser's major role in the developing art world of Pittsburgh in the late nineteenth century. A friend of Andrew Carnegie, Leisser convinced him to include an art program at the Carnegie Institute of Technology (now Carnegie Mellon University).

2 "Pittsburgh Painter of National Repute," *Pittsburgh Gazette-Times*, July 1, 1919.

3 Interview, May 14, 1938.

4 *Pittsburgh Gazette-Times*, January 23, 1919.

MARY STEVENSON CASSATT (1844–1926)
Mother and Two Children, c. 1905
Oil on canvas, tondo, 37 ¼ inches
Signed lower left
Anonymous gift, 1979.1
Provenance: The Artist; Durand-Ruel Gallery, Paris and New York; Harris Whittmore, Naugatuck, CT; José Moraes de Carvalho, Bahiz, Brazil.

SELECTED EXHIBITIONS: Durand-Ruel Gallery, Paris, 1914; *Loan Exhibition of Masterpieces by Old and Modern Painters*, M. Knoedler and Co., New York, 1915; *Mary Cassatt Memorial Exhibition*, Carnegie Institute, Pittsburgh, 1928; Baltimore Museum of Art, 1941–1942; *Mary Cassat*, Wildenstein & Co., New York, 1947; *The Art of Mary Cassatt*, toured by the American Federation of Arts to Kyoto and Tokyo, Japan, 1981; *A Feast for the Eyes: Treasures from the Westmoreland Museum of American Art*, Woodmere Art Museum, Philadelphia, Pennsylvania, 1998; *Mary Cassatt: Friends and Family*, Shelburne Museum, Vermont, 2008–2009; *The Gift of Art*, Westmoreland Museum of American Art, 2009.

One of the most recognized names in American art, Mary Stevenson Cassatt was born on May 22, 1844, in Allegheny City, Pennsylvania—now the North Side section of Pittsburgh—the second daughter of Robert and Katherine Cassatt. By the time she was four years old, the family had moved east, first to Lancaster, then to Philadelphia in 1849. Born to a prominent family, Mary was introduced to Europe when she was just seven years old. Returning to the United States in 1855, the family resettled in Philadelphia by 1857. Cassatt took classes at the Pennsylvania Academy of the Fine Arts from 1860 to 1863, knowing then that she wanted to become an artist. In 1865, she convinced her parents to send her to Europe to further her studies, and in Paris she studied the old masters, copied works in the Louvre, and was invited to become a student of academic painter Jean-Léon Gérôme (1824–1904). She also studied with Thomas Couture (1815–1879) in 1868 and then again in 1874. She had her first painting accepted in the Paris Salon of 1868, having been rejected in 1867 and then again in 1869. Although she came home during the Franco-Prussian War in 1870, she returned to Europe at the end of 1871, only returning to America for brief visits. After studying masterworks in Italy, Spain, and the Netherlands, Cassatt settled permanently in Paris in 1874, drawn to the "modern" artists there, among them Édouard Manet (1832–1883), Edgar Degas (1834–1917), Pierre-Auguste Renoir (1841–1919), and Camille Pissarro (1830–1903). While in Parma, Italy, in 1872, Cassatt was commissioned to paint copies of two paintings by the Italian Renaissance artist Allegri da Correggio (1489–1534) to decorate the interior of the new Saint Paul Cathedral in Pittsburgh. It was her first paying job as an artist.[1]

Cassatt would spend the majority of her life living as an expatriate in France, where her association with the impressionists provided both exhibition opportunities and friendship. The story is often told that when Degas first saw her work in the Paris Salon of 1874, he said, "It is true. Here is someone who feels as I do."[2] Just three years later, Degas invited her to join the Independents (later called impressionists), a group of artists who first showed together in 1874, coming together in reaction to the strict exhibition policies of the Salon. The only American in the group, Cassatt exhibited with them in the Salon des Indépendants of 1879, 1880, 1881, and 1886, and was accepted by them as an equal. Not only was Degas her mentor, but the pair became lifelong friends. They shared a strong interest in light and color, with similar stylistic attitudes emphasizing drawing, asymmetrical design, and painterly brushwork that captured the immediacy of the moment.

Throughout her career, Cassatt experimented with a variety of media, and no matter which she chose to use—oil, pastel, etching, lithography—maternal subjects were a recurring theme and became her hallmark. Her body of work consists entirely of figure studies, for which she employed her own family members—sister, brother, nieces, and nephews—and those of her friends as models, painted in both domestic and urban settings as casual images of everyday life. Cassatt never had a family of her own, as she did not want to compromise her art for marriage; perhaps the focus she chose for her paintings served to satisfy her maternal instincts.

In 1890, she and Degas saw a large exhibition of Japanese

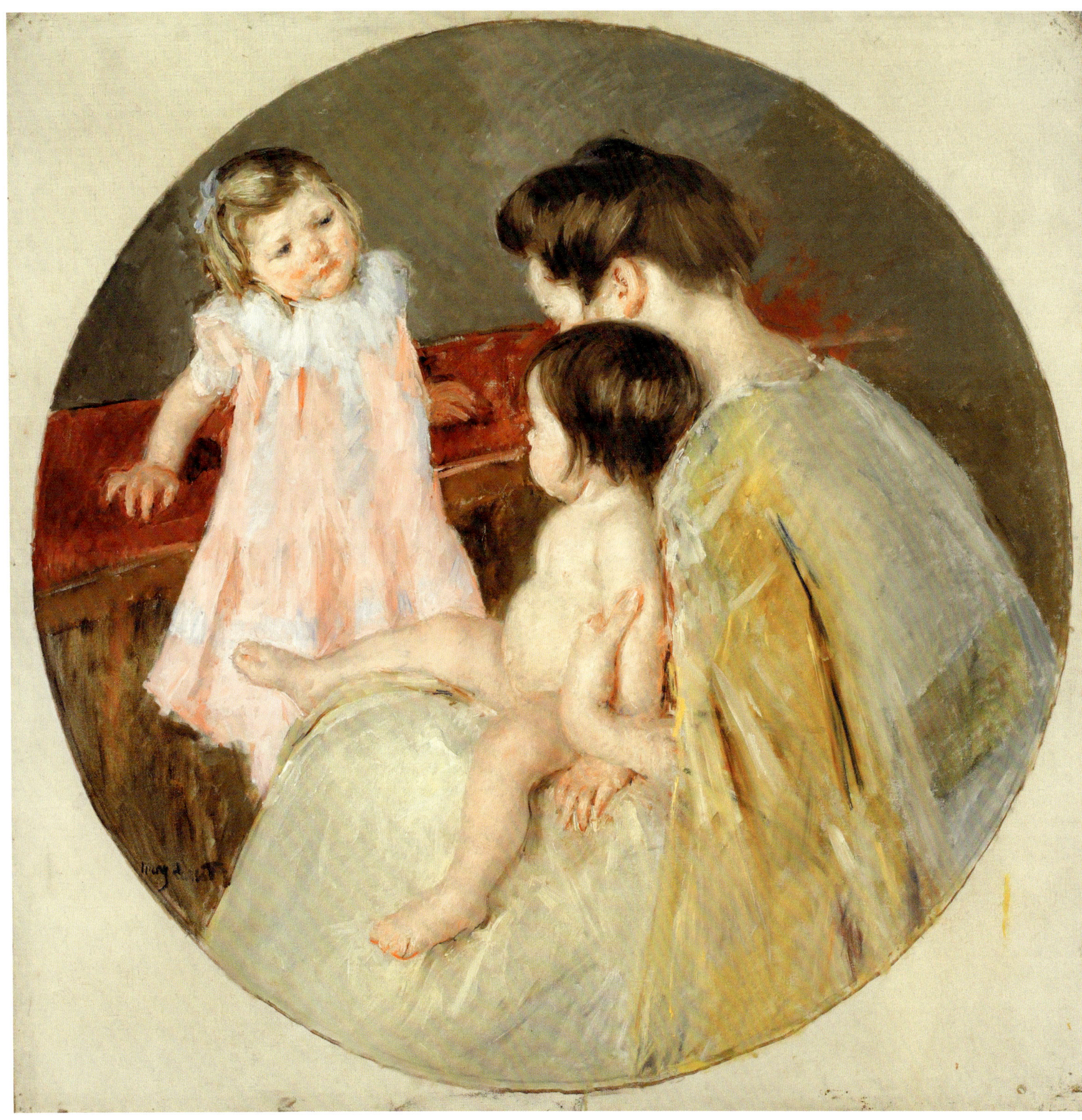

woodblock prints at the École des Beaux-Arts, which had a profound impact on her work. She was so directly influenced by the flat color planes, simplicity of form, strong contours, rhythmic line, and pattern that she adopted those design principles for her most famous suite of ten color prints, which she produced that summer. These prints, in soft-ground etching and aquatint, share the theme she chose for her paintings, depicting women and children in intimate settings.

The Westmoreland's *Mother and Two Children* portrays the artist's signature theme. The tondo shape of the canvas encircling a mother and her two children lends a heightened sense of intimacy to the scene, as if the viewer were peering through a keyhole at the small group. Despite the viewer's inability to see the mother's facial expression, the proximity of the figures to one another, as well as the softness of the brushstrokes, creates a feeling of domestic serenity. The young girl, her blonde hair tied in a bow and all dressed up in her pink dress, waits rather impatiently as her mother, in an elegant yellow peignoir, dresses her younger son, seated on her lap. With his head pressed against her cheek, the nude infant creates a strong bond with his mother, while his projecting right leg connects his sister to this intimate unit. The three figures are tightly grouped together in a shallow setting situated close to the picture plane, accentuated by the nondescript dark background.

This painting has become one of the most popular works in the Museum's collection. It was originally produced as part of a mural commission for the state capitol in Harrisburg, Pennsylvania, one of a pair intended to be installed in the Ladies' Lounge (now the Lieutenant Governor's Suite) when the building was completed in 1906. Philadelphia architect Joseph Huston wanted the capitol to reflect a synthesis of art and architecture, and thus commissioned painters, sculptors, and craftsman to re-create the commonwealth's rich history through murals, stained glass, sculpture, and decorative ornament. Although Huston specified paintings by Cassatt for the Ladies' Lounge, they were never completed because the artist, frustrated with the state of government and the amount of graft involved, withdrew from the project. As a result, tapestries were installed in the room's panel inserts in place of the paintings. The companion painting, also a tondo, is known to exist and was formerly in the collection of the artist's niece. Violet Oakley (1874–1961) would be the artist who completed the largest number of paintings for the capitol—creating a total of forty-three murals for three different spaces—when she replaced Edwin Austin Abbey (1852–1911), who died suddenly (see catalog entry on Oakley's *Unity*, 2005.28).

To benefit women's suffrage, a movement that Cassatt was passionate about, *Mother and Two Children* was included in a *Loan Exhibition of Masterpieces by Old and Modern Painters*, organized by her good friend Louisine Havemeyer and held in 1915 at M. Knoedler and Co. in New York. Critical response to the exhibition and to her work was especially positive.

Cassatt was a respected member of the artistic society in Paris. Her work was celebrated when she had her first comprehensive solo show at the Paris gallery of her dealer, Durand-Ruel, in 1893, and received positive critical attention when her work was shown at his New York gallery in 1895. She was made a chevalier of the French Legion of Honor in 1904, a great honor for an American, and was one of the first women to serve as a juror for the prestigious Carnegie International in Pittsburgh. She also assisted Havemeyer and other major American art collectors in amassing collections of impressionist works, which would eventually be donated to major museums in the United States.

Cassatt continued to exhibit her work both in Europe and in the United States throughout her career, but her critical reception was strongest in her adopted country. When *Modern Woman*—her monumental mural for the Woman's Building at the Chicago World's Columbian Exposition of 1893—was ridiculed by the press because the artist was a woman, she responded, "After all, give me France. Women do not have to fight for recognition here if they do serious work."[3] Severely impaired because of cataracts and diabetes, Cassatt's vision failed completely in 1914, forcing her to give up her art. But even as it was failing, she continued to try different printmaking techniques, including aquatint and lithography. Cassatt purchased the Chateau de Beaufresne in Oise, outside Paris, in 1894, and she lived there until she died on June 14, 1926, at the age of eighty-two. Ten years after her death, the Baltimore Museum of Art organized the first major retrospective of Cassatt's work in the United States.

BLJ

1 Judith A. Barter, *Mary Cassatt: Modern Woman* (Chicago: The Art Institute of Chicago in association with Harry N. Abrams, Inc., 1999), 25.

2 Barter, *Mary Cassatt*, 109.

3 Barter, *Mary Cassatt*, 150.

JOHN SINGER SARGENT (1856–1925)
Base of a Venetian Palace, c. 1904–1909[1]
Watercolor on paper, 23 x 18 inches
Inscribed lower left: to my friend Mrs. Hunter/John S. Sargent
Anonymous Gift, 1978.14
Provenance: Mrs. Charles Hunter; M. Knoedler & Co., New York;
Macbeth Gallery, New York; Mrs. Francis P. Garvan, Roslyn, New York; Dr. John J. McDonough, Youngstown, Ohio.

SELECTED EXHIBITIONS: Possibly *Summer Exhibition,* Royal Watercolour Society, London, 1905; Royal Society of Painters in Water Colours, London, 1910; *Winter Exhibition of the Works of the Late John S. Sargent,* Royal Academy, London, 1926; Tate Gallery, London, 1926; *A Panorama of American Painting: The John McDonough Collection,* New Orleans Museum of Art, 1975; *Americans in Venice: 1879–1913,* Coe Kerr Gallery, New York, 1983; *Venice: The American View, 1860–1920,* The Fine Arts Museums of San Francisco, 1984–1985; *John Singer Sargent,* Whitney Museum of American Art, New York, 1986–1987; *Capturing the Light: A Selection of Twentieth Century American Watercolors,* Palmer Museum of Art of the Pennsylvania State University, University Park, 1997; *John Singer Sargent,* National Gallery of Art, Washington, D.C., 1999; *Sargent and Italy,* Los Angeles County Museum of Art, 2003; *Venice: From Canaletto and Turner to Monet,* Fondation Beyeler, Riehen-Basel, Switzerland, 2008–2009; *The Gift of Art,* Westmoreland Museum of American Art, 2009; *Four Perspectives on Fifty Years,* Westmoreland Museum of American Art, 2009.

As an American expatriate, John Singer Sargent spent the majority of his life abroad, visiting the United States for the first time in 1876, when he was twenty years old. Born in Florence, Italy, he was the son of Dr. Fitzwilliam Sargent—a surgeon at Wills Eye Hospital in Philadelphia—and Mary Newbold Singer Sargent. Following the death of their first child, the couple left Philadelphia for Europe in 1854.

Sargent learned to draw, paint in watercolor, play the piano, and became proficient in four languages at a very young age. American by birth but European by virtue of his cosmopolitan upbringing and lifestyle, Sargent became the premier portraitist of wealthy French, English, and American families. Before settling permanently in London in 1886, his constant travels took him throughout Italy, Switzerland, France, Holland, Spain, and Germany, seeking out the work of artists whom he admired and spending time with his family. He visited Claude Monet (1840–1926) in Giverny on a number of occasions, painting the artist at work (Tate Gallery, London) in 1885 and a portrait of his friend two years later (National Academy of Design).

Sargent began his artistic training in Paris at the independent atelier of Carolus-Duran (1837–1917), who instructed his students in direct drawing on the canvas, without the underdrawing favored at the École des Beaux-Arts. He also worked in the studio of American artist James Carroll Beckwith (1852–1917). In an effort to improve his standing, Sargent sat for the entrance exams to the École three times between 1874 and 1877. Matriculated after each attempt, he succeeded on his third try to place second of all the applicants that year—the highest ranking ever achieved by an American. Among Sargent's early influences were the Spanish artist Diego Velázquez (1599–1660) and the Dutch artist Frans Hals (c. 1580–1666), whose brilliant control of tonal range inspired Sargent's virtuoso technique.

While he is best known for his dramatic oil portraits of society women and men, Sargent was an extraordinary watercolorist. His sure brushwork and brilliant use of color are well evidenced in this lighter, more fluid medium that allowed him greater spontaneity and freedom than oils. His *Base of a Venetian Palace* shows the grand façade of the Palazzo Balbi—built in the 1580s for Nicolò Balbi and situated on the Grand Canal.[2] The oblique angle at which the artist has painted the palazzo suggests that he was seated in a gondola on the canal when he dashed it off. The inscription to "Mrs. Hunter" gives further evidence that it was painted during a pleasurable afternoon and given by the artist as a token of remembrance to his good friend, who was a member of the boating party that day.[3]

As evidenced by most of his other watercolors of Venice, this view from the water was Sargent's preferred vantage point. In contrast to James A. M. Whistler's (1834–1903) views of Venice, Sargent sought out many of the city's historic landmarks, including the Palazzo Ducale (the Doge's Palace) and Santa

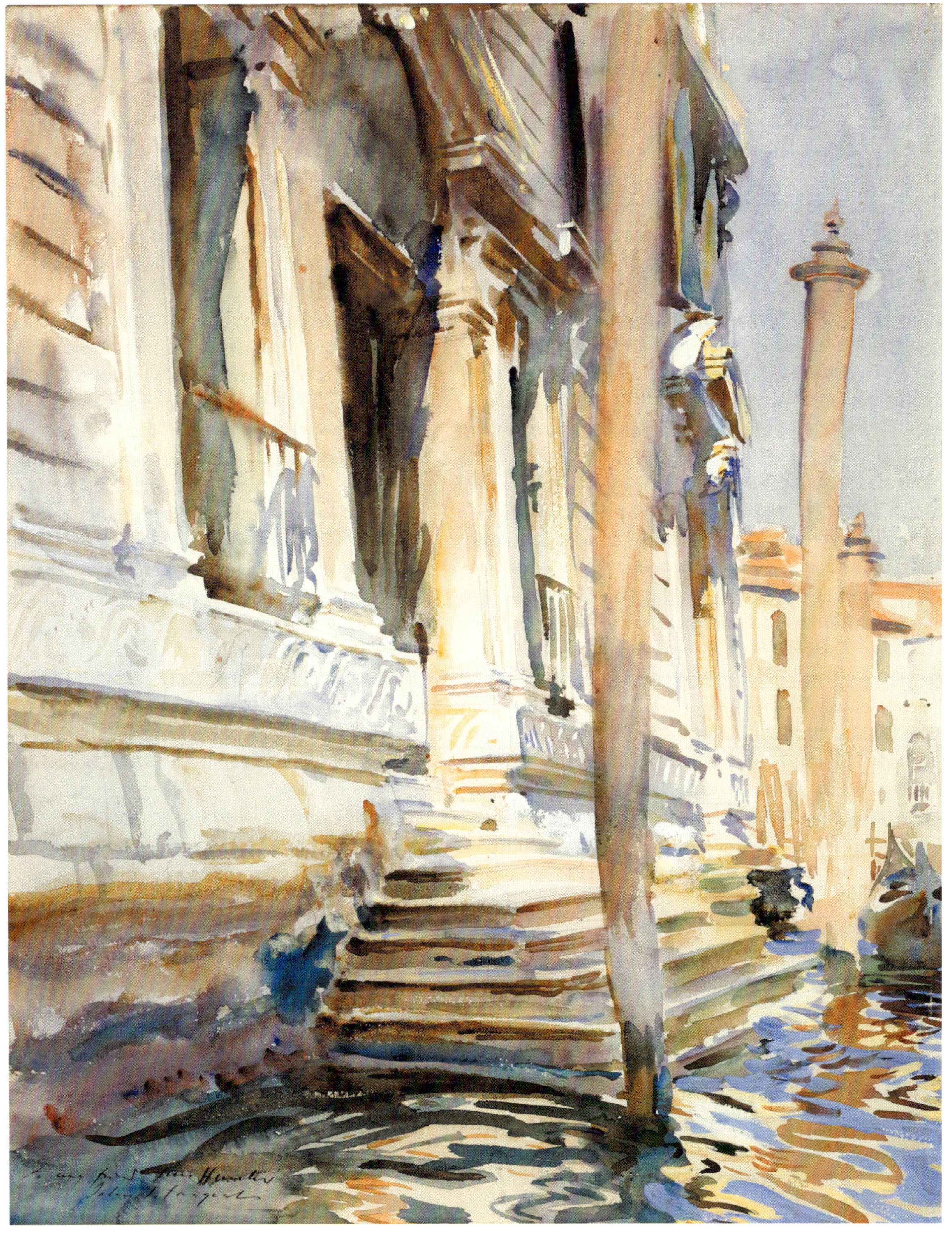

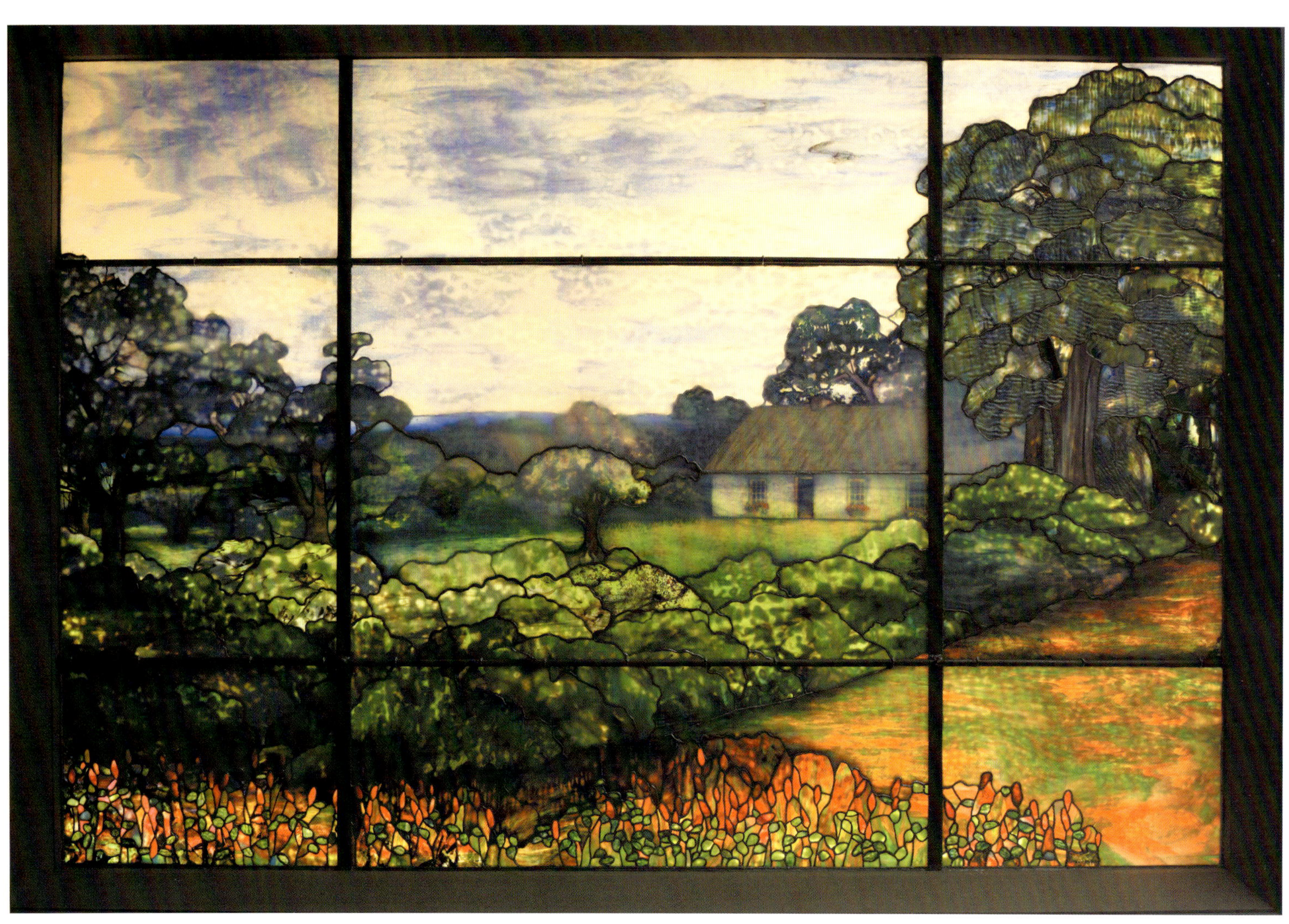

The window is an excellent teaching example in that it includes the variety of glassmaking techniques that Tiffany was noted for, such as the use of mottled, rippled, agate, stringer, and confetti glass to comprise this ambitious scene. Rippled and confetti glass—bits of glass rolled into semimolten glass—evoke the movement and texture of the foliage of the trees and help define the hedgerow. His mottling technique, also called cat's paw or milk spill, suggests the hazy cloud layers in the sky and re-create the subdued light conditions of dusk. In order to achieve depth and a sense of perspective in the landscape, Tiffany treated glass much like the pigment he used as a painter. Incorporating three plating layers overall, he combined them to achieve subtle color gradations that suggest the vista of distant mountains and sky and to capture the atmospheric conditions. To mix his colors and realize his desired effects, some areas on the reverse contain four layers and measure up to 1-inch thick. When the light is turned off behind the window, the artist's plating technique is most visible, as all but the top layer of glass disappears, allowing his range of techniques to stand out. The glass has also been acid-etched in some areas to suggest the subdued light conditions of the time of day and to create details, such as the flowers in the window boxes, without having to add a copper-foiled border. He used a full piece of rose glass to re-create those flowers, masking off the small areas where he wanted color to remain, and then etched away all the color, leaving only the brilliant red accents that represent the blooms. Further, the crimson clover and shamrock patch, together with the lush meadow in the foreground, combine with the diagonal hedgerow placement to create depth and direct the viewer's eye to the cottage—the off-center focal point of the composition. Tiffany often used commercially manufactured Kokomo glass, made in Indiana, in his windows because it contained all the design effects he desired, as can be seen in the colorful meadow in the lower right corner. Blown, sheet, and pressed glass was made at his Stourbridge Glass Company (later called Tiffany Glass Furnaces) in Corona, Queens, and supplied to Tiffany Studios in New York. It was there that he introduced Favrile glass, a type of iridescent glass with which his name would become synonymous and which he trademarked in 1894.

No records remain to specifically identify the designer who produced *The Thomas Lynch Tiffany Window*, as most designers of windows made by Tiffany Studios remained anonymous, with only the studio mark to indicate manufacturer. At the height of its production, Tiffany Studios employed more than three hundred artisans, many of them women, and it is thought that the Museum's window was designed by Agnes Northrop (1857–1953), referred to as one of "Tiffany's girls."[1] Northrop was a floral specialist who worked in Tiffany's window department beginning in 1884, and her authorship was often acknowledged. She was one of six original workers in the Women's Glass Cutting Department, which was created in 1892; before then, only men were involved in glass cutting. Northrop remained with Tiffany Studios until the firm closed in 1909 and was active as a designer of leaded windows until age ninety-four, just three years before her death.

It was important for the Museum to bring this window back to Greensburg both because of its artistic value as a work by an internationally recognized American artist and because it was commissioned for a home in this city and, therefore, a significant piece of Greensburg's history. Moreover, Thomas Lynch Jr. was a founding member of the Board of Trustees, creating an even stronger connection between the window, the family, and The Westmoreland.

BLJ

1 Martin Eidelberg, Nina Gray, and Margaret K. Hofer, *A New Light on Tiffany: Clara Driscoll and the Tiffany Girls* (New York: New-York Historical Society, 2007), 104–5.

COLIN CAMPBELL COOPER (1856–1937)
Pittsburgh, PA, c. 1905
Oil on canvas, 23 1/8 x 30 ¼ inches
Signed lower right
Gift in memory of Alex G. McKenna, 1996.19
Provenance: Private Collection, Philadelphia, Pennsylvania; Concept Art Gallery, Pittsburgh, Pennsylvania.

Selected Exhibitions: *Born of Fire: The Valley of Work,* Westmoreland Museum of American Art, 2006; Oberhausen, Germany, 2007; Chemnitz, Germany, 2008; and Zabrze, Poland, 2009; *Feuerländer: Regions of Vulcan,* LVR-Industriemuseum, Oberhausen, Germany, 2010.

Colin Campbell Cooper was born in Philadelphia, the son of a wealthy surgeon, Dr. Colin Campbell Cooper, and Emily Williams. His mother, an amateur artist herself, was most likely the impetus behind the young Cooper's interest in art, but additional inspiration came from viewing the art at Philadelphia's Centennial Exposition of 1876. He studied at the Pennsylvania Academy of the Fine Arts beginning in 1879 with the great American realist painter Thomas Eakins (1844–1916), and continued his studies at the Académie Julian in Paris, as well as at other art schools in Paris. He met impressionist painter Childe Hassam (1859–1935) in the 1890s, and drew inspiration from the elder artist's expressive paint handling. Cooper spent time in Europe painting figural and architectural subjects for which he drew acclaim; however, many of these paintings were lost in a fire in 1896. Although he taught watercolor for three years at the Drexel Institute in his native city, modern architecture and street scenes became a specialty of Cooper's, and he made his reputation traveling the country painting the modern urban landscape—especially the great skyscrapers of New York City, where he settled in 1898. While living in New York, he and his wife—Emma Esther Lampert (1855–1920), a landscape painter—traveled the world in search of subject matter. Fellow artist Joseph Pennell (1857–1926) encouraged his contemporaries to look both within their country and to one another for inspiration "for the modern rendering of work," and Cooper was one such artist who took his advice.[1] Cooper captured the architectural character of the cities he painted, making him a critical success.

A few of the nationally prominent artists who painted industrial Pittsburgh came to the city for a specific reason. While Cooper's specialty was the architecture of New York City, he presumably he came to Pittsburgh for a Carnegie International exhibition in which his work was included.[2] As a bustling industrial center, Pittsburgh was a natural subject for Cooper, and its powerful visual impact, with its rivers, bridges, steel mills, railroads, and heavy industrial activity, could not be denied. His painting entitled *Pittsburgh, PA*—his only known work of the steel city—is one of the more straightforward and accurate depictions of Pittsburgh at the turn of the century. With an immediacy of paint application, the artist captures the drab and gritty environment that was pervasive at that time. Cooper's vantage point is from a site low on Mount Washington, looking toward the Point, where the three rivers—Monongahela, Allegheny, and Ohio—converge. The Panhandle Bridge, built in 1893 and replaced ten years later, connects the two sides of the Monongahela River. The artist has included the Pittsburgh and Lake Erie (P&LE) station (now Station Square) off to the left of the canvas, and the Oliver and Byers plants—or the "baby plants," as they were referred to—at right. On the far side of the river, the Allegheny County Jail is just visible to the right of the bridge; the spires of St. Paul's Cathedral in Oakland and the main building of Duquesne University can be seen farther to the right, up on the bluff. Jones and Laughlin Steel Works are also shown at the far right.

Cooper's depiction of Pittsburgh is neither idealized nor romanticized but reveals the city's true industrial albeit unseemly nature: steel mills blasting and no fewer than four trains running, adding their smoke to the red-gray sky hanging heavily over the entire scene. In the foreground, we are presented with aging and peeling billboards, the backs of tenements, burned-out buildings, shacks, and a vagrant's tent along the railroad tracks. The artist leads the viewer through this scene with his curvilinear S-shaped composition. With the diagonal curve of the railroad tracks, the eye moves through the immediate

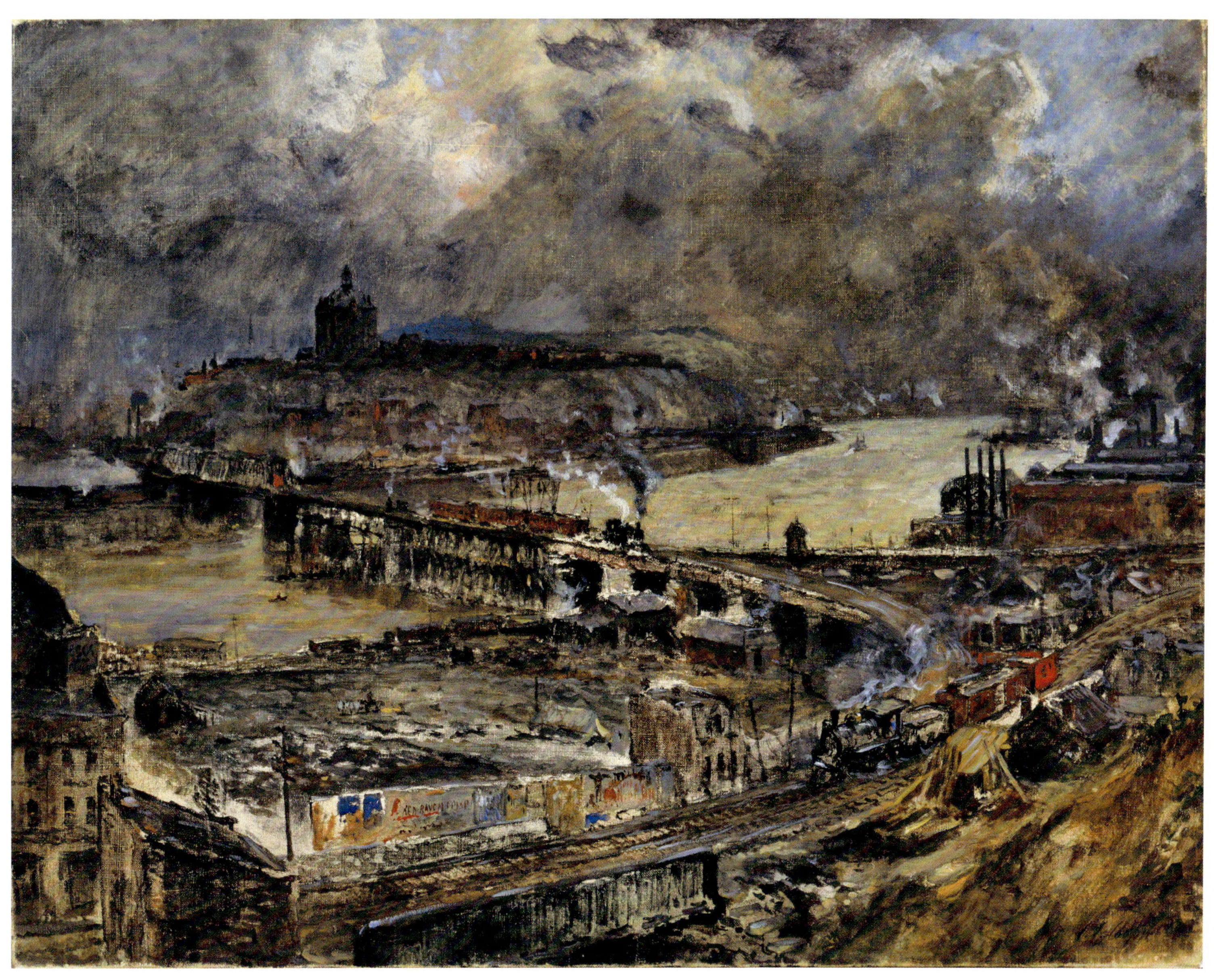

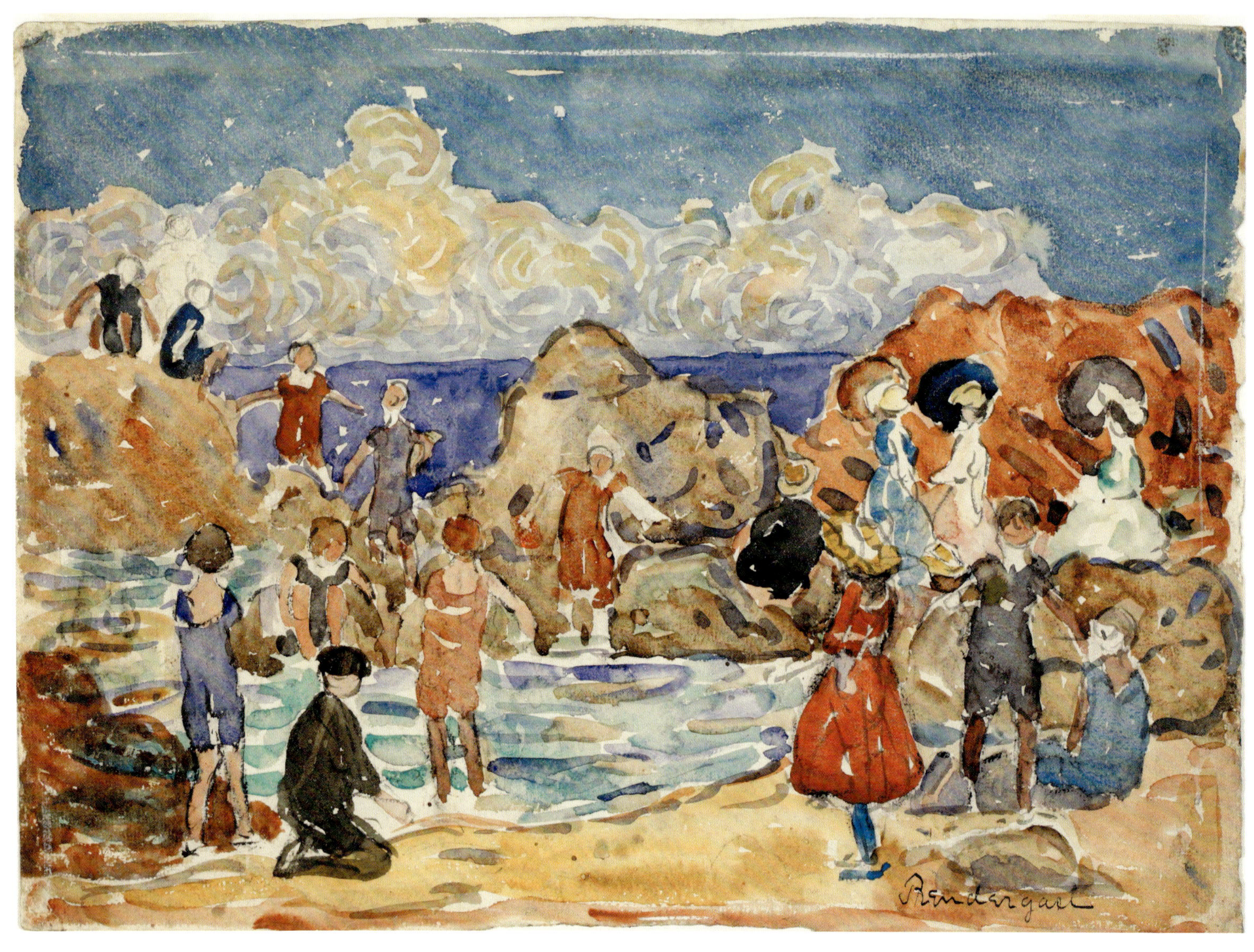

of paint. People enjoying life's pleasures, at leisure or on holiday, and the rhythmic movement of a crowd—in parks, at the beach, or along the boulevards—were his favorite subjects. Painted in vibrant color patches, his scenes come alive with dynamic, visual excitement.

The artist's first solo exhibition, in which he showed forty-two monotypes and twenty-six watercolors, opened in New York at the Macbeth Gallery in March 1900. While a member of the selection committee, Prendergast exhibited seven paintings in the infamous Armory Show of 1913 and was identified by critics as one of the most advanced American modernists in the exhibition. His artistic career, however, did not really take off until 1915, when his first comprehensive exhibition was held at the Carroll Galleries. Consisting of sixty oils and watercolors all painted within the last eight years, the exhibition was a tremendous success, resulting in a large number of sales, with dozens of paintings sold to prominent collectors John Quinn (1870–1924) and Albert C. Barnes (1872–1951). That same year, Quinn commissioned Prendergast to paint two mural-sized paintings, *Promenade* (7 x 11 feet, Detroit Institute of Art) and *Picnic* (7 x 10 feet, Carnegie Museum of Art). The artist's style continued to evolve, and during his final phase, dating from about 1918 onward, his figures grew larger and his outlines became heavier and darker, further containing the movement of his figures.

Bathers, St. Malo is an exceptional watercolor that contains the simplification of form, flat areas of vibrant color, and dynamic surface pattern that were the artist's hallmarks. The composition pulsates with bold color and the lyrical movement of curving lines that form the contours of his many figures. Line becomes color, and the two combined result in a unified, harmonious whole. The Westmoreland's painting can be dated from the period between 1907 and 1909 because of its similarity in style to those shown in the exhibition of the Eight. Prendergast had seen the important Paul Cézanne (1839–1906) exhibition of watercolors in Paris in 1907, and it was Cézanne whom he credited as the most influential to his own work. In this painting, he captures the brightness of the coastal sunlight and the activity of the figures moving through the idyllic scene in long fluid strokes of color. This technique, also evident in the great swirls of clouds in the sky, links the St. Malo painting with that of the French modernists. While his early work owed much to the impressionists, from about 1910, his mosaic-like pictures share a closer relationship to the post-impressionists and the fauves. With its red tonality, simply incised flower pattern, and tarnished gold leaf, the hand-carved frame—believed to have been made by his brother Charles—is in perfect harmony with the color palette of the painting.

The Westmoreland's painting came to the Museum as a gift of Dr. Walter Read Hovey (1895–1981), one of fifteen works of art that he donated in 1978. An art historian who was a member of the Museum's founding Board of Trustees, he was the founder, a professor, and chairman of the Henry Clay Frick Department of Fine Arts at the University of Pittsburgh and served as director of the Henry Clay Frick Arts Building. Hovey was a painter himself, painting landscapes and seascapes on Cape Cod.

With the exception of a few watercolors, Prendergast made very little work after 1922 due to failing health. Maurice died on February 1, 1924, at the age of sixty-five. Margaret Breuning wrote about Prendergast seven years after his death for the Whitney Museum of American Art's American Artists Series, saying that he created "a world of his own, a world of lyrical beauty—gay movement, flickering light, scintillating color woven into exquisite harmonies—where 'unheard melodies' echoed and still echo."[2]

BLJ

1 Letter from Maurice Prendergast to Charles Prendergast, June 13, 1907, quoted in *Maurice Prendergast: Art of Impulse and Color* (College Park: University of Maryland, 1976), 54.

2 Margaret Breuning, *Maurice Prendergast*, American Artists Series (New York: Whitney Museum of American Art, 1931), 8.

JOSEPH PENNELL (1857–1926)
Pittsburgh No. 1, 1909
Etching on paper, 8 ¼ x 11 1/8 inches
Signed and dated in plate lower left
Gift of the Dorothy Lauer Davids Memorial Fund, 1982.19
Provenance: Childs Gallery, Boston.

Selected Exhibitions: *Born of Fire: The Valley of Work*, Westmoreland Museum of American Art, 2006; Oberhausen, Germany, 2007; Chemnitz, Germany, 2008; and Zabrze, Poland, 2009.

One of America's master printmakers and leading illustrators, Joseph Pennell spent nearly fifty years perfecting his technique, resulting in the production of over 1,500 drawings, etchings, lithographs, and mezzotints. Born on the fourth of July in Philadelphia in 1857, the only son of Quaker parents Larkin Pennell and Rebecca A. Barton, Pennell began drawing from his own imaginary stories at the age of four.[1] He got his first art instruction from his father, and later attended the Germantown Friends School in the Philadelphia suburb where his family had moved in 1870. The painter James Reid Lambdin (1807–1889) taught drawing classes there and awarded Pennell first prize for a drawing of a house in his neighborhood. Following his graduation in 1876 (the first boy to graduate), Pennell applied to but was rejected from admission to the Pennsylvania Academy of the Fine Arts (PAFA), so he took a job as a clerk for the Reading Coal and Iron Company during the day and attended the School of Industrial Design (now the Philadelphia Academy of Fine Art) at night. Expelled for non-attendance, he was subsequently accepted at PAFA in 1879, but left after being harshly criticized by his Life Class instructor, Thomas Eakins (1844–1916). Pennell learned to etch from the artist Stephen J. Ferris (1835–1915), who invited him to become a member of the Philadelphia Society of Etchers when it was founded in 1880.

Pennell appeared on the art scene during the golden age of illustration in America, when such leading illustrators as Howard Pyle (1853–1911) and Edwin Austin Abbey (1852–1911) were at work, and magazines including *Godey's*, *Scribner's*, and *Harper's Weekly* prospered. His first commission—illustrations of historic Germantown—was from the Historical Society of Pennsylvania, which published his drawings in its *Pennsylvania Magazine of History and Biography* between 1879 and 1881. By 1882, he was earning an income as an illustrator for the new *Century Magazine* (formerly *Scribner's*). In fact, he met his future wife, Elizabeth Robins (1862–1952), when he was commissioned to make drawings for an article she was writing on Philadelphia buildings. The article was published in 1882, and the two were married just two years later. Together they authored two books, *The Life of James McNeill Whistler* (1911) and *The Whistler Journal* (1921). James A. M. Whistler (1834–1903) became Pennell's friend and mentor when he and Elizabeth lived in London. Although Pennell never studied with Whistler, he frequently acknowledged, "He is and always will be my master—the master of the modern world, the master who will endure."[2] In keeping with Pennell's own artistic philosophy, Whistler "glorified the things about him, the things he knew."[3] Pennell was elected an associate of the National Academy of Design in 1907, achieving full academician status in 1909. The artist's lithographs of the Grand Canyon and Yosemite, made between 1912 and 1915, were purchased by the Uffizi Gallery in Florence, the first such purchase by that venerable institution. Pennell lectured at the National Academy of Design and taught classes in etching and lithography at the Art Students League from 1922 to 1926.

Pennell was a prolific artist and writer, annotating his prints with vivid descriptions of the sites depicted. His prints represent his interest in a broad range of subject matter—cities, factories, steel mills, the Panama Canal, bridges, stockyards, major monuments, and landmark architecture from around the world. Etching and lithography were his printmaking methods of choice, both of which effectively translated his exemplary draftsmanship to paper and allowed him to achieve the atmospheric qualities he felt best represented each subject.

Pennell was fascinated with the "wonder of work" all his life. When he was just twenty-one, Pennell knew the path his career would take: "Even then I knew what I wanted to do, but had no idea that—with certain breaks—all my life would be given to the Wonder of Work—the work that is all about us, the most wonderful thing in the world."[4] From 1881 to 1915, the artist was on a mission to create *Pictures of the Wonder of Work*. Published in 1916, the book contains a series of drawings,

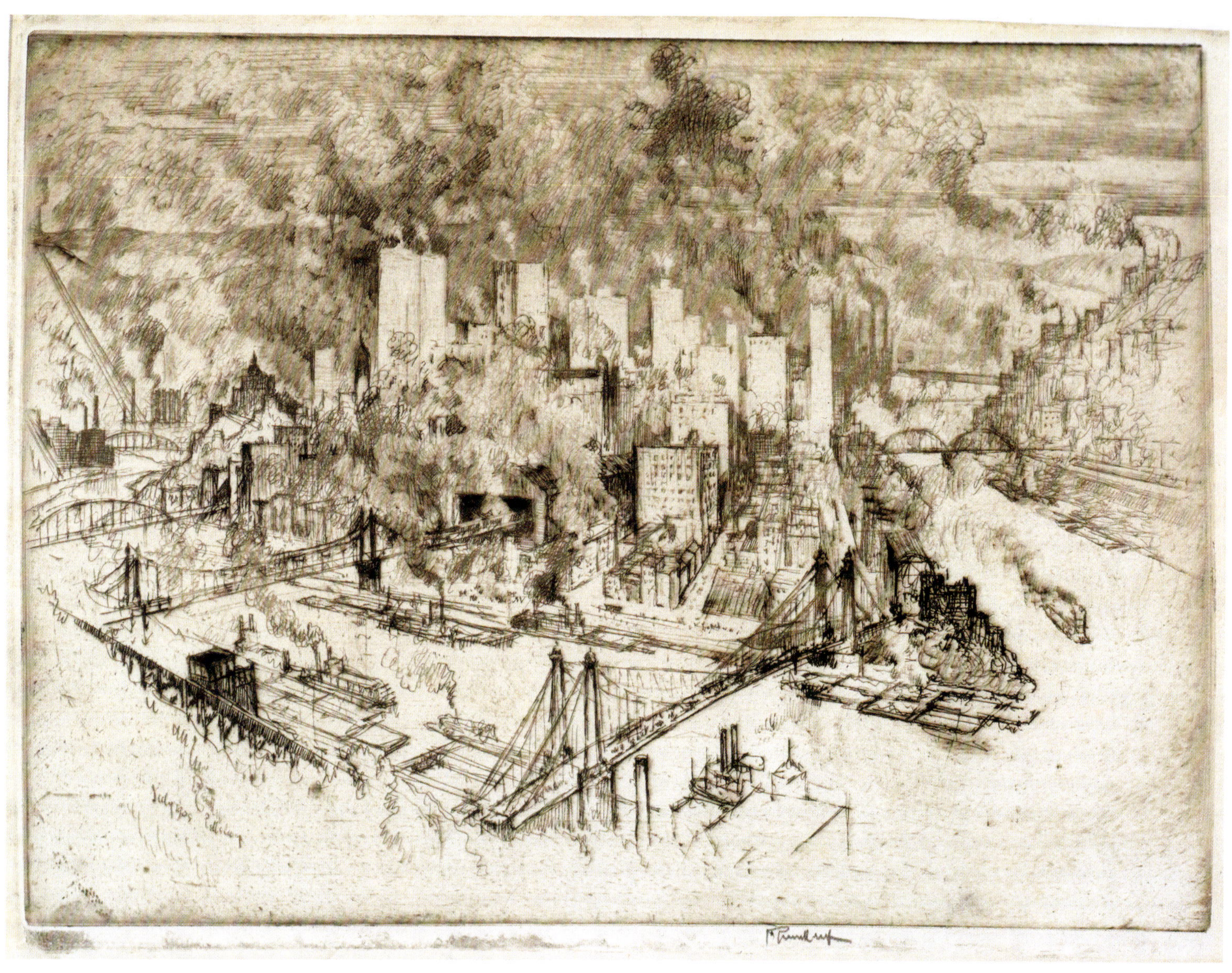

FREDERICK CHILDE HASSAM (1859–1935)
The Outer Harbour, 1909
Oil on canvas, 28 x 26 ½ inches
Signed and dated lower right
Gift of the Mary Marchand Woods Memorial Fund, 1964.1
Provenance: Private Collection; Hirschl & Adler Galleries, Inc., New York.

SELECTED EXHIBITIONS: *Childe Hassam 1859–1935*, Hirschl and Adler Galleries, Inc., New York, 1964; Butler Institute of American Art, Youngstown, Ohio, 1964; The Henry Gallery, University of Washington, Seattle, 1980; *Impressionism: An American View*, Westmoreland County Museum of Art, 1983; Adelson Galleries, Inc., New York, 1999; Meredith Long & Company, Houston, Texas, 2000.

Known as one of America's foremost impressionist painters, Frederick Childe Hassam was born in Dorchester, Massachusetts, into a deeply rooted New England family, the son of a Boston antique collector. While still in high school, he worked in a wood engraver's shop and made illustrations for *Harper's*, *St. Nicholas*, *Scribner's*, and *Century* magazines. While studying at the Lowell Institute and the Boston Art Club, Hassam was introduced to plein air, or open air, painting. Hassam made his first trip to Europe in 1883 and his second in 1886, when he settled in Paris for three years, studying at the Académie Julian with Gustave Boulanger (1824–1888) and Jules Lefebvre (1836–1911). The predominant style of impressionism had its effect on the young artist—he was in Paris when their final exhibition was held in 1886—and his palette brightened and sunlight became an expressive tool. After winning a bronze medal at the Paris Universal Exposition of 1889, he returned to the United States and settled in New York City. There he refined his earlier, more subdued tonal palette to incorporate the impressionist technique of high-key color and flickering brushwork into the life of the city as his subject. New York was a bustling metropolis, and Hassam set out to record his new urban environment and many of its landmarks.

Hassam maintained a studio in the city, but like many of his contemporaries, he vacationed in New England during the summer months, spending time in Gloucester and Provincetown, Massachusetts, and at artist colonies in Cos Cob and Old Lyme, Connecticut. But for Hassam, his favorite summer retreat was Appledore Island, located at the center of a group of tiny, rocky islands known as the Isle of Shoals in the Atlantic Ocean, off the Maine–New Hampshire coast. There he painted waves breaking against huge rock formations from all possible angles and at all times of day, celebrating his love of nature and the New England coastline. With his wife, Maud (Kathleen Maud Doane, 1862–1946), Hassam began visiting the island in 1886 and became a regular at Appledore House, owned and operated by the Laighton family, who advertised it as the "ideal summer resort" with "No noise. No dust. No trolleys."[1] Their daughter, Celia Laighton Thaxter—a poet and gardener, and the subject of many of the artist's paintings, held cultural salons at the hotel, which became a gathering place for a distinguished group of artists, writers, actors, and musicians who summered there. *In the Garden*, (1892; Smithsonian American Art Museum), with Celia poised in her glorious flower garden on the island, is one of Hassam's most renowned works. Hassam produced watercolor illustrations for Celia's book *An Island Garden*, which was published just before she died in 1894.

As Thaxter's garden fell into disrepair after her death, Hassam turned his attention to the island's rocky coast as his subject. *The Outer Harbour* dates from the prime of Hassam's painting career and shows his interest in light, brilliant color and a painterly brushstroke. The almost square format, the high perspective from which the harbor is viewed, and the grand expanse of ocean beyond combine to make it a modern and dramatic scene, giving the illusion that Appledore was completely isolated in the ocean, when in fact it was relatively close to the mainland. His use of sunlight and built-up impasto pigment with myriad daubs and dashes of vibrant color demonstrate his mature understanding and handling of the impressionist and postimpressionist techniques. While his canvases look as if they were quickly dashed off, the artist in fact labored over his work, often entirely reworking a painting until it satisfied him. Filled with light and air, the warmth of the atmosphere radiates through a shimmering rainbow of colors. Broken brushwork creates a prismatic effect, further

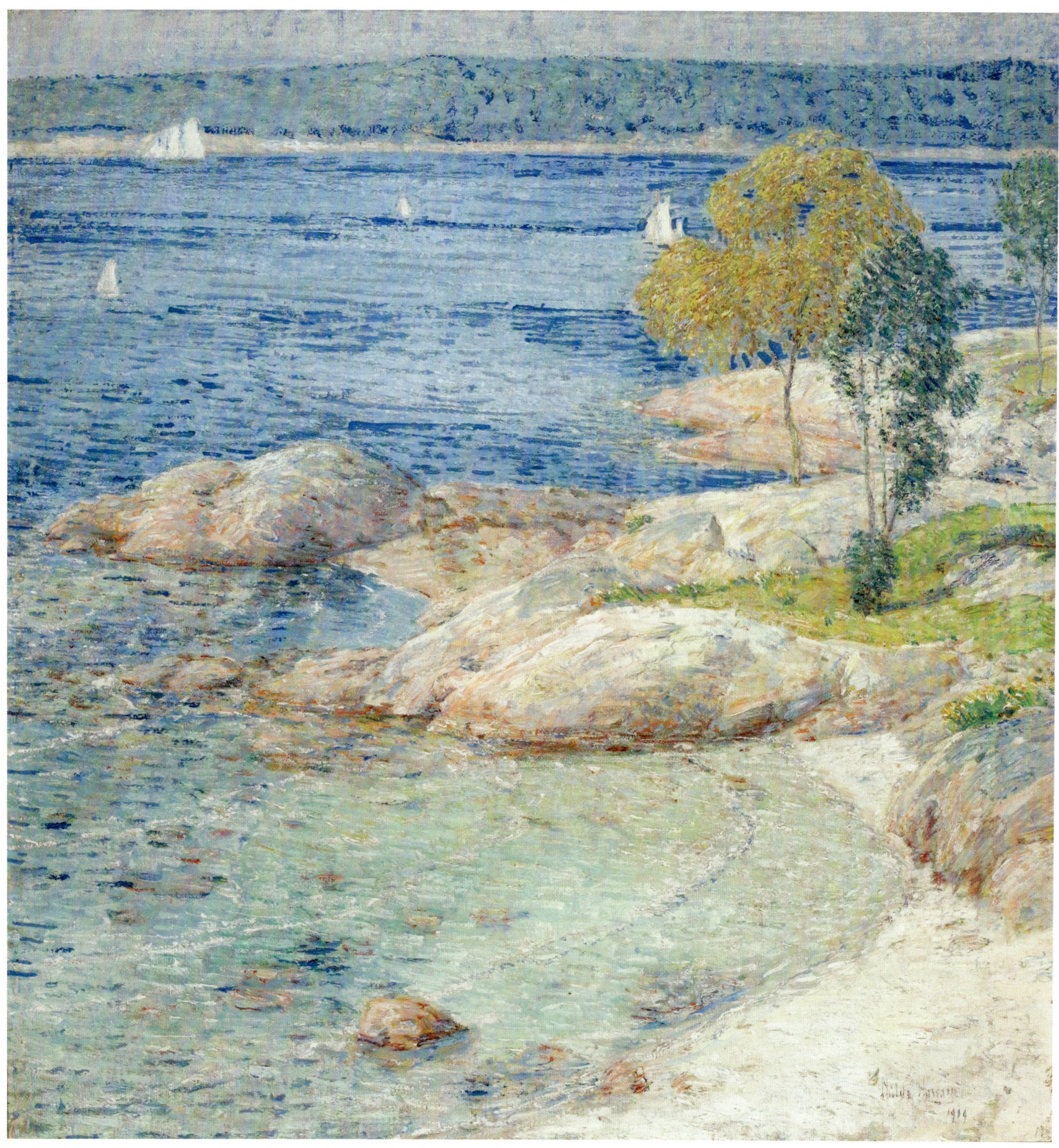

animating the surface.

Hassam is especially well-known for his series of twenty-five flag paintings, created between 1916 and 1919 that both commemorate the United States and its allies during World War I and reveal his patriotism and support of the war effort. Over his lifetime, the artist worked in oils, watercolor, and pastels, turning to the printmaking medium in 1915, through which he created etchings and lithographs of the same cityscape, landscape, and figural subjects he had incorporated in his paintings. The staccato marks made with his etching needle replicate the flickering brushwork of his oils. The Westmoreland owns twenty-two works of art by Hassam, twenty-one of which are etchings created between 1915 and 1933.

Hassam enjoyed a long and lucrative career. In 1897, with fellow impressionist Julian Alden Weir (1852–1919), he co-founded Ten American Painters—an organization of leading impressionist painters known as "the Ten," who exhibited together annually between 1898 and 1919. As members fell away from the group, other painters would be invited in to maintain the group's number at ten. He was also a founding member of the New York Water Color Club in 1889 and was elected its first president in 1890, a post he held for six years. He was elected an associate member of the National Academy of Design in 1902, achieving full academician status in 1906. Carnegie Museum of Art in Pittsburgh owns fifty-six works of art by Hassam, acknowledging the artist's long relationship with the museum, which began with his participation in the first Carnegie International in 1896.

Although Hassam detested modern art, he showed six paintings at the infamous International Exhibition of Modern Art at the New York Armory in 1913. The impressionist style he favored had fallen out of fashion, yet he continued to paint, win prizes in exhibitions, and earn a living from his work until his death twenty-two years later. During his lifetime, Hassam won almost every honor and prize available to him, but his most honored tribute was his election to the American Academy of Arts and Letters in 1920. When he died in 1935, he bequeathed more than four hundred of his works to the Academy to be sold and the proceeds used to create "The Hassam Fund," to purchase the work of living North American artists to be given to museums in the United States and Canada.[2] Jules Kirschenbaum's (1930–2000) painting *The Portrait of My Father* (1959.95) came to The Westmoreland as a gift through the The Hassam Fund in 1959.

BLJ

1 Stephen May, "An island garden, a poet's passion, a painter's muse," *Smithsonian Magazine,* December 1990, 71

2 "Art Fund Created By Hassam's Will," *New York Times,* November 13, 1935: 18.

PAUL WAYLAND BARTLETT (1865–1925)
Peace Protecting Genius (central group from *The Apotheosis of Democracy*), modeled 1911–1914; carved in marble 1914–1916; cast 1927–1931?
Bronze with brown patina, 56 inches high
Signed "SKETCH PWB" on base lower left,
"Fondrie Cooperative Des Artistes, Paris" on base lower right
Gift of Mrs. Armistead Peter III, 1959.27
Provenance: The Artist; Mrs. Armistead Peter III.

SELECTED EXHIBITIONS: *Memorial Exhibition of the Works of Paul Wayland Barlett,* The American Academy of Arts and Letters, New York, 1931; *Paul Wayland Barlett Retrospective,* The Corcoran Gallery of Art, Washington, D.C., 1943–1944; Beaver Junior Women's Club, Beaver, Pennsylvania, 1962.

The son of sculptor, teacher, and critic Truman H. Bartlett (1835–1923), Paul Wayland Bartlett became one of the leading sculptors in the United States and France. Introduced at a young age to the avant-garde of Europe by his father, Bartlett enrolled at the École des Beaux-Arts in Paris at the age of fifteen, the youngest American student there. He also studied in the atelier of renowned animal sculptor Emmanuel Frémiet (1824–1910) and with Auguste Rodin (1840–1917). In his sculptures, whether of human or animal figures, Bartlett remained true to nature and created accurate, detailed depictions of his subjects; and yet his lively, modeled surfaces are expressive forms on which the play of light and shadow reveal the sculpture's emotional content.

Bartlett owned his own foundries in Paris and the United States in which he conducted extensive research on casting methods and patinations. He was involved in every detail of the work, from its creation in the studio to its casting in the foundry. He kept meticulous notes on his experiments for patina colors and, through his thorough investigations, revived interest in color patination techniques and the *cire perdue,* or lost-wax process, of casting bronzes. He kept an eighty-page notebook in which he documented his methods, procedures, and observations, which continues to offer insight into these techniques[1] The color effects that Bartlett achieved on the surfaces of his sculptures by varying the hues of his patinas from blue-green to red to brown-black lend them their expressive quality. His variation of color patinas is fully represented in The Westmoreland's collection.

Bartlett designed numerous public monuments, including three figures for the Main Reading Room of the Library of Congress in Washington, D.C. (1890); General George McClellan for Fairmount Park in Philadelphia (1898–1912), a collaboration with John Quincy Adams Ward (1830–1910) that was never executed; General Joseph Warren (1898–1904) for the city of Roxbury, Massachusetts; the Genius of Man for the Pan-American Exposition in Buffalo, New York (1901); and heroic personifications of Philosophy, History, Romance, Religion, Poetry, and Drama for the attic of the Fifth Avenue façade of the New York Public Library (1908–1916). But it was his equestrian statue of the Marquis de Lafayette, given to France as a reciprocal gift by the United States in return for Frédéric Auguste Bartholdi's (1834–1904) *Statue of Liberty* in 1888, that endeared him to the French people and earned him a substantial reputation as a sculptor of public monuments. The sculpture, which took Bartlett nine years to complete, was installed in the gardens of the Louvre in June 1908.

That year Bartlett was summoned back to the United States from his Paris studio to assist with the pediment of the New York Stock Exchange. At age seventy-seven, John Quincy Adams Ward was unable to complete such a large commission, so Bartlett was chosen to execute the full-size models from Ward's classical design. Because it was not his design, Bartlett conformed his own expressive style to that of the elder artist. Within a year, however, he would be awarded the commission to create his own design for the pediment of the House of Representatives wing of the United States Capitol. The pediment had been empty since the Capitol expansion of the south wing was completed in 1857, and during a period of fifty-four years, eleven other prominent sculptors were invited to submit designs before Bartlett was finally selected in 1909.[2]

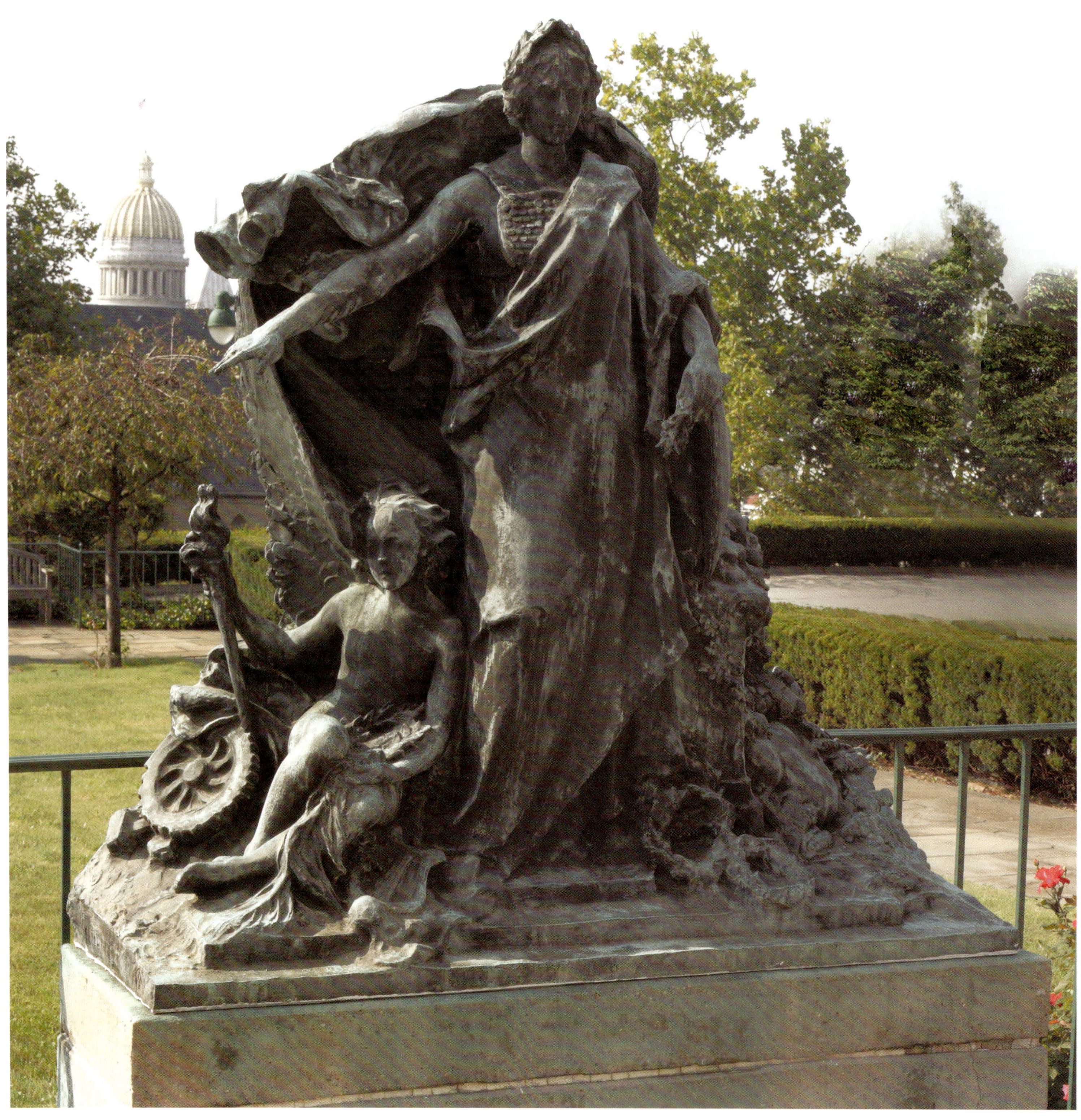

The central pediment of the Capitol had been designed by Luigi Persico (1791–1860) and depicted the personifications of America, Hope, and Justice. Thomas Crawford (1813–1857) designed the Senate wing pediment, reenacting the progress of American civilization. The Congressional Committee mandated that the House pediment be familiar and recognizable to the American people and represent them flourishing "under the benevolent and watchful aegis of a peaceful democracy."[3] For his design entitled *The Apotheosis of Democracy*, Bartlett took inspiration from contemporary American scenes of industry and agriculture.

Peace Protecting Genius is the preparatory sketch for the central group of the House of Representatives pediment. Originally cast in plaster and then carved in marble, this sketch was cast in bronze sometime after the artist's death. The Museum's study is approximately half-scale to the final marble and is virtually identical to the finished pediment, with the exception of a few background details. In both, Bartlett's iconography depicts the personification of *Peace* as a robed woman extending her right arm in a gesture of protection above the head of Genius, a winged child who sits at her feet, holding the torch of immortality. *Peace* wears an armored breastplate, partially exposed by the flowing robe that conforms to her body underneath. Holding an olive branch—the symbol of peace—in her left hand, while her forearm rests on a circular buckler—the symbol of preparedness. On the full-sized pediment, the altar of peace is beside her, and an olive tree stands behind. She is flanked on both sides by figures representing the Power of Labor, with Manufacturing to her right and Agriculture to her left. Breaking waves that reference the Pacific and Atlantic oceans are tucked in to each of the corners. In Bartlett's sketch, a gear and hammers reference the manufacturing side, while fruit and vegetables reference the bounty of agriculture. Light and shadow play a major role in the definition of the figures, which are carved in high relief. Animated in their different poses, they interact with one another across the sixty-foot span. Rather than just presenting frontal views, Bartlett enhanced the three-dimensionality of his figures and their visibility from below by showing side views of them as well, as seen in the figure of Genius, who sits with his upper torso turned to the right, while his knees face front. According to one critic's praise, "Mr. Bartlett has shown, in his work, how sculpture can be modern without ceasing to be monumental, and has pointed out the lines on which American sculpture

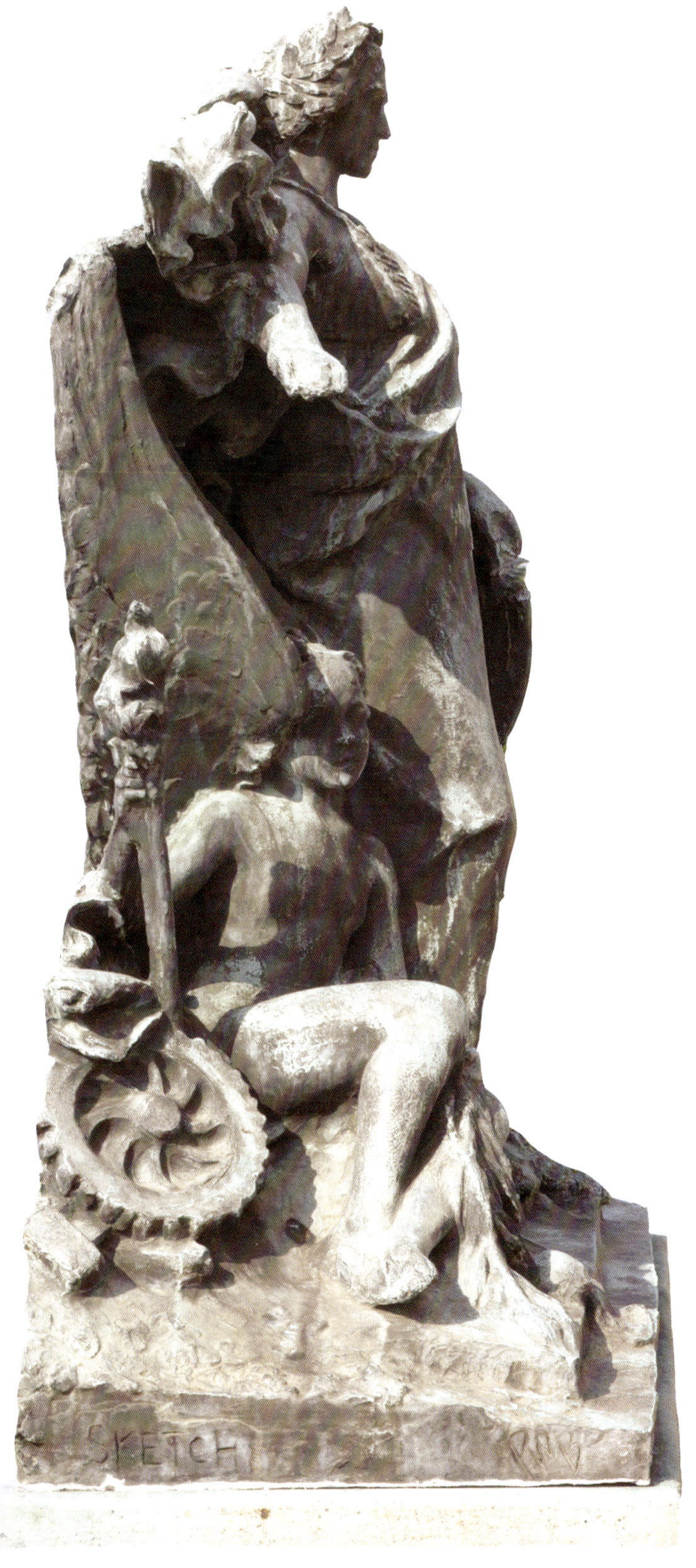

VIOLET OAKLEY (1874–1961)
Unity (Study for International Understanding and Unity: Supreme Manifestation of Enlightenment, Senate Chamber, Pennsylvania State Capitol, Harrisburg), c. 1912
Tempera and gold leaf on panel, 15 5/8 x 19 5/8 inches
Gift of Diana and Peter Jannetta, 2005.28
Provenance: The Artist's Estate; Diana and Peter Jannetta.

SELECTED EXHIBITIONS: Governor's Residence, 1980–1987; *Artists of the Commonwealth: Realism and Its Response in Pennsylvania Painting, 1900–1950,* Westmoreland Museum of American Art, 2006; *Violet Oakley: The Founding of the State of Liberty Spiritual,* Westmoreland Museum of American Art, 2009.

Violet Oakley was an artist, author, and advocate for peace. Born into an artistic dynasty, of which twelve of Oakley's ancestors were artists, she said that her interest was hereditary and that she was "born with a paintbrush in her mouth."[1] Oakley was born in Jersey City and grew up in Bergen Heights, New Jersey, the youngest of three sisters. Suffering from asthma, she did not go to college but stayed at home, copying old masters. When she was twenty years old, Oakley pursued her studies at the Art Students League in New York and briefly in Paris before moving to Philadelphia, where she studied for one semester with Cecilia Beaux (1855–1942) at the Pennsylvania Academy of the Fine Arts. Beaux was the first female instructor at the academy; Oakley would become the second in 1913.[2] Because of the expense, Oakley moved to the Drexel Institute of Art, Science and Industry in 1897, joining her sister Hester to take classes with the gifted illustrator and teacher Howard Pyle (1853–1911). Pyle was a catalyst for a generation of illustrators, including N. C. Wyeth (1882–1945) and Maxfield Parrish (1870–1966), who were among his many students. Oakley gained her own reputation as an illustrator, submitting designs to national magazines such as *Century* and *Collier's Illustrated Weekly*.

Together with Jessie Willcox Smith (1863–1935) and Elizabeth Shippen Green (1871–1954), Oakley's earliest exhibition was held in 1898 at the Plastic Club, the first successful women's art organization in the country, established just the year before. Oakley also designed stained-glass windows, but her first mural was for All Angels' Church on West Eighty-first Street in New York in 1900, which would lead to her greatest achievement—the Pennsylvania capitol murals.

In 1901, she rented the Red Rose Inn in Villanova, a suburb of Philadelphia, with Smith and Green, and was joined by a new friend, Henrietta Cozens, who would manage the household for the three artists. Calling themselves the Cogs, an acronym formed by combining the initials of their last names, the four of them, whom Pyle referred to as the Red Rose Girls, lived there until 1906, when Oakley purchased an estate in Mount Airy, a neighborhood in northwest Philadelphia. The group moved and settled in to their new home, naming it Cogslea, their original acronym with the addition of "lea" to reference the property's surrounding meadow. Oakley would remain there for the rest of her life. All three women dedicated their lives to art, living together and supporting each other's work until 1911, when Green married—the only one of the group to do so. As Jessie Willcox Smith put it, "A woman's sphere is as sharply defined as a man's. If she elects to be a housewife and mother—that is her sphere, and no other. Circumstance may, but volition should not, lead her from it. If on the other hand she elects to go into business or the arts, she must sacrifice motherhood in order to fill successfully her chosen sphere."[3]

In 1902, Oakley received the first of her mural commissions for the Pennsylvania capitol in Harrisburg. She was hired by architect Joseph Huston (1866–1940), believing that choosing Oakley would "act as an encouragement of women and the State." This proved a significant milestone in the history of American art, as it was the largest public commission ever given to a woman in the country. Huston had also hired Mary Cassatt, but she withdrew her work after completing two paintings for the Ladies Lounge. Oakley's first assignment was the Governor's Reception Room, taking four years to complete. Eighteen murals constituted her theme *The Founding of the State of Liberty Spiritual,* which illustrated William Penn's commitment to pacifism and religious freedom.

Huston had selected Edwin Austin Abbey (1852–1911) to create the largest number of murals for the building, but when

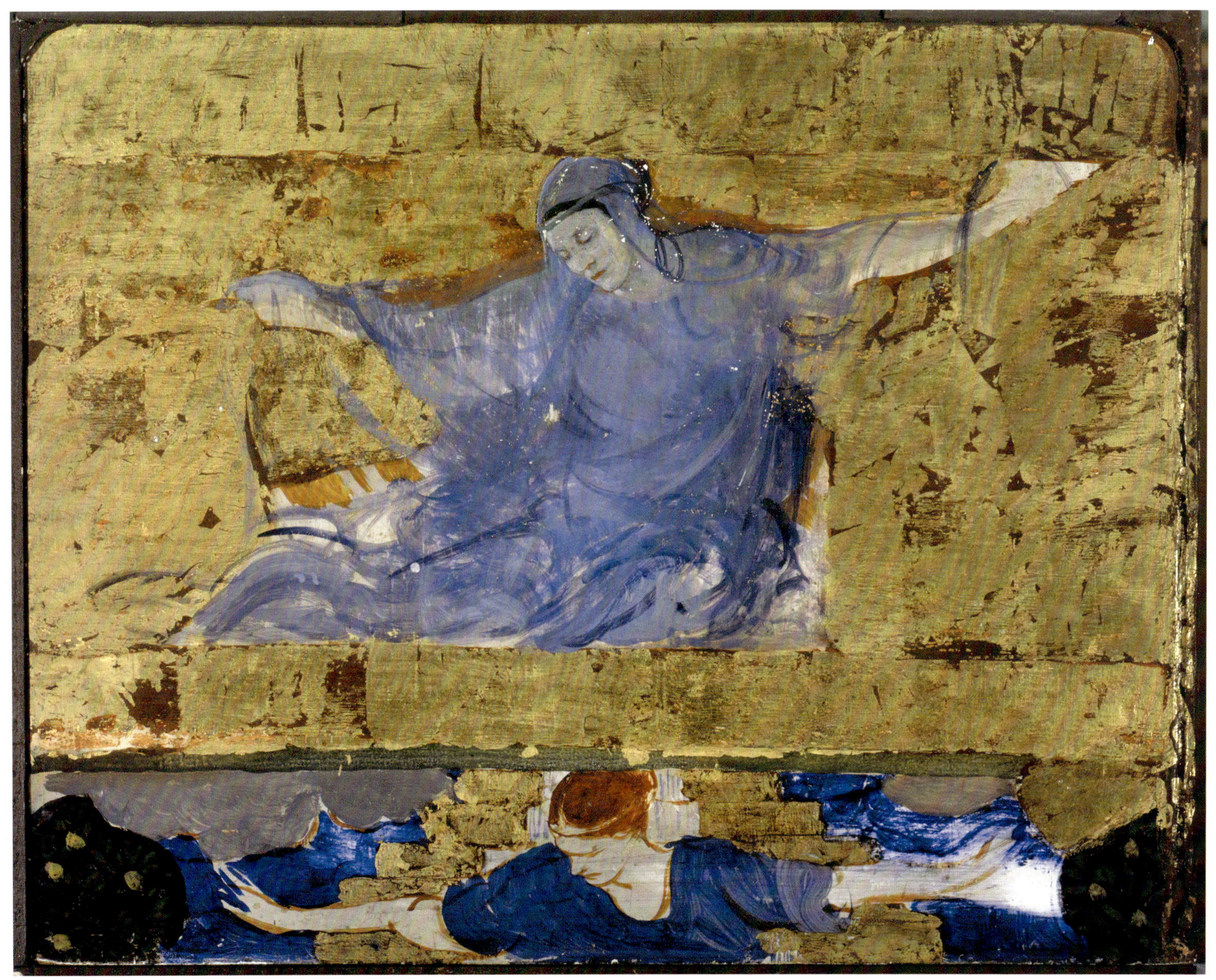

he died unexpectedly in 1911, Oakley was offered the commission and subsequently completed a total of forty-three murals for the capitol—an additional nine for the Senate and sixteen for the Supreme Court. She worked on them almost continuously from 1911 to 1927 and was paid at the same rate that Abbey had been guaranteed, fifty dollars per square foot, or $95,000 to paint the additional chambers.

The Westmoreland's *Unity* is a preparatory study for the central panel of the mural in the Senate chamber. At 9 feet high by 44 feet long, it is dominated by a heroic, allegorical female figure of *Unity*, painted in electric blues to symbolize the waters of life. With outstretched arms, she resolves the atrocities illustrated in panels on either side of her. At right, swords are beaten into ploughshares, prophesying the end of war; at left, slaves of the world are being set free, with a shackle being removed from a woman's ankle.[4] When seven of the murals were unveiled on Abraham Lincoln's birthday in 1917 (February 12), Oakley explained that her work represented the unity of all life, depicting "a world free from war and oppression, united by international cooperation."[5] Ironically, the United States would enter World War I just two months later. When addressing the audience at the dedication of the chamber, Oakley said that the image of Unity came to her in Europe in 1912 while attending a gathering of diplomats from various countries, all of whom were attempting to defuse the impending Balkan conflict: "With striking force came to me messages out of the past, which reached me as I searched, and Lo! I came upon the 'Ideal State,' which was no vain drama, but an actual, historic, rocklike fact. That which so many say 'can't be done,' I found hath already been done."[6] She was referring to William Penn's Holy Experiment of Pennsylvania, the theme she had already addressed in the Governor's Reception Room. Oakley created *Unity* as a testament to the world, a reminder that the power of peace and love is stronger than the power of war. *Unity*, poised in the water of life, is the source of all the unity in the universe. In her remarks, she continued, "I want you to perceive the borders of her garments—the trailing of her veils whenever you look upon the sapphire of the sea . . . when you hear the sound of rushing water she is there; her voice is in the murmuring of the ice floe. She is the witness of dazzling snow; the showers upon the grass; the blue of all the mountains and hills . . . her price is above rubies' for she is the wisdom of Love."[7] Oakley's panel carries an inscription from the Apocalypse: "He carried me away to a great and high mountain and shewed [*sic*] me the Great City and he shewed [*sic*] me a pure river of Water of Life as crystal proceeding out of the throne. The Leaves of the Tree were for the Healing of Nations."[8]

In the Museum's study, the figure of Unity is painted in blue tempera with gold leaf, providing an ornate background for the female figure that floats like a spiritual deity. While small in size, it is powerful in scale, suggesting the strength of the artist as well as the strength of women in general and Oakley's support of the women's suffrage movement.

Violet Oakley lived a long and productive life, one in which she significantly contributed not only to American art, but also to world affairs through her goal of world peace. Her last major mural commission from 1945 to 1949 was for the First Presbyterian Church in Germantown, illustrating *Great Women of the Bible*. Her last public appearance was fittingly made to the United Nations in 1961, when she donated to its library her folio *The Holy Experiment, Our Heritage from William Penn*, which reproduced the paintings from the Governor's Reception Room and Senate. She died on February 25, 1961, at the age of eighty-six, and the epitaph on her headstone, reads simply, "Death Cannot Kill What Never Dies."[9]

BLJ

1 Mahonri Sharp Young, "Violet Oakley: A Message for the World," *American Art and Antiques*, July–August 1978, 51.

2 Beaux was the first woman to be awarded the academy's Gold Medal of Honor in 1898; Oakley was the second, receiving her medal in 1905.

3 Alice A. Carter, *The Red Rose Girls: An Uncommon Story of Art and Love* (New York: Harry N. Abrams, 2000), 52.

4 For more information on the Senate chamber murals, see Pennsylvania Capitol Preservation Committee, *A Sacred Challenge: Violet Oakley and the Pennsylvania Capitol Murals* (Harrisburg: Pennsylvania Capitol Preservation Committee, 2002), 56–79.

5 Patricia Likos, "Violet Oakley," *Philadelphia Museum of Art Bulletin* 75 (June 1979): 7.

6 Pennsylvania Capitol Preservation Committee, *A Sacred Challenge*, 63.

7 Ibid., 65.

8 Patricia Likos, "Violet Oakley," 7.

9 William Penn, *Fruits of Solitude*, The Harvard Classics (New York: P.F. Collier & Son, 1909–14), 127, 128. Oakley is buried in the family plot in Green-Wood Cemetery in Brooklyn, New York.

JOHN MARIN (1870–1953)
Scrub Pine and Rocks, Small Point, Maine, 1915
Watercolor on paper, 16 x 19 inches
Signed and dated lower left
Inscribed verso: Morse Mountain, Small Point, Maine
Gift of Dr. Walter Read Hovey, 1978.99
Provenance: The Artist; An American Place, New York; Downtown Gallery, New York; Dr. Walter Read Hovey, Pittsburgh.

SELECTED EXHIBITIONS: *Contrasts in Impressionism,* Baltimore Museum of Art, 1942; *Pioneers of Modern Art in America,* Whitney Museum of American Art, New York, 1946; *John Marin,* De Young Memorial Museum +, San Francisco, 1949; *Marin, Tobey, Graves,* Contemporary Arts Museum, Houston, 1956; *Forerunners of American Abstraction,* Carnegie Museum of Art, Pittsburgh, 1971–1972; *Paintings and Graphics from the Walter Read Hovey Collection,* Westmoreland County Museum of Art, 1973; *The Gift of Art,* Westmoreland Museum of American Art, 2009.

Born in Rutherford, New Jersey, John Marin was raised by his maternal grandparents and maiden aunts in Weehawken, following his mother's death just nine days after his birth. Marin trained as an architect at Stevens Institute of Technology in Hoboken and worked freelance in that field for several years before pursuing his artistic path. He entered the Pennsylvania Academy of the Fine Arts in Philadelphia in 1899, where he studied for two years with Thomas Anshutz (1851–1912) and Hugh Breckenridge (1870–1937). After further study at the Art Students League in New York from 1901 to 1903, Marin sailed for Europe in 1905, spending the next five years primarily in Paris, but also traveling to Italy, England, Holland, Belgium, Austria, and Germany. Upon his return to America in 1910, he would never again travel abroad.

While in Paris, Marin certainly encountered the avant-garde developments of Paul Cézanne (1839–1906), Henri Matisse (1869–1954), Pablo Picasso (1881–1973), Georges Braque (1882–1963), and Robert Delaunay (1885–1941), which were very much in evidence, but he didn't pay much attention to them. Instead, his early work was inspired by James A. M. Whistler (1834–1903), Paul Signac (1863–1935), and the tonalists. It wasn't until he was back in the United States that he took serious notice of the French modernists through exhibitions of their work at Alfred Stieglitz's Little Galleries of the Photo-Secession at 291 Fifth Avenue—or simply 291, as it was known. In addition to the progressive atmosphere at 291, it was Marin's interaction with American modernists in Stieglitz's gallery stable that provoked his move toward abstraction—artists such as Max Weber (1881–1961), Marsden Hartley (1877–1943), Georgia O'Keeffe (1887–1986), Alfred Maurer (1868–1932), and Arthur B. Carles (1882–1952).

Marin met the photographer Edward Steichen (1879–1973) in France through his friend Carles, who was a fellow student in Philadelphia. Steichen brought Marin's work to Stieglitz's attention and subsequently introduced the two artists. In 1909, Stieglitz exhibited twenty-five of Marin's watercolors in 291's first exhibition of American modernists, paired with fifteen oil paintings by Maurer. This was the artist's first American exhibition. In Paris his work was included in the Salon des Indépendants (1909), and in the Salon d'Automne (1910); the same year as his first solo show in New York, also at 291. From that point on, Marin exhibited annually at 291 until Stieglitz closed the gallery in 1917. Marin and Stieglitz became lifelong friends, the latter supporting Marin by continuing to find him exhibition venues in New York until he opened his Intimate Gallery in 1925 and then An American Place in 1930. As an artist himself, Stieglitz understood the creative impulse and the need for moral as well as financial support.

In 1911, Marin began a series of deftly abstracted scenes of New York that conveyed the frenetic energy of the city, ten of which he exhibited in the infamous Armory Show. Overwhelmed by the force of the ever-changing metropolis, Marin's response to the fast-paced urban environment was conveyed in his paintings of fractured buildings, hectic streets, and bridges. Equilibrium is destroyed in these urban compositions, evoking a topsy-turvy world. Manhattan inspired some of the artist's best-known and most important works, especially his

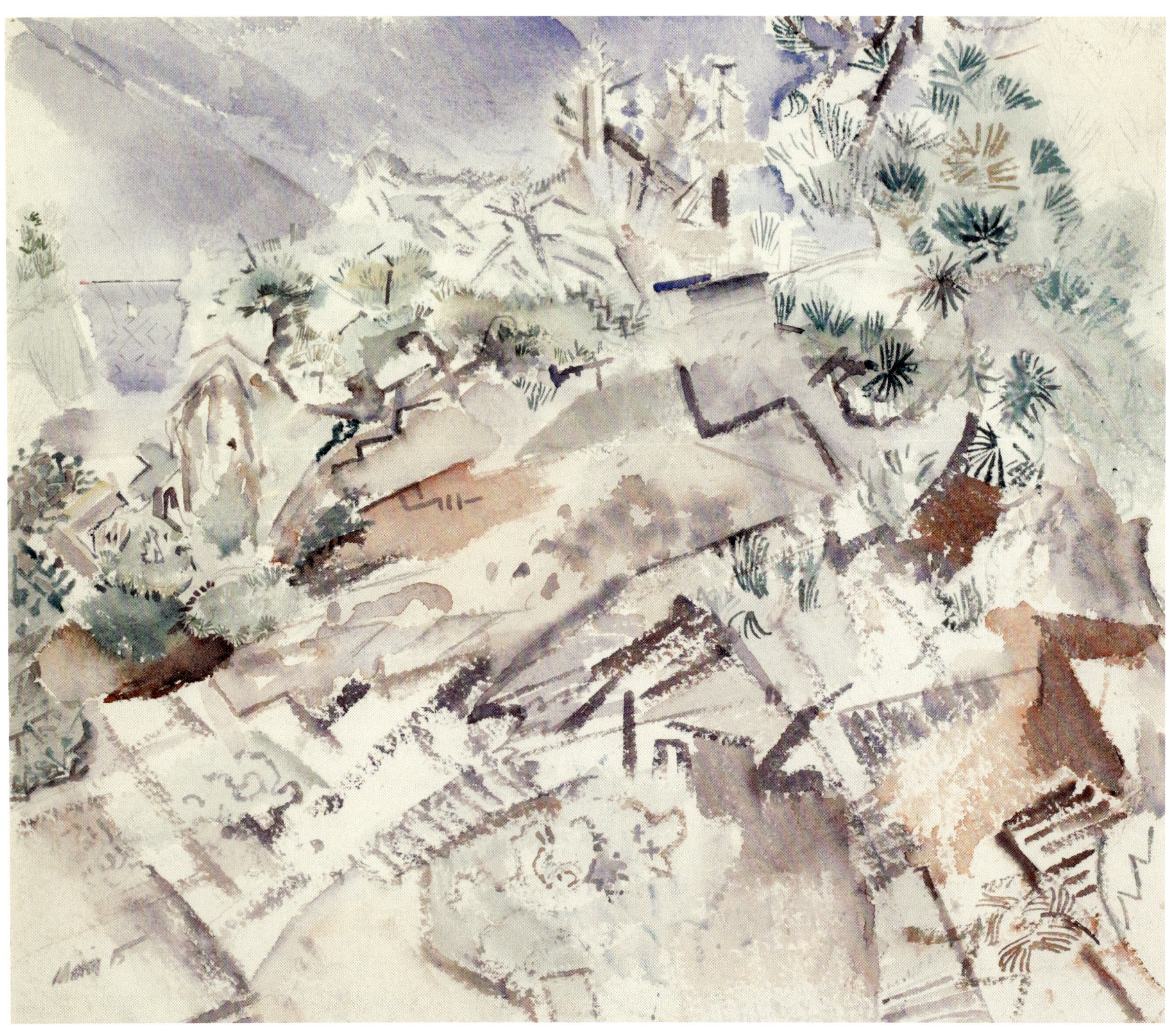

series on the Woolworth Building and the Brooklyn Bridge. According to Marin:

> You cannot create a work of art unless the things you behold respond to something within you. Therefore if these buildings move me they too must have life. Thus the whole city is alive; buildings, people, all are alive; and the more they move me the more I feel them to be alive.[1]

The year 1914 was critical for the artist, marking the moment he discovered Maine where he responded to its dramatic scenery with the same emotion he had for New York. The vitality of the city and the rhythm of the coast would become his primary subjects for the remainder of his career. That summer, he began his series of superbly alive watercolors of the rocky coast; as MacKinley Helm noted, when Marin found Maine, "he found his spiritual home."[2] That year the artist and his pregnant wife, Marie Jane Hughes, whom he married in 1912, summered in Westpoint, a village south of Bath. Their son, John Marin III, was born in November. The following July, the family rented a cottage across the cove near Small Point Beach, where they would spend a total of eight summers between 1915 and 1931. Also in 1915, he purchased an uninhabitable island, which he named Marin Island. With the exception of summer stays in the mountains of Pennsylvania, Massachusetts, New Hampshire, New York, and New Mexico, Marin would spend nearly every summer at four different coastal locations in Maine.[3]

Marin painted The Westmoreland's *Scrub Pine and Rocks, Small Point, Maine* during the summer of 1915. In this watercolor, green hatch marks denote the scraggly scrub-pine trees that were prevalent in the area, while jagged lines suggest Morse Mountain and its rocky terrain. The artist's hand is evident in the thin washes and dense patches of pigment that slowly fade away, while delicate pencil lines still visible underneath the color reveal his initial thought process. The composition builds to a crescendo, architectonically from the base to a central peak, where mountain meets sky. The cream-colored paper becomes an integral part of the whole composition, serving both as negative space and as another color in his palette of blues, greens, and earth tones.

Form, color, and composition in this piece are distilled to essentials, expressive of nature's dynamic forces. In a letter to Stieglitz from Small Point on August 1, 1915, Marin described his new environment: "the rain and the fog, the fog and the rain, torrents, bad roads, mud puddles, high tides and low tides, the bailing out of boats, cold water, you are nearly up to your hips, the dread of the plunge, the shiver of it, oh, but after—oh now I feel bully."[4] The artist wrote about his paintings of this period, explaining: "These works are meant as constructed expressions of the inner senses, responding to things seen and felt."[5]

Marin did not follow any prescribed art movement. His style is a combination of abstraction and representation, a marrying of two opposing forces in early twentieth-century American art. Seen as a precursor to abstract expressionism, he has been referred to as "the single most important bridge between early American modernism and the New York School. In his works, one can follow the rhythm of the hand in his rapid spontaneous brushwork: that gesture enlarged would become the basis for action painting."[6] Signaling his importance, both the Museum of Modern Art and the Whitney Museum of American Art organized large exhibitions of Marin's work in 1936.

Marin is also known for his writings. He and Stieglitz exchanged letters until the latter's death in 1946, many being published in catalogs of An American Place and in *Letters of John Marin* (1931), *The Selected Writings of John Marin* (1949), and *John Marin by John Marin* (1977). After a long and productive career, Marin died on October 2, 1953, in Cape Split, Maine, where he had purchased property in 1934. He was eighty-two years old.

BLJ

1 Larry Curry, *John Marin/1870–1953* (Los Angeles, CA: Los Angeles County Museum of Art, 1970), 10.

2 MacKinley Helm, *John Marin* (Boston: Pellegrini & Cudahy, 1948), 32.

3 Locations Marin lived in Maine: Westpoint, 1914; Small Point, 1915—1917, 1919, 1926—1928, 1931; Stonington, Deer Isle, 1919—1924, 1925, 1928; Cape Split, 1933—1953.

4 Dorothy Norman, *The Selected Writings of John Marin* (New York: Pellegrini & Cudahy, 1949), 21.

5 John Marin, *The Forum Exhibition of Modern American Painters* (New York: Anderson Galleries, 1916), unpaginated.

6 Barbara Rose, *John Marin: The 291 Years* (New York: Richard York Gallery, 1999), 32.

GEORGE BENJAMIN LUKS (1866–1933)[1]
Highbridge Park, not dated
Watercolor on paper, 16 x 19 inches
Signed lower left
Gift of Dr. Walter Read Hovey, 1978.88
Provenance: Kraushaar Gallery, New York; Dr. Walter Read Hovey, Pittsburgh, Pennsylvania.

Selected Exhibitions: *Works of Art From Local Collections,* Westmoreland County Museum of Art, 1962; *Art Since 1900 Privately Owned in the Pittsburgh Area,* Museum of Art, Carnegie Institute, Pittsburgh, 1963; *Paintings and Graphics from the Walter Read Hovey Collection,* Westmoreland County Museum of Art, 1973; *The Gift of Art,* Westmoreland Museum of American Art, 2009.

> It is absolutely impossible to set down on paper any adequate description of [Luks]. He is Puck. He is Caliban. He is Falstaff. He is a tornado. He is sentimental. He can sigh like a lover, and curse like a trooper. Sometimes you wonder over his versatility; a character actor, a low comedian, even song-and-dance man, a poet, a profound sympathizer with human misery, and a human orchestra.[2]

Born the son of central European immigrants in the lumber-mill community of Williamsport, Pennsylvania, Luks was raised in nearby Shenandoah, a coal-mining town. Luks' parents taught him to appreciate the working classes and to enjoy the arts—both of which would later be reflected in his work. His mother's love of music and his own comedic personality combined when he and his older brother toured as the vaudeville team of Buzzey and Anstock in 1885. Although theater did not become his avocation, he would treat his friends to impromptu performances throughout his life, including assuming the persona of Chicago Whitey, a lightweight boxer who existed only in Luks's imagination.

Luks nourished an early love of drawing, and so in 1884, he enrolled at the Pennsylvania Academy of the Fine Arts. Impatient with the tedium and structure of beginning drawing classes, which included drawing from antique casts, he lasted only a month, leaving to go on the vaudeville circuit with his brother. In 1889, he sailed to Germany to study at the Kunstakademie in Düsseldorf, where again the formal structure bored him. Instead of taking classes he toured Europe, going from Germany to France and England, visiting museums and sketching from the masters. Ironically, the young George Luks—who would later think of himself as uniquely American, and who would urge his students not to study the great masters of Europe but the vigorous contemporary life around them—was influenced by two great Dutch artists, Frans Hals (1580–1666) and Rembrandt Van Rijn (1606–1669). The common-man subjects of these artists resonated with the values of his upbringing, and their painterly style attracted him.

Having developed a keen eye and accurate hand, Luks put these to use when he joined the staff at the *Philadelphia Press* in 1894, beginning a ten-year career as a newspaper artist and illustrator. While in Philadelphia, he met fellow artists John Sloan (1871–1951), William Glackens (1870–1938), and Everett Shinn (1876–1953), as well as the charismatic, slightly older painter who would become their mentor, Robert Henri (1865–1929). Meeting at the latter's Walnut Street studio, they became known as the Philadelphia Five. There was great camaraderie among the group—even in their serious discussions of art—and after their critiques, they would stage plays and compose songs with which to entertain one another.

All five eventually moved to New York to pursue their careers. Luks took a job with Pulitzer's *New York World* as an illustrator and cartoonist. There he developed a cartoon called "The Yellow Kid," based on the antics of a street urchin and his pals. He roomed with Glackens, who had encouraged his work in Philadelphia, and together they found the sights and sounds of lower Manhattan a veritable feast for their brushes. They found ready subjects in the small neighborhoods and markets, Luks carrying a sketchpad with him always.

In 1905, Luks painted *The Spielers* (1905; Addison Gallery of American Art, Phillips Academy), an image of two young immigrant girls clasped together in a childish dance, hair flying, mouths laughing, and clearly—despite their abject poverty—enjoying life. It would become one of the images that would make his career and stand as an iconic image in the annals of American painting. It also reflected the kind of subject

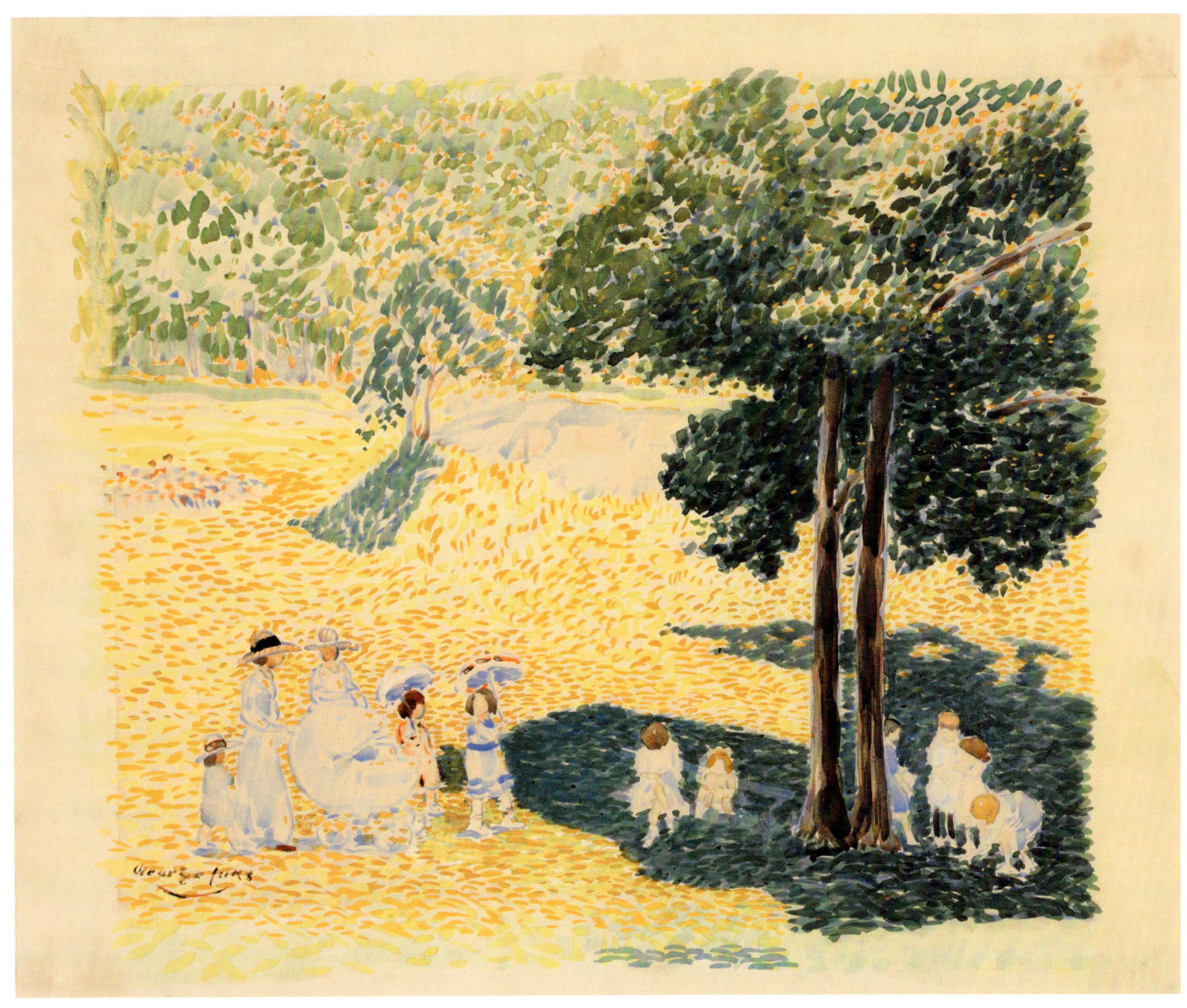

PAUL CORNOYER (1864–1923)
A Rainy Day in the City, c. 1916
Oil on canvas, 32 x 36 inches
Signed lower left
Gift of the Women's Committee, 1977.6
Provenance: Kenneth Lux Gallery, New York.

Selected Exhibitions: Art Club of Philadelphia, 1916; *Recent Acquisitions in American Painting*, Kenneth Lux Gallery, New York, 1977; *A Salute to Pennsylvania's Artistic Heritage*, Pennsylvania Historical and Museum Commission, Harrisburg, Pennsylvania, 1979.

Born in St. Louis, Missouri, Paul Cornoyer attended the city's public schools before moving on to the St. Louis School of Fine Arts. Cornoyer excelled in the academic art program there, encouraged by the school's director, Halsey C. Ives, who also became his friend. From 1889 to 1894, Cornoyer was in Paris pursuing his studies at the Académie Julian, where he studied with Jules Lefèbvre (1836–1911), Louis Blanc (1811–1882), and Benjamin Constant (1845–1902). But rather than the academic foundation he was receiving at the Académie, the major impact on Cornoyer at the time was the prevailing style of impressionism. Scenes in England, France, and Italy reveal his travels through Europe in search of subject matter. Atmospheric street scenes—affected by weather conditions, time of day, and season—fascinated the artist, and he subsequently made a career of translating them in his work. His early style was closer to impressionism, with his use of impasto pigment and broken color, but he later adopted a more subdued tonalist palette that achieves an undeniable color harmony.

While in Paris, Cornoyer exhibited in the 1892 Salon; that same year he won first prize in the American Art Association exhibition. Returning to the United States, he not only won the gold medal of the St. Louis Association of Painters and Sculptors in 1895, but also received a mural commission for the staircase of the Planter's Hotel, describing the founding of the city in 1764. William Merritt Chase (1849–1916), who had purchased one of Cornoyer's paintings when it was exhibited at the Pennsylvania Academy of the Fine Arts in Philadelphia, encouraged the young artist to move to New York, which he did in 1898. Chase's friendship had a profound impact on the developing artist, allowing him to interact with such leading American impressionist artists as J. Alden Weir (1852–1919), John Henry Twachtman (1853–1902), and Childe Hassam (1859–1935). Cornoyer became a member of New York's Salmagundi Club—an organization of the city's artists—and would win many awards there, including its coveted Inness Prize in 1906. The Albright Art Gallery (now the Albright-Knox Art Gallery) in Buffalo, New York, organized a solo show of Cornoyer's work in 1908, and his work was included in the Panama-Pacific International Exposition in San Francisco in 1915. Beginning in 1899, Cornoyer taught at New York's Mechanics' Institute, where he became a respected teacher and mentor to many students. He was elected an associate member of the National Academy of Design in 1909, but he never achieved full academician status.

Cornoyer spent his summer months in Connecticut and Gloucester, Massachusetts, where he taught and painted. His unique impressionist views extended to the harbor and to coastal cityscapes. The artist's best-known works, however, are his intimate scenes of New York City's streets, parks, and buildings, painted in a subdued, tonalist manner. The variety of people who populate his paintings merge with his scenes as they become one with the environment; they are painted not as portraits but as anonymous inhabitants of the neighborhoods he chose, their scale to the tall buildings emphasizing how subordinate they are to the built environment in which they live. Cornoyer's ability at capturing nuances of light—early morning, midday, and moonlight—in combination with fog, mist, rain, or snow, with such a limited color palette was a result of his keen observation skills as well as his passion for portraying the ever-changing moods of the city as dictated by those climatic conditions.

In his cityscape *A Rainy Day in the City*, Cornoyer shows the misty atmospheric effects of the steamy haze rising from the warmed pavement that shimmers in the reappearing sunlight. The storm has passed, umbrellas are put away, and people move along the rain-soaked street that mirrors their passing. The artist presents a dreamlike view of New York's Bryant Park, situated behind the present main branch of the New York Public Library between Fifth and Sixth avenues and

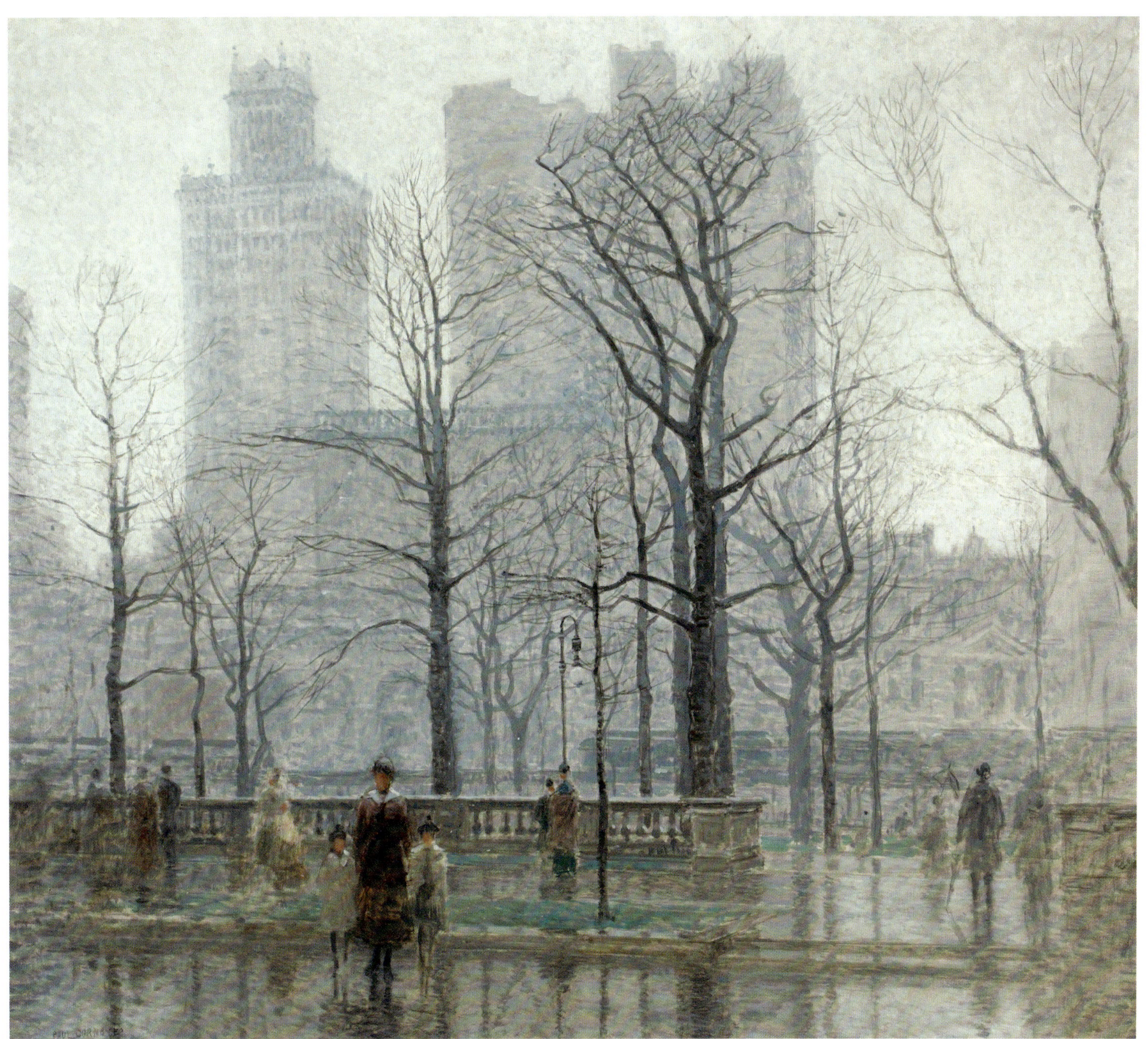

Fortieth and Forty-second streets. From his vantage point on the upper terrace of the library looking toward Sixth Avenue at the southwest corner of the park, Cornoyer records the terrace and its distinctive balustrade in the foreground, the Sixth Avenue Elevated railway running in the middle distance, and a group of ornate buildings in the background. The low, arched building situated in front of the other high-rises is the former Union Dime Savings Bank, built in 1859 on the corner of West Fortieth Street and Sixth Avenue. To its left is the terra-cotta World's Tower Building, erected in 1913 on West Fortieth Street between Sixth Avenue and Broadway. For this composition, Cornoyer has selectively compressed the pictorial space, virtually eliminating the park as it existed between the library and Sixth Avenue, concentrating his attention instead on the manmade as opposed to the natural landscape.[1] Formerly called Reservoir Square and renamed in 1884 following the death of the poet William Cullen Bryant, Bryant Park has a rich history, as the site once held a potter's field, the Croton Distributing Reservoir, and the Crystal Palace Exhibition of the first New York's World's Fair. The reservoir was demolished in the 1890s to make way for the Library, which opened in 1911; and the El was replaced by the Sixth Avenue subway line in 1940. After falling into serious decline, the park was reconstructed in 1933–1934 and to its present state in 1992.

From lower Manhattan to midtown, Cornoyer roamed the streets in search of his preferred subjects. In addition to Bryant Park, his tonalist brush also depicted Madison Square Park, located between Twenty-third and Twenty-sixth streets along Madison Avenue; Columbus Circle at West Fifty-ninth Street; Union Square at Fourteenth Street; and Washington Square in Greenwich Village. Today, the artist's New York work stands as a poetic record of the city's historic architecture, public parks, and picturesque charm of a bygone era.

As the gold plate attached to the frame attests, Cornoyer won Honorable Mention from the Art Club of Philadelphia for this painting in 1916. Founded in 1887, the elegant club was located on South Broad Street and held annual art and architectural exhibitions there until 1940, when patronage suffered and it was forced to close its doors. The distinctive landmark building, which served as a gathering place for the cultural elite—a place where Walt Whitman read his Lincoln poems and Sarah Bernhardt performed—was razed in 1975.[2]

In 1917, Cornoyer moved permanently to East Gloucester, Massachusetts, where he founded the North Shore Arts Association and became acquainted with other artists who visited the area, including John Sloan (1871–1951) and Hugh Breckenridge (1870–1937). Cornoyer continued to paint there, using the picturesque seaside village as his subject, until his sudden death on June 17, 1923, at the relatively young age of fifty-eight.[3]

BLJ

1 With special thanks to Sue Kriete, New-York Historical Society; the New York Public Library Reference Library; Anne Kumer, Bryant Park Corporation; and Dana Jones for their assistance with the identification of this site.

2 Thomas Hine, "To Be Torn Down," *Philadelphia Inquirer,* February 11, 1975.

3 My thanks to Michael Worley for providing the entry on Paul Cornoyer that is included in Richard H. Love and Michael Preston Worley, *Cyclopedia of American Impressionism* (Chicago, IL: R.H. Love Galleries, forthcoming), e-book.

HARRIET WHITNEY FRISHMUTH (1880–1980)
Joy of the Waters, modeled 1917, cast 1920–1971
Bronze, 62 inches
Edition of 44
Signed and dated: HARRIET W. FRISHMUTH SC. 1912 [sic][1]
Foundry mark: GORHAM CO. FOUNDERS
Gift by Exchange, 1990.6
Provenance: Private Collection, New York; Altman/Burke Fine Art, Inc., New York.

Selected Exhibitions: *The Philadelphia Ten,* Art Club of Philadelphia, 1928; Grand Central Art Galleries, New York, 1928; *Garden Sculpture X,* Newhouse Galleries, New York, 1931; *The Philadelphia Ten: A Woman's Artist's Group,* 1917–1945, Galleries at Moore, Moore College of Art and Design, Philadelphia, 1998.

> I have always wished and hoped that anyone who looked at my work would feel a little happier for having done so. My goal was to bring beauty, truth and pleasure into the eye of the beholder.[2]

Harriet Frishmuth was born in Philadelphia on September 17, 1880, to Louise Otto Berens and Frank Beroni Frishmuth. Following her parents' separation in 1888, she moved with her mother and her two older sisters to Europe, where she attended private schools from 1889 to 1894. The family traveled around Europe for much of her childhood, returning for four years to live in Philadelphia with Frishmuth's maternal grandmother. Upon her return to Europe in 1898, Frishmuth reportedly began her artistic career after meeting the American sculptor Lucy Bronson Hinton (1834–1921) while vacationing in Switzerland. As Frishmuth recalled, she was so pleased with her first attempt at a relief sculpture of her mother that she decided to become a sculptor. Frishmuth began her academic training in Paris in 1900, attending an all-women's class at the Académie Rodin, as her mother did not want her daughter in the same class as men. While only there a few months, Frishmuth had direct contact with Auguste Rodin (1840–1917), who critiqued the young sculptors twice a week. When the school closed, Frishmuth continued her studies with Henri Désiré Gauquié (1858–1927) at the Académie Colarossi, then went on to study briefly in Berlin before returning to the United States in 1904. Settling in New York City with her mother, she enrolled in a dissection course for two years at Columbia University and apprenticed with the sculptor Karl Bitter (1867–1915). Continuing her studies at the Art Students League, she worked with sculptors Hermon A. MacNeil (1866–1947) and Gutzon Borglum (1867–1941), and as the latter's studio assistant after winning the Gutzon Borglum Prize. It was Borglum who convinced her to open her own studio in 1908, and it was through him, a Rodin disciple, that she said she drew the most inspiration, garnering much of what would become the trademarks of her work: a strong silhouette, implied movement, and expressive modeling. In 1916, Frishmuth purchased both living and studio space in a converted carriage house and stable at 6 Sniffen Court on East Thirty-sixth Street, where she remained for over twenty years, creating much of her sculptural output as well as taking in some students to supplement her income.

Early in her career, Frishmuth concentrated on making functional objects, such as ashtrays, sundials, bookends, and portrait reliefs of family and friends, but it was the female form captured in motion, often used as garden sculptures and fountains, that would dominate her sculptural expression and become her hallmark. Frishmuth's work surged in popularity during the 1920s—the period of time known as the Roaring Twenties, in which women became free spirits, liberating themselves from the norms of everyday society.

Joy of the Waters is a prime example of Frishmuth's work, employing the elegant form of a nude woman as garden nymph and dancer. Piped as a fountain, this sculpture was intended for either indoor or outdoor use. The idealized female figure was actually derived from a live model, yet it evokes the decorative, curvilinear designs of the Beaux-Arts style along with the streamlined aesthetic of art deco. The artist captures the exuberance and energy of a fleeting moment in time. Her model leaps into the air; the upward thrust of her body, with both arms raised high above her head, her right

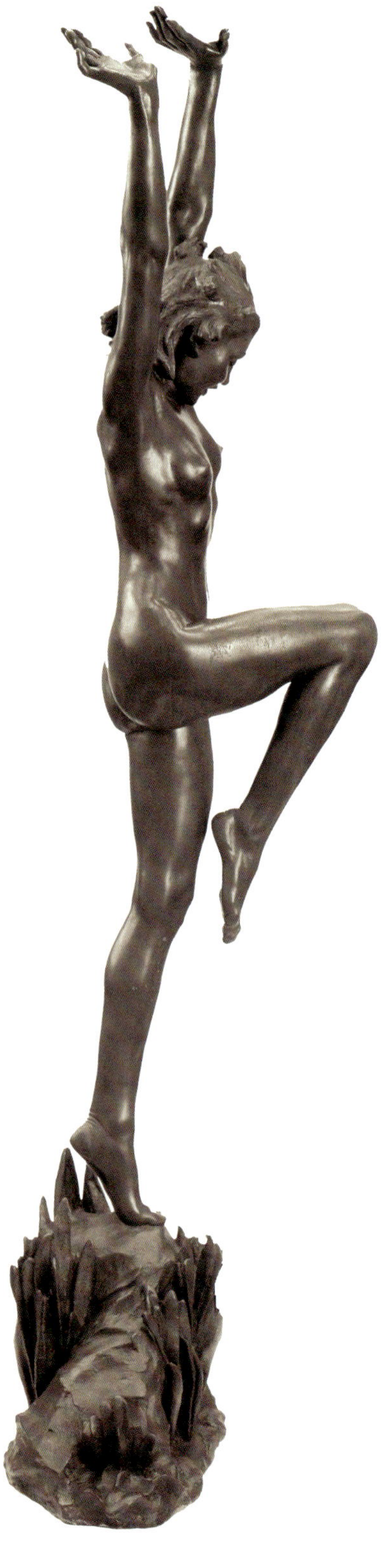

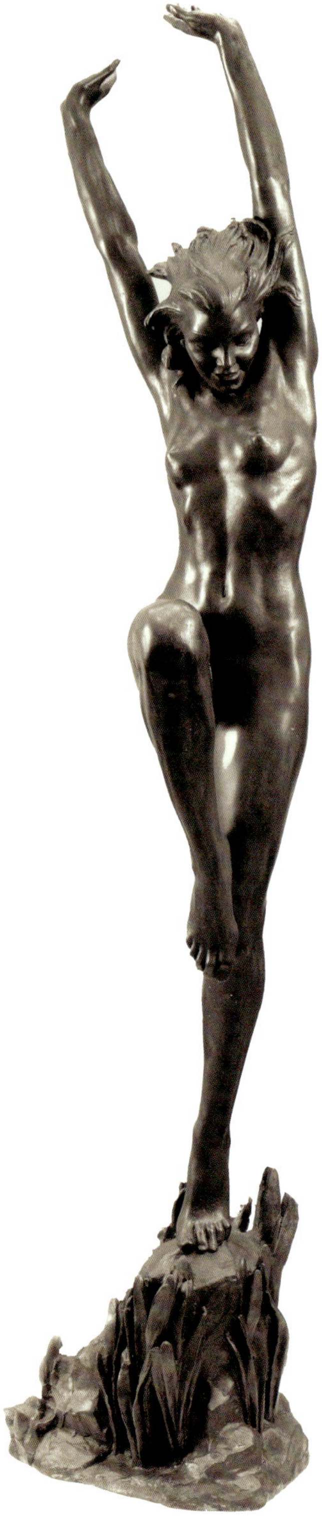

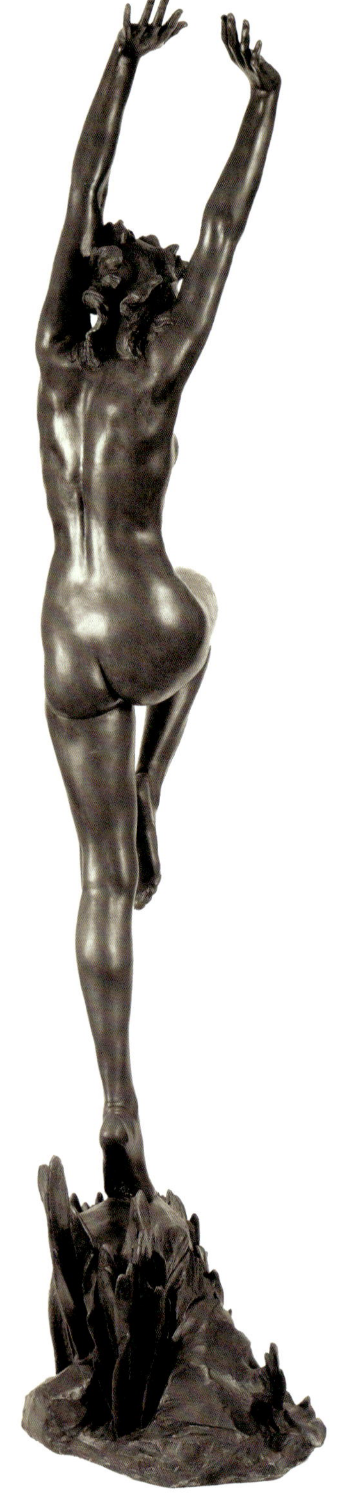

knee drawn up to her waist, and her hair loose and flowing, mimics the motion of the fountain's water as it shoots skyward from the plants that form the base.

Editions of Frishmuth's sculpture were made by the Gorham Company Founders, Providence, Rhode Island, and the Roman Bronze Works, New York, and versions exist in museums throughout the country. *Joy* was made in two versions: 64 inches and 44 inches.[3] While Janette Ransome, a Belgian girl, modeled for the larger version, Frishmuth recounts that it was her favorite model, Desha Delteil (1892–1965)—a ballet dancer whom she met in 1916—who was actually *Joy*'s inspiration. Frishmuth often said that Desha allowed her to sculpt a freer and livelier, more lyrical female form. For her sculptures that were to be used as fountains and in gardens, she chose a green patina that would oxidize naturally over time. The Museum's *Joy* retains only hints of the original green patina, as it has ripened, or darkened, with age, resulting in the rich red-brown that was preferred by the artist.

Reversing her usual working method, Frishmuth modeled the larger, life-size sculpture first (1917) and cast it in an edition of forty-four between 1920 and 1971. She won the Garden Club of America Gold Medal for this version in 1928. The smaller version was made in 1920 and cast in an edition of fifty-four until 1970. Desha posed for this version, one of which was submitted to the National Academy of Design to fulfill her membership requirement when she became a full academician in 1929. The pose of *Joy*'s lower body is nearly identical to another sculpture, *Laughing Waters*, 1929 (2009.23), a recent gift to the collection that now provides the Museum with two fine examples of Frishmuth's working style.

Throughout her career, Frishmuth actively participated in exhibitions around the country, although her first solo exhibition in New York, held at the Grand Central Art Galleries, did not take place until 1928. The artist relocated to Philadelphia in 1937, living there for ten years, and while her sculptural output declined, she continued to supervise the production of her bronzes and exhibit her work. She was a member of the group of women artists known as the Philadelphia Ten from 1939 to 1941, although she had shown with them earlier as a guest in 1928 and 1929. She returned to New York for just four years before moving to Norwalk, Connecticut, with her life companion, Ruth Talcott.

Frishmuth won many awards over the course of her fifty-year career, from her earliest Honorable Mention at the Panama-Pacific International Exposition in 1915 to her latest, a Silver medal from the National Sculpture Society in 1971, when she was ninety-one years old. The artist maintained her prolific career until 1953, when injuries she suffered after falling from a scaffold forced her retirement. In 1973, her patron and friend Charles N. Aronson published *Sculptured Hyacinths* as a tribute to her as an artist of lyric sculpture.[4] Frishmuth was just over nine months shy of her one-hundredth birthday when she died on New Year's Day, 1980, in Connecticut. Always a strong proponent of the Beaux-Arts tradition, Frishmuth was sharply critical of modern art; thus, with the popularity of abstract art came a decline of interest in her work. Fortunately, she lived long enough to see styles change and had the satisfaction of witnessing a revived interest in her work, once again in demand by collectors.

BLJ

1 There is a discrepancy between the date on the base of the sculpture, which clearly reads 1912, and the date when it was first created. According to Leah Lehmbeck, coauthor of *Captured Motion: The Sculpture of Harriet Whitney Frishmuth* (New York: Hohmann Holdings LLC, 2006), Frishmuth recorded in her log book that she paid for models for *Joy* in January 1917, for a plaster sketch in February, and for a plaster cast in May of that year. She did not pay for a bronze until 1920. Lehmbeck believes that stylistically *Joy* belongs with Frishmuth's work of the late teens and that the inscription on the base was most likely applied by a foundry worker rather than by the artist and subsequently a "7" became a "2" in error. My thanks to Leah Lehmbeck for this clarification.

2 Ann V. Masters, "Female Rodin of America: At 87, Harriet Frishmuth Has Laid Aside Sculpture Tools," *Bridgeport (Conn.) Sunday Post*, June 23, 1968, E5, referenced in Janis Conner, Leah Rosenblatt Lehmbeck, Thayer Tolles, and Frank L. Hohmann III, *Captured Motion: The Sculpture of Harriet Whitney Frishmuth* (New York: Hohmann Holdings LLC, 2006), 51.

3 These two sizes were recorded in Frishmuth's order book. The sizes of the versions in the two editions vary slightly, dependant on whether they were cast from the original plaster mold or from a metal pattern that was made later from the plaster, which, due to shrinkage, resulted in a smaller sculpture.

4 Charles N. Aronson, *Sculptured Hyacinths* (New York: Vantage Press, 1973). Frishmuth would denounce this book after its publication.

CHARLES BURCHFIELD (1893–1967)
Coke Oven Homes, 1918
Watercolor on paper, 12 x 26 ½ inches
Signed and dated lower left
Gift of the Women's Committee, 1962.30
Provenance: Kennedy Galleries, New York.

Selected Exhibitions: *Early Watercolors by Charles Burchfield, 1917–1918*, Frank K. M. Rehn Galleries, New York, 1939; Butler Institute of American Art, Youngstown, Ohio, 1964; Henry Clay Frick Fine Arts Department, University of Pittsburgh, 1963, 1966; *Charles Burchfield*, Carnegie Institute, Pittsburgh, 1971; *A Salute to Pennsylvania's Artistic Heritage*, Pennsylvania Historical and Museum Commission, Harrisburg, 1979; *The Gift of Art*, Westmoreland Museum of American Art, 2009.

Artists at work during the first decade of the century—members of the Eight or the Ashcan school of painters—are credited with generating interest in art of the urban landscape, specifically New York City. Edward Hopper (1882–1967) and Charles Burchfield, both students of Robert Henri (1865–1929) and leading painters of the American scene, were lifelong friends and wrote articles for periodicals of the day about each other's work.[1] Hopper described his friend's style: "The work of Charles Burchfield is most decidedly founded . . . on life, and the life that he knows and loves best. From what is to the mediocre artist and unseeing layman the boredom of everyday existence in a provincial community, he has extracted a quality that we may call poetic, romantic, lyric."[2]

Charles Burchfield's "scene" was confined to the rural environs in and around Gardenville, New York, far away from the bustling art center of New York City. He found his greatest inspiration in nature, and when most other artists were working in oil, watercolor became his chosen mode of expression. Using this fluid medium, he conveyed his moods, feelings, memories, and vision. His love of the natural world took root as a child, and as an artist, he celebrated it for a lifetime in his work.

Born in Ashtabula Harbor, Ohio, the fifth of six children, Burchfield grew up in nearby Salem, where the family had moved following his father's death in 1898. He studied at the Cleveland School of Art from 1912 to 1916 with Henry Keller (1869–1949), who was especially influential, and then briefly attended the National Academy of Design in New York, before retreating back to Salem because he disliked the hectic pace of the city. Burchfield served in the army at Camp Jackson, South Carolina, beginning in July 1918, and following his discharge in January 1919, he again returned to Salem. In 1921 he moved to Buffalo, New York, where he worked as a wallpaper designer until 1929. He married Bertha Kenreich in 1922, and the couple moved to the suburb of Gardenville in 1925, where he lived and worked for the remainder of his life.

Burchfield kept personal journals for the better part of his career, and through them one gains access to his daily activities, his observations and experiences in nature, and his thoughts and ideas about his own work over the course of nearly sixty years. According to his son, C. Arthur Burchfield, his father's journals offer "a record of his feelings and thoughts about the subjects of his paintings, expressed with an eloquence that very nearly matched the eloquence found in his art." They afford the public the "opportunity to view an artist's paintings and simultaneously be allowed into his mind through writings that so richly mirror the intense feelings his paintings evoke."[3]

Burchfield loved nature and took great pleasure in expressing the sights, sounds, and smells of each particular time of year. His paintings reflect his moods and memories of specific times and places, and he was particularly attuned to the changing seasons, the variations of weather conditions, and times of day. Whether he was delving into fantasy or translating the natural world, throughout his career his paintings reflect his experiences of the moment. The artist saw the beauty in simple frame houses, tree-lined streets, and surrounding farms of his immediate environment in Ohio and western New York. He translated those forms into his art, evoking through them personality, mood, fantasy, and sometimes the sense of sound.

Coke Oven Homes reflects Burchfield's continued search for ways to express mood in his paintings and anticipates his industrial-themed paintings of the next two years, as well as those that came later, in the 1930s. In his work of this early period, he humanized houses and presented them as expressive visual elements in their own right. They resembled human faces to him, and he tried to capture the unique personality of

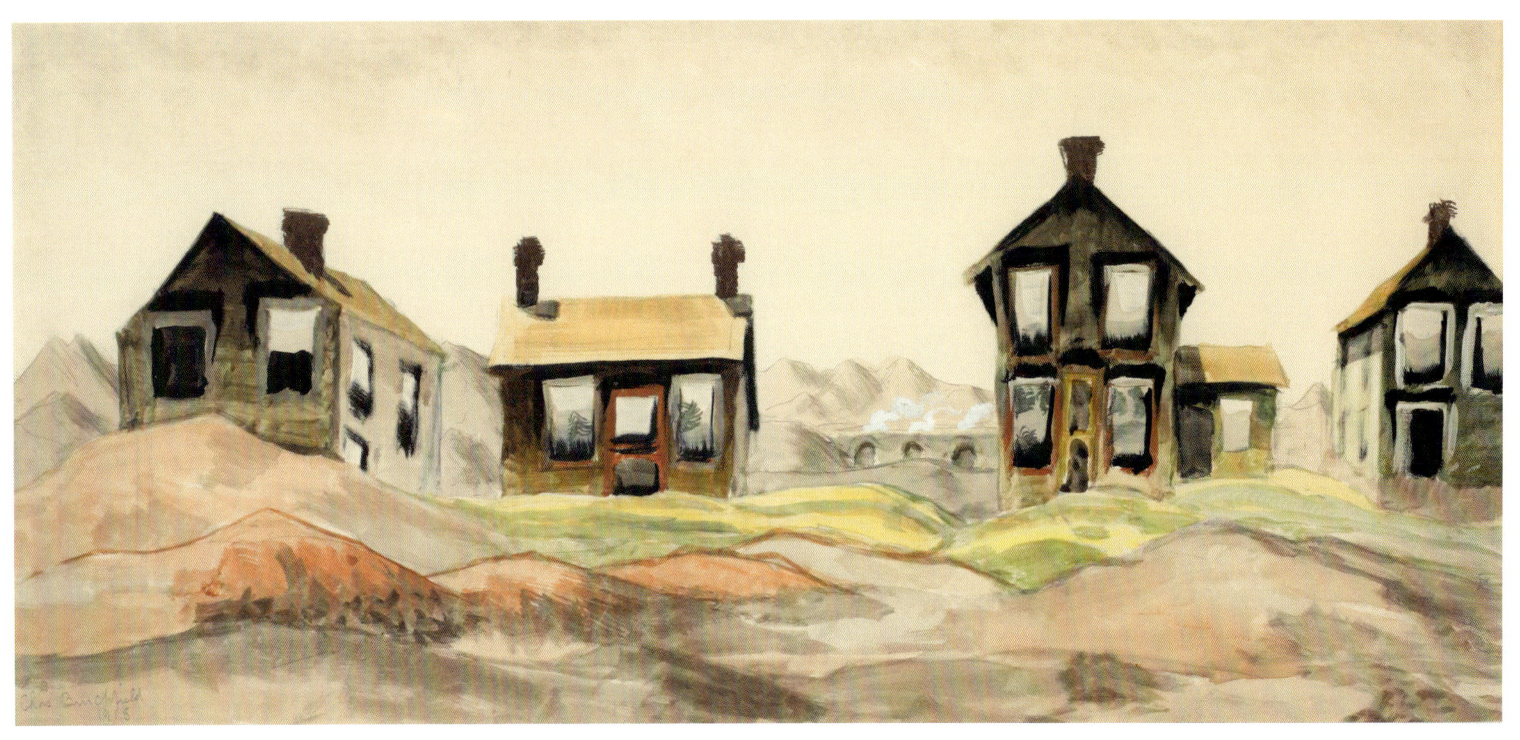

each individual house. In this watercolor, the artist portrays the unexpected beauty of a row of four coal patch houses that populated the Ohio countryside, their windows serving as dark eyes looking onto the rather desolate landscape surrounding them. The only reference to nature are reflections of pine trees in the windows, but the houses come to life with the artist's use of color, use of overall bright light, and fluid handling of the watercolor medium, yet still a somber mood prevails in this painting. Somewhat foreboding in their appearance, the anthropomorphic houses stoically face front, standing as sentinels before the bank of coke ovens in the background—the source of the soot that darkens their facades.

When Burchfield created *Coke Oven Homes* in 1918, he had begun to portray the socioeconomic conditions that small towns were experiencing during war time, perhaps as a personal response to World War I, which the United States had entered just the year before in April. He discussed his 1917–1918 shift in direction in an article he wrote for *Creative Art* magazine in 1928: "Life suddenly became hard . . . and [I] saw everything through a veil of violent dissatisfaction. . . . I was not indicting Salem, Ohio, but merely giving way to a mental mood, and sought out scenes that would express it. . . . Much, however, I hated justly and would like to go on hating to my last breath—modern industrialization, the deplorable condition in certain industrial fields such as steel works and mining sections."[4] Burchfield painted this watercolor while living in Salem, and his inscription on the back identifies the coal patch town as being situated between the villages of Washingtonville and Leetonia in northeastern Ohio. While the artist rarely included figures in his compositions, they are implied here as the unseen occupants of the houses. Ragged curtains hang from the windows, giving a sense of the economic status of the people who live within. At first glance, the houses appear to be abandoned; however, the smoke billowing from the coke ovens behind indicates that they are most likely inhabited by the workers who operate the ovens and manufacture the coal by-product, which was an essential ingredient in steelmaking. The artist would single out the fire-breathing coke ovens in a 1920 watercolor.

Burchfield's first exhibition was held at the Cleveland School of Art in the fall of 1916, and the Museum of Modern Art exhibited his watercolors of 1916–1918 in 1923. He had joined the Frank K. M. Rehn Galleries in 1929 and became part of a stable of artists that included Edward Hopper, Reginald Marsh (1898–1954), Henry Lee McFee (1886–1953), Henry Varnum Poor (1887–1970), and Alexander Brook (1898–1980). Rehn was particularly sympathetic to the work of the American scene painters and representational art in general, and he gave Burchfield an exhibition nearly every year after 1930. Burchfield was the first American artist to receive a solo show at the Museum of Modern Art in 1930, and he was invited to participate in all seven *Painting in the United States* exhibitions at the Carnegie Institute (now Carnegie Museum of Art) from 1943 to 1949. Additionally, his work was singled out in *Life* magazine in 1936; and in 1948, he was cited by *Look* magazine as the seventh best painter in America.[5]

Although Burchfield worked almost exclusively in the watercolor medium, he also made prints that convey some of the same qualities found in so many of his paintings. The Westmoreland owns one of the artist's lithographs, *Summer Benediction* (1961.18), and two of his drawings—*Houses and Wild Roses*, also of 1918 (1984.32), and *The Song Sparrow*, 1946 (1979.117).

Burchfield's art was his subjective response to his own private world. He created a formidable body of work, yet he was reclusive, remaining outside the major metropolitan areas—away from the distractions of the city in favor of the rural environment, where he would find his revelations of nature. His personal vision of his surroundings translated into paintings that convey the artist's extraordinary imagination. He painted until the day before he died in his home in Gardenville on January 11, 1967, at the age of seventy-three.

BLJ

1 Edward Hopper, "Charles Burchfield: American," *Arts*, July 1928, 5–12; Charles Burchfield, "Edward Hopper: Career of Silent Poetry," *Art News*, September 1936, 586–93.

2 Edward Hopper, "Charles Burchfield: American," *Arts*, July 1928, 6–7.

3 J. Benjamin Townsend, ed., *Charles Burchfield's Journals: The Poetry of Place* (Albany: State University of New York Press, 1993), XV.

4 Charles Burchfield, "On the Middle Border," *Creative Art*, September 1928, 25–32.

5 "Burchfield's America," *Life*, December 28, 1936, 24–29; *Look*, February 3, 1948, 44–48.

MARSDEN HARTLEY (1877—1943)
Still Life No. 5, 1918
Pastel on paper, 17 x 27 inches
Signed and dated lower right
Gift of the William A. Coulter Fund, 1962.93
Provenance: Dr. Ralph Meyer Riefstahl; Mr. Elizabeth Riefstahl; M. Knoedler & Co., Inc., New York.

Selected Exhibitions: Henry Clay Frick Fine Arts Department, University of Pittsburgh, 1963; Butler Institute of American Art, Youngstown, Ohio, 1964; Carnegie Institute, Pittsburgh, 1971; *A Salute to Pennsylvania's Artistic Heritage*, Pennsylvania Historic and Museum Commission, Harrisburg, Pennsylvania, 1979.

Marsden Hartley was born Edmund Hartley in Lewiston, Maine. Following his mother's death in 1885, his father married Martha Marsden in 1889 and moved to Cleveland, leaving young Edmund with a fraternal aunt in Auburn, Maine. Edmund joined the family in Cleveland in 1893 and, after studying with several individual artists, enrolled at the Cleveland School of Art (now the Cleveland Institute of Art) in 1898.

Hartley would become an enigmatic artist and a restless, sometimes difficult man, brimming with creativity that found its outlet in the written word as well as in visual imagery. His good friend Carl Sprinchorn (1887–1971), fellow painter and resident of Maine, wrote: "Marsden Hartley was an incurable wanderer upon the face of the earth—a vessel tossing on the multitudinous seas of his own diversified intellectual and emotional horizons."[1]

His piercing blue eyes were noted by all who met him, some saying that it was a relief when he turned his penetrating gaze away. Those who came to know him, however, soon discovered his gentle spirit. Experimentation suited Hartley, and he worked in various styles—from impressionism to cubism to abstraction—before developing his mature style, which is a combination of all three. His life saw periods of great success and abject poverty so extreme that he had to choose between buying bread and art supplies.

When Hartley moved to New York City at the age of twenty-two, he attended classes at both the National Academy of Design and the Art Students League. At the latter, he studied with William Merritt Chase (1849–1916), who was a great influence on the young painter. At this time, he also met the American landscapist and mystic Albert Pinkham Ryder (1847–1917), to whom he would remain close until the latter's death. Ryder's interest in allegory and spiritualism became elements that entered Hartley's aesthetic. In 1908, he dropped the name Edmund and began using his stepmother's maiden name, which he had adopted as a middle name two years earlier.

Alfred Stieglitz (1864–1946), a photographer and dealer who championed modernism, recognized Hartley's talent and exhibited his work at his 291 Gallery as early as 1909. Stieglitz was the first to exhibit works by the then controversial French modernists Paul Cézanne (1839–1906), Pablo Picasso (1881–1973), and Henri Matisse (1869–1954) in the United States. Hartley's exposure to cubism through the work of Cézanne and Picasso changed the way he made art. Stieglitz would keep Hartley in his stable of artists, which included both Europeans and Americans, until Hartley's last exhibition with him in 1937 at An American Place.

In 1912, Hartley discovered Der Blaue Reiter—a group of modernist painters in Munich—through the work of one of their leading members, Wassily Kandinsky (1866–1944). The exploration of these artists into symbolism, spiritualism, and abstraction led Hartley to experiment with these elements in his own art. The following year, Hartley traveled to Europe, stopping in Paris, Munich, and Berlin. It was in Germany that he became enamored of a German officer, Karl von Freyburg. Following Freyburg's death in battle in 1914, Hartley made him the subject of several ambitious, nearly abstract paintings that would become the artist's first signature works. These paintings were mainly composed of iconic symbols, abstracted shapes, rhythmic patterns, and strong color combinations.

In his pastel *Still Life No. 5*, Hartley is seen returning to a more representational style, aligned once again with the principles of cubism. A reduction of forms to simple shapes and distortion of conventional perspective is combined with the flat planes and broken angles typical of that style. The simple footed bowl, filled with fruit and placed among dynamic folds

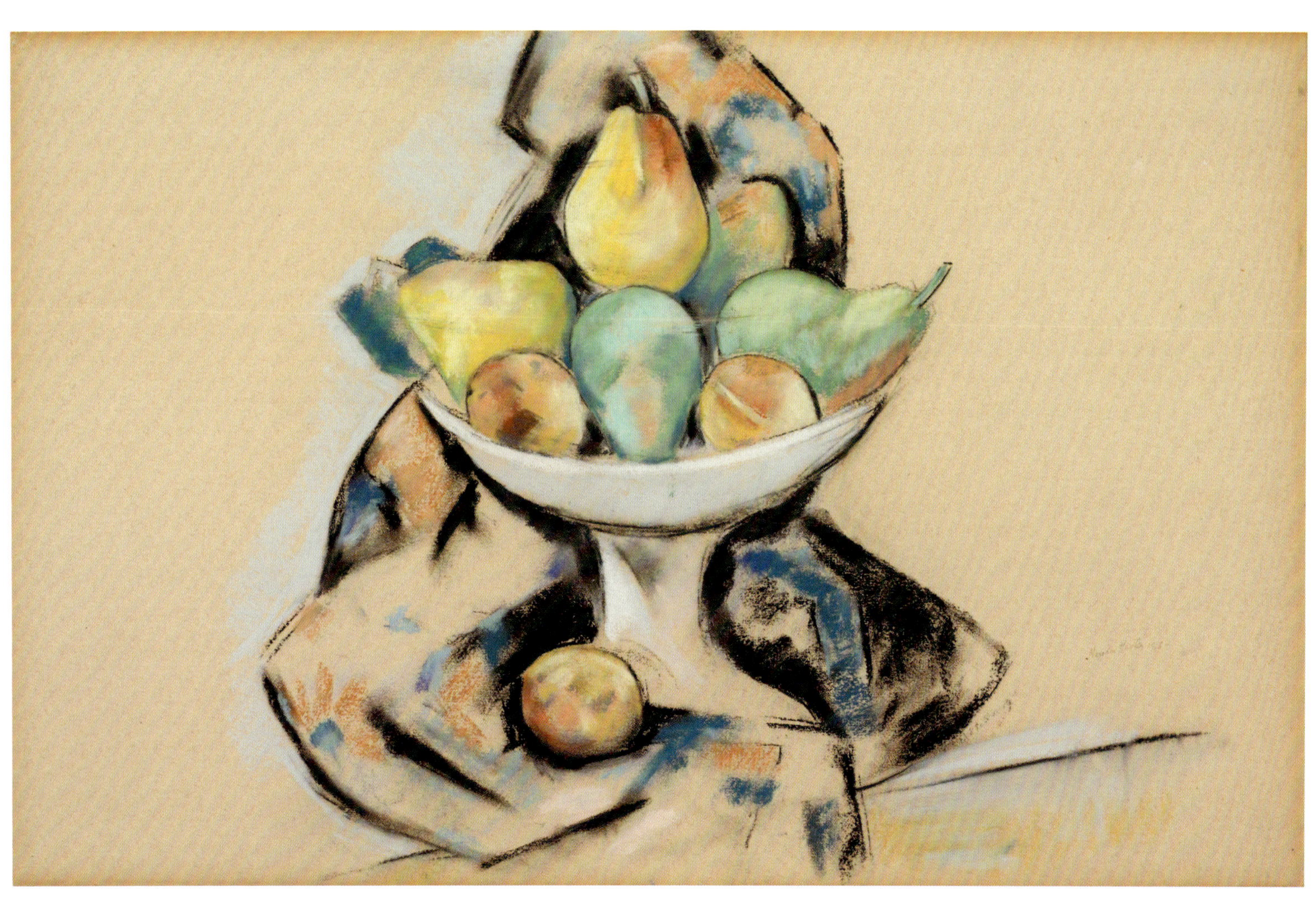

of drapery, is a typical subject favored by still life artists throughout the ages. The piece is composed of domestic objects that could easily and quickly be assembled to serve as a model for the artistic eye or as a platform through which to explore the formalist qualities of art. Hartley's characteristic rugged handling of form and brilliant use of color align with his strong compositional skills give these everyday items an architectural presence. Hartley would continue to work with still life subjects throughout his life, both on paper and in oils. Some of these compositions are among his most powerful in color and form. The Museum owns four lithographs by the artist that reflect his experimentation with printmaking in 1923 and 1933-1934.

The style of this pastel is especially reminiscent of the still lifes of Cézanne, in both subject and execution. Hartley would periodically renew his interest in Cézanne, and in 1926 he found himself in Aix-en-Provence, the longtime residence of the French painter. Hartley wrote that he felt at home under the shadow of Mont Sainte-Victoire, Cézanne's mountain muse.

Hartley continued to travel between the United States and Europe, discontent while in one location yet yearning for it once he had moved on. In the 1930s, he began returning for longer and longer visits to his native Maine. Referring to himself as a prodigal son and a "Maine-iac," it was here that this oft-troubled artist and vagabond finally found peace and acceptance. He continued to paint powerful portraits and still lifes while withdrawing more and more from the art world of New York City. He also found his own mountain muse in Mount Katahdin—an Indian name meaning "greatest mountain"—which served as the subject of many drawings, prints, and paintings during the last three years of his life.

Hartley's style evolved into a blend of representation and expressionism using flat areas of color often surrounded by a dark outline, as in the work of French expressionist painter Georges Rouault (1871–1958). These works usually presented a figure, still life object, or landscape element directly against the picture plane, using little perspective. An unusual use of bold color and broad, thickly applied brushwork add to the intensity of these mature works, which hark back to the dramatic, somewhat confrontational aspect of his German paintings from the mid-teens.

In 1940, as his health continued to fail, he moved in with lobster-fisherman Forrest Young and his wife, Katie, in the small village of Corea on Maine's southeastern coast. An intensely private man for most of his life, Hartley found comfort with the Youngs and their large, extended family, who became the subject of many important paintings executed in the last years of his life. Hartley's respect for their rugged yet simple lifestyle was answered by the Youngs' appreciation for Hartley's talent, creating a strong bond between these otherwise unlikely friends.

Eulogized by many as misunderstood and underappreciated, Hartley is now considered to be one of the greatest painters in the ranks of American artists.

JHO'T

1. Scribner Ames, *Marsden Hartley in Maine* (Orono: University of Maine Press, 1972), 29.

SUSAN HANNAH MACDOWELL EAKINS (1851–1938)
Still Life with Figure, not dated
Oil on canvas, 28 x 21 ½ inches
Gift of Mr. and Mrs. Stuart P. Feld, New York, 1983.179
Provenance: David David Gallery, Philadelphia; Norman Hirschl, New York; Mr. and Mrs. Stuart P. Feld, New York.

SELECTED EXHIBITIONS: *Susan Macdowell Eakins, 1851-1938,* Pennsylvania Academy of the Fine Arts, Philadelphia, 1973; *A Feast for the Eyes: Treasures from the Westmoreland Museum of American Art,* Woodmere Art Museum, 1998; *Passionate Palette: A Celebration of Philadelphia Women Artists, Susan Macdowell Eakins,* Woodmere Art Museum, Philadelphia, Pennsylvania, 2001.

Rather than being recognized as the accomplished artist she was, Susan Hannah Macdowell Eakins is known primarily for her union with the infamous Thomas Eakins (1844–1916), whom she married in 1884. In the late nineteenth century, it was expected and accepted that a woman would support her husband in his endeavors, and because Susan felt that Thomas was worthy of such support and destined to be a great painter, she set aside her own artistic ambitions to focus on his. For about nine years before her marriage, Susan actively participated in exhibitions at the Pennsylvania Academy of the Fine Arts and the Philadelphia Society of Artists. She primarily painted portraits of her family and friends, with an occasional still life in the mix. After the couple married, she painted only sporadically, as her life revolved around her husband's career, taking over all tasks necessary to free him for time in his studio. She made shipping arrangements for his work, answered correspondence, entertained guests, and ran the household. She became his all-around assistant as well as his devoted companion and confidante. Believing in him completely, she became an ally for her husband and helped him survive the controversial years before and after the academy forced his resignation in 1886, when his reputation suffered.[1] Both artists had separate studios in their house, although Susan had little time to spend in hers. She earned additional income for the family by painting copies of portraits on commission. Thomas greatly respected his wife's work, once saying that she knew more about color than he did. In fact, she helped him complete his last commissioned portrait of Rutherford B. Hayes. Following his death in 1916, she took up her brush in earnest once again at the age of sixty-five, painting portraits, still lifes, and genre subjects, creating her largest body of work during the 1920s and 1930s. During these years, she also took on the distribution of Eakins's work to museums and collections in an attempt to secure his reputation as an artist. Once she began painting again, however, she hardly left her studio for over twenty years, when at age eighty-six a fall left her unable to paint.

The fifth of eight children, Susan Macdowell grew up in Philadelphia. Her father, William H. Macdowell, was a respected engraver and consequently knew many of the city's artists. He encouraged his daughter's artistic ambitions, and Susan had her own studio in the home, frequently using her family as models for her portraits. Her sister Elizabeth also became an artist. Susan painted her first self-portrait when she was just ten years old and had one of her early paintings accepted into the academy's annual exhibition in 1876. She studied with Christian Schussele (1824–1879) at his own school before beginning studies with him at the academy in 1876. She also began her studies with her future husband that year, remaining under his tutelage for seven years.

Susan first became aware of Thomas Eakins when one of his now most famous paintings, *The Gross Clinic,* (1875; Philadelphia Museum of Art and the Pennsylvania of the Fine Arts), was exhibited at the Haseltine Galleries. She thought it was one of the best paintings she had ever seen, and as she recounted to Lloyd Goodrich, she fell in love with Eakins shortly thereafter, when she formally met him in Schussele's studio. She asked Eakins to critique her work, and when he did, she said, "His criticism crushed me for awhile, but I realized he was right."[2]

Susan was a talented student and the first to win the academy's Mary Smith Prize in 1879, awarded annually to the best woman painter in memory of Mary Smith, daughter of the artist William Thompson Russell Smith (1812–1896), who had died in 1878. As one of Eakins's most advanced students, she showed seven paintings in a special gallery in the academy's annual exhibition in 1879.

Susan's early work reveals the stylistic influence of her

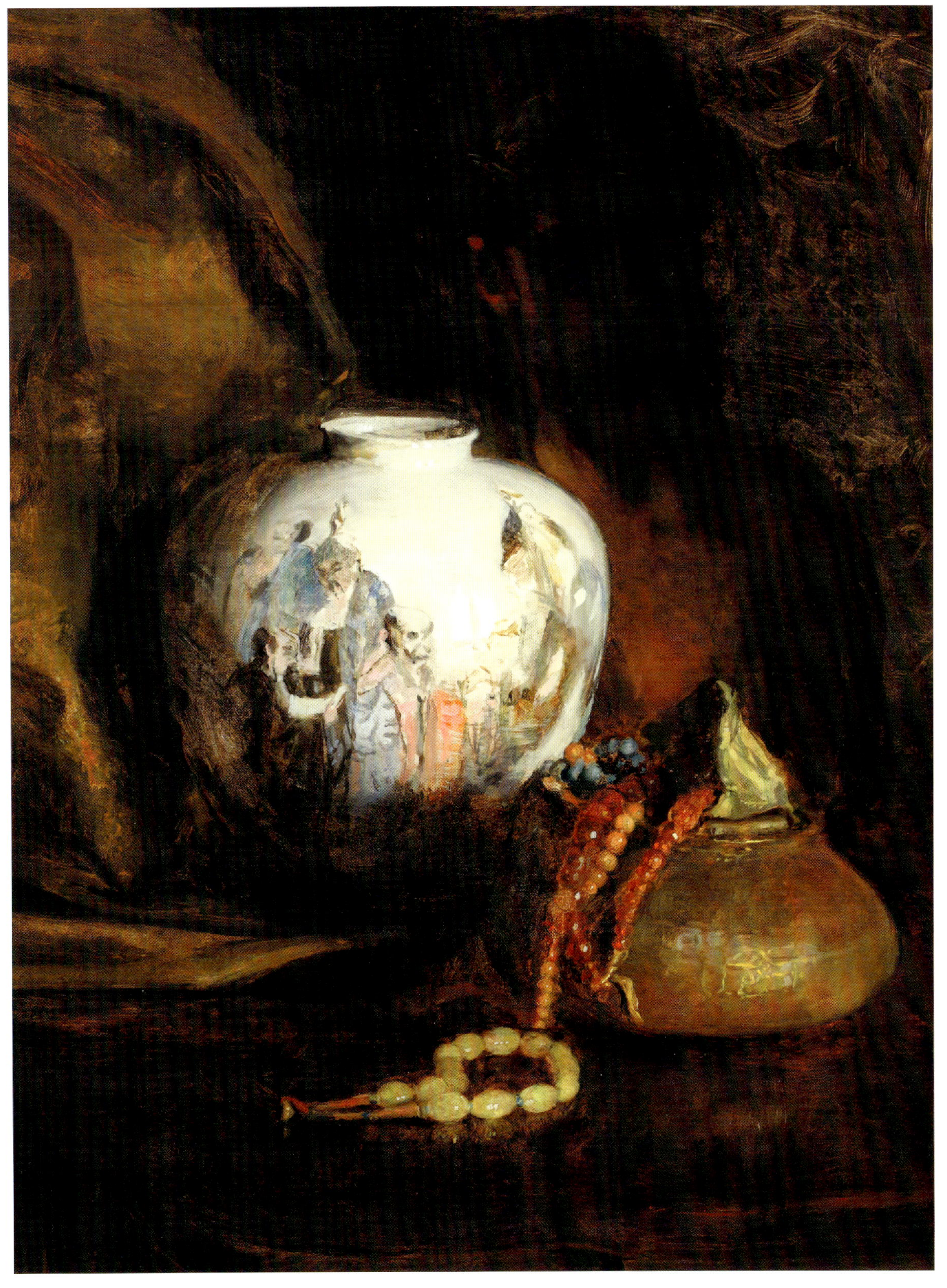

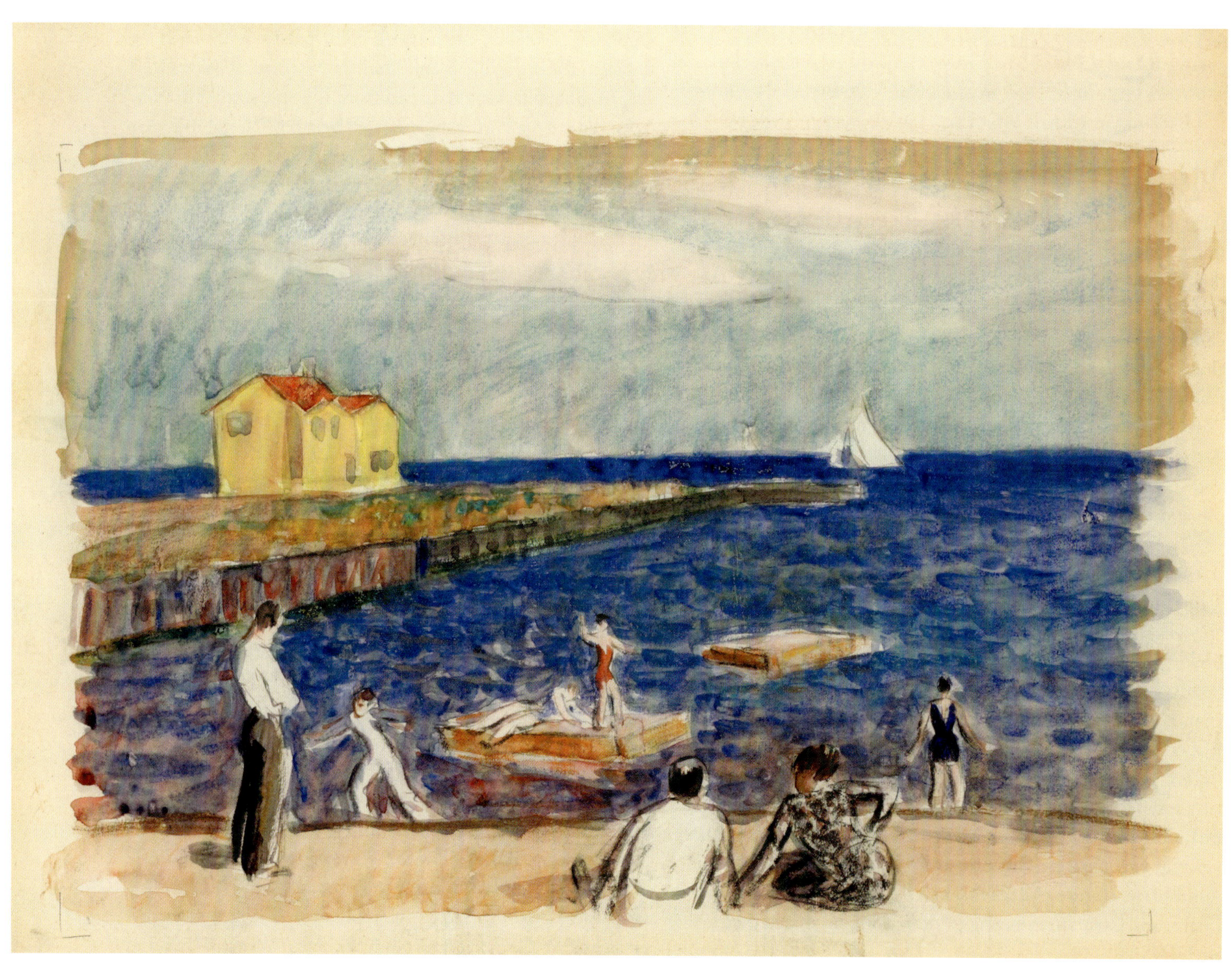

in France, where he became more closely associated with his European counterparts. Works by Renoir, Paul Cézanne (1839–1906), Pablo Picasso (1881–1973), Vincent Van Gogh (1853–1890), and Henri Matisse (1869–1954) were among the first to enter Barnes' collection. Paintings by Americans Ernest Lawson (1873–1939) and Maurice Prendergast (1858–1924), along with works by Glackens himself, were also among the early acquisitions.

Glackens carried either a sketch pencil or watercolors with him almost constantly. His eye was curious, spontaneous, and easily engaged; family and friends were often captured in these quick sketches depicting everyday scenes of American life. His wife, Edith Dimock (1876–1955), also an artist; his son, Ira; and his daughter, Lenna, appear frequently in his work. The family enjoyed excursions to the beaches of Connecticut, Long Island, and many other places on the East Coast and abroad.

The spontaneity of *Bathers and Yellow House* can be seen in the artist's vibrant brushwork, brilliant use of color, and deft handling of the watercolor medium. Like many of the artist's compositions, color has a place in the title, emphasizing its importance. From its perch on an outcropping of land, thrust into waves of blue and purple, the yellow house with its apple-red roof intersects land and sky at the horizon line. Somewhat anthropomorphic, it seems to both observe the foreground figures at play and, by way of its bright color, share in their merriment. The scene is a specific and ordinary afternoon at the seashore transformed by the painter into a marvelous and universally appealing interlude.

Between 1925 and 1936, the Glackens family split their time between France and the United States, with William sending paintings to New York's Kraushaar Galleries, where they sold well. Like the great French impressionist painter Édouard Manet (1832–1883), Glackens turned to painting small still lifes when his health began to fail and he could no longer manage larger-scale works. As Guy Pène du Bois (1884–1958), fellow artist and critic, described them, they were "a single fruit or flower wherein, by main strength or pure joy, he continued to report the glorious fullness of color and light and action which life had been to him."[3] In 1937, the year before his death, Glackens was honored with the Grand Prix at the Paris International Exposition. Picasso's mural-sized canvas *Guernica* was first exhibited at the exposition, commissioned specifically for the Spanish pavilion by the Spanish government to depict the bombing of the small town by German and Italian forces that same year.

Guy Pène du Bois provided an essay for the memorial exhibition of Glackens's work held at the Whitney Museum of American Art in 1938. In it, Du Bois discussed his friend's modesty and dedication to art. He illustrated this by quoting Glackens as having said, "Artists say the silliest things," suggesting that artists should do less talking, especially about themselves, and more art making. Du Bois used this quip as the title of his autobiography in 1940.[4] In his biography of his father, Ira Glackens wrote:

> I cannot think of a happier life than the one my father lived. . . . He had known the best that life has to offer: a peaceful nature, a devoted wife, a happy home, delightful friends, and the contentment that comes from creative work untroubled by anyone's opinion: and he did not leave an enemy, for he had never had one.[5]

Ira died in 1991, leaving his entire personal collection of over two-hundred pieces of his father's work to the Museum of Art, Fort Lauderdale. It is housed in a ten-thousand-square-foot wing built in 2001, a testament to Glackens and his place in the history of American art.

JHO'T

1 They, along with Robert Henri, would form the core of the Eight and become known as the Ashcan school for their particular brand of realism.

2 Painted in 1905, the two figures are Jeanne Louise Mouquin, the owner's wife, and James B. Moore, owner of the Café Francis. Moore was famous for squiring young women around town, and his appearance here with Mouquin's wife hints at the latter's tempestuous marriage.

3 Guy Pène du Bois, introduction to *William Glackens: Memorial Exhibition* (New York: Whitney Museum of American Art, 1939), 6.

4 Guy Pène du Bois, *Artists Say the Silliest Things* (New York: American Artists Group and Duell, Sloan and Pearce, 1940).

5 Ira Glackens, *William Glackens and the Eight: The Artists Who Freed American Art* (New York: Horizon Press, 1957), 260.

ALFRED H. MAURER (1868–1932)
Two Sisters, c. 1925
Oil on board, 26 x 18 inches
Signed upper left
Gift of the Westmoreland Society, 2001.7
Provenance: The Artist; ACA Heritage Gallery, New York; Private Collection, Texas; Kraushaar Galleries, New York.

SELECTED EXHIBITIONS: *Modernist Expressions: Alfred Maurer Heads, 1920-1932,* Kraushaar Galleries, New York, 1998; *Face-to-Face: 20th Century Portraits,* Westmoreland Museum of American Art, 2000.

Alfred Henry Maurer has been called the "first American modernist," having brought the ideas and styles of many early twentieth-century progressive European artists to this country in his own work. The son of prominent illustrator Louis Maurer (1832–1932)—best known for his idealistic, rural American scenes published as prints by Currier & Ives—Alfred was born in New York City. He left school at the age of sixteen to work at Heppenheimer & Maurer, his father's successful lithography firm in Union City, New Jersey. For his formal art training, Maurer took classes at the National Academy of Design between 1885 and 1897, after which, at the age of twenty-nine, he made his first trip to Europe, where he studied briefly at the Académie Julian in Paris. The artist lived in France until 1901, when he officially launched his career with society portraits that generated critical acclaim on both sides of the Atlantic. In that same year, a jury composed of the artists Winslow Homer (1836–1910) and Thomas Eakins (1844–1916) awarded Maurer the gold medal at the Carnegie International for one of his tonalist paintings, entitled *An Arrangement.*

During his second extended stay in Paris (1902–1914), Maurer was strongly influenced by the work of the European modernists—especially Henri Matisse (1869–1954) and the fauves, which he encountered at the 1905 Salon d'Automne. Their use of simplified form and brilliant color had an immediate impact on him. Yet it was not simply this one group of artists or style that affected him; he absorbed the tenets of modernism from impressionism, postimpressionism, and cubism, and would certainly not have missed the opportunity to see the important Cézanne retrospective at the Salon d'Automne in 1907. These new influences resulted in a radical shift in his style.

Up until this time, Maurer had taken a tonalist approach to figurative painting—inspired by James A. McNeill Whistler (1834–1903) and William Merritt Chase (1849–1916). Maurer's early paintings emulate Whistler's symphonies of color and his philosophy about art. Whistler, who spent most of his artistic career in London and Paris, advocated the idea of "art for art's sake," suggesting that art was about aesthetics rather than storytelling or imitations of nature.

Maurer's association and friendship with the American collectors Leo and Gertrude Stein led to his interest in the French avant-garde, which he would incorporate into his work for the remainder of his career. The two expatriates held salons in their apartment in Paris, where they had settled in 1903. Their home was a famous gathering place for both European and American avant-garde artists and writers, who would gain exposure to the work of Matisse, Cézanne (1839–1906), Picasso (1881–1973), and other modernists in the Steins' collection. Maurer may even have met Matisse, then the reigning leader of the fauves, during one of these gatherings. In 1908, Maurer discussed his change in style with a reporter for the *New York Times,* saying: "The transition from the old school to the new is not an easy one. . . . When I decided to make the change, I had to lay aside my brushes for almost a month and think nothing but Impressionism. Then I went at it slowly and timidly, feeling my way. I am still in transition, I know. I can't tell what tomorrow will bring about."[1] The outbreak of World War I in 1914 prompted Maurer's return to America, and while he was never able to return to Europe, he continued to expand on what he had learned in Paris to arrive at his own personal style. Alfred Stieglitz (1864–1946) showed Maurer's fauve-inspired landscapes in his 291 Gallery in 1909, one of the earliest introductions of modernism in America (four years before the famed Armory Show).

During the last two decades of Maurer's life, he painted vibrant floral still lifes, landscapes, and figural studies—particularly heads and half-length portrait studies of women—using the vibrant color vocabulary of the fauves and the

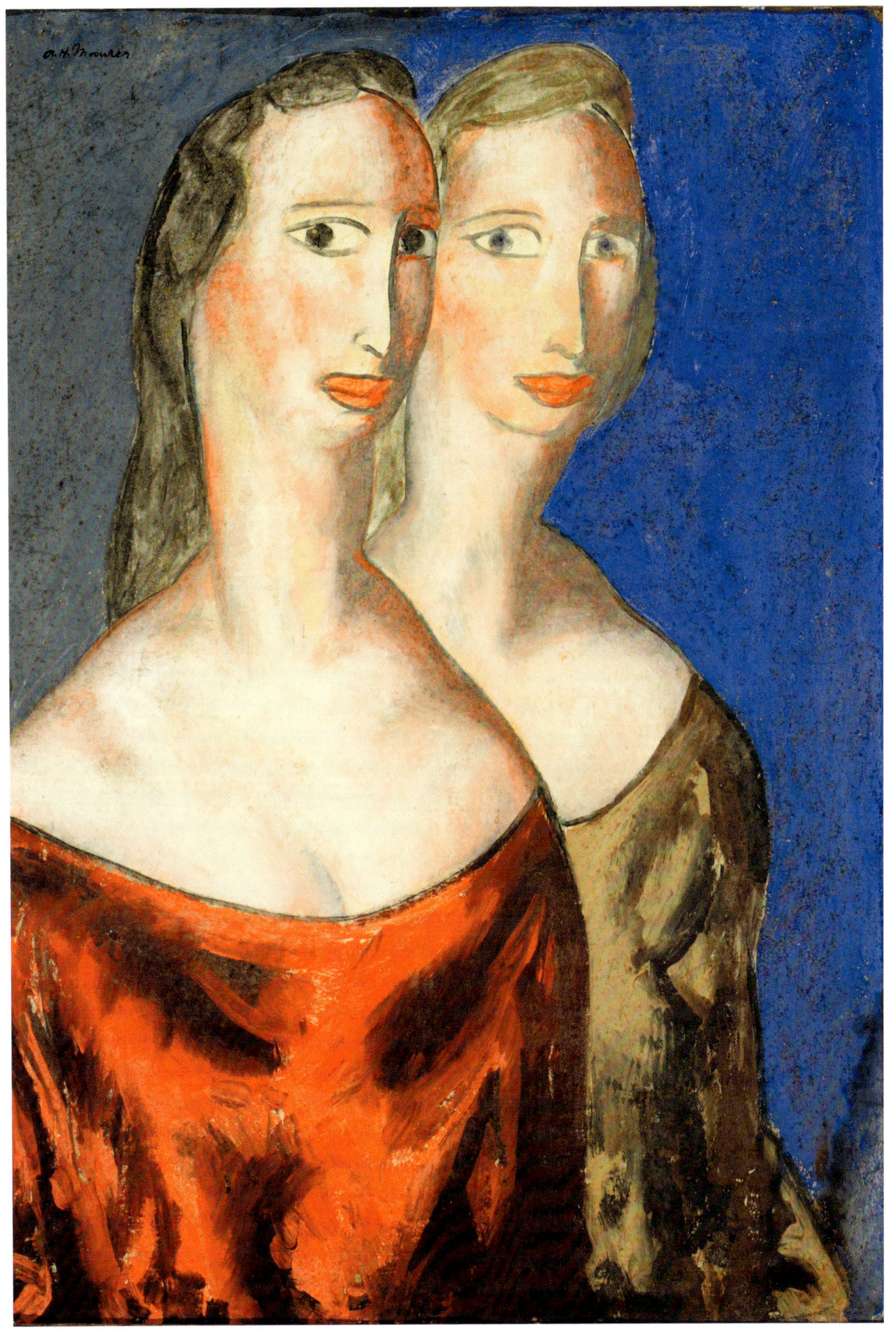

flattened overlapping planes and simplified forms of cubism in his compositions. Maurer's first group of heads, often called "girls," were not drawn from specific models but were more of an amalgamation, representing the successful merging of color, form, and composition into an intimate and emotional experience. Jay Hambidge's compositional theory of dynamic symmetry influenced Maurer in his artistic direction. While they began more realistically, Maurer's heads grew more and more abstract by the end of the decade. In some compositions, two heads merge, suggesting a spiritual or psychological connection, while in others, figures that are paired together seem aloof and disconnected. He created these compositions using simple outlines and broad flat areas of bright color, revealing his keen interest in the formal language of art rather than detailed representation. These works remain the artist's most enigmatic and personal statements. His heads created controversy whenever he showed them, but he enjoyed the reaction.

The Westmoreland's *Two Sisters* demonstrates the dramatic shift in the artist's style during this period. The girls' elongated faces are simplified and mask-like; with their large eyes, the two sisters peer out from the canvas with great curiosity and fix the viewer in their interactive gaze. Whether this mysterious painting actually represents sisters or some psychological duality is unknown.

The frame for *Two Sisters* was specially designed and painted by Maurer, thus providing a complete package. Every Maurer-fabricated frame is unique in form, texture, and coloration because he made each one as a companion to the specific composition it housed. Sometimes Maurer even painted faces on the frames.

In the years prior to his death in 1932, Maurer created an astonishing body of work that further identified his role in shaping American modernist ideals. Louis Maurer was vehemently opposed to his son's choice of modernism, and he publicly expressed this opinion. Living together in New York after the death of his mother in 1917, Alfred was continually under the critical eye of his father. Louis and Alfred had a stormy relationship all their lives, with Alfred always working in the shadow of his more famous father. On July 19, 1932, Louis Maurer died at the age of one hundred, and just sixteen days later, Alfred committed suicide, hanging himself in the home they had shared. He was sixty-four years old. Since their deaths, Alfred Maurer's lasting contributions to the history of American art have eclipsed those of his father. According to critic Lewis Mumford in 1934, "Maurer was one of the handful of genuine moderns who really felt these abstractions as experiences."[2]

BLJ

1 "Artist Maurer Now an Impressionist," *New York Times*, April 19, 1908, C5.

2 Lewis Mumford, *Mumford on Modern Art in the 1930s*, ed. and with an introduction by Robert Wojtowicz (Berkeley, Los Angeles, and London: University of California Press, 2007), 138.

OTTO KUHLER (1894–1976)
Steel Valley, Pittsburgh, c. 1925
Oil on canvas, 45 x 50 inches
Signed lower right
Gift of Richard M. Scaife, 2004.2
Provenance: Private Collection, Vermont; Gilliland's Fine Art, Ligonier, Pennsylvania.

SELECTED EXHIBITIONS: *Born of Fire: The Valley of Work*, Westmoreland Museum of American Art, Greensburg, Pennsylvania, 2006; Oberhausen, Germany, 2007; Chemnitz, Germany, 2008; Zabrze, Poland, 2009; *Feuerländer: Regions of Vulcan*, LVR Industriemuseum, Oberhausen, Germany, 2010.

Just two years after Aaron Harry Gorson (1872–1933) left Pittsburgh, Otto Kuhler arrived on the scene from Germany. According to newspaper accounts, when he landed in the spring of 1923 (fittingly on a steamboat named *Pittsburgh*), he had only eight dollars in his pocket. He had come to Pittsburgh because it was a steel city and because his father's cousin, Gustave Kuhler, had offered him a place to live. From a room in his cousin's house, Kuhler could see "blinding flashes of light whenever a furnace was tapped along the river. This vision of steam and smoke and fire, so familiar from home, assured [him that he] had come to the right place."[1] He was inspired by the sights and sounds he witnessed: "I was deeply impressed by the endless procession of mighty blast furnaces, flame-spawning Bessemer converters, the white-hot snakes of steel crashing back and forth through the rolling mills. This, I realized was the mighty steel-making heart of America!"[2]

Kuhler's love of industrial scenes came naturally to him, as he was born in Remscheid, Germany, to a family who, since 1782, had owned and operated an ironworks in the Ruhr Valley, founded by his great-grandfather. There he said he "learned about steel and trade and the hard facts of life in a society that honored craftsmanship and glorified honest toil."[3] The mill was his playground as a child, and his love of and lessons in the mechanics of locomotives began there. Essentially self-taught as an artist, Kuhler worked in the mills in Germany, with the railroad, and as a commercial artist after World War I. He attempted to study at the Royal Arts Academy in Düsseldorf, but that lasted only three days. "I was disobedient," he said. "They wanted me to draw apples and flowers." Instead, he drew mills and machinery—what he knew best.[4]

Steel Valley, Pittsburgh is an iconic representation of Pittsburgh's steel heritage, impressive in both size and subject matter. Measuring 45 x 50 inches, it is one of the largest known compositions by Kuhler. The artist's vantage point—a site high in the Hill District—provided him with a spectacular view up the winding Monongahela River. The massive mill complex of the Jones & Laughlin Steel Works can be seen along the south side of the river, with the Eliza Furnaces directly across from it—the two connected by side-by-side hot metal bridges (specifically the Monongahela Connecting Railroad Bridge, built in 1887, and the Hot Metal Bridge, constructed in 1900). Hazelwood Coke Works is shown further up the river on the north bank. While it cannot be seen, Panther Hollow is located just off the left side of the composition. The limited palette used by the artist captures the colors of the valley during the height of the steel era, with the sky rendered in gray, ocher, and rust. Similar colors are used in the hillsides, mills, and river, and in other elements comprising the scene. Bright green is the only additional color used on buildings and fields in the landscape. The sun, a pale yellow orb, is struggling to break through the heavy smoke-laden atmosphere—a common sight in the city, where it was often difficult to tell the exact time of day. Its reflection on the river creates a mirrored, opaque surface that is impenetrable to the sun's rays. The "scenes of industry" are fully at work, with tugboats pushing coal barges along the river, and trains crossing the Hot Metal Bridge and steaming through the landscape.

From early childhood, the locomotive fascinated Kuhler. He treasured the Baldwin Locomotive catalog he received from the company's president, who would eventually become his friend and employer. Whenever he traveled, he would gravitate to the rail yards and sketch as many different types of trains as he could. Kuhler ultimately fulfilled his lifelong ambition and became a design engineer for the American Locomotive Company in New York, for which he designed the first streamlined train—the famous Hiawatha engine, unveiled in May

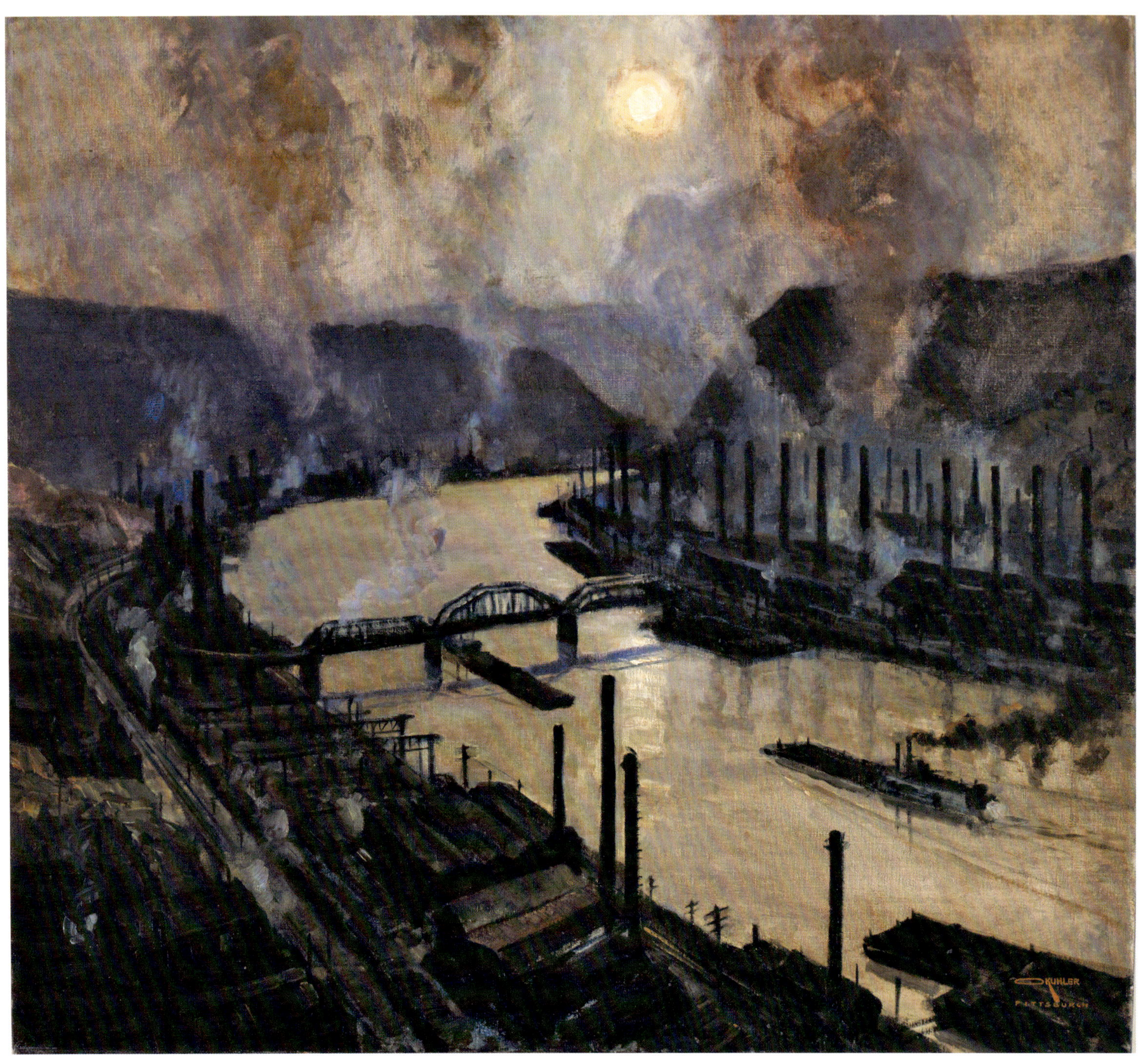

(OPPOSITE) *Pittsburgh,* n.d., Watercolor on paper, 11 ¾ x 8 ¾ inches, Gift of the William A. Coulter Fund, 1967.12

1935—advertised as the "fastest steam locomotive in the world." His portfolio of five etchings entitled *The Iron Horse in the Making* (1985.156-160) was published by Schwartz Galleries, New York in 1930.

When Kuhler left Pittsburgh for New York City in 1928, he vowed: "I shall try to get back to Pittsburgh at least twice a year. When one stays away too long, gets accustomed to the views, it's too easy to miss the beauty of it all.[5] He told a *Pittsburgh Post-Gazette* reporter in 1930: "I've never found such an amazing wealth of subjects as I have seen here. I could draw myself to death."[6] At the age of eighty—more than forty-five years after leaving Pittsburgh—he recalled: "Pittsburgh patterned my future. From my very first days in this country, my enthusiasm for Pittsburgh knew no bounds. It prompted me, armed with canvas, paint box and easel, to use the city's excellent, far-flung streetcar system to explore under a sky of coal smoke an area ten times the size of my homeland in the Ruhr."[7]

While only in Pittsburgh for five years, Kuhler created one of the largest and most accurate records of the industrial center of the country. Even after his move to Denver, Colorado, in 1941, he continued to paint industrial scenes and said he "was still haunted by the rolling hills of Pittsburgh, the busy rivers, puffing and whistling trains endlessly proceeding day and night."[8] He considered it all one "gigantic symphony" and said he did his best "to hold it" in his work. Kuhler worked on the spot to create sketches for his paintings and etchings "to get the very stuff of industry."[9]

Whether using oil, watercolor, or etching techniques, Kuhler was a master at whatever medium he chose, revealing his proficiency at all of them throughout his career. Combined with his love of industry, Kuhler's natural artistic abilities toward rendering technical processes form a body of work that is unrivaled. Following a prolific career in the arts and industry, he died in Santa Fe, New Mexico, at the age of eighty-two. Always the designer, he spent the last years of his life designing mountain-style homes for his friends and family members.

Kuhler's watercolor *Pittsburgh* (1967.12) entered the collection in 1967—one of the first of his works to do so—and *Steel Valley, Pittsburgh*, in 2004. The Westmoreland owns twenty-nine works by the artist—four oils, three watercolors, and twenty-two etchings—which make a significant contribution to the holdings of the Museum's Scenes of Industry collection, an important research and collecting area that spans more than 150 years, from 1851 to the present. This collection supports one facet of the Museum's mission of preserving art that reflects the historic legacy of the region.

BLJ

1 Robert Stearns, "Pittsburgh Patterned My Future," *Pittsburgh Press Roto*, November 24, 1974, 12.

2 Otto Kuhler, *My Iron Journey: An Autobiography of a Life with Steam and Steel* (Denver, CO: National Railway Historical Society, 1967), 202.

3 Ibid., 1.

4 Ibid., 19. Kuhler wanted to attend college to study electrical engineering, but needed one year of practical experience first. He apprenticed with an electrical engineering firm in central Germany, but that didn't last long. He was then hired to design advertisements for trade journals, for which he drew pictures of steam engines. For a short time, he was also a movie-set designer.

5 "The Valley of Work," *Pittsburgh Post-Gazette*, October 20, 1930, 17.

6 Ibid.

7 Ibid.

8 William Gill, "Memories of Pittsburgh," *Pittsburgh Press*, December 3, 1961.

9 "Begins Life as Worker in Big Mills and Mines—Now He Paints Industrial Scenes," *Pittsburgh Sun*, July 31, 1923.

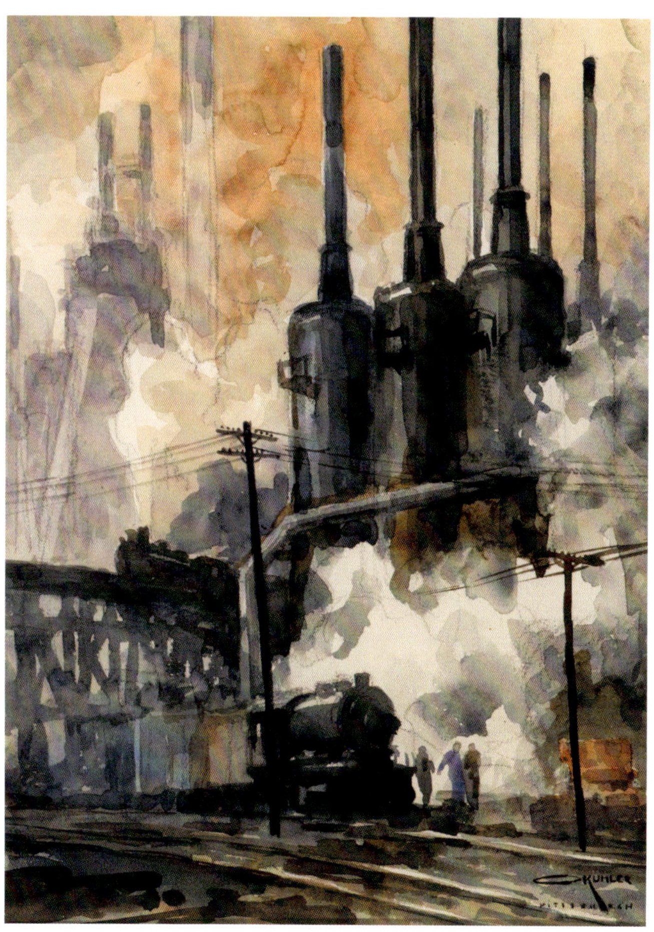

GUY PÈNE DU BOIS (1884–1958)
Studio Window, Anticoli, 1928
Oil on canvas, 37 x 29 inches
Signed and dated lower right
Gift of the William A. Coulter Fund, 1977.84
Provenance: The Artist's Family to his grandson William Lucas, South Carolina; Kenneth Lux Fine Paintings, New York.

EXHIBITIONS: Kraushaar Galleries, New York, 1928; *Guy Pène du Bois and the Art of his Time,* Corcoran Gallery of Art, Washington, D.C., 1980-1981; *Guy Pène du Bois: The Twenties at Home and Abroad,* Sordoni Art Gallery, Wilkes Barre, PA+, 1995; *Face Forward: American Portraiture from Sargent to the Present,* Vero Beach Museum of Art, 2008; *The Gift of Art,* Westmoreland Museum of American Art, 2009.

The son of a writer and critic, Guy Pène du Bois was born in Brooklyn, New York, to a family devoted to the arts. His father, Henri Pène du Bois, wrote on the visual arts, literature, and music, exposing the young Pène du Bois to a life of culture. He studied painting from 1899 to 1905 at the New York School of Art, first with its founder William Merritt Chase (1849–1916) and then with Robert Henri (1865–1929) and Kenneth Hayes Miller (1876–1952). Pène du Bois's mature style reflects in some ways both of the latter artists' work: from Henri he learned to observe contemporary life around him, and from Miller he achieved an abstraction or simplification of form that characterized his figural work.

Following in his father's footsteps, Pène du Bois became a critic and writer, establishing a reputation in the field that eclipsed that of his paintings, at least during his lifetime. Writing and teaching supplemented the artist's income throughout his career, offsetting the financial difficulties that would plague him all of his life. He embarked on a career as a reporter in 1906, working as an art critic for the *New York American*; became an assistant to art critic Royal Cortissoz on the *New York Tribune* for one year; spent two years as the art critic for the *New York Evening Post*; and was the editor of *Arts and Decoration* magazine for about seven years. He married Florence Sherman Duncan, a writer, in 1911. Pène du Bois wrote on many subjects, including fellow artists William Glackens (1870–1938), Ernest Lawson (1873–1939), and John Sloan (1871–1951) for the American Arts Series published by the Whitney Museum of American Art during the 1930s. Pène du Bois was also included in that series, with text by Royal Cortissoz, who wrote, "His art is life seen through a temperament, through a mentality. It is a vital thing."[1]

Pène du Bois made his first trip to Europe with his father in 1905, where he took private art lessons and attended Paris's Atelier Colarossi. As an eager young artist, he either spent his days in the cafés, sketching people as they passed by, or spent hour after hour in the museums and galleries, absorbing all he saw there. Although the style of cubism prevalent in Paris at the time is not immediately apparent in his work of the period, Pène du Bois began to simplify forms, reducing them to pure geometric volumes and incorporating broad areas of modulated color. He first exhibited his work at the Paris Salon in 1905, and was a promoter and an exhibitor at the Armory Show in 1913, but his first solo show in New York, held at the Whitney Studio Club, did not happen until 1918. Kraushaar Galleries, who represented the artist until 1946, gave him a one-man show in 1922.

According to Betsy Fahlman, author of *Guy Pène du Bois: Painter of Modern Life* (2004), the artist "keenly observed the spectacle of social theater he saw around him and deftly captured the spirit of the era in which he worked."[2] Pène du Bois was a sophisticated insider whose subject matter showed the elite of society as they gathered at parties, the theater, art galleries, restaurants, cafés, sporting events, and other urban settings in New York and Paris, where he spent nearly six years as an expatriate. Typically placed close together in groups of two or three, his subjects nonetheless give the feeling of being isolated and estranged. His work is infused with a sense of satire, sometimes subtle, sometimes quite direct, taking a sharp view of contemporary society. His often elegantly dressed figures are not portraits of individuals but serve as generic "society types," situated in characteristic surroundings. A neighbor of F. Scott Fitzgerald in Westport, Connecticut, for a short time, Pène du Bois's paintings reveal something of the lifestyle that the author vividly described in his novels.

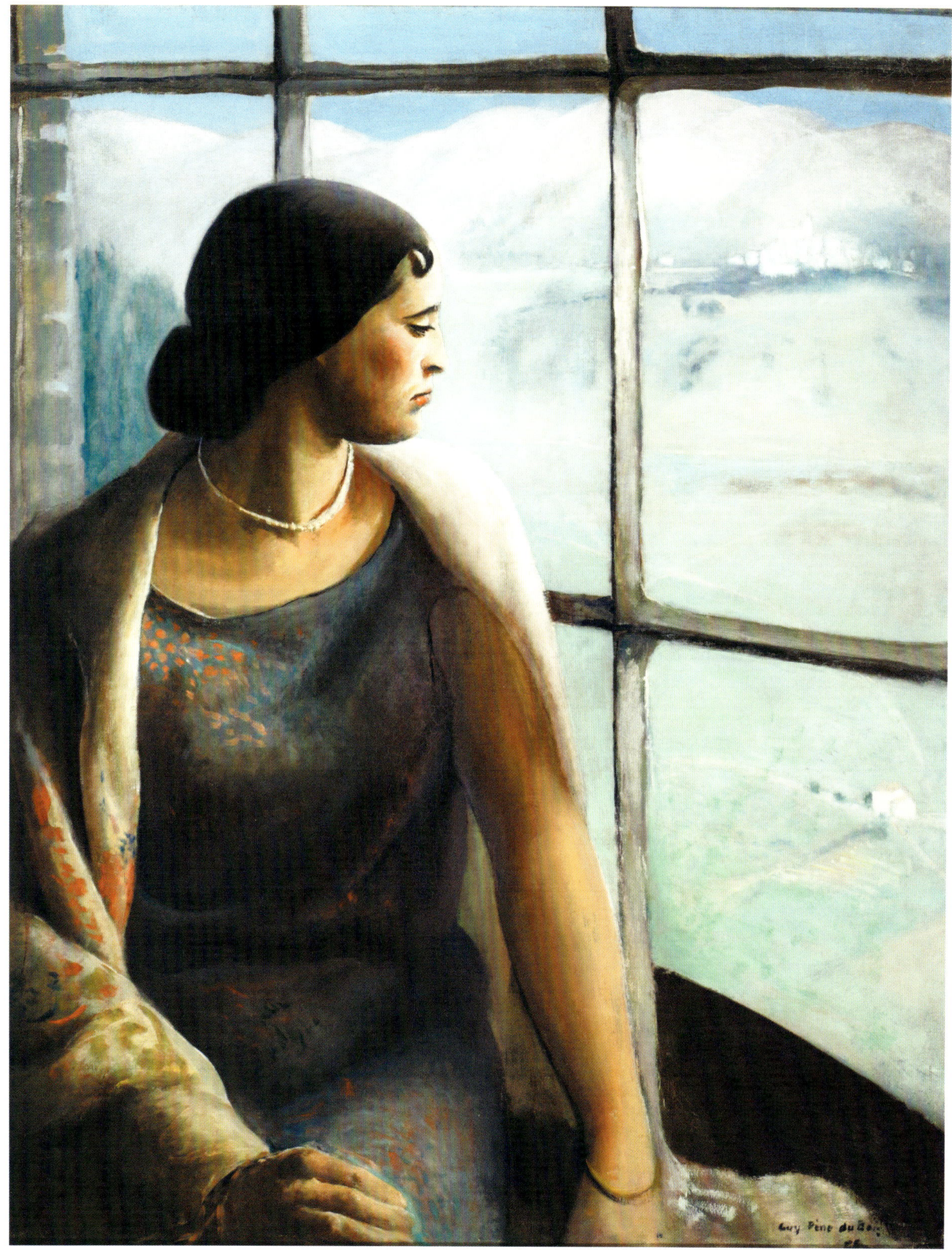

Pène du Bois came to maturity as an artist during the 1920s, a period deemed "the roaring twenties" because of the extravagant parties, raucous speakeasies, and public reaction to prohibition. He made his second trip to Europe in 1924 and was able to remain there for nearly six years. *Studio Window, Anticoli* was painted in 1928, when the artist, who was living in France at the time, took a trip to Anticoli, a charming village in the mountains about two hours from Rome. Du Bois chose an interior view, with his model seated in elegant repose, gazing out from the artist's studio window at the hazy, nondescript Italian landscape beyond. The window is seen more as a barrier to the outside world than as a transparent entrance to it. Furthering that sense of isolation, the model's downcast eyes and mouth elicit a sense of melancholy in the viewer, while also setting the meditative mood of the moment.

Despite the Depression, Pène du Bois's work was well received during the 1930s. He exhibited frequently, including four solo exhibitions at Kraushaar Galleries, which elicited positive critical reviews. Also during those years, the artist was commissioned to paint several murals for the Treasury Relief Art Project (TRAP) and the Works Progress Administration (WPA). Those murals remain today in post offices in Saratoga Springs and Rye, New York, and in Boston, Massachusetts. Pène du Bois was elected an associate member of the National Academy of Design in 1937, and his friend Jerome Myers (1867–1940) painted his portrait submission. He was made a full academician in 1940.

The artist continued his own writing and completed his autobiography, *Artists Say the Silliest Things*, in 1940, chronicling not only his life but the lives of his associates and contemporaries during an important time period in American art history. Pène du Bois taught at the Art Students League from 1930 to 1931 and again in 1935, and opened his own art school, which he named after himself, in 1932; he continued to teach classes in New York and Connecticut until 1950. He died in Boston on July 18, 1958 at the age of seventy-four.

BLJ

1 Royal Cortissoz, *Guy Pène du Bois* (New York: Whitney Museum of American Art), 11.

2 Betsy Fahlman, *Guy Pène du Bois: Painter of Modern Life* (New York: James Graham & Sons, 2004), 8

AARON HARRY GORSON (1872–1933)
Industrial Scene, Pittsburgh, 1928
Oil on canvas, 36 x 40 inches
Signed lower left
Gift in Memory of Roy C. McKenna, 1994.4
Provenance: Roy C. McKenna, Latrobe, Pennsylvania.

SELECTED EXHIBITIONS: *The Legacy of Art and Steel: The Paintings of Aaron Harry Gorson,* Duquesne Club, Pittsburgh, Pennsylvania, 2004; *The Power and Glory: Pittsburgh Industrial Landscapes by Aaron Harry Gorson,* Westmoreland Museum of Art, 1993; *Born of Fire: The Valley of Work,* Westmoreland Museum of American Art, Greensburg, Pennsylvania, 2006; Oberhausen, Germany, 2007; Chemnitz, Germany, 2008; Zabrze, Poland, 2009; *Feuerländer: Regions of Vulcan,* LVR Industriemuseum, Oberhausen, Germany, 2010.

When Aaron Harry Gorson arrived in the United States from Lithuania in 1888, he joined his brother in Philadelphia and was apprenticed to a tailor. His life, however, took a decidedly different turn when he started taking night classes at the Pennsylvania Academy of the Fine Arts in 1894 where he studied under Thomas Anshutz (1851–1912), who was carrying on the realist tradition established by Thomas Eakins (1844–1916).

In 1900, his patron, Rabbi Leonard Levy, arranged for Gorson to study in Paris for a year. While there, he attended the Académie Julian and the Académie Colarossi with many American students and came in contact with the work of James A. McNeill Whistler (1834–1903). Gorson returned from Paris and resettled in Philadelphia, only to pull up stakes in 1903, when he followed Rabbi Levy to Pittsburgh.

Although Gorson painted portraits in Pittsburgh, it was the industrial landscape that captivated him. In an extensive interview with Charles H. Gillespie for the *Pittsburgh Press* in 1908, Gorson commented, "I laugh when I hear people railing at Pittsburg's [*sic*] smoky atmosphere. All painters surely must bear me out when I say the smoke-filled foggy air adds wonderfully to the artistic effectiveness of the view. The darkened atmosphere contributes a wonderfully beautiful tone to the coloring."[1]

Gorson focused his attention on depicting the spectacle of industry via the light effects on water. He lived in the "smoky city" for eighteen years, becoming the best-known painter of industrial subjects during that period (six of the seven Gorson paintings owned by The Westmoreland are industrial scenes). Gorson was a master at depicting the steel mills at night, in all their polytechnic glory. His heavily laden brush, dipped in deep blues, greens, purples, and black, captured the romance and power of the mills as they illuminated the night sky and were reflected in the city's rivers.

Gorson's large canvas, *Industrial Scene, Pittsburgh* dramatizes the Bessemer converter blowing its top at night. As we look up the Monongahela River at the Jones & Laughlin Steel Works on the South Side, flying sparks and the intense glow of the fire offer a spectacular sight that was all too common in the city. Pittsburghers still recall a time when the entire city looked as if it were on fire, due to all the converters and furnaces firing along the river. In this painting, Gorson relies on layers of heavy impasto to emphasize the fierceness of the fire, while using subtle color harmonies of blue, green, purple, and black to create the dramatic contrast between the dark night and reflections of light on the river, making for near Whistlerian symphonic compositions that have little to do with the gritty reality of the steel mills. Hot metal bridges and the high-rise buildings of the city are just visible in the distance. According to Gorson, "At night we have the panoramic view of the outstretched black hills, illuminated by seeming million [*sic*] of lights, while here and there shoots out a mellow white flame with crystal sparks of metal from the furnaces. All of this repeats itself in the water below in a mellower tone, spread by the ripples studded with varied colors of lanterns while here and there are puffs of smoke, glimpses of molten steel in running cars, all busy, dazzling, dancing around the huge straight or pyramidal stacks of very dark hues."[2]

Gorson painted variations of the same subject over and over, making the depiction of mills at night his trademark. The mills operated twenty-four hours a day, giving him myriad opportunities to paint what he loved. Gorson reaffirmed his belief to Gillespie: "In my opinion, there is nothing finer in nature than the rivers here in Pittsburgh. You will not find

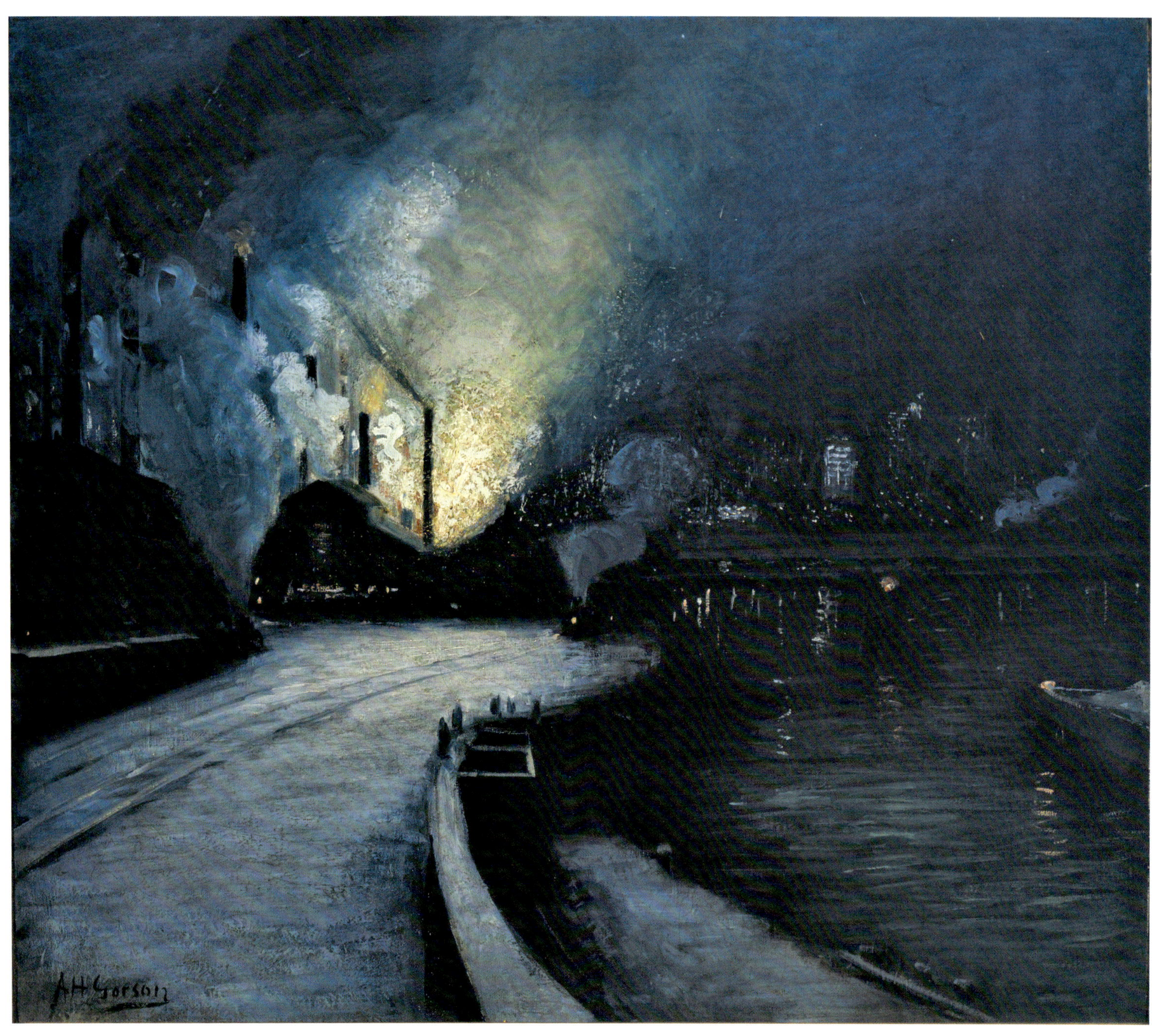
AH Gorson

their equal for artistic possibilities, in all Europe. I have been there, and nowhere did I see any rivers that could compare with them for richness or variety of subjects. True, the waters are not clear and limpid, but their very darkness and muddiness contributes a beauty to the effect. I have stood on bridges hereabout at sunset, or just during the fall of twilight, and never have I seen anything so splendid as the way in which that muddy river water catches the gleam of the dying light, and becomes transformed into running gold. The encompassing hills, stretching picturesquely along these streams, contribute splendid masses of form for the picture."[3]

Gorson loved industrial subjects for their own sake. As he said in 1908, "I am glad that I came, although it is hard to make people see anything beautiful in the scenes around the city. But it is beautiful nevertheless, and I will yet prove it to the world."[4] Color and light were as much the subjects of his paintings as were the mills, the rivers, and the atmospheric conditions. Formal concerns—such as the contrast of light and dark, reflection, texture, and subtle tonal shifts—predominate in his paintings, while cool and warm colors complement each other. Rina Youngner, an independent scholar who has written on the artist and his work, went as far as identifying the colors of the smoke in his canvases: blue smoke came from the open hearth furnaces; white light from the Bessemer converter; and red smoke from the blast furnace.[5] And, once again, the artist had something to say on the subject: "Smoke itself I think is a most graceful thing for its forms and quality of texture, its delicacy of color and vitality of movement. The mills with their ruggedness and activity, and the passing trains loaded with jet-black coal or red-hot ingots, the engines puffing out snow-white steam, add interest to the whole ensemble."[6]

When the John Levy Gallery held an exhibition of Gorson's work in New York in 1926, Royal Cortissoz, art critic for the *New York Herald Tribune*, wrote of his work (after referencing Whistler): "Mr. Gorson may not have felt that fairyland before him, but at all events he has enveloped his Pittsburgh in something that is not grime, investing it with a serene dignity and giving his pictures of it an unusual charm. The artist has borne all his artistic weight upon the delineation of the great steel plants that are one of the wonders of the present day world."[7]

Gorson's interview with Charles Gillespie took place when his industrial painting *Pittsburgh* was hanging in the twelfth annual Carnegie International. He had been submitting work to the International's jury of selection since 1904 but had been rejected each year. He submitted five paintings in 1908, and because *Pittsburgh* was accepted and given the premium hanging position, Gorson began submitting industrial subjects to subsequent Internationals. Although all of his work was rejected in 1909, he was accepted in 1910, 1911, 1912, 1914, 1920, and 1921, all with industrial-themed paintings. In 1921, Gorson left Pittsburgh for New York City because he felt the market for his industrial scenes was shrinking, as later evidenced by his work being rejected by the International juries from 1922 through 1926, and again in 1931. All but two of the twelve submissions over those years referenced Pittsburgh and its steel mills. He was, however, recognized in 1967 for his contributions as a Pittsburgh artist in an exhibition organized by the Carnegie Institute (now Carnegie Museum of Art) that spring.[8]

Upon his move to New York, Gorson turned to depicting the architecture and rivers of that city. However, two years after leaving Pittsburgh, he wrote to a good friend in Etna: "Lots of snow now in New York and it looks fine around the Harlem River and on the Hudson, but have darn Pittsburgh views still on my mind that I couldn't find time enough to go out sketching."[9] William J. Hyett (1876–1952)—a fellow Pittsburgh artist who also painted scenes of industry—organized a memorial exhibition of Gorson's work at J. J. Gillespie Gallery in downtown Pittsburgh just four months after his death in 1933.[10]

BLJ

1 Charles H. Gillespie, "Pittsburgh the Beautiful, A. H. Gorson, Artist," *Pittsburgh Press Sunday Magazine*, June 7, 1908, 3.

2 "Junction of Three Rivers," *Pittsburgh Sunday Post*, September 29, 1912.

3 Gillespie, "Pittsburgh the Beautiful," 13.

4 Ibid., 13.

5 Rina C. Youngner, *The Power and Glory: Pittsburgh Industrial Landscapes by Aaron Harry Gorson (1872–1933)* (New York: Spanierman Gallery LLC, 1989), 9.

6 "Junction of Three Rivers."

7 "What New York Says of Gorson," *Pittsburgh Post-Gazette*, March 26, 1922.

8 *Paintings by Aaron Gorson*, exhibition catalog (Pittsburgh: Carnegie Institute, 1967). The exhibition consisted of twenty-four paintings on loan from New York's Spanierman Gallery and ran from May 25 to June 25.

9 Ruth L. Wilson, "Painters of Pittsburgh...Aaron Gorson," *Pittsburgh Press Roto*, July 31, 1977, 16–18.

10 J. J. Gillespie Company, the name of the gallery when it was established in 1832, remains in operation today after 178 years, now located in the community of McMurray, fifteen miles south of Pittsburgh.

MALCOLM PARCELL (1896–1987)
Portrait of Helen Gallagher [Black and Green], c. 1928
Oil on canvas, 44 ¼ x 40 inches
Signed lower left
Gift of the Estate of Malcolm Parcell, 1987.134
Provenance: The Artist's Estate.

SELECTED EXHIBITIONS: 28th *Annual International Exhibition of Paintings*, Carnegie Institute, Pittsburgh, Pennsylvania, 1929; *Southwestern Pennsylvania Painters 1800-1945*, Westmoreland County Museum of Art, Greensburg, Pennsylvania, 1981; 1996; *100th Anniversary: Malcolm Parcell Retrospective*, Olin Fine Arts Gallery, Washington and Jefferson College, 1996; *Artists of the Commonwealth: Realism and Its Response in Pennsylvania Painting, 1900-1950*, Westmoreland Museum of American Art +, 2006-2007; *The Gift of Art*, Westmoreland Museum of American Art, 2009.

Malcolm Stevens Parcell was born on New Year's Day in Claysville, Washington County, Pennsylvania, and raised in nearby Washington. Malcolm was the youngest child of Stephen and Emma Parcell. His father, pastor of the Broad Street Baptist Church, had studied art before entering the ministry and encouraged his son to pursue his artistic ambitions. His brother, Lindsey Evans Parcell (1891–1959), known as Evans to his family, also became an artist, earning his living as an illustrator.

Parcell attended the Carnegie Institute of Technology (now Carnegie Mellon University) from 1913 to 1917 as a special (non-degree-earning) student, where he studied with artists Arthur W. Sparks (1871–1919) and George Sotter (1879–1953). In 1916, Parcell worked part-time as a mural painter for the Pittsburgh architect John Theodore Comes (1873–1922), a leading designer of churches. George Sotter had worked for Comes earlier in the century, designing and executing windows for numerous churches in and around Pittsburgh, and likely served as Parcell's connection to the architect. The money Parcell earned from mural painting allowed him to move to New York in 1917, following his graduation. In the city, he shared a studio on West Twenty-second Street with his brother, Evans, and continued his work with church architects and as an illustrator for *Scribner's Magazine*. During that same year, he was declared unfit for the draft due to a heart condition. While in New York, leading impressionist painter J. Alden Weir (1852–1919) purchased one of Parcell's paintings and advised him to go back home and paint his native area—advice he would follow in 1920.

Parcell earned his first national acclaim in 1919, when he won the Saltus Medal for Merit from the National Academy of Design for his portrait *Louine* (1918; Board of Public Education, Pittsburgh). A frequent model, Helen Louine Gallagher (1897–1984) was a public schoolteacher in Washington who would become the artist's wife in 1937. Of the portrait, a *New York Times* critic wrote: "Mr. Parcell has awakened interest in the character of his subject and justified his choice of type by his power to realize it."[1] This painting also won first prize at the ninth annual Associated Artists of Pittsburgh exhibition, his first of many showings with the organization.

Parcell's first appearance in the Carnegie International was in 1920, when two of his paintings were selected. Between then and 1950, he was represented twenty-six times, winning the popular prize two consecutive years—1924 and 1925. When the International was suspended due to World War II and replaced with the all-American "Painting in the United States" exhibition from 1943 to 1949, Parcell was invited to participate in all seven exhibitions. The Macbeth Gallery in New York exhibited Parcell's work in 1922, only the second time his work was shown in the city, and although his paintings received mixed reviews, critics cited the artist as showing great promise. A second solo exhibition at Macbeth's would be held in 1927.

Back in Pittsburgh by 1923, the artist exhibited ten paintings at the J. J. Gillespie Gallery, all of which were sold by the close of the third day, prompting a Pittsburgh critic to pronounce Parcell "a prodigy."[2] The following year he exhibited thirteen paintings at Gillespie's, including portraits, mythological fantasies, genre scenes, and autumn landscapes.

Parcell was highly acclaimed for his portraiture throughout his career. Influential to his choice of subject matter were both John Singer Sargent (1856–1925) and James A. McNeill Whistler (1834–1903). Parcell believed that accurate construction of a composition was all-important. "I don't think you can be a successful portrait painter and allow your feeling to enter into it where you twist a nose or an eyebrow to create an

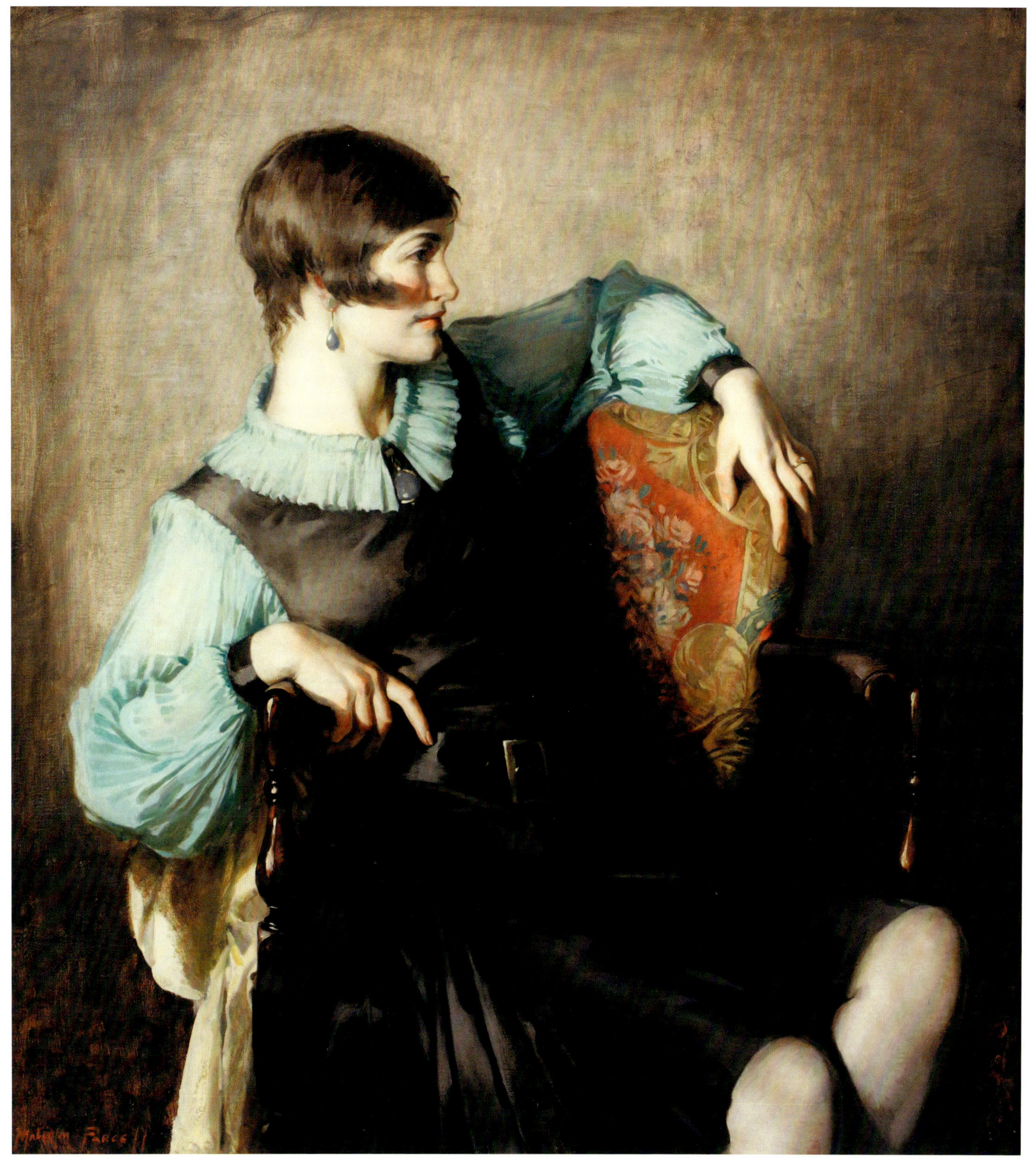

interesting figure."[3] A 1923 article in the French journal *La Revue Moderne* stated: "This painter knows how to place the soul in a glance and feeling in the smallest detail of the face."[4] He was a strong draftsman, attempting a literal likeness of all his sitters, and his drawings and prints reveal his talent for using the simplest line to powerfully describe the human form. In addition to portraits, Parcell painted genre scenes, mythological fantasies, allegories, and landscapes of western Pennsylvania.

Parcell turned to mural painting in 1934, and over the course of his career he painted *The Judgment of Paris* for the Continental Grille at the William Penn Hotel (now the Omni William Penn Hotel) in downtown Pittsburgh, where it was displayed over the Copper Kettle Bar (1934); *The History of the National Road and the Whiskey Rebellion* for the George Washington Hotel in Claysville and *Pegasus and the Amazons* for the Seelbach Hotel in Louisville, Kentucky (1935); *A Future Begins* for the Fidelity Trust Company, Pittsburgh (1949); and *Books Are Many Lives to Live* for the Citizens Library in Washington, Pennsylvania (1964).

When the Carnegie Institute held a one-man show of Parcell's work in 1935, he was the first Pittsburgh artist to be so honored. In his review of the exhibition for *Carnegie Magazine*, John O'Connor Jr. described Parcell as "a painter rich in imagination, strong in the technical requirements of his craft, romantic in his approach to his problems at a time when many of his fellow artist display a tendency to be crudely realistic, and above all . . . an artist of rare personal talent."[5]

Parcell painted his three-quarter-length *Portrait of Helen Gallagher [Black and Green]* nearly ten years before the couple's marriage. Although she was a public school teacher (she retired in 1963), this image—with her stylish bobbed hair and ruffle-pleated sea-green blouse under a black-belted jumper coming just above the knees—suggests a night out rather than a day in the classroom. Parcell's expressive brushwork and superb draftsmanship accurately capture this fashionable and confident woman, who remained his favorite model. Her pose implies some discomfort, as one of her arms rests on the arm of the chair while the other is draped over the back, her tense fingers perhaps signaling impatience with posing. The painting was shown in the Carnegie International in 1929 and is one of about forty known portraits that the artist made of Helen, beginning when she was just seventeen years old.

This portrait is one of two in the Museum's collection, the other being *Emma [Portrait of My Mother]*, 1947 (1987.133), which was shown in the Carnegie Institute's "Painting in the United States" exhibition the year before Emma Parcell died. This rather eerie yet biographical painting shows the disembodied head of Parcell's mother hovering above a scene of his hometown of Claysville, which includes, among other elements, his family home, his father, the family church, and the artist painting at his easel. Both paintings were gifts of the artist's estate upon Parcell's death in 1987 and represent two very different examples of his portrait style. The Westmoreland owns twenty-eight works of art by Parcell—five paintings, ten drawings, eleven etchings, and two sculptures—which encompass the eclectic range of the artist's subject matter and media over the course of his career.

Parcell's romantic realist style fell out of favor in the 1940s and 1950s with the advent of abstract expressionism. He did not waiver, however, in his subject matter or stylistic approach, maintaining his commitment to realism. In 1963, Parcell moved permanently to Moon Lorn, his country home and studio in the scenic hills near Prosperity, Pennsylvania.[6] There, in his trademark black skullcap, Parcell painted almost every day until his death at the age of ninety-one. When he died, an unfinished portrait remained on his easel. The artist received the Washington County Distinguished Citizen Award in 1981, and the largest exhibition to date of his work was shown to celebrate the opening of the new Olin Fine Arts Center at Washington & Jefferson College in 1982. *Malcolm Parcell: Wizard of Moon Lorn* was published by Donald Miller in 1985, and Paul Burgess Edwards's *The Life and Work of Malcolm Parcell: A Catalogue Raisonné* was published by the Washington County Historical Society in 1999.

BLJ

1 *New York Times Magazine*, March 30, 1919.

2 Paul Burgess Edwards, *The Life and Work of Malcolm Parcell, A Catalogue Raisonné* (Washington, PA: Washington County Historical Society, 2002), xvii.

3 Donald Miller, *Malcolm Parcell: Wizard of Moon Lorn*, Pittsburgh, Pennsylvania, 1985, 22.

4 *La Revue Moderne*, October 20, 1923.

5 John O'Connor Jr., "The Carnegie Institute Presents Malcolm Parcell," *Carnegie Magazine*, January 1935, 241.

6 Parcell named the property Moon Lorn because of the tall trees that hid the moon from view.

JOHANNA KNOWLES WOODWELL HAILMAN (1871–1958)
Pittsburgh River Scene, 1929
Gouache and pastel on paper, 21 ½ x 29 7/8 inches
Signed and dated lower right
Gift of Friends of Thomas Lynch Wentling in his memory, with partial funding from the Women's Committee and Museum Acquisition Funds, 1995.3
Provenance: Private Collection, Philadelphia, Pennsylvania; Concept Art Gallery, Pittsburgh, Pennsylvania.

Selected Exhibitions: *Born of Fire: The Valley of Work*, Westmoreland Museum of American Art, 2006; Oberhausen, Germany, 2007; Chemnitz, Germany, 2008; and Zabrze, Poland, 2009; *Feuerländer: Regions of Vulcan*, LVR-Industriemuseum, Oberhausen, Germany, 2010.

Johanna Knowles Woodwell Hailman was the granddaughter of Joseph Woodwell—founder of Woodwell Hardware in Pittsburgh—and the daughter of well-known Scalp Level school landscape painter Joseph Woodwell (1843–1911). She grew up in Pittsburgh, and was the third generation to occupy the Woodwell family estate on Penn Avenue. Although she first studied with her father, she did not completely follow in his artistic footsteps. Instead of concentrating on rural landscape painting, Hailman specialized in floral still life compositions and gardens, painted in a vibrant color palette in both oil and watercolor. From time to time, however, she broke away from that mode of expression to paint the industrial environment in and around Pittsburgh, including a remarkable industrial symphony in paint—*Mills, Trains, and Barges* (Duquesne Club, Pittsburgh)—as well as scenes of Homestead, Clairton, Rankin Mills, the Brady Street Bridge, and Etna. When her work was shown in New York at the John Levy Galleries in 1923, a reporter for *American Art News* wrote: "Mrs. Hailman is perfectly fearless whether she is facing grotesque mechanical forms and the reds and pinks and sun-shot clouds of steam of the 'Eliza Furnace,' the mighty panorama of the 'Pittsburgh Mill,' or a huge cactus plant whose leaves of palest violet under the blazing Bahama sunlight form 'Nature's Jailhouse' through which the spectator glimpses a background of semi-tropical sea and sky."[1] A reporter for the *Pittsburgh Post-Gazette* referenced her industrial watercolors in an exhibition at J. J. Gillespie Gallery in 1935, saying, "What is really notable is the vigor with which this native Pittsburgher has put down her notes on our gray railroad tracks, our sullen rivers, and the smoke which hovers over water and land. For this preoccupation with smoke is, indeed, one of the most fascinating aspects of all her paintings—smoke swirling from trains, from mills, from boats—and adding immeasurably to the balance and beauty of the scenes."[2] Hailman did not adhere to any specific style or school, and she was never afraid to express herself: "I do what I want to do. I've never been afraid of color. I always paint what I want to paint with the color I want and regardless of school."[3]

In *Pittsburgh River Scene*—a cropped view of the second Point Bridge (1927–1970) that crossed the Monongahela River at the confluence of the three rivers—Hailman reveals just a portion of the curving arch and two of the three massive piers that supported the bridge. The smoky atmosphere, the train chugging across the bridge at the forefront of the picture plane, and towboats pushing coal barges in both directions on the river reveal a city at work. Through her choice of large flat areas of color for the piers, shore, and river; long sweeping lines; and hint of detail in the boats and the bridge, Hailman achieves an abstract quality in this composition. She painted on beige paper, which shows through the paint layer in some areas to give the scene its overall warm tonality, but used a palette of bright and rich reds, blues, and greens. In 1937, Jeanette Jena, art critic for the *Pittsburgh Post-Gazette*, wrote, "Nobody but a Pittsburgher would quite realize the shade of that pink, tan dust, the mauve of the sky on a lowering day, the eerie light which strains through the fog. And when the smoke changes color in different pictures, with the mood of the day, one senses the same kindly feeling in the artist's brush, as when one watches familiar moods chase across the face of a very close friend."[4]

Hailman moved even further toward abstraction in her watercolor *Clinton Furnace*, 1924 (1996.21), depicting the oldest blast furnace to operate successfully in Pittsburgh using coke as fuel. Her palette is muted, composed of subtle tones of

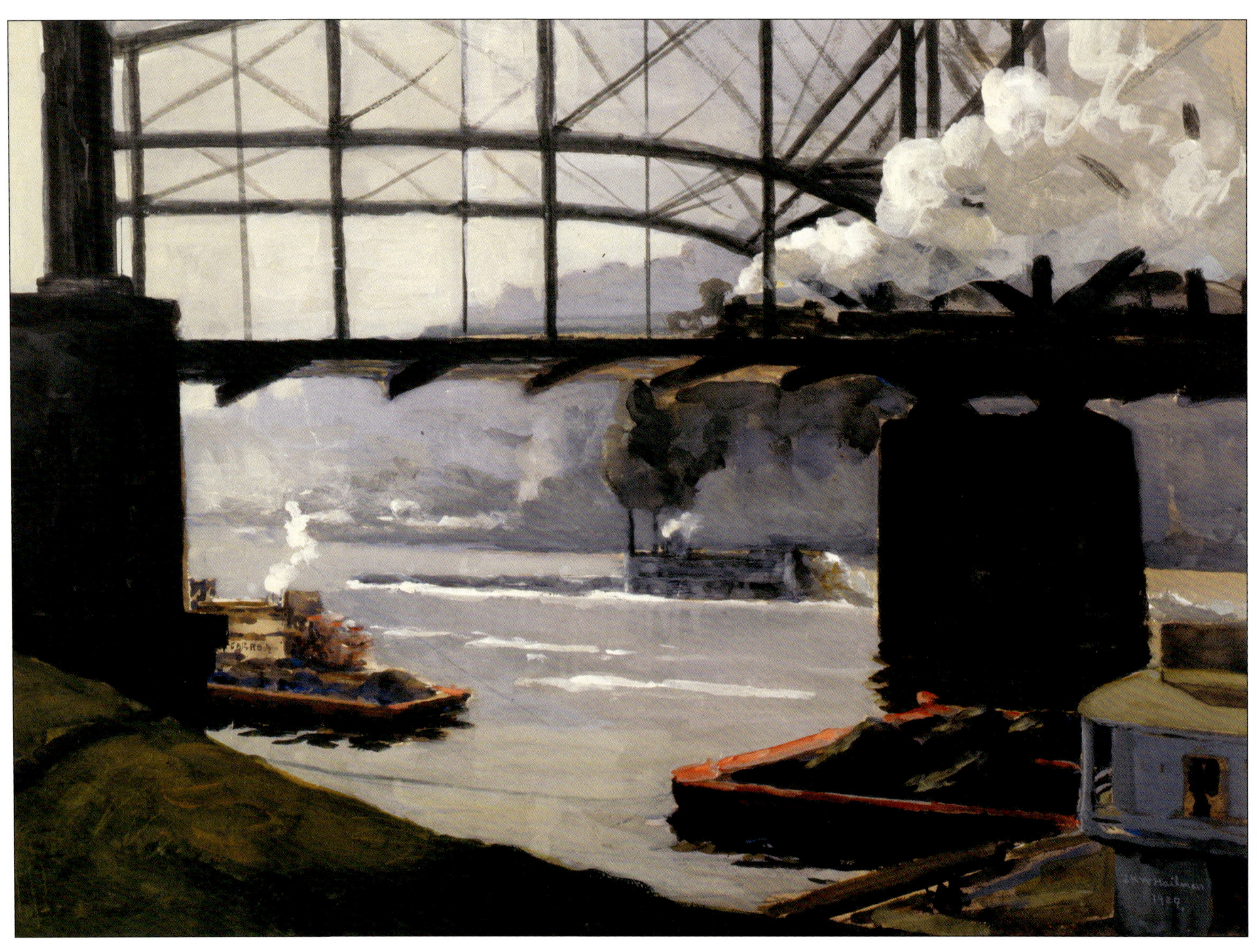

black, white, brown, and gray, and she once again effectively uses the color of the paper to capture the murky atmosphere without painting it, adding only textured patches of yellow and red for the fire of the blast.

Pittsburgh River Scene was given in memory of Thomas Lynch Wentling, who was a president of Southwest Bank (now First Commonwealth Bank) from 1962 until 1981. The Westmoreland owns six paintings by the artist, representing the breadth of her subject areas in portraiture, landscape, and floral still life.

Hailman's only formal art training was at the Pittsburgh School of Design for Women, where George Hetzel (1826–1899) was a leading instructor. She first exhibited in the 1895 exhibition that marked the opening of the Carnegie Library of Pittsburgh, and was included in the inaugural Carnegie International in 1896. She continued showing in all but two of the annual exhibitions until 1955, when she participated in her final International at the age of eighty-four. In January 1927, Hailman was awarded a solo exhibition at the Carnegie Institute (now Carnegie Museum of Art), which included 112 paintings, only 3 of which were industrial subjects. Flower and garden still lifes; portraits; seascapes; and tropical landscapes of Nassau, Jamaica, Miami, and Palm Beach were her primary subjects and the art for which she was best known. She showed her work in exhibitions in Pittsburgh, New York, Chicago, and other venues around the country, winning a silver medal at the Panama-Pacific International Exposition in San Francisco in 1915. In 1905, she married steel industrialist and civic leader James D. Hailman, who was also a patron of the arts. Hailman was a member of the National Association of Women Painters and Sculptors and the Associated Artists of Pittsburgh.

Known as Pittsburgh's First Lady of Painting, Hailman died in Pittsburgh in 1958 at the age of eighty-seven, having made a significant contribution not only to regional art but also to city planning when she crusaded for beautification of the city, leading a conservation effort for its gardens and parks. An avid gardener herself, Hailman helped found the Garden Club of Allegheny County, the Phipps Conservatory, and the Pittsburgh Parks and Playground Society, serving as president of the latter two organizations. In 1936, the Garden Club of America awarded her its gold medal for her efforts with civic gardens. She even started a campaign to have Pittsburgh's many bridges painted different colors "to give Pittsburgh a little life and beauty," she said, "and take away its drab, dull, depressing tone."[5] In her obituary, the *Pittsburgh Press* noted that "she was recognized as an island of normalcy in the ocean of modern art."[6]

BLJ

1 "Is at Home in Atlantic as Much as Native State," *Pittsburgh Post-Gazette*, November 25, 1923. The article quotes from the *American Art News* review.

2 "Show Water Color Works by Johanna K. Hailman," *Pittsburgh Post-Gazette*, April 17, 1935.

3 Dorothy Kantner, "84-Year Old Artist in International," *Pittsburgh Sun-Telegraph*, October 6, 1955.

4 Jeanette Jena, "Show of Johanna Hailman Art Works to Open Today," *Pittsburgh Post-Gazette*, October 12, 1937.

5 "Artist Would Paint Bridges Green or Red in Criticizing Drab Appearance of City," *Gazette Times*, January 13, 1927.

6 "Artist Johanna Hailman Dies," *Pittsburgh Press*, June 30, 1958, 3.

ROY HILTON (1892–1963)
Winter Day, c. 1929
Oil on canvas, 28 3/8 x 35 ¼ inches
Signed lower right
Gift of the Women's Committee through the Westmoreland Society, 2001.5
Provenance: Private Collection, Washington; Gilliland's Fine Art, Ligonier, Pennsylvania.

SELECTED EXHIBITIONS: *Associated Artists of Pittsburgh Nineteenth Annual Exhibition,* Carnegie Institute, Pittsburgh, Pennsylvania, 1929; *Born of Fire: The Valley of Work,* Westmoreland Museum of American Art, Greensburg, Pennsylvania, 2006; Oberhausen, Germany, 2007; Chemnitz, Germany, 2008; Zabrze, Poland, 2009; *Feuerländer: Regions of Vulcan,* LVR Industriemuseum, Oberhausen, Germany, 2010.

Roy Hilton grew up in Winchester, Massachusetts, and attended the Phillips Academy in Andover before entering the Eric Pape School of Art. He came to Pittsburgh in 1928 to take a position as an instructor in the Department of Painting and Design at the Carnegie Institute of Technology (now Carnegie Mellon University), a position he retained for nearly thirty years. He was an active participant in the Pittsburgh art scene, frequently exhibiting in the Associated Artists of Pittsburgh's annual exhibitions and included in invitationals of the work of Pittsburgh artists held at the Carnegie Institute (now Carnegie Museum of Art). Hilton was celebrated in Greensburg with an exhibition organized by the Greensburg Art Club in 1941 and his work was also accepted into the "Artists for Victory" exhibition at the Metropolitan Museum in New York in 1942. Because he was highly thought of, Carnegie Institute awarded him a solo exhibition in 1943, only the eighth contemporary regional artist to be so honored. He was commissioned by the Treasury Department's Section of Fine Arts to paint murals for post offices in Westfield, New Jersey and Rockymount, Virginia, both of which were completed in 1937. Further recognition came for the artist when his study of a night baseball game at Forbes Field was reproduced on the July 1940 cover of the *Saturday Evening Post.*

Pittsburgh—its neighborhoods, industrial sites, and cityscapes—was the source of Hilton's subject matter, and the community responded by embracing both him and his work. He saw the city through a humanist veil, always seeking to include emotion while eliminating detail to extract essential forms. As John O'Connor Jr. wrote, "Roy Hilton is not given to painting traditional subjects in a conventional way. He seeks out the unusual—even what may be considered the unpictorial—and makes a successful composition of it. . . .He demonstrates in his canvases that even the machine age is picturesque and has numerous possibilities for the artist who looks at it with a sympathetic and knowing eye"[1] Like Edward Hopper (1882–1967) and Charles Sheeler (1883–1965) before him, the careful arrangement of simplified form and dramatic use of light were the two most important pictorial elements he employed.

Hilton uses the simplified shapes and geometry of the precisionist style in his two paintings in The Westmoreland's collection, *Winter Day*, and *Pittsburgh Mills* (1982.119). *Winter Day* references the many layers of houses that dot the hillsides of the Pittsburgh landscape, while the latter depicts one of the countless mills that populated the city. The artist found his subjects within his community and painted what he knew best, eliminating all extraneous details. Although there are no figures seen in *Winter Day,* Hilton alludes to the middle-class worker through both the lights glowing in the windows of the homes and the shoveled path up the steep steps leading to the neighborhood. The city's unique topography required creative methods of building to meet the housing needs of the myriad workers who migrated there to work in the steel industry. The famous "steps of Pittsburgh" climb throughout the hilly city, often the only access to some of these homes. With a monochromatic palette, Hilton suggests the smoky atmosphere that permeated Pittsburgh, leaving residents no choice but to turn their lights on even in the middle of the day. His composition is about light, repetitive pattern, and line. Before he initiated a work on canvas, he would often visit the site, taking notes about the light conditions and other details so that he would have a more accurate record when he began to paint. Hilton thought drawing was critical, and was often heard to say: "If

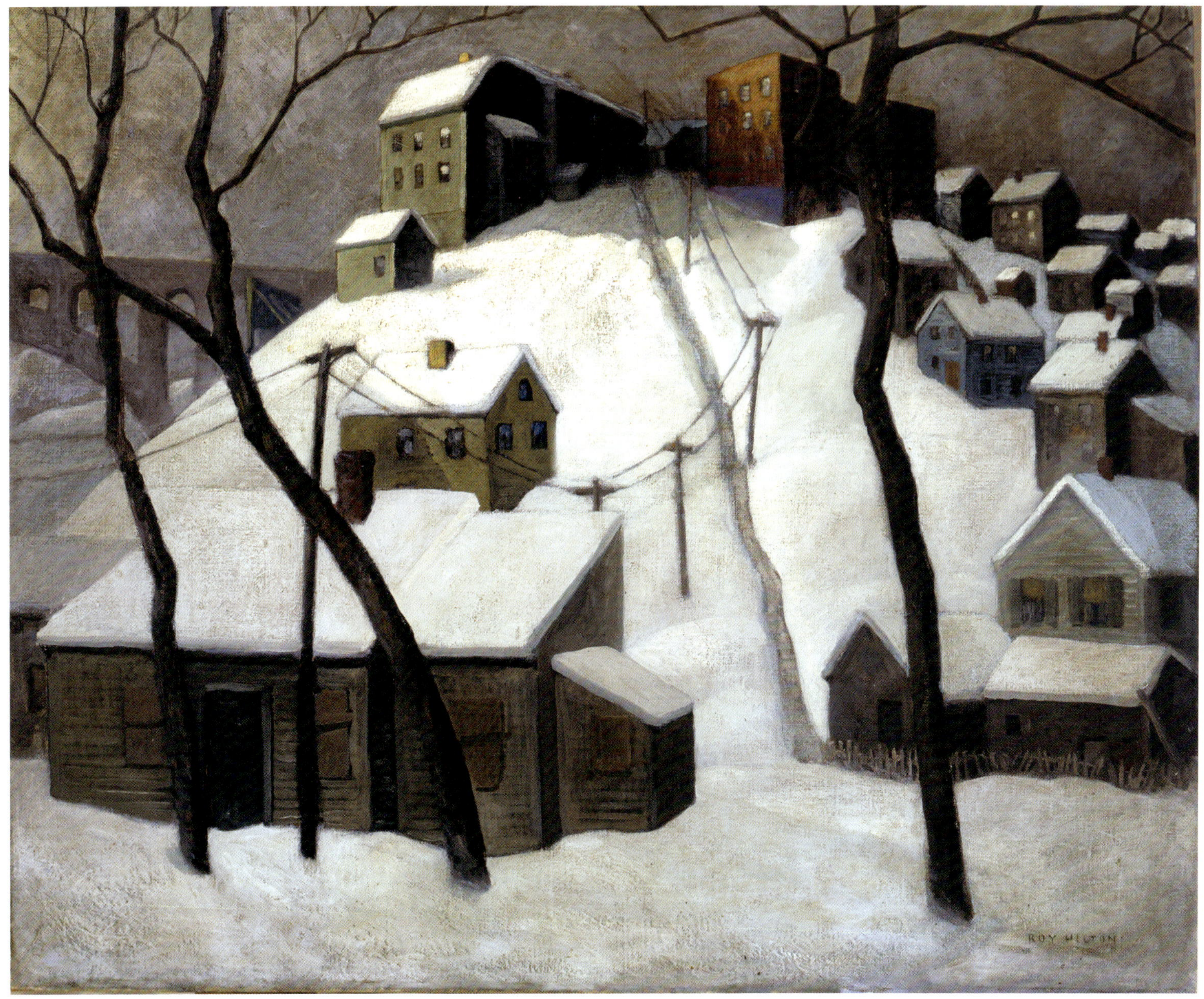
ROY HILTON

you're really serious about your art, you draw it as you see it and as you feel it should be expressed."[2] In this composition, the artist's interest in light and shadow is evident in the flat planes of the dark buildings set against an illuminated snow-covered hillside. The blue door of the house in the foreground lends a spot of color to this otherwise neutral landscape.

Pittsburgh Mills is striking in the artist's use of a predominantly mauve palette. Once again, the play of light is evidenced in the billowing clouds of smoke set against the shadowed foreground of the blast furnace and associated mill. Other furnaces form a line behind; smokestacks continue the extreme verticality, while the mill building stretches out horizontally in both directions. Hilton has included the mill worker in this composition, emphasizing how minute he is in comparison to the giant furnaces that he helps operate. In 2006, the Museum purchased a sketchbook of pencil and charcoal drawings (2006.17) that provides further insight into the artist's working method.

Roy Hilton died suddenly in Pittsburgh on October 10, 1963 at the age of seventy-three, doing what he loved best, making art. In his obituary, Ralph Brem wrote: "Art for him was neatness and order. Art for the looking; the search for a familiar scene that recalls past experience and send the looker on his way a bit happier for the reminder.[3]

BLJ

1 John O'Connor Jr., "Paintings by Roy Hilton," *Carnegie Magazine,* May 1943, 47.

2 Ralph Brem, "Brief Death Notice Not Enough," *Pittsburgh Press,* October 12, 1963.

3 Ibid.

ERNEST LAWSON (1873–1939)
Pittsburgh Mills, Monongahela River, c. 1930
Oil on canvas, 20 x 23 ¾ inches
Signed lower right
Gift of the William A. Coulter Fund, 1984.44
Provenance: The Artist; Mr. Bertram Bloch; Robert Schoelkopf Gallery, New York.

Selected Exhibitions: *Impressionism: An American View,* Westmoreland County Museum of Art, 1983; *Born of Fire: The Valley of Work,* Westmoreland Museum of American Art, Greensburg, Pennsylvania, 2006; Oberhausen, Germany, 2007; Chemnitz, Germany, 2008; Zabrze, Poland, 2009; *Feuerländer: Regions of Vulcan,* LVR Industriemuseum, Oberhausen, Germany, 2010.

Ernest Lawson came to Pittsburgh on at least three occasions: as a member of the jury of selection for the Associated Artists of Pittsburgh's annual exhibitions in both 1927 and 1932, and as a member of the jury of award for the Carnegie International in 1928. With his trademark color palette, Lawson created a view along the Monongahela River that captures his emotional response to the industrial environment he encountered. The artist clearly found inspiration in the smoke-filled atmosphere of the steel city.

Lawson was born in Halifax, Nova Scotia, the son of a doctor who did not like the idea of his son becoming an artist. Lawson went ahead anyway, studying with John Henry Twachtman (1853–1902) and J. Alden Weir (1852–1919) at the Art Students League in New York and at their summer art school in Cos Cob, Connecticut. While briefly attending the Académie Julian in Paris in 1893, Lawson became intrigued with the work of James A. McNeill Whistler (1834–1903). While in France, he sought the advice of impressionist painter Alfred Sisley (1839–1899), who told him to "put more paint on your canvas and less on yourself!"—a suggestion Lawson took to heart.[1] Prominent art critic Edward Alden Jewell wrote about the artist in the *New York Times*: "Founded upon the principles of French Impressionism, Lawson's art became a truly original embodiment of the adventure of eye and heart and mind. It was not Impressionism at all in any narrow, hidebound, derivative meaning of the term. It was the vigorous, brilliantly realized, unique expression of a poet of finely sensitive vision."[2] Lawson made few preliminary drawings; rather, he worked directly on the canvas, using a palette knife, sometimes a brush, or even his thumb, scraping and manipulating the paint to achieve the effect he wanted.

When painting his *Pittsburgh Mills, Monongahela River,* Lawson saw colors in the landscape that no other artist saw. While essentially painting the same view of the river that Otto Kuhler (1894–1977) had painted several years earlier (see page 192), Lawson created his view in an entirely different style and color palette. Unfamiliar with the area, Lawson originally titled his painting *Mon River at Allegheny, PA* (now the North Side and part of Pittsburgh), when in reality the painting depicts the Monongahela River and the South Side of the city. Like the artists before him, Lawson included no figures in his scene, which is purely about the unique topography, the winding river, and the riverbanks lined with steel mills and factories. His color palette is composed entirely of jewel tones, which he effectively utilized: brilliant emerald greens, ruby reds, sapphire blues, and golden topazes, applied in a heavy impasto technique that makes the painting vibrate and the river seem to flow. Lawson built his paintings using layer upon layer of thickly applied pigment. Because of his brilliant color combinations and impasto technique, art critics of the period repeatedly said the artist painted with "a palette of crushed jewels."[3] There is a vitality to Lawson's landscapes that was not achieved by other artists of the industrial scene. His paintings are lyrical creations of land, sky, and atmosphere. According to the artist, "Movement in nature is my creed as a landscapist and light and air are my delight."[4]

Lawson remained committed to his chosen mode of expression throughout his career, using the same high-key color combinations, layering of impasto pigment, and bravura brushwork in all of his landscape compositions. To explain his ideas and theories about painting, the artist wrote his own credo, entitled, "The Power to See Beautifully and Idealistically," in which he discussed his use of color: "Color is my specialty in art. That's my special technique; experiment with color. I did it from the beginning. . . . It affects me like music affects

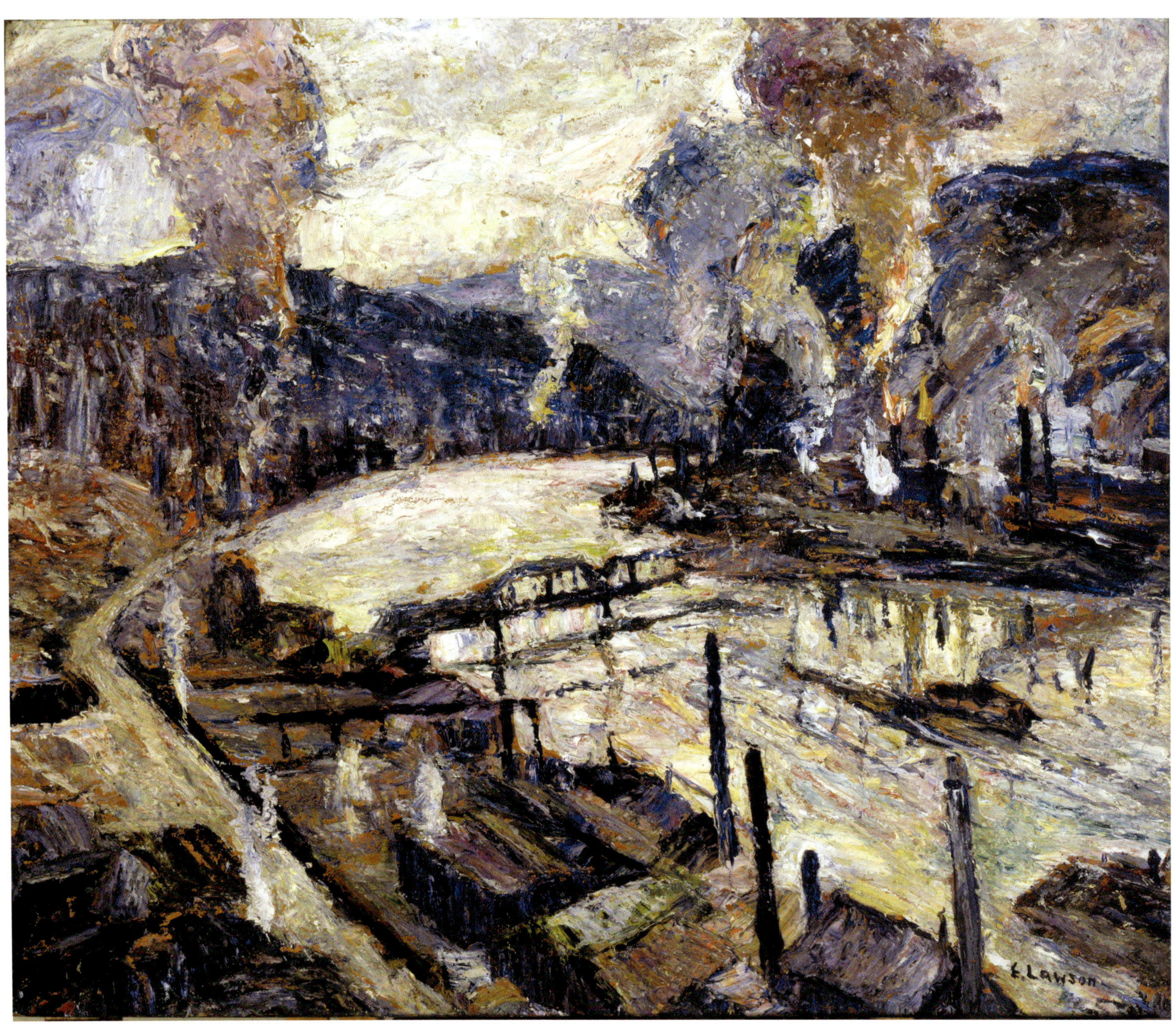
E. Lawson

some persons—emotionally. I like to play with colors like a composer playing with counterpoint in music. It's sort of rhythmic proportion. You try one color scheme in a sort of contrapuntal fashion, and you get one effect. We don't actually copy nature in art. Nature merely suggests something to us, to which we add our own ideas. Impressions from nature are merely jumping off points for artistic creations."[5] In letters to his friend and dealer Frederic Newlin Price, president of the Ferargil Galleries in New York, Lawson revealed even more about his use of color: "I believe man's emotions can be expressed in a clear understandable way with color. I believe I can take one simple well-balanced landscape, use it as a foundation and paint in three keys and depict the three major emotions in a man's life—anticipation, realization and retrospection. Take anticipation—early dawn, tender color, etc. Realization—intense key with vivid brilliant color. Retrospection—restful twilight or colorful night, low key, violet tones."[6]

Drawing inspiration from scenes of industry was not unusual for Lawson, as he also painted the less-than-attractive scenes along the Harlem River in upper Manhattan, making them beautiful with his vibrant color palette. Few images in his oeuvre are like *Pittsburgh Mills*; however, bridges remained one of his favorite subjects and are seen in many views recorded from both his studio around High Bridge on the Harlem River and Washington Heights.

J. N. Laurvik wrote of the artist's work: "Lawson's canvases open one's eyes to the beauty of everyday scenes and the innate charms of familiar places as the work of few American painters has ever done . . . supremely investing the commonplace actualities of life with the hitherto unsuspected glamour, a poetry and a charm quite personal."[7] In 1896, William Merritt Chase (1849–1916) referred to Lawson as "America's greatest landscape painter," and in 1907, Robert Henri (1865–1929)—leader of the Ashcan school of painters—paid him a great compliment: "Lawson is the biggest man we have had since Winslow Homer."[8] Although Lawson was well known during his lifetime and exhibited his work frequently—taking part in the famous exhibition of the Eight at Macbeth Gallery in New York in 1908, as well as the Armory Show of 1913—he died in relative obscurity in Miami, Florida, in 1939. Lawson was elected a member of the National Academy of Design in 1917.

BLJ

1 Henry and Sidney Berry-Hill, *Ernest Lawson: American Impressionist, 1873–1939* (Leigh-on-Sea, England: F. Lewis Publishers, 1968), 22.

2 Peyton Boswell, "Ernest Lawson Departs," *Art Digest*, 1 January 1940, 3.

3 Berry-Hill, *Ernest Lawson*, 29, referring to James Gibbons Huneker, a New York journalist who coined the expression in reference to Monet's "palette of diamonds and precious stones" and Renoir's "rainbow palette."

4 Ibid., 22, referring to Lawson's credo, "The Power to See Beautifully and Idealistically."

5 Ibid., 21, 46.

6 Peyton Boswell Jr., "As Ever Ernest," *Art Digest*, 15 April 1943, 10.

7 Berry-Hill, *Ernest Lawson*, 26.

8 Peyton Boswell Jr., "As Ever Ernest," 10; Berry-Hill, *Ernest Lawson*, 26.

OSCAR FLORIANUS BLUEMNER (1867–1938)
Untitled (House Cluster), 1930
Inscribed verso: "stumpy shapes in a pattern"
Gouache on paper, 4 ¾ x 5 ¾ inches
Gift of the Westmoreland Society, 1999.7
Provenance: Estate of the artist; Hirschl & Adler Galleries, New York; Private Collection, California; Kraushaar Galleries, Inc., New York.

Selected Exhibitions: *The Gift of Art*, Westmoreland Museum of American Art, 2009.

> Landscape painting speaks to the soul like a poem or music, more intimately than any other kind of painting. I present a surprising vision of landscape by the daring new use or colors. . . .
>
> —Oscar Bluemner, *Oscar Florianus Bluemner*

Born in Hanover, Germany, Oscar Florianus Bluemner immigrated to the United States in 1892 after receiving a degree in architecture from the Royal Academy of Design in Berlin. Following in the path of his father and grandfather, he began his career as an architect. However, he became disillusioned with the field and shifted his focus to painting between 1908 and 1910 after meeting influential art dealer and photographer Alfred Stieglitz (1864–1946). Stieglitz sealed Bluemner's fate by introducing him to European and American modernism through his 291 Gallery exhibitions in New York.

By the time Bluemner arrived in America to set up his architectural practice, he had designed both a theater and a post office in Germany. The watercolor and colored-pencil sketches that Bluemner made as preliminary studies for his building designs would anticipate his later painting style. He lived and worked in New York, Boston, and Chicago, ultimately settling in New York City. While living in Chicago in 1896, he married Lina Schumm, with whom he had a son. Following Lina's death in 1926, Bluemner would move to South Braintree, Massachusetts, and live a much more secluded life, away from the hustle and bustle of city life.

After his move to New York City in 1901, Bluemner started sketching urban views in an impressionist style similar to that of Maurice Prendergast (1858–1924). This early work was realistic, as he depicted the man-made and natural landscape environment of houses, barns, and factories surrounding the city, venturing often into New Jersey, where he moved in 1916. An extended trip to Europe in 1912 allowed him to experience modernism firsthand through exhibitions of the latest avant-garde artists of the period, including the futurists in Italy; Die Brücke and Der Blaue Reiter in Germany; and the postimpressionists, fauves, and cubists in Paris. This direct exposure had a profound and immediate effect on him as an artist, prompting a radical shift in his style. His color palette intensified, edges and details sharpened, forms became solid, and pictorial space—although never denied—was compressed and became somewhat claustrophobic.

Upon his return to the United States in 1913, Bluemner submitted one of his newest landscape paintings to the landmark Armory Show and wrote an article in defense of modernism and the infamous exhibition for Stieglitz's *Camera Work* magazine. Stieglitz gave Bluemner a solo show at his 291 Gallery in 1915, the artist's first in New York. His work had become more and more abstract after his return from Europe, prompting him to rework his more realistic compositions to conform to his new style.

Bluemner's preferred subjects were architectural forms set in the landscape—both urban and rural—and his hard-edged, unpopulated landscapes of buildings, factories, and water towers of this period are a precursor to his precisionism in the next decade. During the 1920s, more mystical elements—large suns and moons, evocative night views—permeated his art, tempering his structured forms with an element of fantasy. His paintings from this point on convey mood and emotion through abstracted, simplified shapes and intense color. Bluemner's work was featured in a solo exhibition at the Whitney Studio Galleries in 1929, but despite his success with exhibitions during this period, he did not sell much and spent most of his life plagued with financial difficulties. During the 1930s, the artist was employed by the short-lived Public Works of Art Project and the Federal Art Project, but the paintings

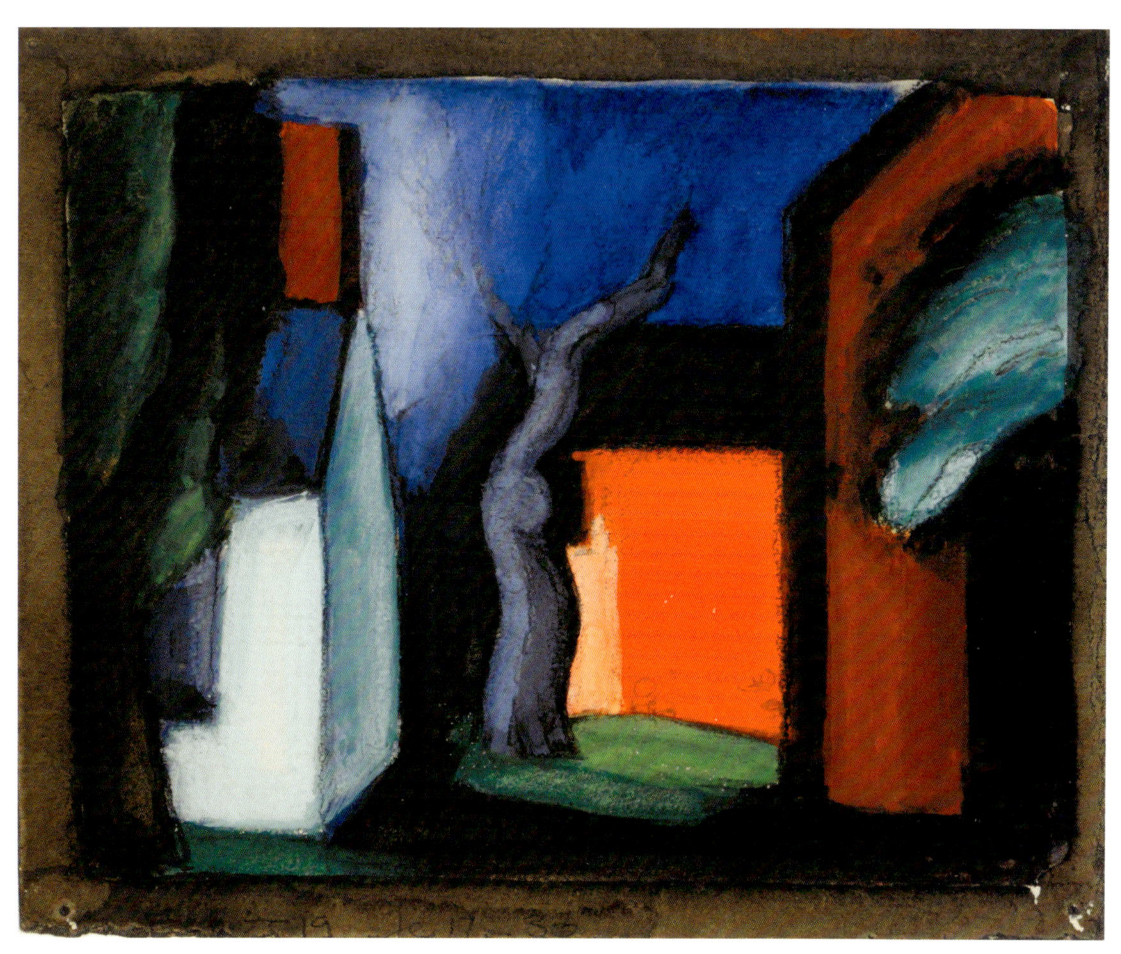

he made for the government have been lost.

Bluemner painted both large and small canvases, and many are especially tiny—including The Westmoreland's *Untitled (House Cluster)*, which measures only 4¾ x 5¾ inches—yet dynamic in their scale due to the color combinations chosen by the artist. Throughout his life, Bluemner kept annotated notebooks, or "painting diaries," in which he expressed both his interest in color theory and his philosophy about art. In them, he worked out diagrams of color and media combinations that would be used in his paintings. He associated each color with a particular meaning or emotion, thereby giving him a reference guide for the mood he wanted to convey. Many of the diaries include color studies and sketches for his paintings as well as early architectural illustrations of homes he had designed. Fascinated with the formal, emotional, and spiritual qualities of color, Bluemner developed his own color system in which he assigned individual properties to specific hues. Red, for example, represented "power, energy, life, blood, passion, majesty, rage."[1] In referencing his reliance on bright red hues for his houses and barns, Bluemner dubbed himself "the Vermillionaire."[2]

The structure and order of Bluemner's compositions derive from his architectural training, but it is his highly personal style and use of color that so strongly convey mood in his paintings. Geometric patterns of color constitute *Untitled (House Cluster)*. A black wash outlines the composition, directing the eye to three tightly organized buildings set in a shallow wooded landscape. Full foliaged trees frame the cluster of houses on both the left and the right, while a biomorphic leafless tree form suggests a human presence in this otherwise unpopulated landscape. Heavy black outlines create shadows on the buildings and add depth to the composition. The artist's signature red draws the eye in to the central most building, while the expanse of blue sky overhead relieves the claustrophobic nature of the scene. With the intensity of his blue, red, and green color palette, this diminutive painting achieves enormous impact.

Critics often referred to Bluemner's compositions in musical terms because of his bold color harmonies and theories of the subconscious, and the artist approved. Bluemner wrote about how to view his work for what would turn out to be his posthumous exhibition at the University of Minnesota in 1939: "Look at my work in a way as you listen to music—look at the space filled with colors and try to feel; do not insist on 'understanding' what seems strange. When you 'FEEL' colors, you will understand the 'WHY' of their forms. It is so simple."[3] The artist died by his own hand on January 12, 1938, and although he was far from appreciated during his lifetime—and suffered financially because of it—Oscar Florianus Bluemner has since become known as one of the premier practitioners of American modernism.

BLJ

1 Painting Diary, April 21, 1918, Series 3: Painting and Theory Diaries, Painting Diary, 1916–1918 (box 1, folder 35), Oscar Bluemner Papers, 1886–1939, 1960, Archives of American Art, Smithsonian Institution, Washington, DC.

2 Oscar Bluemner, *What and When Is Painting? Today* (South Braintree, MA: privately printed, 1929), quoted in Barbara Haskell, *Oscar Bluemner: A Passion for Color* (New York: Whitney Museum of American Art, 2005), 200.

3 "Conclusion," *Oscar Florianus Bluemner*, exhibition catalogue (Minneapolis: University Gallery, University of Minnesota, 1939).

EVERETT LONGLEY WARNER (1877–1963)
Panther Hollow, c. 1930
Oil on canvas, 26 x 32 inches
Signed lower right
Museum purchase, 1983.85
Provenance: Mrs. Beatrice Nash Marshall, Pittsburgh, Pennsylvania.

Selected Exhibitions: Governor's Mansion, Harrisburg, Pennsylvania, 1992; *A World Observed: The Art of Everett Longley Warner 1877-1963*, Old Lyme, Connecticut + 1992-1993; *Born of Fire: The Valley of Work*, Westmoreland Museum of American Art, Greensburg, Pennsylvania, 2006; Oberhausen, Germany, 2007; Chemnitz, Germany, 2008; Zabrze, Poland, 2009.

Born in Vinton, Iowa, Everett Longley Warner studied at the Corcoran School of Art in 1897, spent two years at the Art Students League beginning in 1898, and went to Paris to study at the Académie Julian in 1903. He served in the navy in World War I, in charge of the design section of navy camouflage, within which he created one of the camouflage systems for battleships. He was recalled to service during World War II to perform the same duties. Upon moving from New York to Pittsburgh in 1924 to accept a teaching position at the Carnegie Institute of Technology (now Carnegie Mellon University), Warner began painting the industrial environment around him in earnest—the mills, the Bessemer converters, worker housing, and the ever-running trains, sometimes combining all in one painting. Color and atmosphere were his strengths, and he possessed the ability to transform the dreary gray landscape before him into one filled with color and light.

To his students he stressed close observation—a technique he used in his own work. Warner made sketches on the spot but completed his canvases in the studio. Before settling down to paint, he sometimes visited a site twenty or thirty times, to familiarize himself with the scene for easier recall back in his studio.[1] Warner was an expert at looking and seeing; he wrote manuals and articles on perspective, reflections, highway markings, and gallery lighting. As an American scene painter, Warner painted what he knew and the life around him with an impressionist's flair. His acute sense of perception allowed him to paint his landscapes with great accuracy and, at the same time, explore all aspects of color. He enjoyed painting the seasons, different times of day, and atmospheric conditions. Like Monet (1840–1926) before him, Warner painted a view of Notre Dame outside his window in Paris at different times of day and in different seasons, absorbed with trying to transcribe the same scene under varying effects of light, including the cathedral at night, inspired by James A. McNeill Whistler (1834–1903). Childe Hassam (1859–1935) also exerted an influence on Warner when he came in contact with him in 1909 at Florence Griswold's boardinghouse and art colony in Old Lyme, Connecticut—the center of impressionist painting in America at that time.

In *Panther Hollow*, Warner interpreted this neighborhood in the Oakland section of Pittsburgh as a light and vibrant winter landscape. Except for the train puffing through the hollow in the foreground, Warner shows few signs of the industry that surrounded this neighborhood along the rivers. Warner uses a high-key palette of impasto whites, blues, greens, and yellows to create this bright impressionistic scene. Though not necessarily the most accurate description of those particular surroundings, it was conceivably painted on a day when the sky was clearer than usual and the landscape was covered with a clean blanket of freshly fallen snow. His painting is about the effects of light, color, and atmosphere: billowing smoke from the train softens the entire scene, illuminated by afternoon sunlight. The train dramatically bisects the composition and draws attention to the community of colorfully painted houses that line the hillside on the left. The landmark St. Paul's Cathedral with its twin spires is prominently depicted in the background. In the midst of the industrial urban environment, Warner has created a peaceful bucolic scene that shimmers with the effects of color: opaque snow, blue sky, and candy-colored houses.

In 1937, when asked by an art reviewer about his painting *Progress and Poverty* (location unknown), he took the opportunity to discuss his nonsocial or political motivation: "If my pictures faithfully reflect the world about me they can hardly escape being in some sense a commentary on it, but I have no

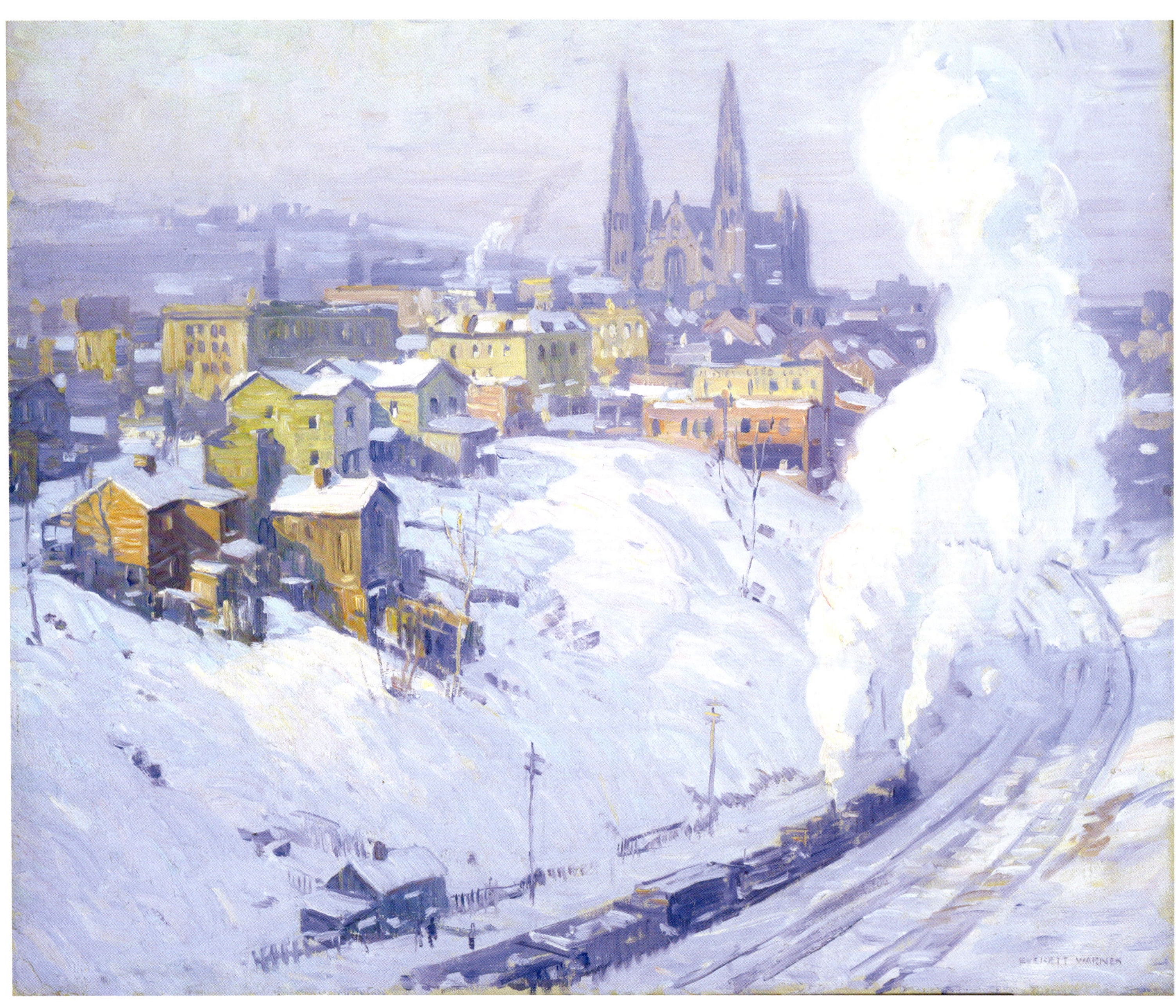
EVERETT WARNER

intention of trying to solve the problems of our civilization in my paintings . . . as an artist I am interested in contrasts of another kind. I am interested in the contrast between the formal vertical and horizontal lines of the mills with the curved lines of the ground forms and smoke masses. I am concerned with the opposition of light and dark, and with the contrast between warm color and cool color, and between soft and sharp edges. I wish to make my picture an artistic document . . . not a social document."[2]

Warner was awarded a solo exhibition at the Carnegie Institute (now Carnegie Museum of Art) in 1941, the seventh artist in the Institute's series of annual exhibitions of contemporary western Pennsylvania artists. The thirty paintings on view represented his work from 1912 to 1940 and included many industrial subjects painted in Pittsburgh. Acting director John O'Connor Jr. titled his article about the exhibition for *Carnegie Magazine* "Everett Warner: Painter of Pittsburgh" and discussed the artist's choice of subjects: "Wherever he may be he finds his subjects in his general or immediate surroundings. They may be as commonplace and homely as a simple washstand, an old rush-bottomed chair, or a frame house clinging to a hillside, but with his brush and color he gives them a dignity and a beauty that they do not seem to possess in themselves."[3]

Warner excelled as a painter, printmaker, and teacher, and is represented in The Westmoreland's collection with three oil paintings and two etchings. The artist favored trains, and four of the five works in the collection include them. Prints paralleled his paintings in subject, as can be seen in two undated etchings, *Halstead Hills* (1990.239) and *Roundhouse* (1990.238), in which a train figures prominently. In the former, the train divides the composition; and in the latter, workers—diminutive in scale—repair giant locomotives. In his panoramic vista of Pittsburgh entitled *Monongahela River* (c. 1941) (2000.30), the artist depicts a sweeping view of the river that includes its many bridges, Station Square, and Jones & Laughlin Steel Works.

Warner cut back his teaching load in 1937 to devote more time to painting. He painted slowly and deliberately, producing only two to three canvases per year. In 1943, one of his last paintings was included in the first "Painting in the United States" exhibition, organized by the Carnegie Institute. (This exhibition replaced the Carnegie International, which was suspended during World War II.) He was discharged from the navy in 1945, at which time he retired from Carnegie Tech and moved permanently to Westmoreland, New Hampshire. Unhappy with his painting, he turned to writing. At the age of eighty-one, he wrote "The Visibility of Highway Markers in the Atlantic Seaboard States" for *Traffic Quarterly* and "An Artist Looks at Gallery Lighting" for *Atlantic Monthly*, condemning the poor quality of light in modern galleries. He received success in fits and starts throughout his career. Today Warner is recognized as an important American impressionist painter, but at the time of his death in 1963, he and his work were all but forgotten.

BLJ

1 "'Snow Flurries' by Everett Warner," *Carnegie Magazine*, May 1940, 41.

2 Helen K. Fusscas, *A World Observed: The Art of Everett Longley Warner, 1877–1963* (Old Lyme, CT: Florence Griswold Museum, 1992), 34.

3 John O'Connor Jr., "Everett Warner: Painter of Pittsburgh," *Carnegie Magazine*, May 1941, 50.

HENRY LEE MCFEE (1886–1953)
Interior with Still Life, 1931
Oil on canvas, 46 x 40 inches
Signed and dated lower right
Gift of Dr. and Mrs. John J. McDonough, Youngstown, Ohio, 1982.114
Provenance: Dr. and Mrs. John J. McDonough, Youngstown, Ohio.

SELECTED EXHIBITIONS: *Henry Lee McFee,* Frank K. M. Rehn Galleries, New York, 1933; *Henry Lee McFee and Formalist Realism in American Still Life, 1923–1936,* The Center Gallery of Bucknell University, Lewisburg, Pennsylvania, 1986–1987.

Order, symmetry, and balance—three words that describe his carefully thought out compositions—reveal Henry Lee McFee's formalist approach to realism. He explained what he was trying to do in his painting: "I am endeavoring, by analysis, to find the essential planes of the emotional form of my motif, and to realize these planes by right placing of color and line, and by such a just relation of shape to shape, that the canvas will be, when completed, not a representation of many objects interesting in themselves, but a plastic unit expressive of my understanding of the form-life of the collection of objects."[1] McFee's reference to "form-life of the collection of objects" reveals his knowledge of the concept in the work of Paul Cézanne (1839–1906), which he studied thoroughly. In his article *My Painting and Its Development,* McFee acknowledged reading, among other sources, Roger Fry's *Essay on Aesthetics* (1909) and Clive Bell's *Art* (1914), who both explained Cézanne's concepts, which he noted were influential to his style during his formative years.[2]

Born in St. Louis, McFee spent most of his adult life in Woodstock, New York. At the age of twenty-one, he came into a family inheritance from his mother's cousin, the Pittsburgh industrialist Henry Lee Mason, which allowed him to forgo his day job as a surveyor and devote all his attention to painting. He spent 1908–1909 studying at the Stevenson Art School in Pittsburgh and then joined an Art Students League summer class in landscape painting in Woodstock. Enjoying the quiet of the country, he remained in Woodstock rather than moving to New York City to continue his formal education, staying for over thirty years. In 1920, together with Andrew Dasburg (1887–1979) and other artists, he founded the Woodstock Artists Association, which remains today one of the oldest continuing organizations of its kind.

McFee painted still lifes for the better part of his career, and the subject dominated his output from 1913 until his death in 1953. He crafted them in the tradition of Cézanne, based on the late nineteenth-century artist's principles of spatial organization, which led to the development of analytic cubism by Pablo Picasso (1881–1973) and Georges Braque (1882–1963) in the early twentieth century. At first glance, they are simply arrangements of commonplace objects—a turned leg table, apples in a ceramic compote, a cut melon with its brilliant orange flesh, a faceted vase containing dried foliage, a blue tablecloth, an onion—but on further examination, you no longer see those objects but see an arrangement of design elements—a combination of geometric shapes with color and tonal relationships, and the abstract voids that both surround and connect them. In The Westmoreland's *Interior with Still Life,* McFee sets up just such a composition of spatial relationships, creating a dynamic rhythm with the inclusion of multiple angles, facets, and curves. He applies cubist principles, such as the tilted tabletop and the ability to see several sides of an object simultaneously, to create and enhance the visual relationships. The unruly, twisting branch of leaves and the folds of the cloth add a sense of movement, and combined with the hard-edged, faceted objects of wood and ceramic that contrast with the softer, curvilinear forms of fruit and cloth, the artist creates dynamism throughout his composition. The objects exist in a shallow space; however, his placement of other objects—a portion of a large canvas in the left foreground, a framed painting on the wall behind, and an easel—allude to the deeper space within the room in which the still life arrangement is situated. Reducing his forms to their geometric essentials, McFee designed his paintings much like an architect, all the while maintaining the integrity of the whole.

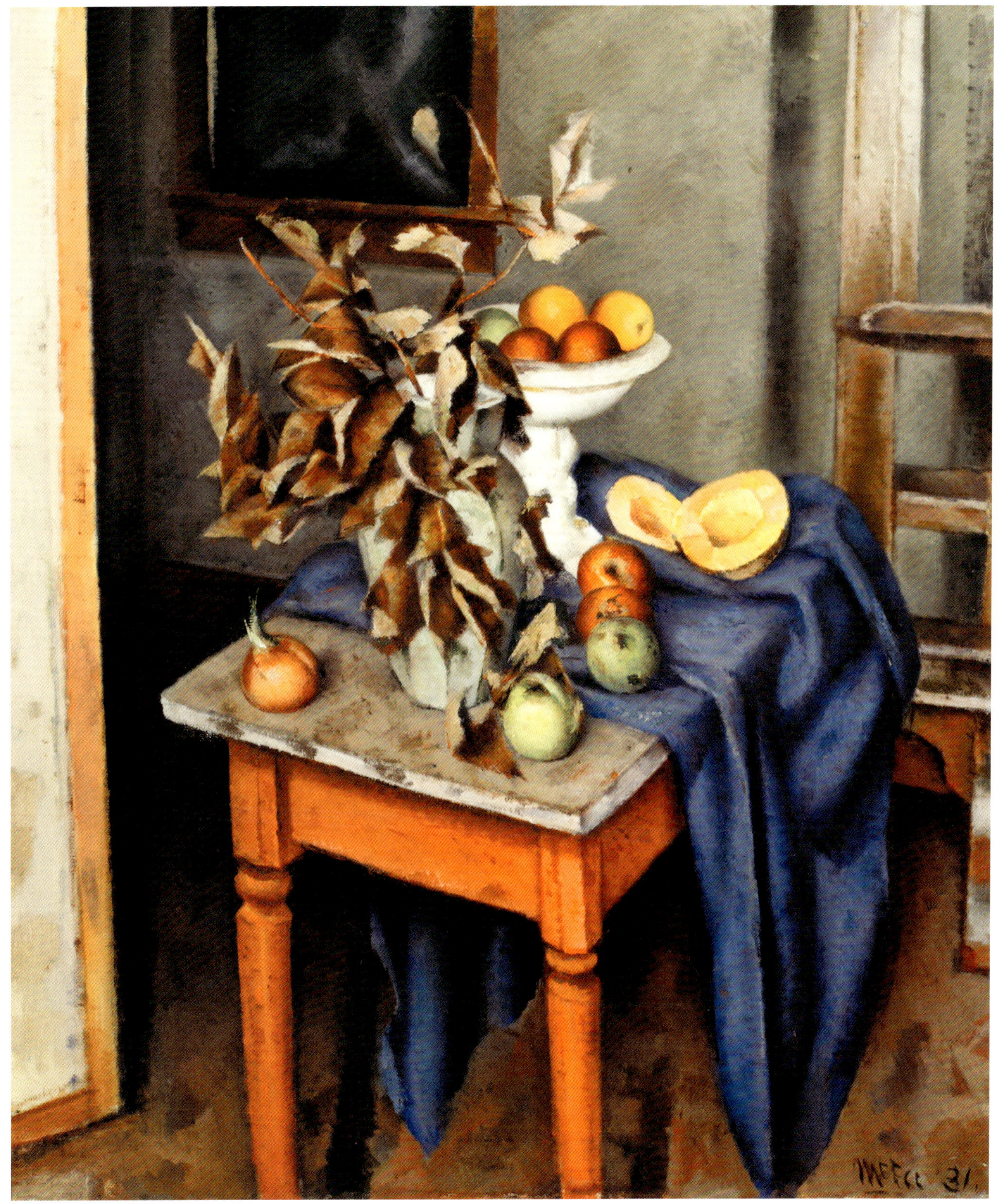

According to the artist: "If the component parts of a canvas are not essential parts of the whole, if the picture appears substantial only to the uncritical eye of one searching for pleasing effects, then it is a bad job, a jerry-built house."[3] Further, he is not conscious of painting objects but "kinds of color," making relationships of form, shape, and color on a two-dimensional plane while creating the illusion of three-dimensional solidity and volume with light and shadow rather than line. Each fold of the cloth and each piece of fruit achieves volume through built-up paint layers that slowly and steadily take their shape. Edwin Alden Jewell called McFee's painting "flawless architecture" and his still life paintings "noble creations, superbly organized and alive throughout. . . . They have in them the carefully planned grace and the completed thought of a successful sonnet."[4]

Dated 1931, *Interior with Still Life* represents the artist's shift from his more formal abstract cubist arrangements of the 1920s. Like others of the same period, McFee incorporates a larger interior space and more objects in his composition, not simply to enlarge it but to increase the number of significant form relationships. When this painting was included in McFee's solo show at Frank K. M. Rehn Galleries in 1933, a critic for *Art News* referred to it as "a stunning scene accented with warm notes of a halved melon," and "another McFee work that contains all his best qualities."[5] Writing about the same exhibition for the *New York Times*, Edwin Alden Jewell referred to the Museum's painting as "particularly strong" and his still lifes in the exhibition as "noble creations, superbly organized and alive throughout."[6]

During the thirties, McFee's reputation as an artist reached a high point. In 1930, the still life for which he won two prizes in the Carnegie International was purchased by Mrs. John D. Rockefeller Jr.; he won a gold medal at the Paris International Exposition in 1937; examples of his work were purchased by the Whitney Museum of American Art (1931–1936), the Metropolitan Museum of Art, and the City Art Museum in his native St. Louis (1933); and the Whitney selected McFee as one of the artists for its American Art monograph series in 1931. His paintings were included in two exhibitions at the Museum of Modern Art in 1931 and 1932, and having been represented by the Frank K. M. Rehn Galleries since 1927, his first solo show in four years was held there in 1933.

McFee was a well-known, mature artist when he was invited to participate in all seven *Painting in the United States* exhibitions at the Carnegie Institute (now Carnegie Museum of Art) between 1943 and 1949. *American Artist* magazine published an article on his still lifes in 1948, in which Ernest Watson quoted the artist: "Still life I have always with me. I find beginnings of a picture that interests me most in the corner of my studio or living room. I keep about me things that I like—common things mostly—shapes that touch me; inanimate objects that take on life when seen with understanding. I suppose I am more interested in still life because it does not bother me. It does not have to rest every so often as models do, nor do I have to keep up a pretended interest in a personality. And I do not have to gossip as I work."[7] Critics continually commented on the exceptional quality of his still lifes and that they represented the artist's best work. In 1942, McFee moved to California, where he began teaching in the Department of Painting and Design at Scripps College in Claremont. He remained there for the next eleven years, until his death in 1953 at the age of sixty-seven.

BLJ

1 Henry Lee McFee, *The Forum Exhibition of Modern American Painters* (New York: Anderson Galleries, 1916).

2 Henry Lee McFee, "My Painting and Its Development," *Creative Art*, March 1929.

3 Ernest Brace, "Henry Lee McFee," *American Magazine of Art*, July 1934, 376–77.

4 Edwin Alden Jewell, *New York Times*, January 7, 1933.

5 "Henry McFee, Rehn Galleries," *Art News* 31, January 1933, 6.

6 Edward Alden Jewell, "Henry L. McFee Opens His First One-Man Show in Four Years at Rehn Galleries," *New York Times*, January 7, 1933.

7 Ernest W. Watson, "Still Life Paintings by Henry Lee McFee," *American Artist*, February 1948, 20.

SAMUEL ROSENBERG (1896–1972)
God's Chillun, 1934
Oil on canvas, 36 x 48 inches
Signed and dated lower right
Gift of the William A. Coulter Fund, 1974.67
Provenance: The Artist; Mrs. Samuel (Libbie) Rosenberg, Pittsburgh, Pennsylvania.

SELECTED EXHIBITIONS: *Second Biennial Exhibition of Contemporary American Painters,* Whitney Museum of American Art, 1934; Associated Artists of Pittsburgh Annual, 1935; *Survey of American Painting,* Museum of Art, Carnegie Institute, 1940; *Samuel Rosenberg Retrospective,* Westmoreland County Museum of Art, 1960; Pittsburgh Plan for Art, 1963; Hewlett Gallery, Carnegie Mellon University, 1965; Sewickley Academy, 1974; *Southwestern Pennsylvania Painters,* Westmoreland County Museum of Art, 1981; *American Art of the Great Depression: Two Sides of the Coin,* The Wichita Art Museum, 1985; Historical Society of Western Pennsylvania, 1992; *Samuel Rosenberg: The Early Years,* Jewish Community Center, Pittsburgh, 1994; *Pittsburgh Rhythms,* Historical Society of Western Pennsylvania, 1997; Governor's Residence, Harrisburg, 1998; *Samuel Rosenberg: Portrait of a Painter,* Westmoreland Museum of American Art, 2003; *Artists of the Commonwealth: Realism and Its Response in Pennsylvanian Painting, 1900-1950,* Westmoreland Museum of American Art +, 2006.

Known as both the Dean of Pittsburgh painters and Pittsburgh's Painter Laureate, Samuel Rosenberg devoted his life to his art and his teaching for nearly sixty years, disseminating a wealth of knowledge and understanding through both. From 1915 to 1972, he created over five hundred paintings, over four hundred preparatory sketches and drawings, and over one hundred collages. His work can be divided into four periods, with frequent overlapping or transitional episodes within each: 1915–1930, portraits (and a few still lifes); 1930–1942, American scene and Pittsburgh's urban landscape; 1942–1952, allegory to abstraction; and 1949–1972, abstract expressionism.

Rosenberg chose to teach so that he could have summers free to paint while earning enough money to support his family. Whether spending summers in Woodstock, New York; Somerset County, PA; Rockport, MA; Arizona; California; Mexico; or Europe, Rosenberg never ended a day without making, looking at, or talking about art. His art permeated his life, and his life, in turn, permeated his art: his family, neighborhoods, the light and color of the natural world, were the subjects of his paintings that are filled with his images of the visible world, his emotions, and his imagination. From his early portraits—commissioned and otherwise—through his social-realist studies of the Hill District where he grew up; his allegorical subjects and universal themes of suffering; and, finally, his enigmatic abstract expressionist canvases of light and color, Rosenberg's growth as an artist was a slow and steady, ever-evolving progression. Although a shy and thoughtful man, his reticence did not translate into his painting, for he painted with an authority that surpassed his personality.

Born in Philadelphia on June 28, 1896, the fifth of six children, Rosenberg showed an early interest in art. His father, Solomon, had emigrated from Vienna around 1890 to Philadelphia, where he had presumably met his second wife, Anna Dickstein Turetsky, from Minsk, with whom he had three children.

Rosenberg spent his early childhood in Erie, Pennsylvania, and when Samuel was eleven, the family moved south to the Oakland neighborhood of Pittsburgh, which, according to the artist, was much like living in the country at that time. When the Rosenbergs arrived in Pittsburgh, the city was a booming industrial center, commonly referred to as Steel Town or the Smoky City. Years later, Rosenberg would say, "You can hate and like Pittsburgh at the same time. It is not the most pleasant place in the world, for the atmosphere here is not particularly clean. But from an artist's standpoint, I contend that it is one of the most interesting cities in the United States."[1]

In 1912, the family moved to the Lower Hill District, where Rosenberg would live until 1924—the year he married Libbie Levin (1898-1987). Together the couple moved back to Oakland, then settled permanently in Squirrel Hill in 1952.

Throughout his artistic development, Rosenberg resisted conforming to a single signature style. After years of experimentation, his own style emerged in his mature work of the late 1950s and early 1960s, when he finally, as he said, "came into his own." The importance of the edge of the canvas, balance, color harmony, and working on the composition as a

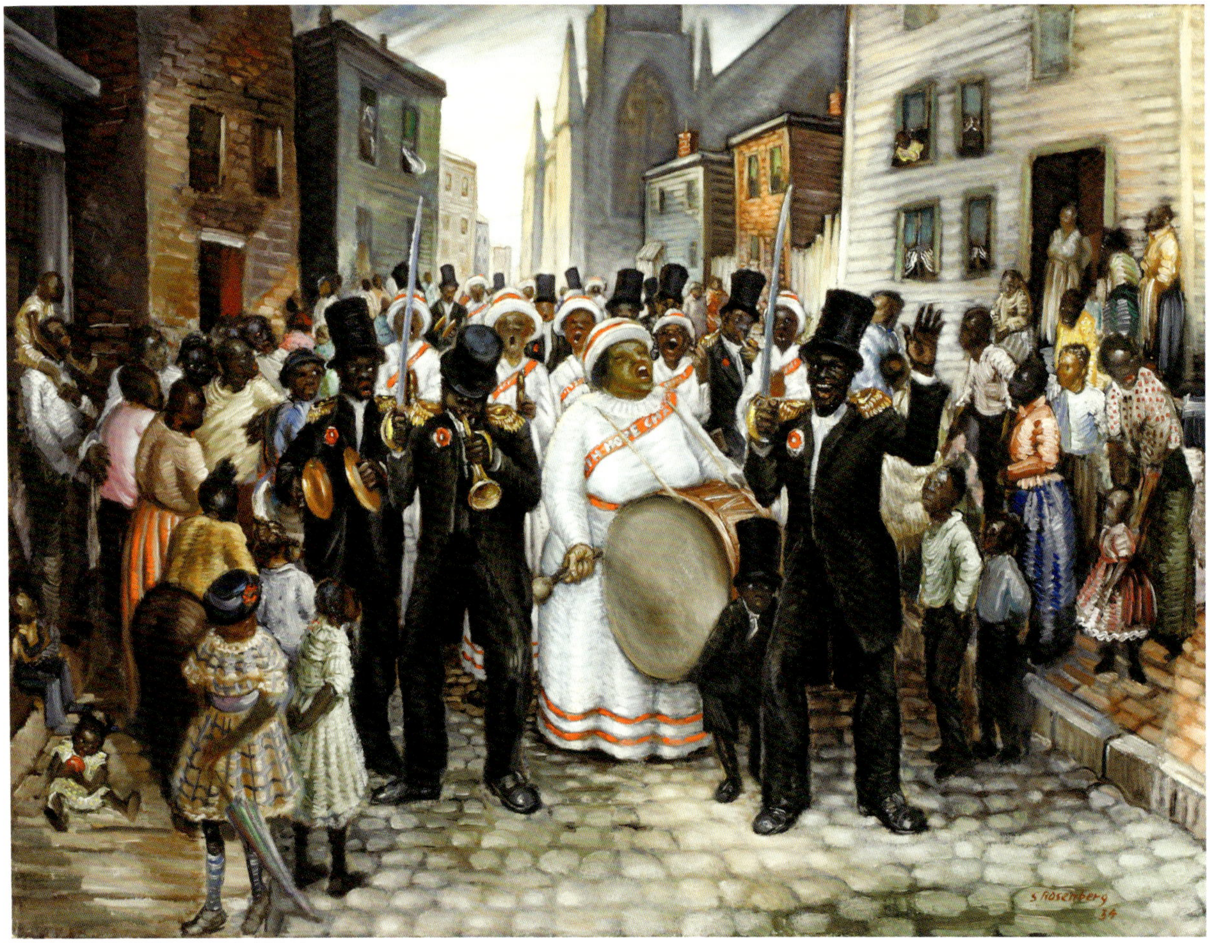

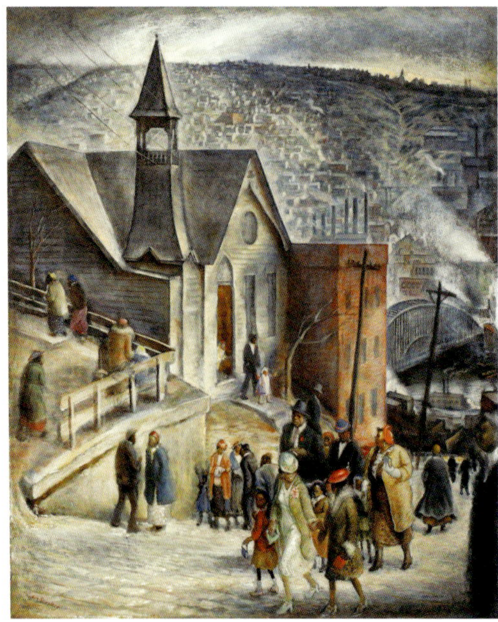

Sunday Morning, 1937, Oil on masonite, 56 x 46 inches,
Gift of Arline Rosenberg (Mrs. Murray), 2003.21

whole became his mantra, both to himself and to his students. Despite the diversity of his subject matter, his paintings through the years share a consistency in style and purpose, attempting to convey his feelings and the effects of light through the application of paint. It can be seen in the chiaroscuro of his early portraits, in the light and shadow of his genre paintings of Pittsburgh's urban landscape, and most predominantly in his later abstractions. Light as the sole subject of his painting, however, did not take precedence until the early 1950s, when Rosenberg began his search for a universal, and perhaps spiritual, truth.

When other artists were leaving Pittsburgh and traveling to Paris or New York, Rosenberg made the conscious decision to remain at home. During the 1930s, Rosenberg documented the socioeconomic life of the inner city, portraying the conditions of the urban poor during the Depression as well as the ethnic neighborhoods of Pittsburgh's Hill District. *God's Chillun* portrays an incident of African American street life on Crawford Street in the Hill District, where a spiritual revival or rally is commencing. The large woman at the center of the composition wears a sash that reads "Faith, Hope, and Charity." You can almost hear the sounds of the gospel music emanating from the mouths of the participants and the instruments they play. Rosenberg situated himself in front of the large group, representing the congestion of the crowd as far as the eye can see. As noted in *The WPA History of the Negro in Pittsburgh*: "Weekly, in summer months, the men and women of this faith don their bright-colored garb—women in white dresses, red or blue sashes, poke bonnets and broad white hats trimmed with chenille ball braid; men in uniforms pieced together from gold braided trousers, epaulettes that never match, plumed hats, and flashing swords. A woman beats a bass drum; a girl shakes a tambourine. One man blows a trumpet; another plays a triangle. Cow bells, dinner bells, rattles or guitars make music unto the Lord."[2]

The Holy Trinity Church (now St. Benedict the Moor) looms behind the participants on the right, who might also be members of the congregation of St. Benedict the Moor, which at that time was located just three blocks away on Heldman Street. Together with two other paintings, *God's Chillun* won the Carnegie Prize for best group of oil paintings in the Associated Artists of Pittsburgh's 25th annual exhibition in 1935. A *Pittsburgh Post-Gazette* critic described the painting as "riotous and bubbling with the ecstasy of a street corner revival, with a canvas crowded with rhythmic figures which seem themselves the visual embodiment of hallelujah!"[3] Rosenberg's many canvases of this area of the city remain a vital record of the once vibrant neighborhood. The Whitney Museum of American Art was interested in purchasing *God's Chillun* after it was shown in their 1934 Biennial exhibition, but they were without funds at the time to do so.[4]

The Westmoreland owns twenty-nine works of art by Rosenberg, which span the artist's stylistic career. Nine of the seventeen paintings were gifted by the artist's son, Dr. Murray Z. Rosenberg, in 1977. Since its founding, the Museum has organized two retrospective exhibitions of the artist's work—in 1960 and 2003. During his lifetime, Rosenberg's work was reviewed in nearly all the periodicals of the day, and he participated in a variety of notable exhibitions at the Whitney Museum of American Art, the New York World's Fair, and the Museum of Modern Art. Two solo exhibitions of his work were held at New York's Associated American Artists Gallery in 1944 and 1948, and he participated in group shows in cities throughout the country. Rosenberg was recognized twice for solo exhibitions at the Carnegie Institute (now Carnegie Museum of Art), first in 1937—only the third Pittsburgh artist to be so honored—and again in 1956. He was named "Man of the Year" by the Arts and Crafts Center (now the Pittsburgh Center for the Arts) in 1950, only the second artist to receive that distinguished award. He was accepted by the jury of the Carnegie International in 1920 and 1925, and was subsequently invited to participate in every International from 1933 to 1964.

Rosenberg's teaching career spanned forty years, and his spirit continues to live on through his students. He taught at the Carnegie Institute of Technology (now Carnegie Mellon University) from 1924 to 1964, earning his own degree there in 1926; at the Pennsylvania College for Women (now Chatham College) from 1937 to 1945; and at the Irene Kaufmann Settlement and the Young Men & Women's Hebrew Association from 1926 to 1964.

BLJ

1 Douglas Naylor, "Art for Life's Sake," *Pittsburgh Press* (27 July 1937).

2 Laurence A. Glasco, ed., *The WPA History of the Negro in Pittsburgh* (Pittsburgh: University of Pittsburgh Press, 2004), 237.

3 Unidentified author, *Pittsburgh Post-Gazette* (9 February 1935). Scrapbook volume I, 17. Samuel Rosenberg Family Papers and Photographs, MSS#567, Rauh Jewish Archives, Senator John Heinz History Center, Pittsburgh.

4 Information from a letter in Samuel Rosenberg Artist File, Whitney Museum of American Art Library, New York.

WILLIAM ZORACH (1887–1966)
Reclining Cat, 1935
Bronze, edition 5 of 6
Signed on lower left edge
Gift of the Westmoreland Society, 2000.18
Provenance: The Artist; The Zorach Children.

Born in Euberick, Lithuania, Zorach Samovich was four years old when his family immigrated to Ohio, ultimately settling in Cleveland. The family had taken the name Finkelstein upon their arrival in America, but the future artist's name was Americanized to William Zorach by one of his early teachers. To help support the family and learn a trade, Zorach left school in the eighth grade and joined the W. J. Morgan Lithograph Company, while studying nights at the Cleveland School of Art. He apprenticed with the same firm from 1903 to 1906, and for many years he supported himself as a lithographer. Determined to become an artist, however, in 1907 he traveled to New York, where he began two years of study at the National Academy of Design. During the summer months, he returned to his lithography job in Cleveland. On a trip to Paris in 1910, he saw firsthand the work of the fauves and cubists, which from that point on would influence him in both painting and sculpture. Zorach studied at the English-speaking Académie de la Palette, where he met and became enamored of fellow student Marguerite Thompson (1887–1968), an accomplished artist who had been in Paris for over two years. Zorach returned to his job in Cleveland in 1911, remaining until he had saved enough money to move back to New York in December 1912. Marguerite left Paris around the same time but traveled around the world before returning to her home in California. William and Marguerite were married on December 24, 1912, and set up a home and studio together. Their marriage created a strong artistic partnership that lasted for fifty-three years. While they collaborated on some work during their years together, they remained individual artists, each with his or her own distinct identity. They both wanted to live by their art alone, and although it was a financial struggle, they succeeded, raising their son, Tessim, and daughter, Dahlov, in the process.[1]

Zorach began his artistic journey as a painter, first in the academic style taught at the National Academy, and then in the modernist styles of fauvism (Matisse) and cubism (Picasso) he experienced in Paris. Both William and Marguerite were represented in New York's landmark Armory Show of international modern art in 1913 and were among the seventeen artists included in *The Forum Exhibition of Modern American Painters* in 1916.

In 1917, both Zorachs abandoned fauvism for cubism, using darker color palettes and overlapping planes in a flattened pictorial space. According to William, Max Weber (1881–1961) "broadened the range of my vision; he made me conscious of a more three-dimensional vision. To him it meant the third dimension that Cézanne saw in the world about him. To me it opened a new vista that led me away from painting and into my true medium of sculpture."[2] William carved his first sculpture in wood relief that year; however, he would continue painting until 1922, when he turned his full energies to sculpture, working in both wood and stone. Although he stopped painting in oil, he would, however, continue to paint in watercolor for the remainder of his career.

In 1923, both Zorachs were mentioned in a *Vanity Fair* article titled "Among the Best of American Painters"; however, only William's work was reproduced, highlighting the tendency at the time to identify the female artist as subordinate to her male counterpart.[3]

In his first years as a sculptor, William's interest was in direct carving with wood, inspired by African and Oceanic sculpture, Eskimo carvings, and folk art. While his two-dimensional work was heavily influenced by abstraction and the fractured perspectives of cubism, his sculpture reveals this influence in a much more subtle manner. Softened angles and smooth and simplified forms shape his naturalistic sculpture with a dignity and monumentality that echo classical and Egyptian styles. He admired the sculpture of Constantin Brâncusi (1876–1957) and wrote about the artist in an article for *The Arts* in 1926. When William began carving in stone in 1923, he said, "I felt perfectly at ease carving stone because of my experience with wood. Stone seemed natural to me. I liked it better than wood. I liked the effort, the hard resistance. I liked the time it required; one could dream and organize while the

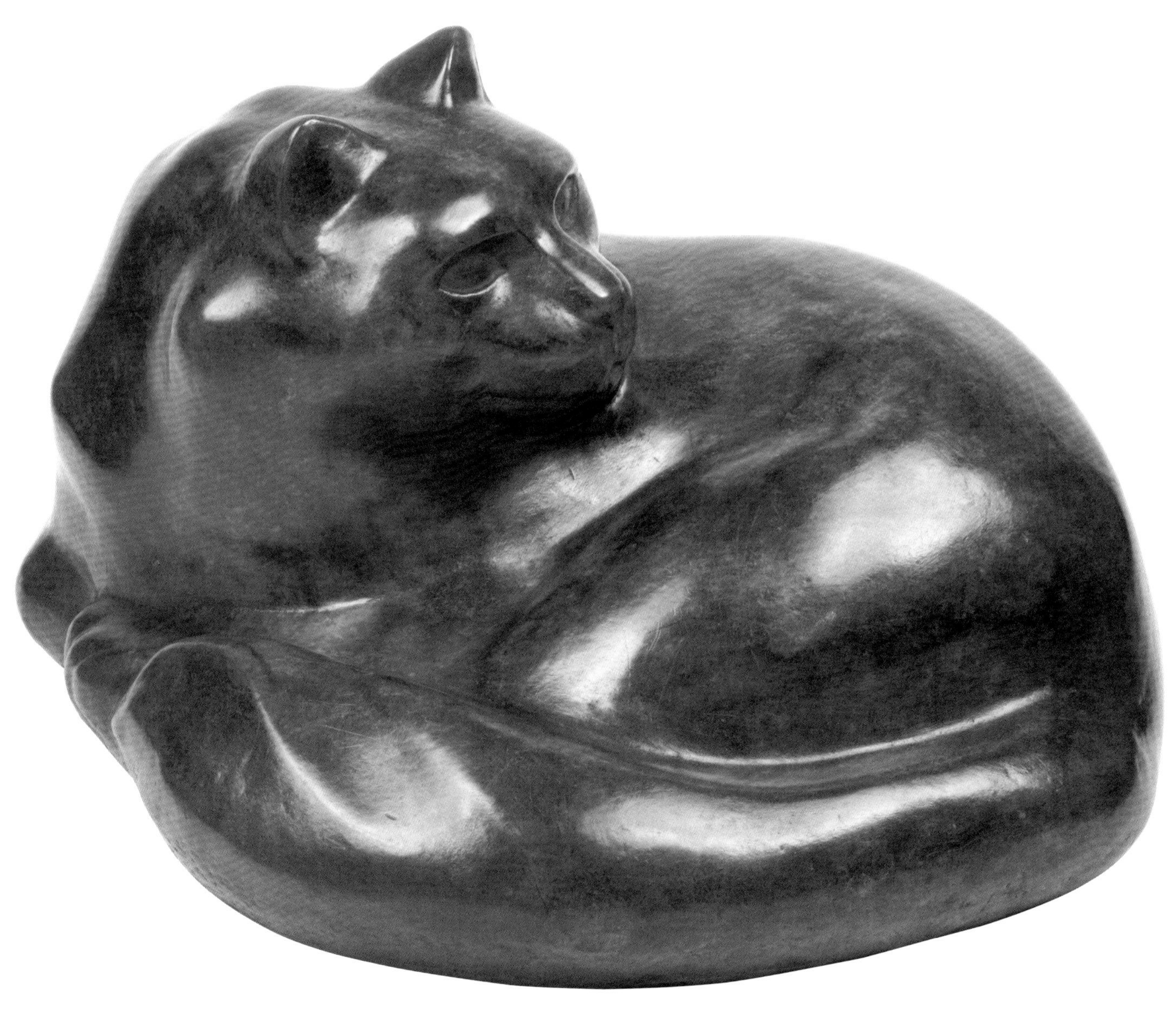

stone slowly took form and life."[4] He loved the painstaking process of direct carving and enjoyed seeing the form emerge from the material. In 1930, he elaborated further on his sculpting method for an article in *Creative Art* magazine: "You cannot make changes easily and what you do you do with great consideration and thought. Your senses are continually alive, you are constantly on guard, you cannot take ill-thought-out chances, for there is no putting back tomorrow what was cut away today."[5] He could often visualize the subject of his resulting sculpture before he carved it, selecting his materials for their innate qualities. He employed the grain in his wood sculpture, and in his marble and granite pieces he contrasted the rough and smooth textures that were inherent in the different stones. He also worked in clay, which he modeled in preparation for casting pieces in bronze or aluminum, used primarily for his public commissions. The marks of his chisel on the surface of some of his sculptures reveal the hand of the artist, while on others he completely eliminates that evidence by smoothly polishing the surface, as seen in the Museum's *Reclining Cat.*

Much of Zorach's sculpture is his response to the world around him. He is most well-known for his larger-than-life sculptures of single nudes or embracing couples, but his family—Marguerite, their children, and pets—were favorite models. He created loving, timeless images of those closest to him. His subjects of men and women, motherhood, children, and animals were crafted, however, in such exquisitely reduced forms that they evoke universal images of these subjects, which speak to any of us who share these familiar relationships.

Although cast in bronze, The Westmoreland's *Reclining Cat* shares the exact pose as the artist's *Reclining Cat* of 1934–1935, carved out of Maine granite, and is similar to his *Black Cat* of 1941, made from black porphyry. Zorach said that he loved to carve cats. "Cats are subtle and lovable and have no objections to being studied and sketched; whereas a dog, if you look at him, is immediately all over you for attention. A cat, who is imbued with dignity and has a mysterious and aloof quality, also has a beautiful, flowing form."[6] Zorach's words accurately describe the Museum's *Reclining Cat,* as just enough information remains in this exquisitely simple form to identify it as such. With subtle curves and minimally incised details, he portrays a cat at rest, curled in on itself, relaxed yet alert and ready to pounce, with head slightly raised, as if something has just caught its attention. The mottled patina on the sculpture is reminiscent of the texture and variegated coloring of a cat's fur.

The Zorachs always lived in the city during the winter months but spent summers in the countryside, first in upstate New York, then in Massachusetts, and finally in Maine, where in 1923 they purchased a large sea captain's house and property on Robinhood Cove in Georgetown, near their friends Isabel and Gaston Lachaise (1882–1935).

Zorach's voice was heard through his writing. He wrote *The Artist Explains Sculpture* in 1947, culminating in his autobiography, *Art Is My Life,* published posthumously in 1967. He taught art to fellow students at his children's school and to young artists at the Art Students League from 1929 to 1960.

William and Marguerite Zorach became leaders of the avant-garde in American art. They both had productive careers even though hers became inextricably woven with her household duties and caring for the children. William died on November 15, 1966, at the age of seventy-nine, and less than two years later, on June 27, 1968, Marguerite joined him.

Referencing the two mediums in which he worked for nearly fifty years, Zorach wrote, "There are things one does for the pure love of form and color, in the easy abandonment to the moods and the fancies of the moment. These are my watercolors. Then there are the visions imprisoned in the rock and the visions deep in one's soul—the things one does in seeking for the inner rhythm of nature and life, in the journeys into an unknown region where one can grasp only mystic fragments from the great subconscious that surrounds us. There is much of pain and exaltation in creative work. A resistless, relentless power that makes one ever create. This is my sculpture."[7]

BLJ

1 For an excellent examination of the artist couple, see *Marguerite and William Zorach: Harmonies and Contrasts* (Portland, ME: Portland Museum of Art, 2002).

2 William Zorach, *Art Is My Life* (Cleveland: The World Publishing Company, 1967), 134.

3 *Vanity Fair,* March 1923, 52.

4 Zorach, *Art Is My Life,* 68.

5 William Zorach, "Views and Methods," *Creative Art,* June 1930, 444.

6 Zorach, *Art Is My Life,* 170.

7 Ibid., 193.

ERNEST FIENE (1894–1955)
Coal Breaker, Pennsylvania, c. 1935–37
Oil on canvas, 26 x 36 inches
Signed lower right
Gift of the Westmoreland Society and the Thomas Lynch Fund, 2005.26
Provenance: The Artist; his wife, Jeanette Fiene; her nephew; CIGNA Corporation, Philadelphia; D. Wigmore Fine Art, Inc., New York.

Selected Exhibitions: *The Industrial Scene,* First National Bank, Pittsburgh, 1937; Associated American Artists Gallery, New York, not dated; *Art of the City,* 1925–1955, ACA Galleries, New York, 1981; *Born of Fire: The Valley of Work,* Westmoreland Museum of American Art, 2006; Oberhausen, Germany, 2007; Chemnitz, Germany, 2008; and Zabrze, Poland, 2009.

Born in Elberfeld, Germany—an industrial region of the Ruhr River valley—Ernest Fiene immigrated to the United States in 1912 at the age of eighteen, settling in New York City and becoming a citizen in 1928. He studied at the National Academy of Design from 1914 to 1918 under Leon Kroll (1884–1974), overlapping at the Beaux-Arts Institute of Design from 1916 to 1918, and then furthering his studies in printmaking at the Art Students League in 1923. Fiene was successful early in his career, with exhibitions at the MacDowell Club in 1919; the Whitney Studio Club in 1923; and the New Gallery in 1925, at which he sold all of his fifty-two paintings. With the proceeds from those sales, he and his brother, sculptor Paul Fiene, built studios in Woodstock, New York, and joined the artist colony there. This small upstate town served as the subject of the majority of Fiene's landscape paintings during the twenties. Gradually, however, his interest in industrial and urban environments replaced that of the natural landscape, and Fiene turned to architecture and industry as his subjects. Frank K. M. Rehn gave Fiene a solo show in 1926, and Fiene remained in the modern art dealer's stable until he joined Edith Halpert's Downtown Gallery in 1933. Fiene was also a mural painter, learning the Renaissance technique of fresco while in Italy in 1932 on a Guggenheim Fellowship. Two studies that he completed for his *Mechanical Progress* mural were shown in an exhibition of American mural painters at the recently founded Museum of Modern Art in 1932. He won both public and private mural commissions, including a four-panel mural for the new Department of the Interior building in Washington, D.C., in 1938, but his largest mural in fresco was made for the Central High School of Needle Trades in New York, painting not for the government—although he was employed by the Federal Art Project—but for the industry itself. Unveiled in 1940 and containing over two hundred oversized figures, it took the artist two and a half years to complete. During the war years, Fiene concentrated his efforts on painting industry in relationship to the war, referencing oil and optical instruments. Fiene was one of fourteen leading American artists who were commissioned in 1946 by Gimbel Brothers Department Stores in Pittsburgh and Philadelphia to create a portrait of the post–World War II years in the Commonwealth.[1] He became an associate member of the National Academy in 1948, achieving full academician status in 1952.

Fiene was a highly respected artist who was a member of the faculty at several institutions, including Cooper Union and the Art Students League in New York, teaching at the latter from 1938 until his death in 1955. Drawing on his over fifty years as a painter, Fiene wrote a book entitled *Complete Guide to Oil Painting,* which was published the year before his death.

The coal industry in Pennsylvania is represented in the Museum's scenes of industry collection by Ernest Fiene's *Coal Breaker, Pennsylvania.* Although Fiene is most well known for his New York cityscapes and harbor scenes, he concentrated on industry as a subject in the winter of 1935–36, when he made a sketching trip through the steel and coal-mining areas of Pennsylvania and West Virginia, seeking, as he put it, icons of the machine age. According to the artist, "Pittsburgh fascinated me. It was a symphony in gray, brown, and black. The rising hills of the city wrapped in snow, a heavy ceiling of snow clouds gathering smoke from the belching chimneys and the saffron colored rivers winding their way through these populous hills; in their magic setting all objects became

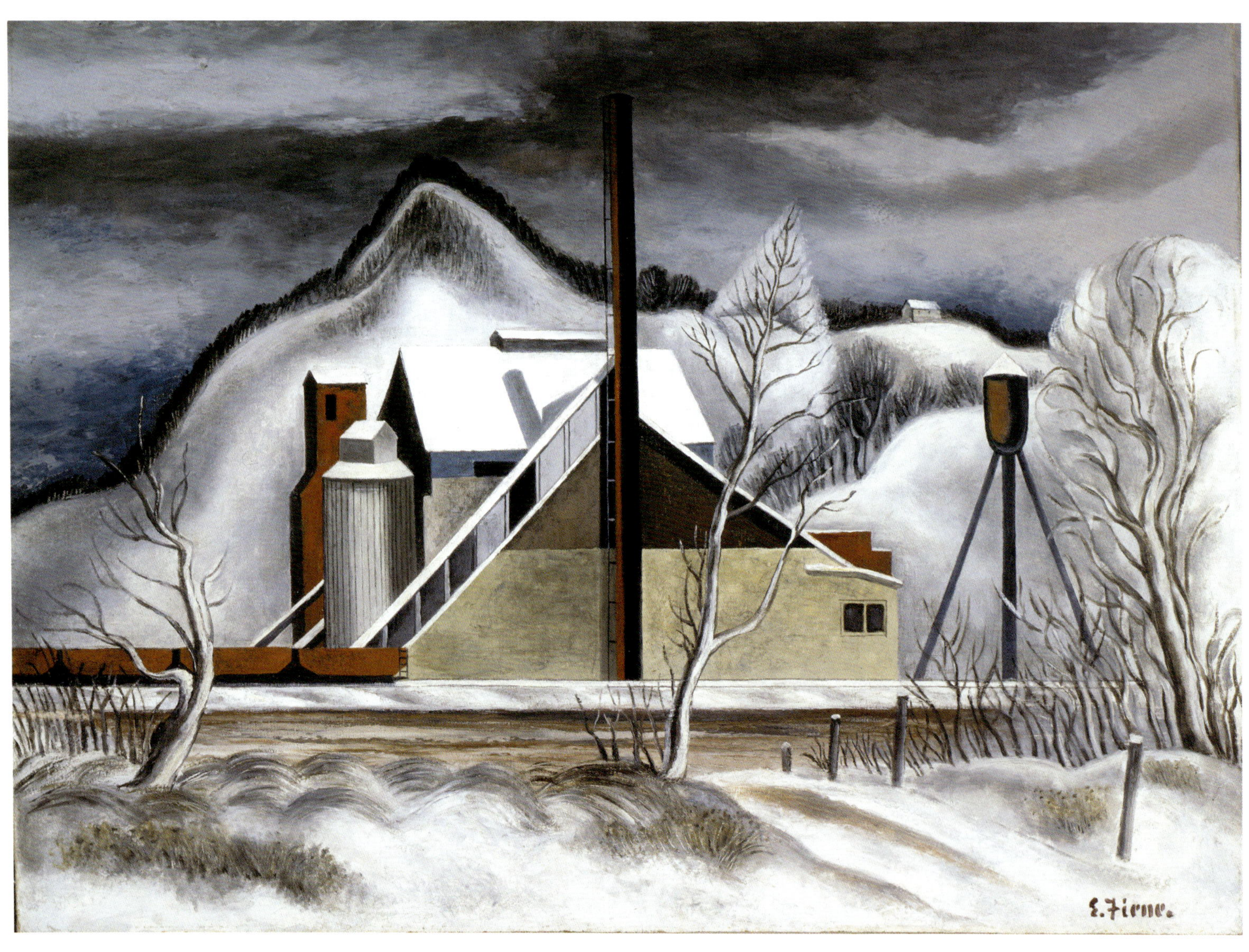

imbued with a new significance."[2] Having spent his youth in Germany's Rhineland, his attraction to industrial subjects is not surprising. Twenty-four paintings, including *Coal Breaker, Pennsylvania*, resulted from this trip and were shown in an October 1937 exhibition at the First National Bank in Pittsburgh, organized by the Pittsburgh Commission for Industrial Expansion. The author of a brief review of the exhibition in *Art News* referred to Pittsburgh as the "World's Industrial Center," and considered the collection of paintings "an important record of our period," adding that "Fiene has successfully interpreted industry in relation to its environment."[3] Visitors to the exhibition thought Fiene's work "a vision of the soul of their region."[4] When referencing the exhibition in the *Pittsburgh Post-Gazette*, Jeanette Jena commented that "because Fiene was an outsider, brought face to face with a new town and a new experience, he made us natives see new colors and new forms in our rivers and smoke, which had escaped our accustomed eye before."[5] The trip served more of a purpose than Fiene had realized when, in December 1935, he made a sketch of the Lucy blast furnace, built in 1872 on the banks of the Allegheny River in Lawrenceville. Less than two years later, in August 1937, Carnegie-Illinois Steel Corporation dismantled the mighty furnace. Sixty-five years earlier, Lucy and Isabella—her twin furnace across the river in Etna—were the ranking blast furnaces in Pittsburgh, and mill workers made bets on the amount of iron each could produce in a single day.[6] Fiene made paintings of Lucy in both oil and watercolor, and *Factory on the River* (1936)—a watercolor in The Westmoreland's collection (1995.40)—references the mill complex, with the blast furnace prominently featured. Fiene became a historian the day he chose Lucy as his subject, preserving her as a record of Pittsburgh's industrial landscape.

From coal breakers to blast furnaces, Fiene recorded the industrial environment in simplified compositions that focus on the subject at hand, with minimal detail or distraction. Painted in a precisionist style, *Coal Breaker* calls attention to the angular geometry of the building itself, set in a pristine winter landscape. His use of flat areas of bright color was a stylistic approach he adopted following a trip to Paris in 1928–29, where he came under the influence of the decorative work of Henri Matisse (1869–1954). Fiene worked in layers of paint, applying first a monochrome layer, mixing one color with white to create a uniform background, then applying layers of the colors of his subject. A final layer of varnish tinted with the background color gives his paintings their overall luminous quality and continuity.

With the production of coal so prevalent surrounding Greensburg, *Coal Breaker, Pittsburgh* was a significant addition to the Museum's collection, documenting the coal mining industry, which played a substantial role in the steelmaking process in this region.

BLJ

1 The commission resulted in a total of 115 works, of which 48 depicting Pittsburgh and western Pennsylvania were given to the University of Pittsburgh; 67 that referenced Philadelphia and the eastern part of the state went to the University of Pennsylvania. Fiene's painting of a mother and son in Ephrata is in the collection of the University of Pennsylvania.

2 Quoted with *Coal Breaker*, lot number 9, in Sotheby's Arcade Auction catalog, December 15, 2004, taken from the files of CIGNA Corporation.

3 "Pittsburgh: Paintings of the Coal and Steel Region by Fiene," *Art News*, October 9, 1937, 19.

4 D. Wigmore Fine Art, Inc., *Ernest Fiene (1894–1965)*, unpaginated.

5 Jeanette Jena, "Show of Johanna Hailman Art Works to Open Today," *Pittsburgh Post-Gazette*, October 22, 1937.

6 Blast furnaces associated with the steel mills were typically given women's names, after a special woman in the life of the mill's manager or owner. Lucy, Isabella, Ann, Dorothy, Carrie, and Eliza were some of the names of the furnaces in the Pittsburgh region.

JOHN SLOAN (1871–1951)
Mary Regensburg, 1939, 1947
Tempera underpaint, oil-varnish glaze on panel,
24 x 20 inches
Signed and dated lower right
Gift of Mary Regensburg Feist, 2007.3
Provenance: Gift of the artist to Mary Regensburg Feist.

SELECTED EXHIBITIONS: *Face-to-Face: Twentieth-Century Portraits*, Westmoreland Museum of American Art, 2000; *Painting in the United States 2008*, Westmoreland Museum of American Art, 2008; *The Gift of Art*, Westmoreland Museum of American Art, 2009.

John French Sloan was born in the north central Pennsylvania community of Lock Haven but grew up in Philadelphia, where he was a classmate of William Glackens (1870–1938)—future fellow member of the Eight—and Albert C. Barnes (1872–1951)—future art patron and founder of the Barnes Foundation. His father was unable to hold a job and provide for his family, forcing Sloan, the eldest child and only son, to leave school at age seventeen and take a job at the bookstore Porter & Coates. This turned out to be fortuitous in that it allowed Sloan to peruse the art books when the shop was not busy. He began to make drawings based on their illustrations and in turn began making etchings, which he could sell.

In 1889, Sloan began teaching himself to paint from John Collier's *A Manual of Oil Painting*, using an inexpensive set of oils. His first realized painting, completed the following summer, was a self-portrait that captured his likeness well.[1] Two years later, he met the charismatic artist and teacher Robert Henri (1865–1929), who urged him to continue painting. Although Henri was initially a mentor to Sloan, both men are credited with having defined the tenets of the Ashcan school in the early decades of the twentieth century. In addition, both were to become inspirational teachers, thereby affecting several generations of American artists.

In 1892, Sloan went to work as an illustrator at the *Philadelphia Press* and later the *Philadelphia Inquirer*, where he also made art posters in the art nouveau style. He began taking night classes at the Pennsylvania Academy of the Fine Arts from Thomas Anshutz (1851–1912)—a realist painter and former student of Thomas Eakins (1844–1916). He met George Luks (1866–1933) and Everett Shinn (1876–1953), reunited with Glackens, and cofounded with Henri the Charcoal Club, which met at Henri's Walnut Street studio for informal art instruction.

In 1901, Sloan married Anna Maria Wall, affectionately referred to by all as Dolly. At four feet nine, she was petite in stature but fiery in temperament. Dolly was a manic-depressive and an alcoholic but proved to be a devoted partner to Sloan. It was she who convinced Sloan to leave Philadelphia in 1904 to join the rest of the Philadelphia Five in New York City.[2] Once there, Sloan began to establish a reputation for himself. He joined forces with Henri to organize the 1908 exhibition of the Eight at the Macbeth Gallery, served as treasurer for the 1910 Exhibition of Independent Artists, and contributed to the Armory Show of 1913. He was a founding member of the Society of Independent Artists and served as its president for over twenty years. He had begun keeping a diary in 1906, which would prove to be an important record of a tumultuous era in American art.[3]

Sloan became enamored of the city, observing and recording its life through painting and prints. His etching *Night Windows* (1910) reveals this preoccupation. This scene is drawn from the perspective of the artist's window at dusk, when the city's buildings have fallen into shadow. The view looks across to the building next door and a brightly lit window, through which a woman is drawing in the day's laundry. Perched atop the roof of the building is the figure of a man in silhouette. His gaze is directed toward the window of a distant building, where an attractive young woman is leaning into the night air, arms holding her hair above her head in a sensual manner. Both Sloan and the unidentified man appear to be voyeurs of the city at night. As in this image, Sloan often inserted his sense of humor and love of humanity into his work.

Also in the Museum's collection are fourteen prints dating from 1905 to 1946, including a portrait of Robert Henri from 1905. A watercolor sketch of the Pittsburgh skyline from 1907

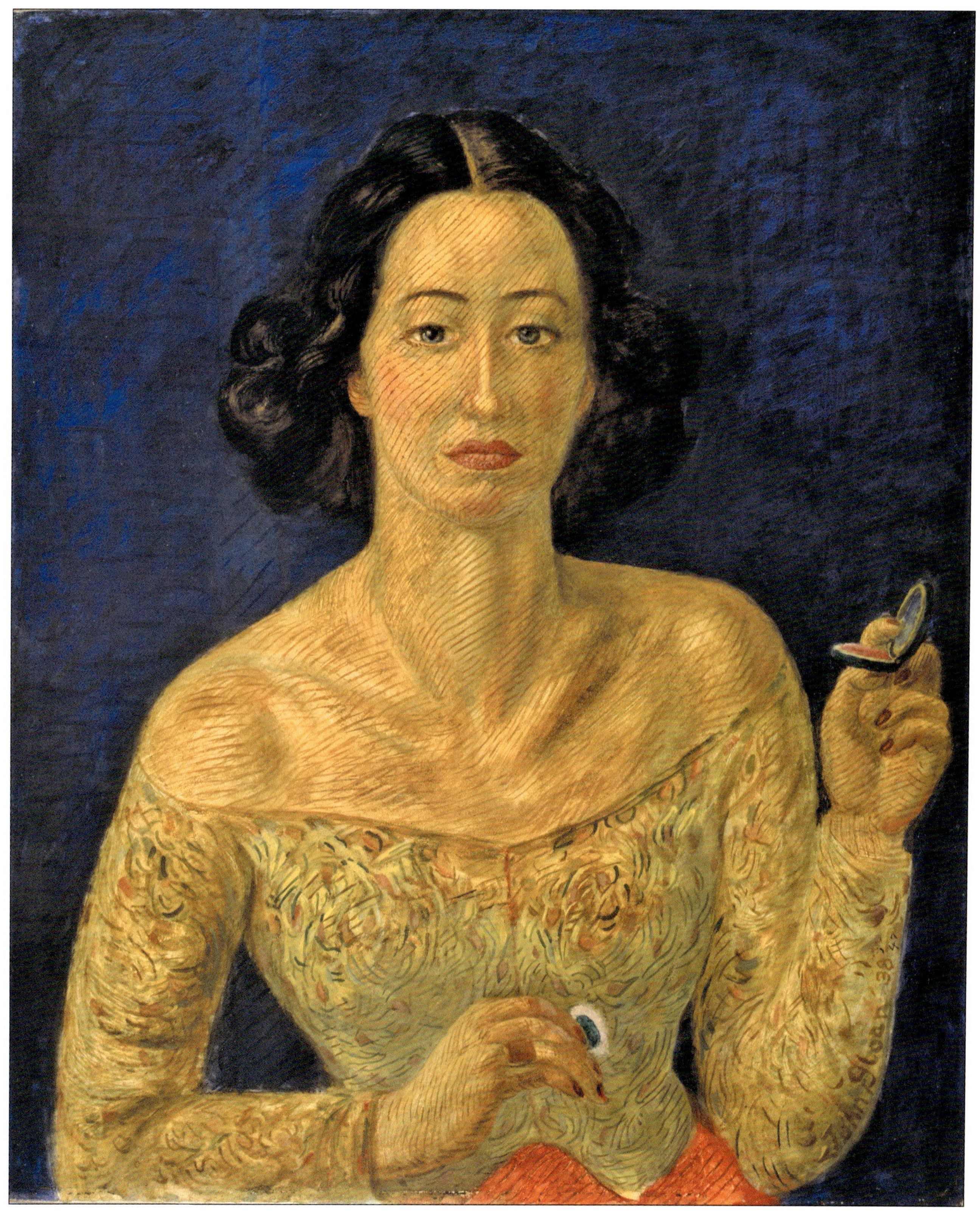

when he taught at the Carnegie Institute of Technology (now Carnegie Mellon University) is of special interest to our scenes of industry collection.

Sloan taught at the Art Students League off and on for nearly thirty years. He was a demanding teacher who believed in giving his students a basic understanding of techniques and materials while encouraging them to find their own style. He gave his students no illusions about greatness and warned that his teachings would not offer them the ability to make a living. His lectures were compiled by a young art student named Helen Farr (1911–2005) and published in 1939 under the title *Gist of Art*. The book is still in publication today and is widely appreciated by art students.

In 1914, Sloan become the art editor of the *Masses*, a socialist magazine in which his drawings frequently appeared as illustrations. He and Dolly had been politically active in the Socialist Party since 1909. However, Sloan's interest in politics had always been stimulated by his desire to better the plight of New York's indigent, and he balked as the magazine became increasingly propagandistic. He quit at the outbreak of World War II.

Sloan's exposure to European artists through the 1913 Armory Show changed both his subject matter and his palette. He turned to landscape and figure painting with an interest in color, pattern, and texture. He began working with oil glazes to add depth to his images. The summers he spent in Santa Fe, beginning in 1919 and lasting through the 1940s, also contributed to his interest in color, form, and landscape. He took a keen interest in Native American crafts and jewelry, and advocated on behalf of Native American artists.

Mary Regensburg (b. 1914) was a private student of Sloan's in the late 1930s. Her portrait was presented to her as a wedding gift and is executed in the painter's later style. Sloan had begun using in his oil paintings the crosshatch marks typically employed in printmaking to build volume. Their use here causes the figure to stand out from the background. Sloan's use of oil tempera and glazes casts the sitter in an overall golden appearance which is extremely effective set against the intense blue of the background. The fashionable bodice—elaborately decorated in green and gold—sets off her well-coifed dark hair and pale complexion. The artist reworked the painting in 1947, when he borrowed it to re-glaze the background. Where the sitter had held a cigarette, he now placed an open compact. Mary had never liked the cigarette, as she was not a smoker, but she had accepted it as an endearing reference to her father, who kept Sloan well supplied with his favorite pipe tobacco. Interestingly, she also disliked the compact, as she had never worn makeup.

A second oil in the Museum's collection is *Old Man of the Rocks*—a painting dating from the summer of 1915, during which Sloan experimented with the Maratta color system in Gloucester, Massachusetts.

In 1943, Dolly passed away; the following year, Sloan married his former student Helen Farr, now a teacher and practicing artist. He continued painting and resumed his diary after some encouragement from Helen. He felt somewhat embittered that critics and collectors did not appreciate his current work, and was constantly fielding questions about why he wasn't continuing to work in the Ashcan style. In 1951 while summering at Dartmouth at the invitation of his cousin and namesake John Sloan Dickey—then president of the college—he was diagnosed with cancer. A number of visitors came to his bedside, including George Luks's son, Kent Crane, and the poet Robert Frost, who was teaching at Middlebury College in Vermont that summer. Sloan died in Hanover, New Hampshire, due to complications from surgery that September. A retrospective exhibition was held at Dartmouth and at the Whitney Museum of American Art the following year.

Helen created the John Sloan Memorial Foundation, through which she supported research and publications. She also established a collection and library relating to the Eight at the Delaware Art Museum. Although Sloan died believing that his life's work was no longer understood or relevant, Helen's dedication ensured that this was not the case.

JHO'T

1 Sloan kept this portrait with him throughout his life. It was later donated by his widow, Helen Farr Sloan, to the Delaware Art Museum. A notation on the verso states that the stretcher was made by Sloan's father.

2 Sloan, Glackens, Luks, Shinn and Henri are sometimes referred to as the Philadelphia Five

3 See *John Sloan's New York Scene: From the Diaries, Notes, and Correspondence, 1906–1913* (New York: Harper & Row, 1965).

FRANCIS L. KOMPERDA (1914–1996)
Portrait of Mike Kessel, c. 1938–1940
Oil on canvas, 28 x 40 inches
Signed lower right
Gift of the Thomas Lynch Fund, 2004.8
Provenance: The Artist; William Goldbach, Pittsburgh, Pennsylvania.

SELECTED EXHIBITIONS: *Born of Fire: The Valley of Work,* Westmoreland Museum of American Art, 2006; Oberhausen, Germany, 2007; Chemnitz, Germany, 2008; and Zabrze, Poland, 2009; *Feuerländer: Regions of Vulcan,* LVR-Industriemuseum, Oberhausen, Germany, 2010.

Born in Pittsburgh, Francis L. Komperda lived in both Hays and Hazelwood. For the better part of his career, he worked as a production artist and model maker for the Gardner Display Company in Oakland and for the former GRS &W, a display company in East Liberty. Two of his early assignments for Gardner included painting the comic strip characters in the Old Mill at Kennywood Park and the 4-foot hot dogs for the walls above the concession stands at Three Rivers Stadium. One of his largest works was a 15 x 127 foot industrial exhibit for the Carrier Corporation, depicting buildings—including the Empire State Building in New York and the Palmer House in Chicago—that contained Carrier air-conditioning units. He was a longstanding member of Pittsburgh's Sign, Pictorial and Display Artists Local Union no. 479, which he joined in 1949.

Komperda attended night school at Carnegie Institute of Technology (now Carnegie Mellon University) in 1930, working during the day as a shipper for a carpet company in downtown Pittsburgh, lugging hundred-pound rolls of carpet up and down steps all day. He received his bachelor's degree in fine arts from the College of Painting and Design in 1938. His instructors included Robert Lepper (1906–1991), Wilfred Readio (1895–1961), and Alexander Kostellow (1897–1954), all of whose styles are reflected in Komperda's work—especially in those reflecting his interest in industrial technology. At the same time he was painting realistically, albeit in a simplified, abstract style, he was creating small abstract paintings and drawings in a precisionist, architectural manner in keeping with the modernist aesthetic of the period. During the early twentieth century, these two opposing stylistic camps—realism and modernism—shared the spotlight, as artists worked to express themselves. In addition to portraits of steelworkers and other laborers, Komperda painted a variety of subjects, from the deserted downtown streets of Pittsburgh, to the modern roadways surrounding the city, to the backyards of Coal Hill houses.

Komperda began painting during the Depression in the 1930s, and first exhibited at Carnegie Institute (now Carnegie Museum of Art) in 1936. As a member of the Associated Artists of Pittsburgh, he exhibited with them from 1938 to 1941 and again from 1957 to 1960. He served in the Air Force Medical Corps in New Guinea during World War II, sending home a landscape that he drew on silk pieces retrieved from a Japanese parachute. Because he had limited colors to work with, he ground colored pills to use as pigment. A small show of his work was organized by Studio Z Gallery on the South Side in 1996, and upon his death that year, a memorial retrospective exhibition was held at the Associated Artists of Pittsburgh Gallery, the only two solo shows of his career.

Komperda created a larger-than-life image of his late brother-in-law in his *Portrait of Mike Kessel,* c. 1938–40, and pays homage to and celebrates the workingman, whose blood and sweat powered industry in Pittsburgh during the Big Steel Era. Heroic in scale, this man symbolizes the ordinary laborer who, like the sitter, worked every day in the mills, keeping them in continuous operation. According to the artist, "Mike would come in after work filled with dirt and grime and dirty welding goggles on his head." Kessel worked for the Baltimore & Ohio Railroad in Glenwood, and Komperda thought his brother-in-law was "typical of the hard-working men and women who made this city."[1] His model wears a cap, welding goggles, and heavy gloves, but only his undershirt besides, with no other protective clothing to shield his body from the heat and other dangers of the workplace. Kessel's solid, muscular build signifies human strength, while the pipe and casting he holds in his hands represent the industrial parts produced by Pittsburgh mills every day. The heavy rope draped over his shoulders symbolizes how completely tied he is to the industry

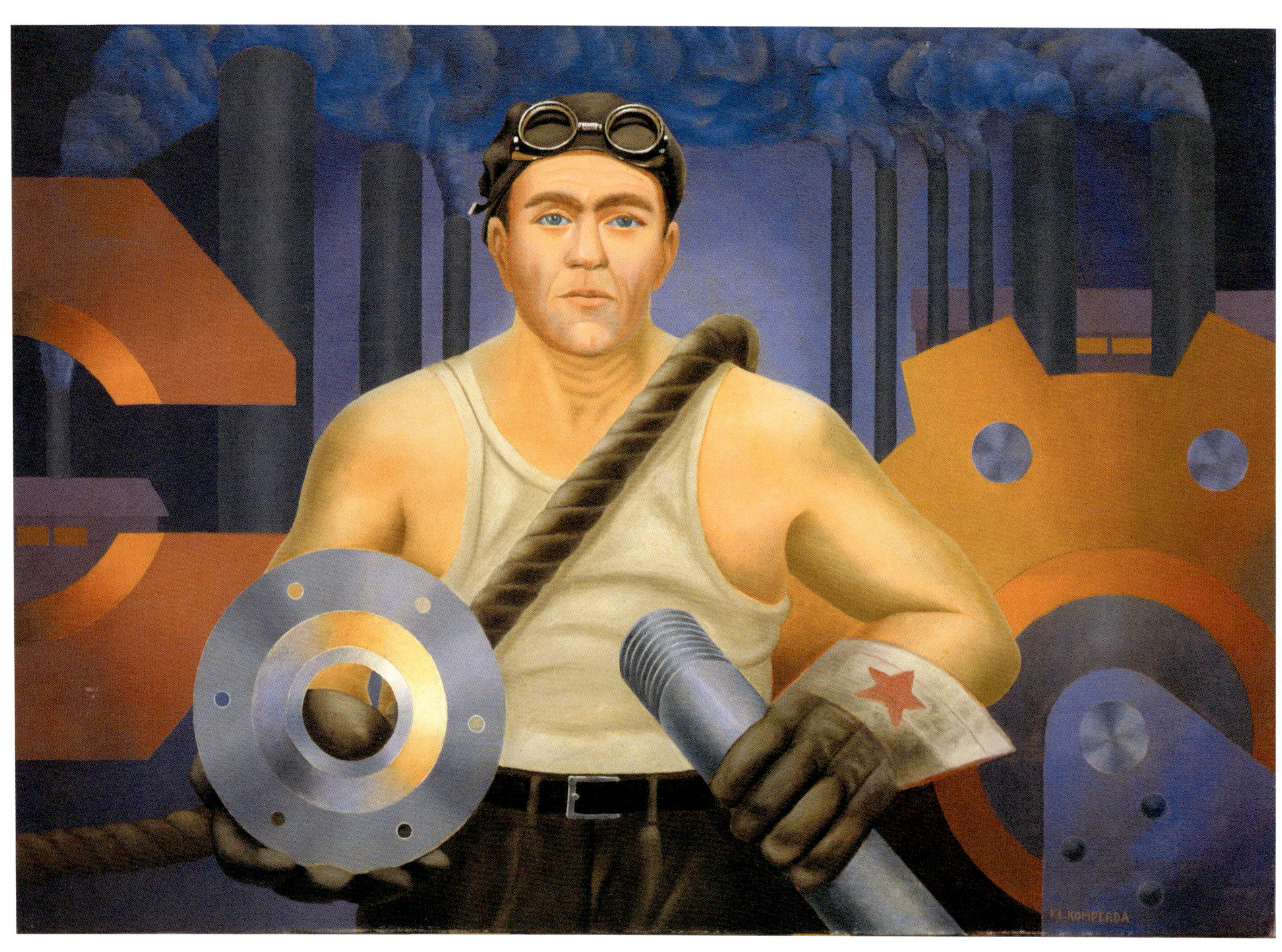
F.L. KOMPERDA

that exists outside the picture plane. Colorful gears and bearings surround him, all products produced by Pittsburgh's foundries, pipe mills, and finishing mills. Belching smokestacks behind him further emphasize that he is in the midst of a heavy industrial environment. Komperda accentuates his sitter by placing him solidly in the center of the composition under bright illumination, while high key combinations of complementary colors call attention to his surroundings.

Portrait of Mike Kessel is one of two works by the artist in the Museum's collection; the second is an untitled abstract charcoal-and-ink drawing (2004.19), which reveals a very different stylistic approach for Komperda.

Following a heart attack in 1973, Komperda was forced to retire from his production work but kept on painting. In 1988, at the age of seventy-four, he painted a 7 x 24 inch watercolor entitled *Pittsburgh—Steel City*, which is essentially a miniature panoramic version of The Westmoreland's painting, with Mike Kessel once again as its central character. In a much more graphic and illustrative manner, the artist's congested composition includes specific Pittsburgh landmarks—the tunnels under the surrounding hills; the three rivers; Mellon Arena; the former Three Rivers Stadium; Mercy Hospital; the Point; the inclines; various bridges and boats; a plane—all to celebrate the vitality of his native city and the blue-collar worker who labored in it. Komperda received the first award of his career from the American Association of Retired Persons (AARP) for this painting, and it was reproduced in the June–July 1990 issue of *Modern Maturity* magazine. The jury of selection for the AARP exhibition included the curator from the Whitney Museum of American Art, an art critic, and an artist. According to them, they were "looking for works that were a genuine expression of the artists' lives."[2] The painting, together with the other thirty-nine entries, subsequently made a four-city cross-country tour in 1991.

BLJ

1 Jerry Vondas, "Artist, 76, Feels Good with First Winner," *Pittsburgh Press*, December 26, 1990, A2.

2 "The Seasoned Eye 3, Winning Works of Art," *Modern Maturity*, June–July 1990, 48.

BALCOMB GREENE (1904–1990)
Organic Forms, 1939
Oil on canvas, 33 7/8 x 46 inches
Initialed lower right
Anonymous gift with additional funds from the William Jamison Art Acquisition Fund, 2005.27
Provenance: The Artist's Estate; D. Wigmore Fine Art, Inc., New York.

Born John Wesley Greene in Millville, New York, Balcomb Greene was the son of Methodist minister Bertram Stillman Greene—a descendant of the Revolutionary War general Nathanael Greene (1742–1786)—and Florence Stover Greene, who died when he was just a child.[1] Greene grew up in small towns in Iowa, South Dakota, and Colorado, where his father preached. He pursued his undergraduate degree in philosophy at Syracuse University from 1922 to 1926, intent on following his father's path into the ministry. While on a field trip during his final year, he met the artist-sculptor Gertrude Glass (1904–1956) at the Metropolitan Museum of Art, thus beginning his journey into art rather than religion. The two married following his graduation, then traveled to Paris, where they immersed themselves in the avant-garde culture of the day, especially the art of Piet Mondrian (1872–1944), Juan Gris (1887–1927), and the Abstraction-Création group. While in Paris, Greene devoted more time to writing than art, and in fact would earn his living through writing during the 1930s. He studied philosophy in Vienna for a year before returning to New York in 1927 and entering Columbia University to pursue his master's degree in English literature. Rather than completing his degree, he took a position teaching English at Dartmouth College from 1928 to 1931. He had his first show at the College Art Gallery in 1931, and that same year, he and Gertrude moved back to Paris, where he sketched independently at the Académie de la Grande Chaumière. According to Greene, he took no formal instruction there, as it was costly, learning instead from the avant-garde artists he associated with and by studying the street life of the city. His second show was held in Paris in 1932. Returning to New York, Balcomb continued to pursue his writing, promoting abstract art in articles for *Art Front*, the publication of the Artists' Union. He wrote eloquently, and sometimes condescendingly, in the defense of abstract art, stating that it could not be explained to a "John Doe" any more than could the meaning of existentialism or the character of pure science. "In an era of such stupendous knowledge-accumulation, the painter when he is informative through exact detail becomes tedious."[2] In other words, those up to the task of looking seriously at abstraction would benefit from being invited into the creative act by way of their own imagination.

Beginning in 1936, Greene earned additional income working on the Federal Art Project of the Works Progress Administration. While in the government's employ, he produced a stained-glass window in 1937, and two years later created abstract murals for the Federal Hall of Medicine at the New York World's Fair.

A founding member of the American Abstract Artists (AAA) group in 1937, he was its first president, a post he held for three consecutive terms until 1941. The mission of the group—which included such artists as George L. K. Morris (1905–1975), Ibram Lassaw (1913–2003), and Carl Holty (1900–1973)—was to foster the public's appreciation of abstract art. As a group, they exhibited annually together, issued a charter, and published a magazine to further advance their cause. In 1940, Greene went back to school to pursue a master's degree in art history from New York University, but in 1943, before it was awarded, he accepted a position at the Carnegie Institute of Technology (now Carnegie Mellon University), where he taught art history and aesthetics. Andy Warhol (1928–1987) and Philip Pearlstein (b. 1924) were among his students. Greene remained on the faculty until 1959, maintaining studios in both Pittsburgh and New York. For his last eight years at Carnegie Tech, he taught only during the spring semester, spending the winter months in New York and the summer months on Montauk Point, Long Island, where he had built a home and studio in 1947.

Organic Forms is a representative example of the type of painting that Greene was doing during the 1930s. While the

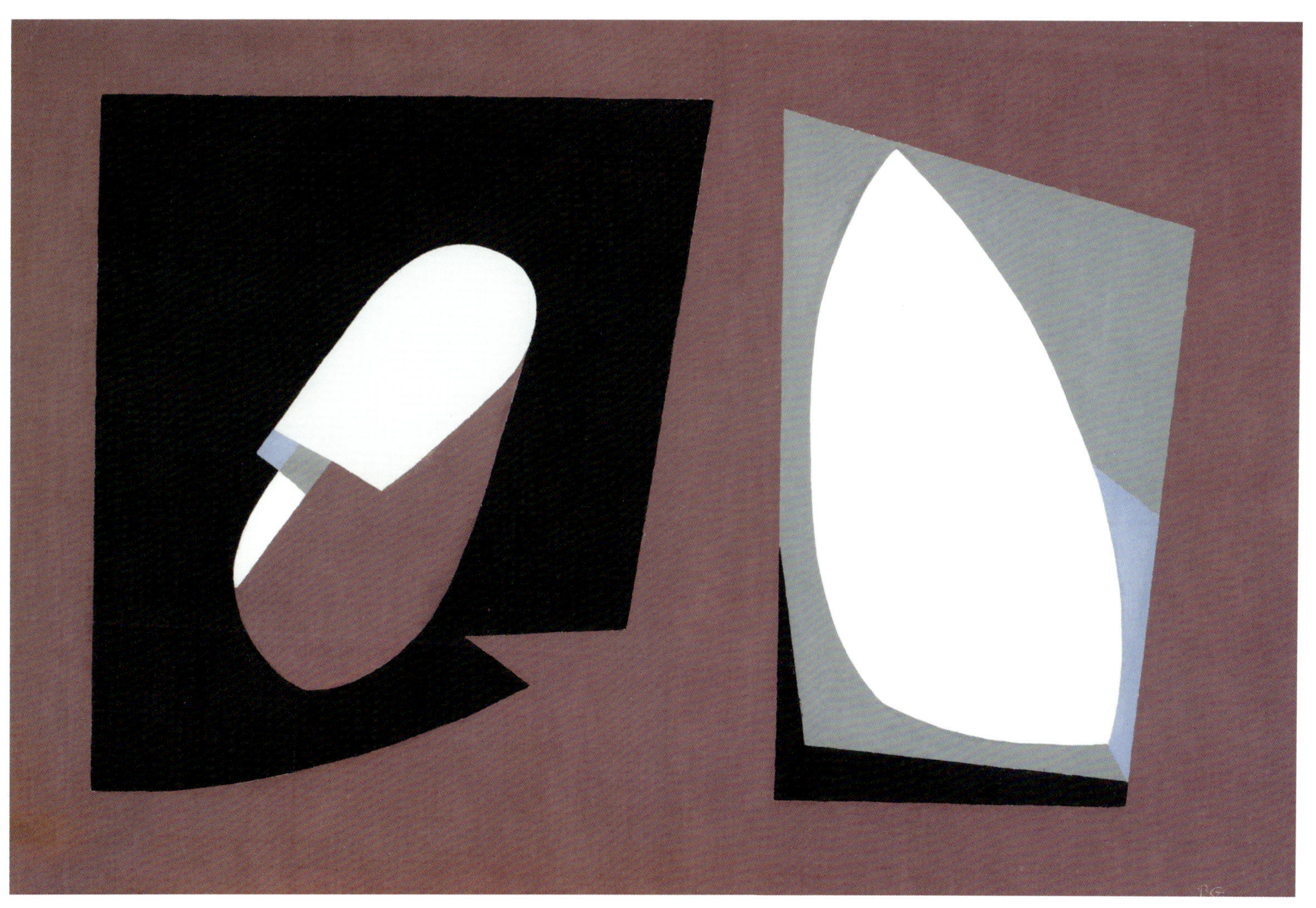

figure emerges and disappears in his work throughout his career, he worked on both figural abstraction and geometric abstraction concurrently for the first half of the decade. By 1935, however, the figure disappeared entirely from his work in favor of geometric abstract compositions composed of hard-edged overlapping shapes and linear patterns on a tilted picture plane. Unlike his figural abstractions, there is no evidence of the artist's hand in these paintings. Greene felt that Mondrian was "the greatest painter of the century," and his influence is clearly evident in this work. Greene described his abstractions of this period as rhythmic arrangements in color and space, yet noted that they required solid and planned geometric structure in order to succeed. His interest was in the formal concerns of art—line, plane, composition, and color. He called them "straight line, flat paintings," using color to define space in these non-objective compositions.[3] He said his only purpose was to make good paintings, and to do so, he felt it was easier to remove subject matter from the equation. In 1941, a studio fire destroyed most of his early paintings, but a group of his collages that served as preparatory studies for those paintings survived.

By the 1940s, the figure reemerges in Greene's painting, appearing collage-like, with ragged edges, as though they had been torn from pieces of paper. In this work, the marks of Greene's brush reveal a more expressionistic surface while light, color, texture, and gesture remain the artist's primary concerns over subject matter. During this decade, Greene began photographing the female nude using dramatic lighting situations to produce sharp contrasts between light and dark. His interests merge in his paintings of the decade and beyond, with his use of anthropomorphic figural forms and high contrasts of white, black, and primary colors. From 1948 on, the figure continues to play a dynamic role in his work but becomes more and more ambiguous.

Greene was invited to participate in all seven of the Carnegie Institute's *Painting in the United States* exhibitions, which replaced the Carnegie International from 1943 to 1949, when it was suspended due to World War II. His first New York solo exhibition was held at J. B. Neumann's New Art Circle gallery in 1947; in the same year, he had a solo show at the Arts and Crafts Center, Pittsburgh (now the Pittsburgh Center for the Arts). In addition, he exhibited in the Associated Artists of Pittsburgh (AAP) annual exhibition at the Carnegie Institute (now Carnegie Museum of Art) and was awarded first prize by the jury that year. Writing about the exhibition, fellow artist and AAP president C. Kermit Ewing called Greene "one of Pittsburgh's leading abstract painters." Directing readers' attention to the purely abstract manner of the painting and their ability to understand it, Ewing wrote, "Until the spectator readjusts his set of values by purging it of its dependency upon objective forms, he will continue to be confused by the type of painting with which Mr. Greene is preoccupied."[4] Greene participated in the International exhibition when it was reinstated in 1950 and then periodically until 1964.[5] In 1949, Greene became the first artist to be named Artist of the Year by the Arts and Crafts Center, an award that is still given today.

In 1959, Greene wrote "The Doctrine of Pure Aesthetic" for the *College Art Journal*, outlining his painting philosophy. During this period, abstract expressionism was at its height, and Greene, like artists such as Larry Rivers (1923–2002) and Jim Dine (b. 1935), embraced the figure when other artists did not. All three artists were among those included in the Museum of Modern Art's *New Images of Man* exhibition that year, which revealed that not all artists chose the path of non-objectivity for their art.

Three years after Gertrude Greene's death in 1956, Balcomb resigned his position at Carnegie Tech and went back to Paris, eventually returning to New York, where his surroundings at Montauk Point inspired his late paintings of the landscape and the sea. In 1972, he referenced his early collages to re-create some of his abstract oil paintings that had been lost in the fire. Greene continued to paint until illness forced his retirement in 1985, and although he said he was never completely satisfied with his accomplishments, since his death in 1990 he has been widely recognized as one of the great abstract artists of the twentieth century.

BLJ

1 Christened John Wesley after the founder of Methodism, Balcomb took his grandmother's surname after becoming disillusioned with religion. The city of Greensburg, Pennsylvania, was named after General Greene.

2 Balcomb Greene, "The Problem of Expression in Art," *Carnegie Magazine*, February 1949, 213.

3 Robert Beverly Hale and Nike Hale, *The Art of Balcomb Greene* (New York: Horizon Press, 1977), 12.

4 C. Kermit Ewing, "Out of the Smog," *Carnegie Magazine*, March 1947, 229.

5 Greene was included in the 1952, 1955, 1958, 1961, and 1964 Carnegie Internationals.

EVERETT SHINN (1876–1953)
The Green Ballet, 1943
Oil on canvas, 19 ¾ x 30 inches
Signed and dated lower left
Gift of the William A. Coulter Fund, 1958.35
Provenance: Mr. Victor D. Spark, New York.

SELECTED EXHIBITIONS: *A Salute to Pennsylvania's Artistic Heritage,* Pennsylvania Historical and Museum Commission, Harrisburg, 1979; *Impressionism: An American View,* Westmoreland County Museum of Art, Greensburg, 1983; *Dance, Dance, Dance:* Nassau County Museum of Art, Roslyn, New York, 2000.

Everett Shinn, like his friend and fellow artist George Luks (1866–1933), demonstrated a natural childhood talent for drawing, possessed a remarkable visual memory, and showed an interest in the theatrical. These attributes served both artists well as observers of contemporary life.

Shinn was born the middle son of Quaker parents near Woodstown, New Jersey, a small community surrounded at the time by farmland.[1] After a happy childhood, he left home to enroll in mechanical drawing classes at the Spring Garden Institute in Philadelphia (now Spring Garden College) and later worked briefly as a technical draftsman. Noting his interest in drawing people rather than machinery, his supervisor at the Thackery Gas Fixture Works advised him to seek other employment, which Shinn found at the *Philadelphia Press* in 1893 and shortly thereafter at the *Inquirer.* Along with fellow artist-journalists George Luks, William Glackens (1870–1938), and John Sloan (1871–1951), Shinn became a regular at the Charcoal Club, which met in Robert Henri's (1865–1929) Walnut Street studio. Between the tips on painting he received from Henri and the immersion in drawing he experienced on the job, Shinn developed an observant eye and an adept hand. Classes at the Pennsylvania Academy of the Fine Arts honed his artistic talent and introduced him to his future wife, a young art student named Florence Scovel.[2]

In 1897, Shinn moved to New York, where he worked for various newspapers and magazines. Off duty, he drew his artistic subject matter from the teeming metropolitan streets, public parks, fashionable restaurants, and theatrical productions. Like other members of the Eight, he was stimulated by the spectacle, diversity, excitement, and sheer size of the city. A trip to London and Paris in 1900 confirmed his interest in the figure, modern life, and the theater. Upon returning home, he constructed a stage in his studio at 112 Waverly Street, where he, Glackens, Luks, and others would perform for audiences of fifty-plus, continuing what had begun on a smaller scale in Henri's Walnut Street studio in Philadelphia. Known as the Waverly Street Players, Shinn enthusiastically performed multiple roles of playwright, director, scene designer, and actor.

Some of Shinn's best graphic work is executed in pastels, such as *Orchestra Pit* (1978.82), also in The Westmoreland's collection. He would have been introduced to this medium as an art student, used it as an illustrator, and developed it as a medium for fine art. Pastels permitted him to work quickly, blending one color over another until the desired image was achieved. In 1899, Shinn began work on a never-published book called "New York at Night," containing pastel drawings of everything from bowery bums to the city's glitterati. His nighttime views of the city are perhaps most popularly recalled in murals for the Oak Bar at the Plaza Hotel, which he completed in 1944. Central Park South, the Vanderbilt mansion (formerly located across from the hotel), and a view of the Pulitzer Fountain, figure prominently in these murals.

As a member of the Eight, Shinn participated in the group's exhibition at the Macbeth Gallery in 1908 and in the first exhibition of the Independents—organized by John Sloan and Robert Henri, among others—in 1910. He declined, however, to contribute to the Armory show in 1913.

Due to their overlapping interest in subject matter, Shinn is sometimes referred to as an American Degas. He was, in fact, an admirer of Edgar Degas (1834–1917), having rented a studio in Paris's Latin Quarter near the French painter's residence. Both artists were interested in the dynamic created between audience and performer, and both favored images of the ballet, symphony, and café concert. Shinn was a man of many talents, but his diverse interests eventually contributed to a dilution of skill in any one area, resulting in his work being uneven—masterful at times and careless at others. Shinn's

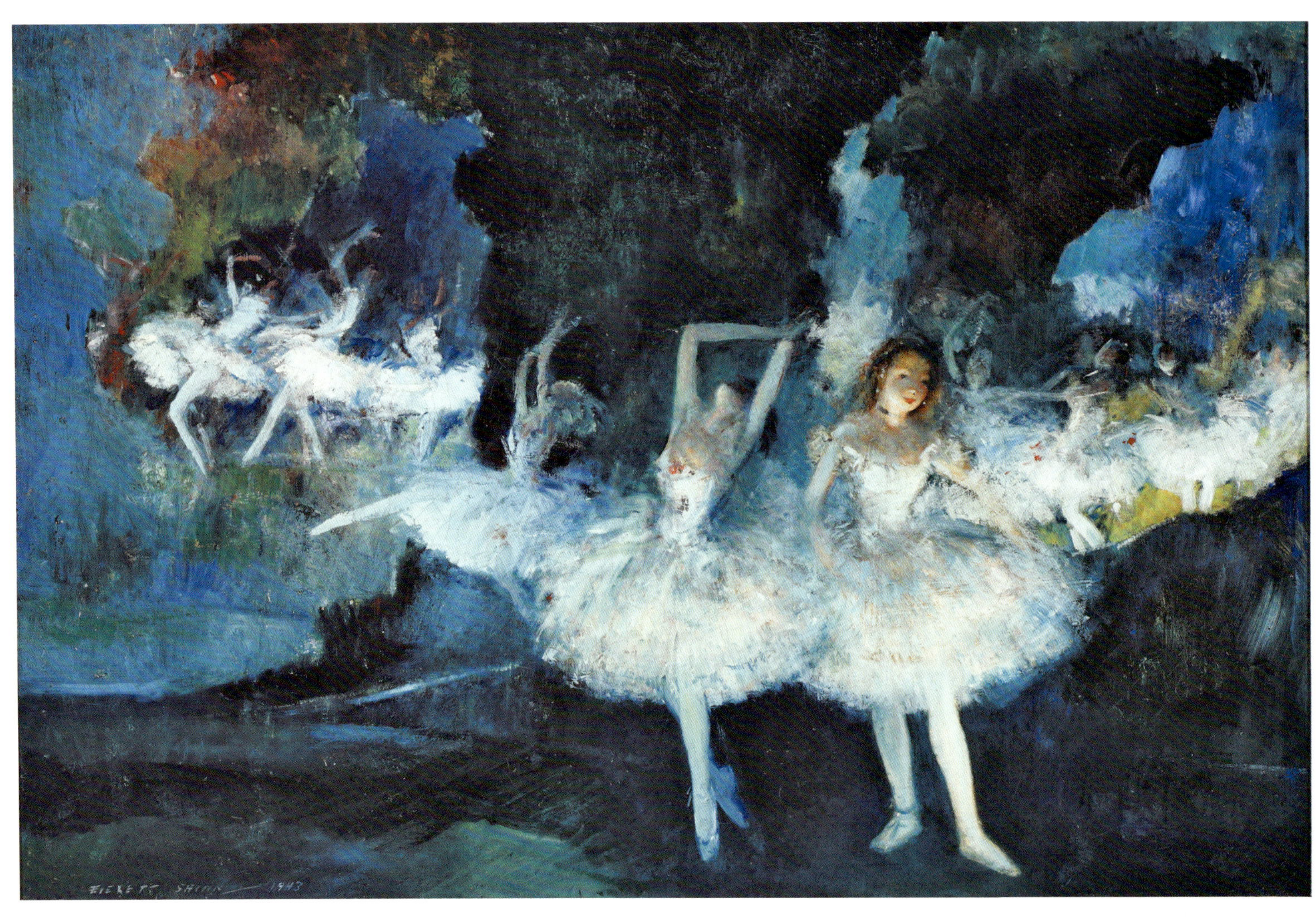
EVERETT SHINN 1943

reputation has suffered because of this. The preponderance of circus images—especially clowns—in his later work often appear hackneyed and sentimental. However, when he was on his game, he was remarkable.

The Green Ballet shows three clusters of dancers on what is assumed to be a stage. There is no clear definition of space or references to curtains, proscenium, orchestra pit, or audience. Surrounded by abstract patterns of color, the dancers perform almost as one dancer in a time-lapsed image, working her way across the composition. Only one dancer's facial features are defined: reds lips in a gentle smile, with brow and chin lit from underneath. The brushwork is lush in the dancers' skirts and pleasingly scumbled in the background.

Shinn's lifelong fascination with popular entertainment—vaudeville, the circus, the café concert, even shopping—manifested itself not only in an important body of visual work but in the authorship of over thirty-five plays and the creation of set designs for Goldwyn Pictures and other movie houses. Alone among his colleagues of the Eight, he continued magazine illustration in his later years, working for *Harper's Weekly* and other publications. Having outlived John Sloan by two years, Shinn was the last surviving member of the group when he died in New York City in 1953.

JHO'T

1 There has been some confusion about his birth year, sometimes recorded as 1873, but a birth certificate in the New Jersey State Library, Archives and History Bureau, confirms November 6, 1876.

2 An artist-illustrator in her own right, Florrie or Flossie, as she was variously known to friends, married Shinn in 1898, divorced him in 1912, and amicably attended his three subsequent weddings.

DORIS EMRICK LEE (1905–1983)
Oranges and Avocados, not dated
Oil on canvas board, 16 x 20 inches
Signed lower right
Gift of Mr. and Mrs. Charles H. Booth Jr. and Burrell Group, Inc., 2009.10
Provenance: The Artist's Estate.

Selected Exhibitions: *Doris Lee: Form and Color,* D. Wigmore Fine Art, Inc., New York, 2004.

Born in Aledo, Illinois, Doris Emrick Lee was one of the most successful artists of the Depression era. The fourth of six children, she grew up in a family that encouraged her in the arts. Her great-grandfather began painting after retiring from farming, and she watched her great-aunts and grandmothers embroider, quilt, and carve, all of which inspired her in her later art. She attended Ferry Hall—a finishing school in Lake Forest—and then Rockford College in Illinois. After graduating in 1927, she married photographer Russell Lee (1903–1986) and traveled to France and Italy to study art. Back in the United States, she pursued her studies at the Kansas City Art Institute with well-known American impressionist Ernest Lawson (1873–1939) in 1929. The next year she was back in France, where she studied in Paris with cubist painter André L'Hote (1885–1962) and, later that year, at the California School of the Fine Arts in San Francisco with painter Arnold Blanch (1896–1968). Upon her return from Paris, Lee was painting abstractly, but Blanch encouraged her to move away from abstraction and to paint subjects from her own life. In an interview with Harry Salpeter for *Esquire* magazine in 1938, Blanch referred to Lee "as a combative student who helped make teaching interesting by entering into disputes with her teacher and expressing differences of opinion."[1] Following her divorce, Lee and Blanch were married in 1939.

In 1931, Lee had settled permanently in rural Woodstock, New York—an active artists' colony north of New York City—and the proximity of the city to Woodstock guaranteed a regular flow of artists between the colony and the urban environment, allowing her to keep in touch with current developments in the arts. The countryside surrounding her Woodstock home became the subject of many of her paintings and prints.

Lee loved gardening and growing things, as evidenced in her landscapes as well as her still life paintings. The Westmoreland's *Oranges and Avocados,* a simplified composition consisting of two oranges, one whole and one cut avocado, three lemons, and one sprig of leaves, is fundamentally about shape, pattern, and color. Lee has simplified forms to their most essential natures: oranges become circles, avocados and lemons become ovals, and the background becomes two rectangles, the whole more like abstract cutouts than a naturalistic depiction of fruit. As the artist stated in 1950, "Quite a few people have liked the subject and this discomforts me somewhat, for I like shapes best, or, at least that is what I work hardest for."[2]

The eight objects in *Oranges and Avocados* exist in a flattened pictorial space that is divided into two unequal horizontal bands: the top, representing one-third of the background, is painted in a colorful pointillist technique, with the remaining two-thirds a subtly modulated neutral gray. Two oranges and one lemon bridge the two backgrounds, connecting them while also suggesting the illusion of a tabletop and backdrop. The colors of the different fruit are echoed in the multi-colored daubs that make up the top band. Lee has succeeded in suggesting the sense of volume and irregular shape of all three fruits without including a single outline to define them.

The 1930s marked the beginning of a long and productive career for Lee. An early abstractionist, Lee developed a mature style based in realism, described as a "sophisticated fusion of folk and modernist painting."[3] Her career was launched in 1935 when she received the Logan Medal from the Art Institute of Chicago for her painting *Thanksgiving,* which features a farm kitchen bustling with preparations for the forthcoming feast. Even though the style of this painting prompted a controversy initiated by Josephine Logan, wife of the benefactor of the prize, the museum subsequently acquired it for its collection. Calling the painting "atrocious," Mrs. Logan sponsored the

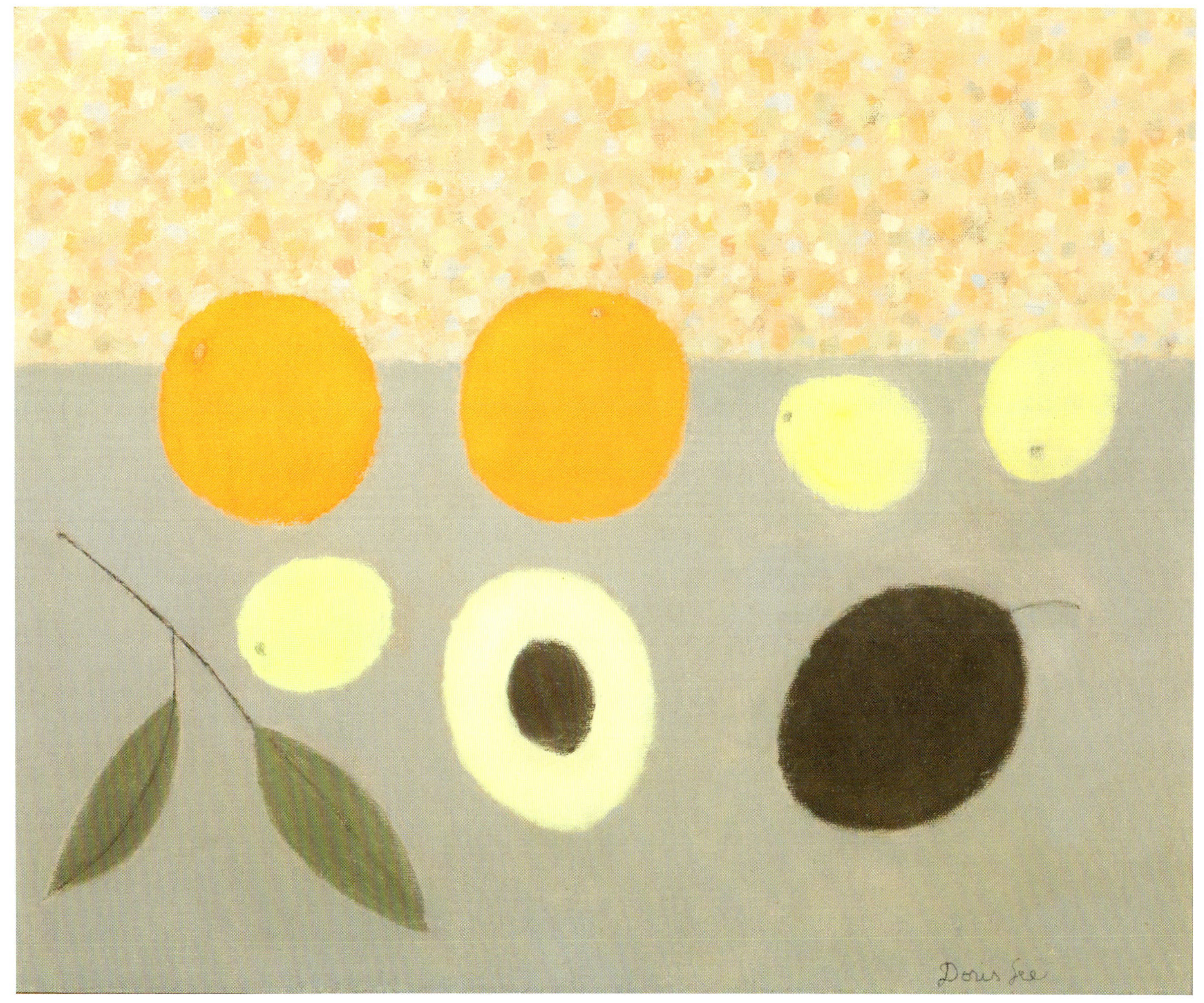
Doris Lee

Sanity in Art Movement in an attempt to abolish modern art in its various forms.[4]

Lee won two mural commissions in 1935 for the Post Office Department Building in Washington, D.C., sponsored by the Treasury Department Section of Painting and Sculpture. *Country Post* and *General Store and Post Office* appealed to the section's and the publics' preference for paintings of the American scene, but not without major modifications and compromises by the artist with regard to style.

Beginning in 1935, Lee traveled to Florida each year with Blanch, who taught throughout the state, spending the winter months there with artist couple Milton (1885–1965) and Sally Avery (1902–2003), who shared Lee's sensibility toward simplified, flattened shapes and forms that merge with a further simplified landscape background. In a statement made to *Artists* magazine in 1966, Lee said, "Years ago I studied modern dance with Martha Graham. It all tied up completely with my own painting because Martha Graham makes one so conscious of one's form and the shapes that are made while dancing."[5]

Lee worked as an illustrator on assignments for *Life* magazine during the 1940s and 1950s, creating paintings to accompany essays on a variety of subjects, including "The Southern Negro as a Source of Fashion Inspiration" (1941), Hollywood (1944–1945), and North Africa (1952). She won third prize for her painting *Siesta* in the Carnegie Institute's *Painting in the United States* exhibition in 1944, and was invited to participate in all seven of these exhibitions from 1943 to 1949, during which time they replaced the Carnegie International exhibitions due to World War II.

Lee's work included easel paintings, murals, prints, and illustrations, as well as costume, textile, and ceramic design. She was concerned with life in rural America, and with her simplified style and ideology, her work had much in common with American scene painting—the prevailing style of the 1930s and 1940s in this country. Lee painted realistic subject matter with an emphasis on form, color, and pattern, while adapting aspects of the regionalist style, folk art (which she actively collected), modernism, and abstraction to create her own unique painting style that is both primitive and modern simultaneously. Her subjects include portraits, landscapes, genre scenes, and still lifes, choosing the people around her and ordinary objects that caught her attention, rendering them to their simplest forms and employing a flattened perspective—an indication of her continued interest in the tenets of abstraction. Her paintings are enlivened with a fresh, remarkable use of color and infused with good-natured nostalgia. They often have a narrative quality, as if there were a good story behind them—perhaps a by-product of her work as an illustrator.

Critics have referred to Lee's style as "crisp, witty, ebullient, joyous, purposefully simplified, primitive-naive, sophisticated."[6] Grace Pagano wrote about the artist when Lee's painting *Arbor Day* was included in the Encyclopaedia Britannica's collection catalog in 1945: "For the same reason that a bird sings—sheer joy of living—Doris Lee paints her exuberant and subtly humorous legends of the rural scene. In a sad world of too many complexities, one breathes a sign of relief and feels free to admire, to enjoy and even to chuckle a little at the 'busy' but delicious whimsy of her canvases."[7]

Lee coauthored the book *Painting for Enjoyment* with Blanch in 1947. After a career that spanned over fifty years, she died in Clearwater, Florida, in 1983 at the age of seventy-eight. A memorial retrospective of eighty-three works was held at the Woodstock Artists Association in 1984. When *Life* magazine published an article on her in 1937, the author ended with a comment on her vitality as a woman: "As vigorous as she is attractive, she spent a large part of one winter improving the view from her hilltop studio by chopping down trees all by herself."[8]

The Westmoreland owns two other works by Lee: *Autogyro*, an undated etching (1983.96), and *Vineland*, an abstract oil painting (2009.35) from around 1940 that was a gift from William P. Emrick, the artist's nephew, in 2009.

BLJ

1 Salpeter, Harry, "Doris Lee," *Current Biography*, January 1954, 35.

2 Alice Lewis, *Doris Lee, 1905–1983* (Woodstock, NY: Woodstock Artists Association catalog, 1984), unpaginated.

3 Roberta Smith, "Offering a Painter for History's Reconsideration," *New York Times*, April 7, 2008.

4 Salpeter, "Doris Lee," 35.

5 Ibid.

6 Lewis, *Doris Lee, 1905–1983*.

7 Grace Pagano, *The Encyclopaedia Britannica Collection of Contemporary American Painting* (Chicago: Encyclopaedia Britannica, 1945), 68.

8 "Doris Lee: An American Painter with a Humorous Sense of Violence," *Life*, September 20, 1937, 44.

MILTON AVERY (1885–1965)
Arrangement with Plants, 1948
Oil on canvas, 26 x 42 inches
Signed and dated lower right
Gift of Mr. Michael Ross, 1975.77
Provenance: Mr. Michael Ross, Hewlett Bay Park, New York.

SELECTED EXHIBITIONS: *Milton Avery,* The Baltimore Museum of Art, 1952–1953; *A Salute to Pennsylvania's Artistic Heritage,* Pennsylvania Historic and Museum Commission, Harrisburg, Pennsylvania, 1979; *The Flower,* Southern Alleghenies Museum of Art, Loretto, Pennsylvania, 1987.

Born in Altmar, New York, in 1885, Milton Avery grew up in Hartford, Connecticut, where he studied at both the Connecticut League of Art Students and the School of the Art Society of Hartford. Avery was committed to his art from a very early age, taking on a variety of jobs to support his passion. Over the course of twenty years, he was employed as assembler, latheman, mechanic, file clerk, tire salesman, and construction worker. In 1925, he moved to New York City to be near his future wife, fellow artist Sally Michel (1902–2003), and they were married the following year. Both artists enrolled at the Art Students League and attended sketch classes there until 1938, when they began hiring models to pose for them and their friends so that they could work at home. In addition to being Avery's life partner, Sally served as his art dealer and financial supporter, earning a regular income so that he could concentrate solely on his art. He and Sally had a daughter, March, in 1932, and reflecting the two women in his life, the maternal relationship of mother and child became a frequent subject.[1]

As an artist, Avery is seen as a transitional figure between representation and abstraction, between early twentieth-century modernism and abstract expressionism. Avery was an early admirer of the work of Albert Pinkham Ryder (1847–1917), who was ahead of his time in his creation of emotionally charged abstract compositions in the late nineteenth century and influential to many artists who came after him. Although Avery did not travel abroad until his sixties, he was aware of European art through his personal studies in museums and galleries. He entered the art world in the 1920s, when modernism was at odds with both realism and American scene painting, which still dominated the art scene. Many artists of the period who were working in abstraction felt the same rejection.

Avery's work is a unique combination of figural subjects and nonobjective formal concerns. His early work reflects the influence of the European avant-garde artists, especially Pablo Picasso (1881–1973) and Henri Matisse (1869–1954), whose work was accessible in New York. Avery responded strongly to Matisse, who was creating flattened planes of all-over color and pattern as early as 1910, and though his influence is evident, Avery's painting style evolved into one that was uniquely his own. Matisse and Avery shared a common attitude about art making and achieving balance and harmony in their paintings through the use of color, pattern, and shape.

Avery's early work was more painterly, composed of texture, modeling, pattern, and arbitrary color. As his style matured, he eliminated more and more detail and pattern, his paintings evolving into a harmony of form and color. Simple flat planes defined his subjects and were combined with transparent washes of color that resulted in luminous abstract compositions. As they grew in size, they became even more sparse. Avery's intuitive sense of color and his ability to reduce his subjects to their barest essentials resulted in lyrical abstractions that were more about universal experiences than specifics. But no matter how abstract his work became, Avery never totally abandoned representation.

Avery painted portraits, landscapes, seascapes, and still lifes throughout his career, continually painting the life around him. Sally, March, their dog Picasso, and friends figured prominently in his work, serving as models for his figural and landscape compositions, involved in such everyday activities as playing a game of checkers, table tennis, or cards; talking on the telephone; reading; or lying on the beach. According to Barbara Haskell, Avery sketched everything around him, and those sketches became a kind of diary of his activities throughout his lifetime.[2]

Avery participated in a group show at the Opportunity Gallery in 1928 that included the work of Mark Rothko (1903–1970), and it was there that the two artists' long friendship began. Avery joined the Valentine Gallery in 1935, which also represented Matisse, and had his first solo show there that

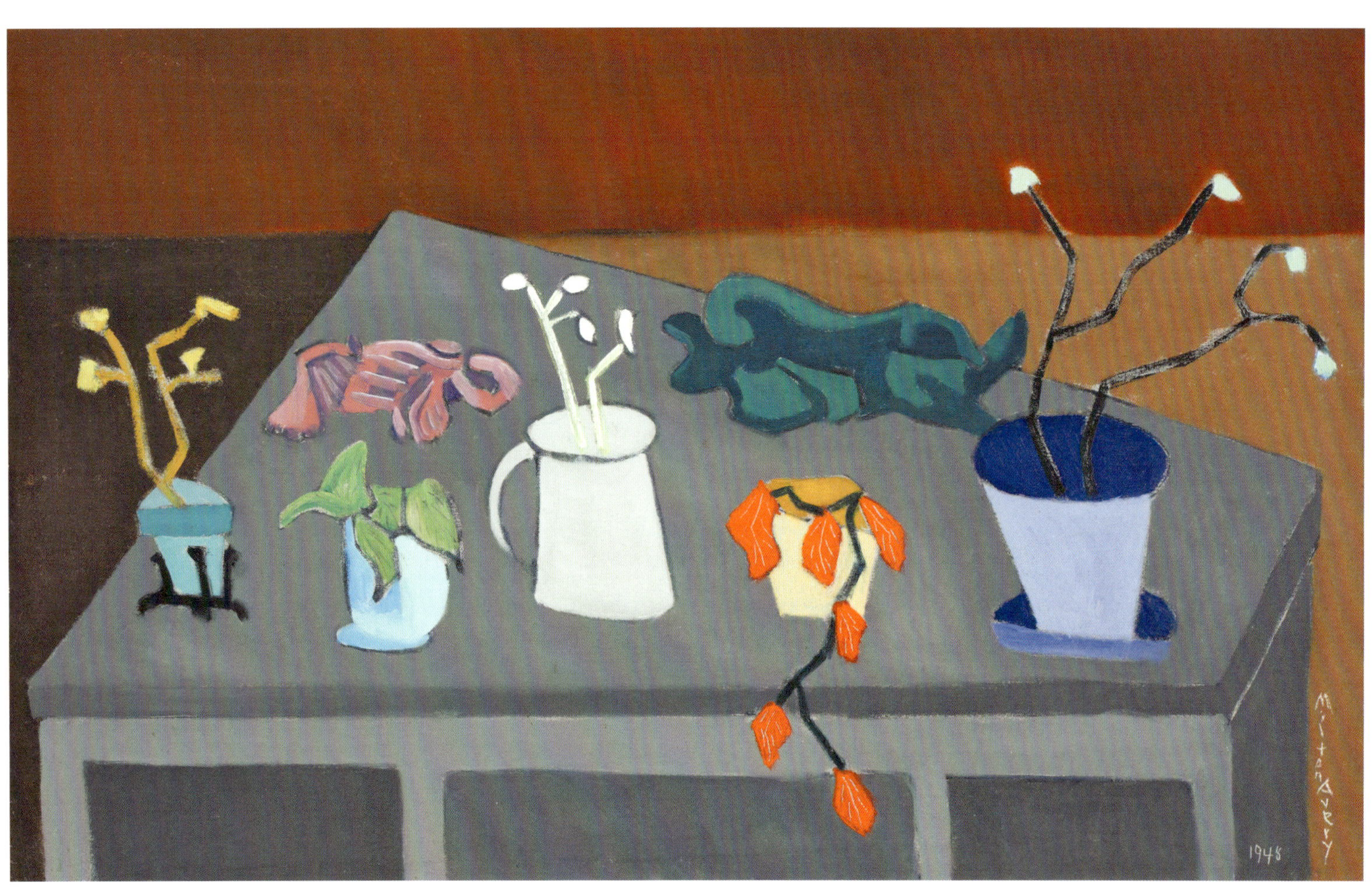
Milton Avery
1948

year. In 1943, Avery left Valentine and joined the gallery of Paul Rosenberg, who promoted the European avant-garde and had previously operated a gallery in Paris. Fernand Léger (1881–1955), Picasso, and Georges Braque (1882–1963) were among Rosenberg's stable of artists he brought with him to New York after fleeing Paris in 1940, allowing Avery to study them firsthand. Avery's first solo show there was held in 1943. Four years later, when he was sixty-two years old, the artist's first retrospective in New York was held at the gallery of Durand-Ruel, who also operated a gallery in Paris. From 1944 to 1949, Avery's work was shown at both galleries.

Rothko introduced Avery to Adolph Gottlieb (1903–1974) in 1929, and in 1932, Avery vacationed in Gloucester, Massachusetts, with Rothko, Gottlieb, and Barnett Newman (1905–1970). All three were Avery disciples, and all would become leading abstract expressionist artists, founding the Federation of Modern Painters and Sculptors in New York in 1940. Avery had summered in Gloucester for the first time in 1920, where he met Sally, and would spend summer months there periodically during the twenties and thirties. Other summers were spent in Vermont; Maine; Provincetown, Massachusetts; the artists' colony in Woodstock, New York; and MacDowell Colony in Peterborough, New Hampshire.

While still life paintings were a relatively limited subject area in Avery's body of work, he painted them occasionally throughout his career. Like his landscapes, his still lifes became more simplified as his work matured, featuring fewer and fewer objects in arrangements of flat planes and colors, with household objects, food, fruit, and houseplants serving as the different shapes in his compositions, set in a shallow pictorial space. In The Westmoreland's *Arrangement with Plants,* Avery used a muted yet harmonious color palette, reducing the composition to the barest essentials of color, shape, and form. His early still life paintings of the twenties and thirties are more academic in their approach and include realistically rendered objects, but by the 1940s, he had eliminated objective references in favor of large areas of flattened color shapes configured in abstract patterns. His paintings became more about the formal concerns of color relationships and expression rather than subject. In *Arrangement with Plants,* five different yet equally straggly plants, in five separate containers, are set on a tilted tabletop close to the front of the picture plane. The artist includes no extraneous details to identify plant type; instead, the plants constitute a balanced composition of simple, biomorphic shapes that reference nature. Evenly modulated color bands define a neutral background that not only is in harmony with the foreground objects but also accentuates them and the tabletop. Avery had his first major heart attack in January 1949 at the age of sixty-three, and while recuperating at a friend's house, he continued painting still life arrangements of objects and furniture that were readily available to him.

Avery experimented with printmaking techniques starting in 1932, and throughout his career, he made etchings, monotypes, lithographs, and woodcuts. The Museum's collection contains one of the artist's woodcuts (1970.80) and two of his drypoint etchings—one depicting his wife (1982.60); the other, his daughter (1962.38).

A retrospective of Avery's work opened at the Whitney Museum of American Art in February 1960, and in October, he suffered his second heart attack. His health remained fragile over the next few years, and he returned to the hospital on March 6, 1964, remaining there until his death ten months later on January 3, 1965. Mark Rothko delivered the memorial address at the New York Society for Ethical Culture four days later, commenting on the artist's greatness and the importance he held to younger artists like himself. Although not highly acclaimed during his lifetime, Avery is now seen as one of the premier American modernists of the twentieth century. Nearly twenty years after his death, Barbara Haskell noted Avery's enduring legacy: "As one of the first and most accomplished American exponents of color and its structural function, Avery paved the way for later generations of American colorists. Applying thin layers of paint, he created chromatic harmonies of striking subtlety, delicacy, and invention. The range and originality of his achievement established him unequivocally as one of America's greatest color poets."[3]

BLJ

1 For an in-depth chronology and exhibition history, see Barbara Haskell, *Milton Avery* (New York: Whitney Museum of American Art in association with Harper & Row, 1982); and Robert Hobbs, *Milton Avery* (New York: Hudson Hills Press, 1990).

2 Haskell, *Milton Avery,* 30.

3 Haskell, *Milton Avery,* 14.

BEN SHAHN (1898–1969)
Byzantine Isometric, 1951
Tempera on canvas mounted on masonite, 40 x 26 ½ inches
Signed lower right
Museum purchase, 2007.21
Provenance: The Downtown Gallery, New York; Mr. and Mrs. Stanley J. Wolf, Great Neck, New York; Milton and Adrienne Porter, Pittsburgh, Pennsylvania.

SELECTED EXHIBITIONS: *1951 Annual of Contemporary American Painting*, Whitney Museum of American Art, New York, 1951–1952.

Ben Shahn remains one of the most well-known social-realist artists in the United States, for the often troubling content of his paintings, war posters, photographs, prints, commercial illustrations, and murals that call attention to tragedy, injustice, politics, and poverty. He championed many causes and brought them to a public forum through his art, his writing, and his lectures, voicing his personal concern for human rights and his commitment to world peace.

Born in Kovno, Lithuania, Shahn settled in the Bronx with his family in 1906, when he was eight years old. He studied briefly at the Art Students League, New York University, City College of New York, and the National Academy of Design before completing an apprenticeship in lithography, which supported him for many years. He traveled to Europe and was aware of the modernist developments there but chose his own brand of realism, one that he felt would best portray the themes he was trying to communicate.

During the 1930s, Shahn painted government-sponsored murals and made thousands of photographs that he said "cried out to be taken" for the Resettlement Administration and the Farm Security Administration, joining photographers Roy Stryker (1893–1975), Dorothea Lange (1895–1965), and Walker Evans (1903–1975) in an effort to document the effects of the Depression on rural areas of the country.[1] He took up photography because he "felt strongly that [he] could arrive at broad generalizations about human beings through sharpened observation of the specific."[2]

An artist and political activist, Shahn was a member of the Artists' Union and joined the editorial staff of the group's publication, *Art Front*, with his second wife, artist-activist Bernarda Bryson (1903–2004). He contributed illustrations to such publications as the *Nation*, the *New Republic*, *Fortune*, and *Harper's Weekly*, and this commercial work made him accessible to millions of Americans. In the early forties, he created a series of compelling posters for both the Office of War Information, to assist in explaining to the public the United States' involvement in the war, and the Congress of Industrial Organizations, highlighting the labor crisis in the country. In his renowned series of paintings *The Passion of Sacco and Vanzetti* (1931–1932), Shahn portrays the notorious arrest, trial, and subsequent execution of Italian immigrants Nicola Sacco and Bartolomeo Vanzetti for a robbery and murder that many believe they did not commit. Shahn participated in the picket line outside the courthouse in Boston in protest of the executions. His interest in this subject culminated in a large-scale mosaic mural for Syracuse University in 1967.

World War II had an enormous impact on the artist, and it is during this period that his style shifted direction. Years later, Shahn explained:

> The change in art, mine included, was accomplished during World War II. . . . During the war I worked in the Office of War Information. We were supplied with a constant stream of material, photographic and other kinds of documentation of the decimation within enemy territory. There were the secret confidential horrible facts of the cartloads of dead; Greece, India, Poland. There were the blurred pictures of bombed-out places, so many of which I knew well and cherished. . . . I had once believed that the incidental, the individual, and the topical were enough; that in such instances of life all of life could be implied. But then I came to feel that that was not enough. I wanted to reach farther; to tap some sort of universal quality. . . . A symbolism which I might once have considered cryptic now became the only means by which I could formulate the sense of emptiness and waste that the war gave me, and the sense of the littleness of people trying to live on through the enormity of war.[3]

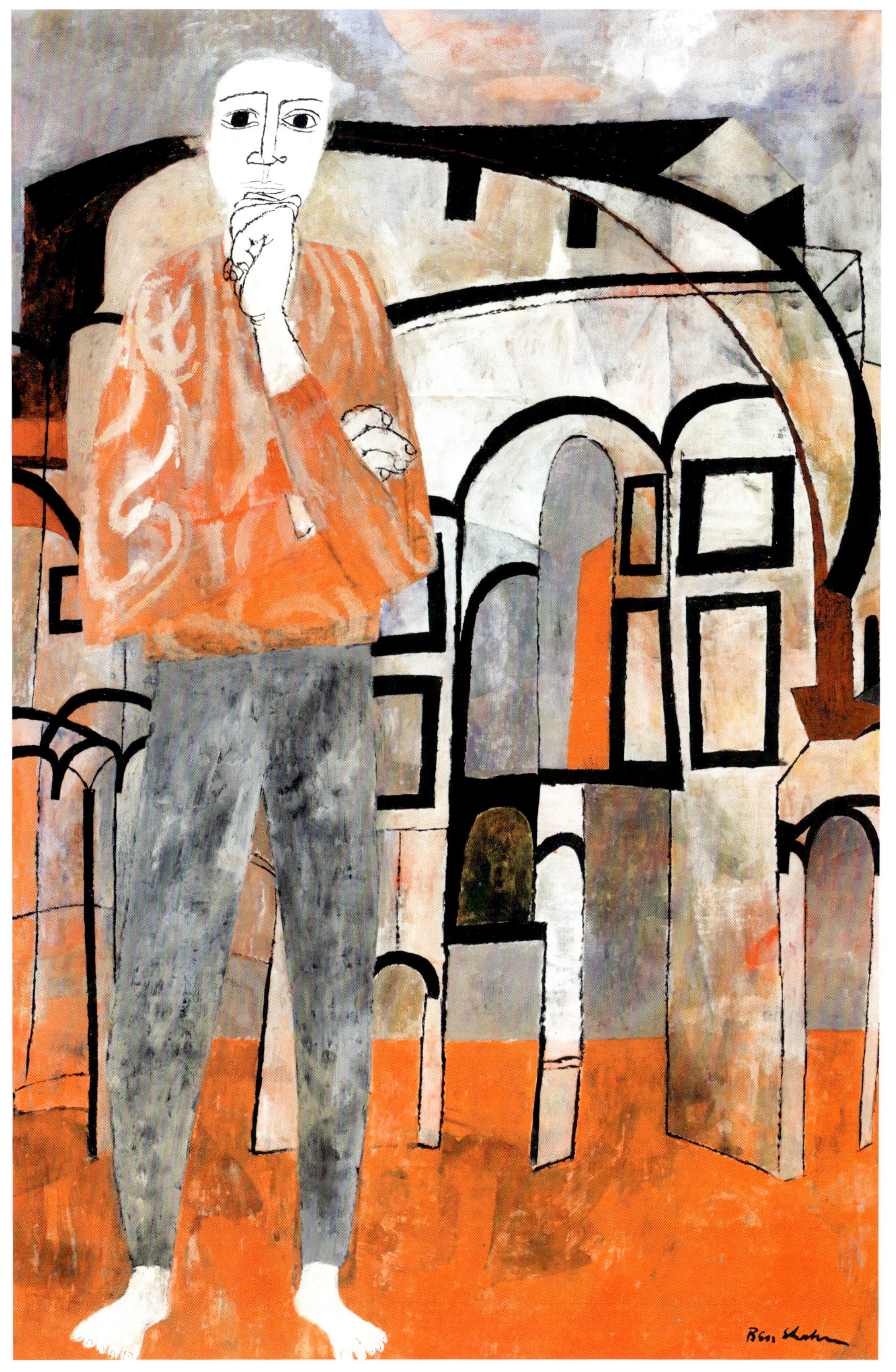

He became embroiled in issues surrounding the cold war of the late 1940s and 1950s, and the paranoia surrounding the red scare, and because of his affiliations of the 1930s, he became a target. Accused of being a Communist, he was investigated by the FBI, blacklisted by CBS network television, included in the list of artists attacked by Representative George Dondero in his diatribes to Congress on modern art, and called before the House Un-American Activities Committee in 1959.

The Museum of Modern Art selected eleven of Shahn's works for its *American Realists and Magic Realists* exhibition in 1943, and his *Retrospective* exhibition was shown there in 1947. The following year, Shahn was categorized as number five in *Look* magazine's list of the ten best American painters in the country, and in 1954, he and Willem de Kooning (1904–1997) were selected to represent the United States at the Venice Biennale. The two artists characterized the opposing stylistic tendencies of the period—realism and abstract expressionism—and although the response to de Kooning's style was generally negative, the Italians related to Shahn's work, as one lawyer wrote, "Shahn sees things from the inside; we feel he is one of us."[4] In 1956, the artist was invited to give a series of lectures at Harvard University, which resulted in the publication of his book, *The Shape of Content*, the following year.

Shahn's work of the 1950s and 1960s reflects some of the same ideas of his earlier period, and while continuing to reference death, destruction, anger, and political discord, he portrayed his themes symbolically rather than specifically. The Westmoreland's *Byzantine Isometric* was painted in 1951 and represented a new direction in Shahn's work that began that summer, prompted by a teaching session at Black Mountain College in North Carolina. He was now approaching the human figure less realistically, and although the clothed body of the man in the painting remains anatomically referential, his head has been simplified to a line drawing, his face mask-like. During that same year, Shahn painted the enormous eight-foot-high image entitled *Nicholas C*, in which he caricatures the human body, its skeletal framework compartmentalized with heavy black outlines that are filled in with bright colors, much like the flat, linear structure of a stained-glass window. These cartoon-like characters represent everyman. The image of *Nicholas C* appeared in different contexts, as Shahn recycled his imagery during this period. Not only are the figure's head, hands, and feet found on the body of the man in *Byzantine Isometric*, but his head and torso appear again in *Man* (c. 1961). The figure's same facial expression and contemplative pose, with hand to chin, are also used in *Artists and Politicians* (1953) and in his small watercolor *Distressed Man* (1963). The overlapping isometric diagrams that constitute the background are incorporated once again in *Byzantine in Israel* (1965). This arrangement of abstract architectural fragments makes reference to the repetitive arched porticoes and arcades of early Christian and Byzantine basilica design and the artist's recycling of the historical past. Shahn was also interested in tracings left in a picture when changes were made. Those marks intrigued him, and traces of his earlier design are evident in the background of *Byzantine Isometric*, as is his looser application of paint. Our "man" stands alone in the foreground, pondering his place in this mysterious architectural landscape.

"Shahn was among a number of Americans who consistently pressed for and defended change through social reform. It is out of this social reform tradition that Shahn's work emerged and from which it continues to derive its strength and its meaning."[5] Ben Shahn continued to work, teach, exhibit, and participate in causes that he believed in until 1968, when his health deteriorated. He died on March 14 the following year at the age of seventy.

BLJ

1 Frances K. Pohl, *Ben Shahn* (San Francisco: Pomegranate Artbooks, 1993), 16.

2 Katharine Kuh, *The Artist's Voice: Talks with Seventeen Artists* (New York: Harper & Row, 1960, 1961), 206, 208.

3 Ben Shahn, "The Biography of a Painting," in *The Shape of Content* (Cambridge: Harvard University Press, 1957), 40–41, 45, 47.

4 Francis K. Pohl, *Ben Shahn: New Deal Artist in a Cold War Climate, 1947–1954* (Austin: University of Texas Press, 1989), 172.

5 Ibid., 178.

Staff of The Westmoreland

Amy Baldonieri, Assistant Director for Advancement
Aileen Barnard, Senior Visitor Services Representative and Greeter
Sue Beaver, Visitor Services Representative
Charlene Bidula, Communications Specialist
Malinda Brighton, Visitor Services Representative
Frances Browning, Accounts Manager
Edward Bunting, Senior Visitor Services Representative
Casey Dugan, Visitor Services Representative and Greeter
Pat Erdelsky, Assistant for Public and Financial Development
Douglas Evans, Collections Manager
Tim Ferencz, Custodian
Jeremy Holdorf, Visitor Services Representative
Barbara L. Jones, Chief Curator
Darlene Konvalinka, Administrative Assistant to the Chief Curator
Virginia Leiner, Museum Shop Manager
Nan Loncharich, Senior Visitor Services Representative and Greeter
Soji Olowofoyeku, Museum Shop Sales Associate
Judith H. O'Toole, Director/CEO
John Peterson, Senior Visitor Services Representative
Katie Resch, Visitor Services Representative and Greeter
John Richardson, Visitor Services Representative
Marianne Roskosh, Assistant to the Director/CEO
Judy Ross, Director of Marketing and Information Technology
Audrey Wright, Housekeeper
Jessica Zamiska, Visitor Services Manager
Maureen Zang, Public Programs Coordinator
Michael Zimmerlink, Facilities Manager
P.J. Zimmerlink, Preparator

Selected Bibliography

Adelson, Warren, et al. *Sargent's Venice*. New Haven: Yale University Press, 2006.

Alfred H. Maurer: Aestheticism to Modernism. New York: Hollis Taggart Galleries, 1999.

Anderson, Nancy K. *Thomas Moran*. Washington: National Gallery of Art, 1997.

Aronson, Charles N. *Sculptured Hyacinths*. New York: Vantage Press, Inc., 1973.

Art in the United States Capitol. Washington, DC: United States Government Printing Office, 1976.

Baker, John. *Henry Lee McFee and Formalist Realism in American Still Life 1923-1936*. Cranbury, NJ: Associated University Presses, 1987.

Barter, Judith A., Erica E. Hirshler, George T. M. Shackelford, Kevin Sharp, Harriet K. Stratis, and Andrew J. Walker. *Mary Cassatt: Modern Woman*. New York: The Art Institute of Chicago/Harry N. Abrams, Inc., Publishers, 1998.

Baur, John I. *Life and Work of Charles Burchfield 1893-1967, The Inlander*. Cranbury, NJ: Associated University Presses, Inc. and Cornwall Books, 1982.

Beaux, Cecilia. *Background with Figures*. Boston: Houghton Mifflin Company, 1930.

Beggs, Thomas M. *Paul Manship*. Washington, DC: Smithsonian Institution, 1958.

Bolger, Doreen, Marc Simpson, John Wilmerding, and Thayer Tolles Mickel. *William M. Harnett*. New York: Amon Carter Museum, Fort Worth/The Metropolitan Museum of Art/ Harry N. Abrams, Inc., 1992.

Breeskin, Adelyn D. *Milton Avery*. Washington, DC: The National Collection of Fine Arts, Smithsonian Institution, 1969.

Breuning, Margaret. *Maurice Prendergast*. New York: Whitney Museum of American Art, 1931.

Carter, Alice A. *Cecilia Beaux: A Modern Painter in the Gilded*. New York: Rizzoli International Publications, Inc., 2005.

———. *The Red Rose Girls: An Uncommon Story of Art and Love*. New York: Harry N. Abrams, Inc., 2000.

Catalogue of the Memorial Exhibition of Portraits by Thomas Sully. Philadelphia: The Pennsylvania Academy of the Fine Arts, 1922.

Chambers, Bruce W. *The World of David Gilmour Blithe (1815-1865)*. Washington, DC: Smithsonian Institution Press, 1980.

Chevlowe, Susan. *Common Man: The Paintings of Ben Shahn*. New Jersey: Princeton University Press, 1999.

Cikovsky, Nicolai, Jr. and Franklin Kelly. *Winslow Homer*. Washington, DC: National Gallery of Art, 1995.

Clark, Vicky A., Bruce Altshuler, Lois Marie Fink, Kay Larson, Kenneth Neal, and Susan Platt. *International Encounters: The Carnegie International and Contemporary Art, 1896-1996*. Pittsburgh: Carnegie Museum of Art, 1996.

Conrads, Margaret C. *Winslow Homer and the Critics: Forging a National Art in the 1870s*. Princeton: Princeton University Press, 2001.

Cooper, Helen A. *Winslow Homer Watercolors*. New Haven, CT: Yale University Press, 1986.

Cortissoz, Royal. *Guy Pène du Bois*. New York: Whitney Museum of American Art, n.d.

Craven, Wayne. *Sculpture in America*. New York: Thomas Y. Crowell Co., 1968.

Curry, Larry. *Eight American Masters of Watercolor*. New York: Los Angeles County Museum of Art/Frederick A. Praeger, Inc. Publishers, 1968.

Dearinger, David B. *Rave Reviews: American Art and Its Critics, 1826-1925*. Hanover: University Press of New England, 2000.

Deeds, Daphne Anderson. *Alfred Maurer: The First American Modern*. Minneapolis: Frederick R. Weisman Art Museum, University of Minnesota, 2003.

DeLue, Rachael Zaidy. *George Inness and the Science of Landscape*. Chicago: The University of Chicago Press, 2004.

Denker, Eric. *Whistler and his Circle in Venice*. London: Merrell Publishers Limited in association with The Corcoran Gallery, 2003.

Dorment, Richard and Margaret F. MacDonald. *James McNeill Whistler*. London: Tate Gallery Publications, 1994.

du Bois, Guy Pène. *Ernest Lawson*. New York: Whitney Museum of American Art, 1932.

———. *William Glackens*. New York: Whitney Museum of American Art, 1931.

Edwards, Paul Burgess. *The Life and Work of Malcolm Parcell, A Catalogue Raisonné*. Washington, PA: Washington County Historical Society, 1999.

Eidelberg, Martin, Nina Gray, and Margaret K. Hofer. *A New Light on Tiffany: Clara Driscoll and the Tiffany Girls*. New York: The New-York Historical Society in association with D. Giles Limited, London, 2007.

Fahlman, Betsy. *Guy Pène du Bois: Painter of Modern Life*. New York: James Graham & Sons, 2004.

Falk, Peter Hastings. *Record of the Carnegie Institute's International Exhibitions 1896-1996*. Madison: Sound View Press, 1998.

Fort, Ilene Susan. *The Figure in American Sculpture, A Question of Modernity*. Los Angeles: Los Angeles County Museum of Art, 1995.

———. *The Flag Paintings of Childe Hassam*. Los Angeles: Los Angeles County Museum of Art, 1988.

Gerdts, William H. *Painters of the Humble Truth, Masterpieces of American Still Life 1801-1939*. Columbia: University of Missouri Press, 1981, 1983.

Goode, James M. *The Outdoor Sculpture of Washington, D.C.* Washington, DC: Smithsonian Institution Press, 1974.

Goodyear, Frank H., Jr. *Cecilia Beaux: Portrait of an Artist*. Philadelphia: The Pennsylvania Academy of the Fine Arts, 1974.

Grand, Stanley I. *Guy Pène du Bois: The Twenties at Home and Abroad*. Wilkes-Barre: Sordoni Art Gallery, 1995.

Green, Eleanor. *Maurice Prendergast: Art of Impulse and Color*. College Park: University of Maryland Art Gallery, 1976.

Grieve, Alastair. *Whistler's Venice*. New Haven: Yale University Press, 2000.

Haskell, Barbara. *Milton Avery*. New York: Harper & Row, Publishers, Inc., 1982.

———. *Oscar Bluemner: A Passion for Color*. New York: Whitney Museum of American Art, 2005.

Hayden, F. V. *The Yellowstone National Park, and the Mountain Regions of Portions of Idaho, Nevada, Colorado and Utah*. Tulsa: Thomas Gilcrease Museum Association, 1997.

Helm, MacKinley. *John Marin*. Boston: Pellegrini and Cudahy in association with The Institute of Contemporary Art, 1948.

Hoopes, Donelson F. *The American Impressionists*. New York: Watson-Guptill Publications, 1972.

Hubbert-Kemper and Jason L. Wilson, ed. *A Sacred Challenge: Violet Oakley and the Pennsylvania Capitol Murals*. Harrisburg: The Pennsylvania Capitol Preservation Committee, 2002.

James-Gadzinski, Susan and Mary Mullen Cunningham. *American Sculpture in the Museum of American Art of the Pennsylvania Academy of the Fine Arts*. Seattle: University of Washington Press, 1997.

Johnston, Sona. *In Monet's Light: Theodore Robinson at Giverny*. London: Philip Wilson Publishers Limited, 2004.

Kinsey, Joni L. *Thomas Moran's West, Chromolithography, High Art, and Popular Taste*. Lawrence: The University Press of Kansas, 2006.

Kramer, Hilton. *Milton Avery: Paintings 1930-1960*. New York: Thomas Yoseloff, Publisher, 1962.

Little, Carl. *Winslow Homer and the Sea*. San Francisco: Pomegranate Artbooks, 1995.

Lovell, Margaretta M. *Venice: The American View, 1860-1920*. San Francisco: The Fine Arts Museums of San Francisco, 1984.

MacDonald, Margaret F. *Palaces in the Night: Whistler in Venice*. Hampshire, England: Lund Humphries, 2001.

Mathews, Nancy Mowll. *Maurice Prendergast*. Williamstown: Prestel in association with Williams College Museum of Art, 1990.

Miller, Donald. *Malcolm Parcell: Wizard of Moon Lorn*. Pittsburgh: Donald Miller, 1985.

Miller, Dorothy. *The Life and Work of David G. Blythe*. Pittsburgh, PA: The University of Pittsburgh Press, 1950.

Miller, Lillian B. *In Pursuit of Fame: Rembrandt Peale, 1778-1860*. Washington, DC: National Portrait Gallery, Smithsonian Institution, 1992.

Murtha, Edwin. *Paul Manship*. New York: The MacMillan Company, 1957.

Neal, Kenneth. *A Wise Extravagance: The Founding of the Carnegie International Exhibitions, 1895-1901*. Pittsburgh: University of Pittsburgh Press, 1996.

Norman, Dorothy. *The Selected Writings of John Marin*. New York: Pellegrini and Cudahy, 1949.

Pennell, Elizabeth Robbins. *The Life and Letters of Joseph Pennell, I*. Boston: Little, Brown, and Company, 1929.

———. *The Life and Letters of Joseph Pennell, II*. Boston: Little, Brown, and Company, 1929.

Pennell, Joseph. *Joseph Pennell's Pictures of the Wonder of Work*. Philadelphia: J. B. Lippincott Company, 1916.

Pisano, Ronald G. *A Leading Spirit in American Art: William Merritt Chase, 1849-1916*. Seattle: Henry Art Gallery, University of Washington, 1983.

———. Completed by Carolyn K. Lane and D. Frederick Baker. *William Merritt Chase, Portraits in Oil*. New Haven: Yale University Press, 2006.

Pohl, Frances K. *Ben Shahn*. San Francisco: Pomegranate Artbooks, 1993.

———. *Ben Shahn: New Deal Artist in a Cold War Climate, 1947-1954*. Austin: University of Texas Press, 1989.

Prown, Jules David. *John Singleton Copley in America 1738-1774*. Cambridge, MA: Harvard University Press, 1966.

Reich, Sheldon. *John Marin: Part I, A Stylistic Analysis*. Tucson, AZ: The University of Arizona Press, 1970.

———. *John Marin: Part II, Catalogue Raisonné*. Tucson, AZ: The University of Arizona Press, 1970.

Richardson, Edgar P., Brooke Hindle, and Lillian B. Miller. *Charles Willson Peale and His World*. New York: Harry N. Abrams, Inc., 1983.

Roof, Katharine Metcalf. *The Life and Art of William Merritt Chase*. New York: Charles Scribner's Sons, 1917.

Rutledge, Anna Wells. *Cumulative Record of Exhibition Catalogues, The Pennsylvania Academy of the Fine Arts, 1807-1870*. Philadelphia: The American Philosophical Society, Independence Square, 1955.

Schoelwer, Susan P. *Lions and Eagles and Bulls, Early American Tavern and Inn Signs from the Connecticut Historical Society*. Hartford: The Connecticut Historical Society in association with Princeton University Press, 2000.

Sellers, Charles Coleman. *Portraits and Miniatures by Charles Willson Peale*. Philadelphia: American Philosophical Society, 1952.

Sessions, Ralph. *The Poetic Vision: American Tonalism*. New York: Spanierman Gallery, LLC, 2005.

———. *The Shipcarvers' Art: Figureheads and Cigar-Store Indians in Nineteenth Century America*. Princeton: Princeton University Press, 2005.

Shanes, Eric, Marc A. Simpson, and Judith C. Walsh. *Winslow Homer: Poet of the Sea*. Giverny: Terra Foundation for American Art, 2006.

Smith, Helene. *Catalog: Tavern Signs of America.* Greensburg, PA: McDonald/Swärd Publishing Company, 1988.

————. *History: Tavern Signs of America.* Greensburg, PA: McDonald/Swärd Publishing Company, 1989.

Somma, Thomas P. *The Apotheosis of Democracy 1908-1916.* Newark: University of Delaware Press, 1995.

Staley, Allen. *Benjamin West, American Painter at the English Court.* Baltimore: Baltimore Museum of Art, 1989.

Sweet, Frederick A. *Sargent, Whistler and Mary Cassatt.* Chicago: Art Institute of Chicago, 1954.

Talbott, Page and Patricia Tanis Sydney. *The Philadelphia Ten: A Women's Artist Group, 1917-1945.* Kansas City: American Art Review Press, 1998.

Terhune, Anne Gregory, Sylvia Yount, and Naurice Frank Woods, Jr. *Thomas Hovenden (1840-1895): American Painter of Hearth and Homeland.* Philadelphia: Woodmere Art Museum, 1995.

Terhune, Anne Gregory and Patricia Smith Scanlan. *Thomas Hovenden, His Life and Art.* Philadelphia: University of Pennsylvania Press, 2006.

Townsend, J. Benjamin, ed. *Charles Burchfield's Journals: The Poetry of Place.* Albany: State University of New York Press, 1993.

Trovato, Joseph. *Charles Burchfield: Ctalogue of Paintings in Public and Private Collections.* Utica, NY: Museum of Art, Munson-Williams-Proctor Institute, 1970.

von Erffa, Helmut and Allen Staley. *The Paintings of Benjamin West.* New Haven: Yale University Press, 1986.

Ward, David C. *Charles Willson Peale: Art and Selfhood in the Early Republic.* Berkeley: University of California Press, 2004.

Watson, Forbes. *Mary Cassatt.* New York: Whitney Museum of American Art, 1932.

Wattenmaker, Richard J. *Maurice Prendergast.* New York: Harry N. Abrams, Inc., in association with The National Museum of American Art, Smithsonian Institution, 1994.

Wick, Peter A. *Maurice Prendergast: Water-color Sketchbook, 1899.* Cambridge: University of Fine Arts/Harvard University Press, 1960.

Wuerth, Louis A. *Catalogue of the Etchings of Joseph Pennell.* Boston: Little, Brown, and Company, 1928.

Yount, Sylvia. *Cecilia Beaux, American Figure Painter.* Berkeley: University of California Press, 2007.

Zorach, William. *Art is my Life: The Autobiography of William Zorach.* Cleveland: The World Publishing Company, 1967.

Index of Artists

The typeface Centaur

was designed by Bruce Rogers, the most important American typographer of the early twentieth century. Centaur is his masterpiece. The uppercase was first used in 1914 by the Metropolitan Museum of Art, which had established its own excellent press for announcements, posters, labels, etc. Centaur was then roman only, but at the request of some fine printers, Rogers added an italic typeface based on drawings by Frederic Warde. Warde's italic is an interpretation of the work of the sixteenth-century printer and calligrapher Ludovico degli Arrighi. The process took over a year. The most famous use for the new type came in 1935 when a special 22-point size was cast to set the 1,238-page Oxford Lecturn Bible. Since then Centaur has been one of the most widely praised roman types of our time. A noted typographer wrote, "Centaur is a beautiful type, delicate and subtle. . .[It] has been used with elegant effect by sensitive designers."

Cecilia Beaux

Robert Henri

G. Inness

Geo. Hetzel.

J.F. Francis.
Pt

H F King.

Mary Cassatt

A H Gorson

Chase

Louis C. Tiffany

E. Lawson

Guy Pène du Bois

L.W. Prentice.

R. Peale

W M Harnett.